# THE CICS PROGRAMMER'S GUIDE TO FEPI

## TITLES IN THE IBM McGRAW-HILL SERIES

OPEN SYSTEMS AND IBM
Integration and Convergence
Pamela Gray
ISBN 0-07-707750-4

OS/2 PRESENTATION MANAGER PROGRAMMING: HINTS AND TIPS
Bryan Goodyer
ISBN 0-07-707776-8

THE IBM RISC SYSTEM/6000
Clive Harris
ISBN 0-07-707668-0

THE IBM RISC SYSTEM/6000 USER GUIDE
Mike Leaver, Hardev Sanghera
ISBN 0-07-707687-7

PC USER'S GUIDE
Simple Steps to Powerful Personal Computing
Peter Turner
ISBN 0-07-707421-1

DYNAMIC FACTORY AUTOMATION
Creating Flexible Systems for Competitive Manufacturing
Alastair Ross
ISBN 0-07-707440-8

MVS SYSTEMS PROGRAMMING
Dave Elder-Vass
ISBN 0-07-707767-9

THE NEW ORGANIZATION
Growing the Culture of Organizational Networking
Colin Hastings
ISBN 0-07-707784-9

COMMONSENSE COMPUTER SECURITY
2nd Edition
Your Practical Guide to Information Protection
Martin Smith
ISBN 0-07-707805-5

CICS CONCEPTS AND USES: A MANAGEMENT GUIDE
Jim Geraghty
ISBN 0-07-707751-2

RISK MANAGEMENT FOR SOFTWARE PROJECTS
Alex Down, Michael Coleman, Peter Absolon
ISBN 0-07-707816-0

INVESTING IN INFORMATION TECHNOLOGY
Managing the Decision-making Process
Geoff Hogbin, David Thomas
ISBN 0-07-707957-1

THE ADVANCED PROGRAMMER'S GUIDE TO AIX 3.x
Phil Colledge
ISBN 0-07-707663-X

THE CICS PROGRAMMER'S GUIDE TO FEPI
Robert Harris
ISBN 0-07-707793-8

BUSINESS OBJECTS
Ease of Programming for Client Server
Oliver Sims
ISBN 0-07-707957-4

RESHAPING IT FOR BUSINESS FLEXIBILITY
The IT Architecture as a Common Language for Dealing with Change
Mark Behrsin, Geoff Mason, Trevor Sharpe
ISBN 0-07-707984-1

Details of these and other titles in the series are available from:
The Product Manager, Professional Books, McGraw-Hill Book Company Europe,
Shoppenhangers Road, Maidenhead, Berkshire SL6 2QL
Telephone: 0628 23432 Fax: 0628 770224

# THE CICS PROGRAMMER'S GUIDE TO FEPI

**ROBERT HARRIS**

**McGRAW-HILL BOOK COMPANY**

**London** · New York · St Louis · San Francisco · Auckland · Bogotá
Caracas · Lisbon · Madrid · Mexico · Milan · Montreal
New Delhi · Panama · Paris · San Juan · São Paulo
Singapore · Sydney · Tokyo · Toronto

Published by
McGRAW-HILL Book Company Europe
Shoppenhangers Road, Maidenhead, Berkshire SL6 2QL, England
Telephone: 0628 23432 Fax: 0628 770224

**British Library Cataloguing in Publication Data**
Harris, Robert
CICS Programmer's Guide to FEPI. — (IBM
McGraw-Hill Series)
I. Title II. Series
005.329

ISBN 0-07-707793-8

**Library of Congress Cataloging-in-Publication Data**
Harris, Robert
The CICS programmer's guide to FEPI / Robert Harris.
p. cm. — (IBM McGraw-Hill series)
Includes bibliographical references and index.
ISBN 0-07-707793-8:
1. CICS (Computer system). 2. Emulators (Computer programs)
3. Computer interfaces. I. Title. II. Series.
QA76.76.T45H37 1994 93-38086
005.7'13—dc20 CIP



1234 CUP 97654

Typeset by Paston Press Ltd, Loddon, Norfolk
and printed and bound in Great Britain at the University Press, Cambridge

*This book is dedicated to my parents and to the Reverend Noel Battye*

# Contents


| | | |
|---|---|---|
| | **IBM Series Foreword** | xiii |
| | **Preface** | xv |
| **PART 1** | Design overview | 1 |
| **CHAPTER 1** | **General information**<br>**Key points:** What is FEPI? ■ How FEPI fits into a system | 3 |
| **CHAPTER 2** | **LU2 and LU0 access methods**<br>**Key points:** Emulator concepts ■ FEPI and access methods ■ LU2 (3270) ■ LU0 (SLUP) | 6 |
| **CHAPTER 3** | **Datastream and Formatted**<br>**Key points:** FEPI access techniques ■ Formatted techniques ■ Keystroke Interface ■ Screen Image Interface ■ Datastream techniques | 8 |
| **CHAPTER 4** | **Passthrough and Coded** | 11 |
| **CHAPTER 5** | **Scatter/Gather** | 13 |
| **CHAPTER 6** | **Use of FEPI's asynchronous facilities**<br>**Key points:** Conversations and tasks ■ EXEC CICS FEPI STARTs ■ CICS resource constraints | 16 |
| **CHAPTER 7** | **Use of Timeouts**<br>**Key points:** Timeouts on EXEC CICS FEPI ALLOCATEs ■ Timeouts on EXEC CICS FEPI RECEIVEs ■ Timeouts on EXEC CICS FEPI STARTs | 18 |
| **CHAPTER 8** | **Handlers** | 20 |
| **CHAPTER 9** | **FEPI Monitor Transient Data Queues**<br>**Key points:** FEPI Monitors | 21 |
| **CHAPTER 10** | **FEPI Conversation types**<br>**Key points:** FEPI Conversations ■ Normal FEPI Conversations ■ Single transaction Conversations ■ Full asynchronous Conversations ■ Handler Conversations ■ Temporary FEPI Conversations | 22 |
| **PART 2** | System definition and the SPI | 25 |
| **CHAPTER 11** | **FEPI resource concepts**<br>**Key points:** The FEPI resources ■ FEPI Nodes ■ FEPI Targets ■ FEPI Propertysets ■ FEPI Pools ■ FEPI Connections ■ FEPI Conversations | 27 |
| **CHAPTER 12** | **VTAM definitions for Nodes**<br>**Key points:** VTAM and FEPI Nodes ■ VTAM's APPL statement ■ VTAM Node Activation and Control ■ VTAM Session parameters ■ VTAM and FEPI Targets | 31 |
| **CHAPTER 13** | **FEPI resource definition**<br>**Key points:** A general review of CICS resource definition ■ FEPI Dynamic Resource Definition ■ Definition of FEPI resources ■ Enabling FEPI in CICS ■ CICS initialization ■ Order of installing the FEPI resources | 34 |
| **CHAPTER 14** | **EXEC CICS FEPI INSTALL/ADD**<br>**Key points:** EXEC CICS FEPI INSTALL commands ■ EXEC CICS FEPI ADD command | 38 |
| **CHAPTER 15** | **EXEC CICS FEPI DISCARD/DELETE**<br>**Key points:** EXEC CICS FEPI DISCARD commands ■ EXEC CICS FEPI DELETE command | 46 |

**CHAPTER 16** **Choosing the Propertyset options** 49
**Key points:** Propertyset attributes ■ BEGINSESSION ■ CONTENTION ■ DEVICE ■ ENDSESSION ■ EXCEPTIONQ ■ FJOURNALNUM ■ FORMAT ■ INITIALDATA ■ MAXFLENGTH ■ MSGJRNL ■ STSN ■ UNSOLDATA and UNSOLDATACK

**CHAPTER 17** **Resource Definition Examples** 57
**Key points:** Standard Pool ■ Creating the Pool and Connections at the same time ■ Pool Connections not Bound until use ■ Pool containing usable and unusable Connections

**CHAPTER 18** **Resource manipulation** 60
**Key points:** Status transitions ■ Resource Status ■ EXEC CICS FEPI SET commands ■ EXEC CICS FEPI INQUIRE commands ■ Browsing FEPI Resources ■ Browsing FEPI Nodes, Targets, Pools, and Propertysets ■ Browsing FEPI Connections

**CHAPTER 19** **CEMT** 70
**Key points:** CEMT Usage ■ CEMT examples

**PART 3** Application programming techniques and the API 75

**CHAPTER 20** **Introduction to 3270 Datastream** 77
**Key points:** Query Structured Field ■ 3270 and VTAM indicators ■ CD ■ EB

**CHAPTER 21** **Terminal emulation and what is on the screen** 80
**Key points:** Knowledge of the position ■ First flows ■ Asynchronous operation ■ Contention State

**CHAPTER 22** **Scatter/Gather techniques** 83
**Key points:** Scattering the emulations ■ The scattered transactions ■ Returning the scattered transactions' data ■ Gathering the data ■ Scattered updates

**CHAPTER 23** **Knowing when you have all that you need** 86
**Key points:** The problem ■ The EXEC CICS FEPI CONVERSE commands ■ General warning

**CHAPTER 24** **The difference between Unexpected and Unsolicited input** 88
**Key points:** Things are not what they seem! ■ Unsolicited data ■ Processing the Unsolicited data ■ Actions for Datastream Conversations ■ Actions for Formatted Conversations ■ Unexpected data

**CHAPTER 25** **IMS partners** 91
**Key points:** IMS message protocols ■ Unsolicited and Unexpected data ■ IMS transactions ■ MFS paging ■ VTAM indicators ■ Session acquisition ■ Session termination ■ Message logging ■ IMS conversational transactions

**CHAPTER 26** **FEPI command sequences** 95
**Key points:** General command sequence ■ Command overview

**CHAPTER 27** **Full description of the API-type commands** 101
**Key points:** Return Codes ■ EXEC CICS FEPI ALLOCATE a new Conversation ■ EXEC CICS FEPI ALLOCATE an existing Conversation ■ EXEC CICS FEPI SEND formatted ■ EXEC CICS FEPI SEND Datastream ■ EXEC CICS FEPI RECEIVE formatted ■ EXEC CICS FEPI RECEIVE Datastream ■ EXEC CICS FEPI FREE a Conversation ■ EXEC CICS FEPI START a new FEPI Transaction ■ EXEC CICS FEPI EXTRACT Field ■ EXEC CICS FEPI EXTRACT Conversation details ■ EXEC CICS FEPI EXTRACT STSN Sequence Numbers ■ EXEC CICS FEPI ISSUE SNA Responses ■ EXEC CICS FEPI CONVERSE Formatted ■ EXEC CICS FEPI CONVERSE Datastream ■ EXEC CICS FEPI AP NOOP ■ EXEC CICS FEPI SP NOOP

**CHAPTER 28** **EIBRESP2 codes and what to do with them** 116
**Key points:** Universal errors ■ General API errors ■ Sequence errors ■ Datastream errors ■ Allocation errors ■ Send errors ■ Receive/Start errors ■ Issue errors ■ General errors on the SPI-type commands ■ Install errors ■ Browse errors

**PART 4** Formatted programming 129

**CHAPTER 29** **EXEC CICS FEPI ALLOCATE options** 131
**Key points:** Starting a FEPI Conversation ■ EXEC CICS FEPI ALLOCATEing a new FEPI Conversation ■ Timeouts ■ The Convid ■ Target selection ■ Order of Connection usage ■ How the Connection started ■ EXEC CICS FEPI ALLOCATEing an existing FEPI Conversation

**CHAPTER 30** **Sending with Keystrokes** 136
**Key points:** Keystroke concepts ■ The escape sequences ■ The FEPI Keystroke command ■ Keystroke techniques ■ Starting from a known point ■ Multiple Attentions ■ Keystrokes without Attention keys ■ Keystroke errors

**CHAPTER 31** **Sending with Buffers** 141
**Key points:** Buffer concepts ■ Obtaining the Buffer ■ The EXEC CICS FEPI SEND command for Formatted Buffer usage ■ Attribute Byte processing ■ Protected and Unprotected fields ■ The cursor position ■ Buffer example

**CHAPTER 32** **Receiving with Buffers** 144
**Key points:** Concepts ■ The EXEC CICS FEPI RECEIVE FORMATTED command ■ Buffer reception ■ Screen parameters ■ Knowing when you have everything ■ CICS usage ■ IMS usage ■ VTAM responses ■ Obtaining Attribute Bytes and field information

**CHAPTER 33** **Receiving with Fields** 148
**Key points:** Field concepts ■ The EXEC CICS FEPI EXTRACT FIELD command ■ Specifying the field of interest ■ Obtaining the field's contents ■ Obtaining the Attribute Bytes

**CHAPTER 34** **The effect of Receive TIMEOUT usage** 151
**Key points:** Recovering from a Timeout ■ Unsolicited Data Handler's first Receive ■ EXEC CICS FEPI STARTed transaction's first Receive ■ The Begin Session Handler's first Receive

**CHAPTER 35** **EXEC CICS FEPI START and asynchronous operation** 154
**Key points:** What the started transaction should do ■ Detecting that FEPI initiated the transaction

**CHAPTER 36** **EXEC CICS FEPI FREE** 156
**Key points:** Concepts ■ Free options ■ Application programming usage ■ Begin Session Handler usage ■ End Session Handler usage ■ Unsolicited Data Handler usage ■ STSN Handler usage

**PART 5** Datastream programming 161

**CHAPTER 37** **3270 Datastreams and VTAM** 163
**Key points:** VTAM flows ■ SNA RU indicators ■ SNA Chains ■ Brackets ■ EXEC CICS FEPI RECEIVE DATASTREAM options ■ 3270 Command codes for FEPI Inbound data ■ Write Control Character for FEPI Inbound data ■ 3270 Data format for FEPI Outbound data ■ 12-bit cursor position

**CHAPTER 38** **Structured Fields** 168
**Key points:** FEPI Inbound Structured Fields ■ FEPI Outbound Structured Fields

**CHAPTER 39** **The EXEC CICS Terminal Control API for FEPI Passthrough operations** 170
**Key points:** EXEC CICS RECEIVE ■ EXEC CICS SEND ■ EXEC CICS CONVERSE

**CHAPTER 40** **Datastream programming considerations** 172
**Key points:** 3270 orders ■ 3270 format control orders ■ 3270 Attribute Bytes ■ 3270 Extended Attribute Bytes ■ Datastream errors ■ Asynchronous processing

**CHAPTER 41** **Datastream programming techniques** 176
**Key points:** Datastream techniques ■ 3270 Command Codes and EXEC CICS Terminal Control Commands ■ EXEC CICS Terminal Control Commands for Writes ■ EXEC CICS Terminal Control Commands for Reads ■ EXEC CICS Commands for Structured Fields ■ FEPI Outbound operations

**CHAPTER 42** **Passthrough program** 180
**Key points:** Headers ■ Variables ■ Initialization ■ Processing loop ■ MAPIN ■ Generating a 12-bit cursor position ■ MAPOUT data reception ■ Deciding what action to take ■ Write ■ Erase Write ■ Erase Write Alternate ■ Write Structured Field selection ■ Write Structured Field operation ■ Read Buffer ■ Read Modified ■ Read Modified All ■ Erase All Unprotected ■ Unknown command ■ MAPOUT end of processing ■ End of program

**PART 6** The use of Monitors and Handlers 201

**CHAPTER 43** **Introduction to Handlers and Monitors** 203
**Key points:** The Handler and Monitor transactions ■ Defining the Handlers ■ Defining the Monitors

**CHAPTER 44** **Handler descriptions** 205
**Key points:** The Begin Session Handler ■ What the Handler should do ■ The End Session Handler ■ End of Conversation ■ End of Connection ■ What the Handler should do ■ The Unsolicited Data Handler ■ What the Handler should do ■ The STSN Handler

**CHAPTER 45** **Pool-specific Monitors** 211
**Key points:** List errors ■ What the Monitor program should do (1) ■ Usability errors ■ What the Monitor program should do (2)

**CHAPTER 46** **CSZX Monitors** 215
**Key points:** Resource management errors ■ What the Monitor program should do (1) ■ Resource Acquisition Error ■ What the Monitor program should do (2) ■ Unsolicited Bind Arrival ■ What the Monitor program should do (3)

**CHAPTER 47** **How to use Monitors and Handlers** 219
**Key points:** Designing with Handlers ■ Design decisions ■ The Begin Session Handler ■ The Unsolicited Data Handler ■ The End Session Handler (End of Conversation) ■ The End Session Handler (End of Connection) ■ The STSN Handler ■ Designing with Monitors ■ Pool-specific Monitors ■ The number of Connections ■ VTAM failures ■ CSZX Monitors ■ Install and discard errors ■ Set failures ■ VTAM acquisition failures ■ Unsolicited Bind occurrence

**PART 7** Hints and tips 227

**CHAPTER 48** **Resource tuning with the SPI** 229
**Key points:** Pool organization ■ The number of Connections ■ Detecting that there is a problem ■ Needing more Connections ■ Adding more Connections ■ Making more Connections usable ■ Adding another target to a Pool ■ Removing Connections ■ Timed operations ■ CEMT operations

**CHAPTER 49** **Using STARTs effectively** 233
**Key points:** The problem ■ A failing work-around ■ The solution

**CHAPTER 50** **USERDATA** 237
**Key points:** Userdata on FEPI resources ■ Userdata on FEPI starts

**CHAPTER 51** **FEPI and CLSDST(PASS) operation** 239
**Key points:** CLSDST(PASS) concepts ■ Known and unknown third-party systems ■ Pool arrangements ■ Known third-party PLU name ■ Unknown third-party PLU name ■ CLSDST(PASS) processing during EXEC CICS FEPI ALLOCATE processing

**CHAPTER 52** **SLUP topics** 245
**Key points:** SLUP sequence numbers ■ SNA considerations ■ FEPI STSN processing ■ The STSN Handler ■ The FEPI EXTRACT STSN command ■ Responding to the STSN request ■ IMS and sequence numbers ■ SLUP VTAM definitions

**CHAPTER 53** **DRn responses, and how to cope with them** 248
**Key points:** FEPI and SNA responses ■ Responding manually ■ Responding negatively

**CHAPTER 54** **IMS response and nonresponse modes** 250
**Key points:** Types of IMS transactions ■ IMS definitions ■ Coping with IMS response mode transactions ■ Coping with IMS nonresponse mode transactions

**CHAPTER 55 Security** 252

**CHAPTER 56 Journalling** 254
**Key points:** Journalling facilities ■ Layout of FEPI journal records ■ Printing FEPI journal records

**CHAPTER 57 Global User Exits** 258
**Key points:** FEPI Global User Exits ■ Usage of the Global User Exits

**CHAPTER 58 Debugging** 263
**Key points:** The FEPI environment ■ FEPI tracing ■ FEPI dump interpretation ■ FEPI and CICS debugging facilities ■ GTF tracing

**CHAPTER 59 Shutdown** 268
**Key points:** Normal shutdown ■ Immediate shutdown ■ Forced shutdown

**CHAPTER 60 XRF** 271
**Key points:** VTAM and XRF concepts ■ XRF takeover of FEPI CICS ■ Effect in the alternate ■ XRF takeover of partner CICS ■ Effect on FEPI application programs ■ Effect on FEPI Connections

**CHAPTER 61 Convid management** 277
**Key points:** Partner signons ■ Obtaining the password ■ Signon overheads ■ Security implications ■ Reducing signon overhead by Convid management ■ Convid management code overview ■ Saving away the last userid ■ Pool arrangement ■ EXEC CICS FEPI FREE processing ■ Begin Session and End Session processing ■ Convid management coding

**PART 8** Reference material 281

**APPENDIX A Listing of the API and SPI** 283

**APPENDIX B Listing of CVDAs used by FEPI** 314

**APPENDIX C Listing of FEPI Return Codes and names** 315

**APPENDIX D Start Data and Transient Data Queue Record layouts** 319

**APPENDIX E Listing of FEPI Command Codes** 323

**APPENDIX F FEPI States** 324

**APPENDIX G Listing of FEPI formatted keystroke escape sequences** 325

**APPENDIX H Listing of FEPI XSZARQ and XSZBRQ GLUE parameter lists** 327

**GLOSSARY** 329

**INDEX** 339

# Foreword

**The IBM McGraw-Hill Series**

IBM UK and McGraw-Hill Europe have worked together to publish this series of books about information technology and its use in business, industry and the public sector.

The series provides an up-to-date and authoritative insight into the wide range of products and services available, and offers strategic business advice. Some of the books have a technical bias, others are written from a broader business perspective. What they have in common is that their authors—some from IBM, some independent consultants—are experts in their field.

Apart from assisting where possible with the accuracy of the writing, IBM UK has not sought to inhibit the editorial freedom of the series, and therefore the views expressed in the books are those of the authors, and not necessarily those of IBM.

Where IBM has lent its expertise is in assisting McGraw-Hill to identify potential titles whose publication would help advance knowledge and increase awareness of computing topics. Hopefully these titles will also serve to widen the debate about the important information technology issues of today and of the future—such as open systems, networking, and the use of technology to give companies a competitive edge in their market.

IBM UK is pleased to be associated with McGraw-Hill in this series.

Sir Anthony Cleaver
Chairman
IBM United Kingdom Limited

# Preface

## How to use this book

This book is a companion to the IBM *SC33–0804 CICS/ESA Front End Programming Interface User's Guide*. You should understand the idea of FEPI as presented in this IBM book, and be familiar with the concepts of CICS/ESA.

This publication should be used as a source of Hints and Tips for FEPI usage. Therefore, I recommend that you *do not* read this book from start to end—the unrelenting series of facts will probably prove too much. Rather, I have written the text with lots of cross-references to facilitate a drop-in approach.

First, go to the part of this book which most closely describes the information you are after. The first page of each part contains a list of the following chapters, so you should easily be able to determine the information required. Alternatively, consult the index if the required information is more narrowly defined.

**ADVICE**

This book contains advice on FEPI usage as well as information on FEPI's facilities and functions. Where something like *'I recommend'* appears, this denotes a preferred course of action that the author thinks is appropriate.

As these recommendations are purely the author's responsibility, IBM does not assume any responsibility for their accuracy.

## Warranty

No warranty of any kind, either explicit or implied, is provided by this book. In all cases, you should consider the IBM book *SC33–0804 CICS/ESA Front End Programming Interface User's Guide* as the prime reference for FEPI. In case of conflict between this book and SC33–0804, the information in SC33–0804 should be taken to be correct.

The author acknowledges IBM's *SC33–0804 CICS/ESA Front End Programming Interface User's Guide* as the source of the information presented within this book.

## Acknowledgements

I would like to thank one of my co-developers of FEPI, Keith Andrews, for his efforts in reviewing this book. Also thanks to Robin Drew for his encouragement in writing this book.

# Trademarks

CICS, CICS/ESA, CICS/MVS, IBM, IMS/ESA, Netview, VTAM, ACF/VTAM, MVS/ESA, PS/55 are trademarks of International Business Machines Corporation.

# PART 1

# Design overview

**GUIDANCE**

This part of the book provides a brief overview of FEPI's facilities. See the *CICS/ESA FEPI User's Guide* for more information.

The following FEPI facilities are discussed in this part of the book:

- General information
- LU2 and LU0 access methods
- Datastream and Formatted
- Passthrough and Coded
- Scatter/Gather
- Use of FEPI's asynchronous facilities
- Use of Timeouts
- Handlers
- FEPI Monitor Transient Data Queues
- FEPI Conversation types

# CHAPTER 1 General information

**GUIDANCE**

This chapter provides a *brief* introduction to opportunities for emulation with FEPI. See *CICS/ESA FEPI User's Guide* for more information.

## 1.1 What is FEPI?

The CICS/ESA Front End Programming Interface (FEPI) is a terminal emulator for CICS/ESA version 3.3. It provides the ability to write CICS application programs that communicate to CICS/ESA, CICS/MVS or IMS systems.

FEPI is completely integrated into CICS processing. Its function is provided via a set of `EXEC CICS FEPI` commands.

FEPI's 'Front End' nomenclature comes from its ability to act as a terminal emulator, and so provide the equivalent of a real terminal to a partner system. The 'Programming Interface' part comes from the way FEPI is accessed via the `EXEC CICS FEPI` commands.

Therefore, FEPI provides the ability to mimic completely the behaviour of a real terminal within a CICS/ESA 3.3 system.

## 1.2 How FEPI fits into a system

FEPI is an integrational tool. By this, I mean that FEPI is used to glue disparate systems together into a seamless whole. The crucial thing is that these systems do *not* have to be changed in any way to be operated via FEPI.

As these existing systems remain unchanged, you can use systems *outside* of your control in differing ways. Thus, if you need to use a credit reference agency's system, but its information is presented in an uninspiring fashion, you drive the credit agency's system via FEPI and reformat the data to your desired pattern.

Change in a computer system is a risky business, therefore it may not be possible to arrange for an enhancement to an existing application to be made in a timely fashion. FEPI may be able to reduce the risk by adding new function without disturbing the existing processing.

The advantage of using FEPI is that existing systems and applications can be used as they stand, and that you provide integrational benefits by driving them in new ways.

### 1.2.1 Corporate takeover

The first example of FEPI usage presented in the *CICS/ESA FEPI General Information Book* is that of corporate takeover.

Often when two companies merge, the easy bit is all the financial dealings—after all, just a few bits of virtual paper move from place A to place B! However, joining the two computer systems is another matter. Each ex-company will have its own systems, which they operate in their own (peculiar) ways. Yet, the new company needs to use both sets of systems immediately. Ultimately, the new company may decide to rewrite the systems, but this is of no use in the short term.

FEPI comes into the picture by providing a new application that accesses the existing disparate applications in a new fashion. The great advantage of using FEPI is that the existing systems remain unchanged for those who need access to only one of them. The coding of a new FEPI Front End is much quicker than rewriting everything, and so the integration can be speedily accomplished.

### 1.2.2 Background functions

In this scenario, FEPI is used to hide system access from the End User. The *CICS/ESA FEPI General Information Book* calls this 'Function Bundling'.

There are existing applications within your system, but now you want to run them in background mode, and not at a terminal, in order to join them together. Consequently, you use a FEPI application program to access this existing function and join up the data before presenting it to the end user.

The great advantage to using FEPI to join up these systems, is that the systems themselves are unchanged. This permits existing usage of the systems to continue, while new users have access to the same information in a different fashion *without* any coding changes.

### 1.2.3 New function

Another scenario is where existing systems need exending, but you do not not have the time or opportunity to recode. Perhaps the existing system is ages old (and thus too stable to change), or it came from a supplier who has gone bust, or the existing system is on someone else's system, and cannot be changed.

For whatever reason, an existing system cannot be touched, but you need to extend it. FEPI provides the solution whereby the existing function can be run through FEPI emulation, and the new function provided separately.

FEPI can therefore be used to drive old applications, and fit the data into a new system.

### 1.2.4 Parallelism

Another use for FEPI is to provide a degree of parallelism within your processing. As FEPI emulations can run in parallel, using FEPI's asynchronous facilities, existing applications can be recoded to work via FEPI and thus gain a quicker response.

## 1.2.5 Changing PF keys

Another idea for using FEPI is to convert whatever PF keys are used by an application to other ones.

For example, some office systems do not use PF7/8 for paging backwards and forwards. Therefore, consider using FEPI processing to change between users keying PF7/8 and the office system's PF key usage.

## 1.2.6 Syncpoint trees

In addition to the preceding examples of FEPI application usage, FEPI can be used to solve complex or esoteric technical problems.

When running a Distributed Transaction using LU6.2, all elements of the net should Syncpoint at the same time. However, suppose that some element in the Distributed Processing net is somewhat suspect, and you need to Syncpoint that element more frequently. LU6.2 does not permit this processing.

However, consider replacing the LU6.2 link to the dodgy system with a FEPI link (using LU2). You can quite happily Syncpoint this component without affecting the other distributed components—because FEPI does not take any notice of Syncpoints.

When the Distributed Set of transactions really Syncpoints (or backsouts) you should ensure that the FEPI-linked component has done what is required.

I *strongly emphasize* that this technique is not for the faint-hearted. It will take a degree of coding to ensure that all the Distributed Transaction Syncpoints properly (and more to the point, backsout appropriately). Getting things wrong will lead to integrity problems. However, that being said, you can do this sort of complicated processing using FEPI.

# CHAPTER 2 LU2 and LU0 access methods

| GUIDANCE |
|---|
| This chapter briefly discusses the access methods that FEPI supports. |

## 2.1 Emulator concepts

FEPI is a Terminal Emulator. Consequently, it is designed to mimic fully the behaviour of a 'real' terminal. However, the facilities thus provided are too complex for normal usage. Consequently, FEPI supports three different ways of operating the emulation, depending upon how much of the underlying VTAM behaviour you need to know about:

- *High-level operations* provide a very straightforward way of running an emulation. These techniques are used via *Formatted* access.
- *Datastream operations* expose more of the VTAM emulation, and you have to provide functions that understand the access-method flows.
- *Special functions* are available for those who require access to the underlying VTAM control flows.

## 2.2 FEPI and access methods

FEPI supports emulation using two access method protocols:

- LU2
- LU0

### 2.2.1 LU2 (3270)

LU2 is the normal 3270 Datastream used for communication to terminals like 3278s, 3279s, and 3290s. Host communication to these terminals is either via BSC or SNA. FEPI performs as if it is either a 3278 or a 3279 terminal in SNA mode.

This 3270 protocol, and the way FEPI uses it to communicate, are the subject of this book. The structure of a 3270 Datastream can be complex, thus FEPI provides a layered set of services to hide this complexity. The FEPI Formatted facilities (discussed in Chapter 3) are only available for LU2 operations, but FEPI Datastream techniques are also available if required.

### 2.2.2 LU0 (SLUP)

LU0 is a very basic access method that many types of device use to communicate to many host systems. Consequently, there are lots of varieties of LU0 communication.

The only flavour of LU0 supported by FEPI is that used for SLUP communication to IMS. This provides FEPI with the ability to emulate a 4700 automated teller machine to IMS.

FEPI's Formatted facilities are *not* available for LU0 emulations; all coding is done with the Datastream-level commands, maybe using some of the special functions.

The concepts involved with writing these SLUP emulations are outside the scope of this book. However, Chapter 52 contains a brief description of the SLUP facilities provided by FEPI.

CHAPTER 3

# Datastream and Formatted

| GUIDANCE |
| --- |
| This chapter discusses the techniques available for FEPI emulation. |

## 3.1 FEPI access techniques

FEPI supports a layered set of services to hide complexity from the application programmer:

**Formatted** commands yield the simplest emulation, with all complexity hidden from the application program. Formatted commands are only available for LU2 (3270) emulations.

**Datastream** commands allow the application program to manipulate the VTAM Datastreams directly.

**Special** commands provide additional facilities to Datastream communication that permit the manipulation of underlying VTAM control flows.

All FEPI commands are prefixed by `EXEC CICS FEPI`, and the CICS Translator option `XOPTS(FEPI)` must be specified for the translator to accept these FEPI commands.

### 3.1.1 Formatted techniques

The formatted commands provide facilities for the application programmer to manipulate a copy of the LU2 (3270) emulated screen which is controlled by FEPI. The application program does not concern itself with the underlying 3270 protocols, merely accessing the screen as a chunk of data.

The formatted facilities fall into two areas:

- The keystroke interface
- The screen image interface

## KEYSTROKE INTERFACE

This interface permits the application program to manipulate the screen by 'pressing' keys that would have been used by a 'real' user of the screen. However, use of keystrokes requires a knowledge of the layout of the screen. An example command is shown in Fig. 3.1.

```
SEQUENCE DC   C'!CL!HOceot!EN'
SEQLEN   DC   A(L'SEQUENCE)

EXEC CICS FEPI SEND FORMATTED KEYSTROKES FROM(SEQUENCE)
                                        FLENGTH(SEQLEN)
                                        ESCAPE('!')
```

**Figure 3.1** Example of a Keystrokes command

Figure 3.1 clears the screen (`!CL`), puts the cursor on the first unprotected field (`!HO`), and sends the CEOT transaction with a press of Enter (`!EN`). It shows various things:

- The `ESCAPE` character precedes a two-character mnemonic that defines a special key press. In this case, the default setting has been changed from & to `'!'`.
- Multiple Attentions can be sent in one operation (thus losing any intermediate screens).
- The use of the Keystroke Interface is specified on the `EXEC CICS FEPI` command.

When the sequence of keystrokes is sent to FEPI, it is converted into a 3270 Datastream and sent to the partner system. This flow occurs when an Attention key (Enter or a PF key, etc.) is specified.

The full Keystroke Interface to formatted facilities are discussed in Chapter 30.

## SCREEN IMAGE INTERFACE

This interface operates by using a buffer representing the fields of the screen. You do not have to worry about 3270 Attribute bytes, but you do have to know where the fields are located on the screen (and so in the buffer).

Unlike the Keystroke Interface which only permits screen updates, the Screen Image Interface is used for both reading and updating the screen. In fact, if using formatted techniques, it is the only way to read the screen (but there are several ways of performing this operation).

The example command shown in Fig. 3.2 performs the same sequence as Fig. 3.1 (clear the screen, key in CEOT, and press enter). In this case:

- Three commands are required:
  The first clears the screen.
  The second receives the updated (empty) screen.
  The third sends the CEOT transaction.
- Each command processes one screen's worth of data.
- The Attention Key pressed is specified via the `AID` parameter.

```
SCREEN   DS   CL1920
         ORG  SCREEN
TRANSID  DS   CL4
         ORG  *

EXEC CICS FEPI SEND     FORMATTED AID(CLEAR)

EXEC CICS FEPI RECEIVE  FORMATTED INTO(SCREEN)
                                  MAXFLENGTH(=A(L'SCREEN))

         MVC  TRANSID,=CL4'ceot'

EXEC CICS FEPI SEND     FORMATTED FROM(SCREEN)
                                  FLENGTH(=A(L'SCREEN))
                                  AID(ENTER)
```

**Figure 3.2** Example of screen image commands

When screen image (the buffer) is sent to FEPI, it is converted into a 3270 Datastream and sent to the partner system. A similar process occurs in the reverse direction.

The full screen image interface to formatted facilities are discussed in Chapter 31 and subsequent chapters.

### 3.1.2 Datastream techniques

The Datastream techniques provide the application programmer with full access to the VTAM Datastream. FEPI does not provide any facilities to assist in building or parsing this data.

Datastream techniques are useful when running a passthrough application (see Chapters 4 and 42), as you are simply obtaining a 3270 Datastream from the real end-user terminal, and (with a bit of manipulation) passing it to the partner system. The reverse happens when the partner system responds with its flow.

However, Datastream programming is also useful if you connect FEPI with any facility that manipulates 3270 Datastreams.

Usage of the FEPI Datastream facilities permits the creation of a sophisticated windowing environment, whereby each window is communicating with a different partner. This is an extension of the techniques discussed in Chapter 5.

CHAPTER 4

# Passthrough and Coded

**GUIDANCE**

This chapter provides information on the way you use FEPI to run an emulation.

## 4.1 Introduction

When you run any type of terminal emulation (not necessarily using FEPI), you need to do two things:

- Connect the 'real' end-user terminal to a partner system (and change which partner system is being used).
- Do processing in the background, presenting the results to the 'real' terminal on an ad hoc basis.

The first technique is called *Passthrough*, and the second *Coded*.

### 4.1.1 Passthrough

In this technique, the 'real' end-user terminal is connected to various partner systems. The flow from a partner system is simply sent to the 'real' terminal unchanged (and vice versa).

FEPI supports Passthrough techniques using the Datastream-level commands, as the user is primarily concerned with 3270 Datastreams being passed to and fro. Passthrough techniques for FEPI are discussed in Chapter 41, and a sample program in Chapter 42.

Passthrough techniques are fairly straightforward. You just grab the flow from the partner system, do a little manipulation on it to change into a form suitable for CICS usage, and then use CICS Terminal Control commands to send the flow to the 'real' end-user terminal. A similar process operates in the other direction. Chapter 49 reveals some programming hints for Passthrough designs to get round CICS resource constraints.

### 4.1.2 Coded

Coded techniques are most suitable for applications that want to hide interactions from the 'real' end-user terminal. For example, you may wish to replace a complex sequence of interactions (like a database inquiry) with a single PF-Key press, with information for the operation being obtained from existing fields on the 'real' screen.

The crucial thing about Coded FEPI applications is that they involve some intelligence on the part of the FEPI application program. The application program *has* to know what is on the emulated screen at all times, and so take the appropriate action to recover from things like error messages (see Chapter 24).

You can use either Formatted or Datastream commands to perform Coded applications, but if you know the layouts of the panels that you are hiding (which you should), then Formatted access is best.

More information about the usage of Coded techniques is discussed in Chapter 5. One use of Coded techniques is to provide a windowing environment for the 'real' end-user terminal. (However, this implies sophisticated processing of the overlaid attribute bytes!)

## **4.2** A FEPI example

You have an existing set of transactions which are accessed from a menu. You now need to restrict the options on the menu to some of the users. Unfortunately, you cannot change the processing of the menu to ensure that only the allowed options appear to the privileged operators. Thus, you code up a FEPI front end to the menu. You blank out references to the privileged actions when the operator is not allowed to run them.

This FEPI application will probably use the Passthrough techniques to run via an emulated terminal. The flow from the emulated terminal is scanned for the menu screen, and amended if the user is not suitably authorized.

You may think this is a bit of a complicated way of stopping operations; you might think it easier to write a replacement menu system. This is true, but in the case where you cannot do this, FEPI provides the answer.

# CHAPTER 5 Scatter/Gather

**GUIDANCE**

This chapter provides some ideas about techniques to generate multiple FEPI requests from a single end-user request. These techniques are called Scatter/Gather.

## 5.1 Introduction

Scatter/Gather is a term taken from the messaging arena. A single message can contain many subrequests, all of which have to succeed for the prime request to succeed. Therefore, the prime request *Scatters* into many other requests (which themselves may explode into many subrequests), and then *Gathers* the results into one whole, this single gathered response forming the answer to the original prime request.

In the FEPI environment, Scatter/Gather is realized by the end user initiating a request which does lots of processing in the background before returning the results.

### 5.1.1 Scatter/Gather example (Utility)

A customer comes into a utility shop and orders a fire. Before processing the order, the utility needs to run a credit check on the customer (for credit worthiness), and examine the customer's energy account (to see if the customer is a bad payer).

Therefore, the following things need to be done:

1. Get customer's name and address.
2. Look up customer's credit rating and save it.
3. Look up customer's energy account and note speed of payment.
4. Look up stock to see if the fire is available.
5. Process the fire order.

Without FEPI, the shop assistant needs to run five different terminal interactions (on different hosts), writing down information from each one. This is not only tedious, but it also has to be done synchronously. Using a windowed environment does not reduce the complexity, or the writing down, but it permits a degree of overlap if all the systems are online at the same time.

This scenario may be acceptable (but slow) if all the systems are all online and rapidly respond, but what should happen if one of them is down, or takes ages to respond? How do you get rid of the low-tech image of pieces of paper? How do you prevent the customer from becoming fed up with waiting for the simple order to be processed?

As you have probably guessed, the answer is to use FEPI in a Scatter/Gather mode. The way to do this is to write a CICS transaction that simply asks for the customer's name and address, and records the order. As soon as the name and address are known, start some FEPI accesses that emulate the credit check, and payment check functions. These accesses will run in parallel to obtain the required information. As soon as either one completes, then update the order screen (at the 'real' terminal) with some indicator to say what credit or payment is OK/NOGO. In the meantime, another FEPI access can be accessing the order system to see if the fire is available. When all three functions (credit check, payment check, fire availability) have completed, the order can be processed.

FEPI gives these benefits:

- It reduces the keying involved—so improving accuracy and speed.
- It reduces the elapsed time—as operations proceed in parallel.
- It removes the manual copying of data—so improving accuracy and image.
- It removes shop assistant decisions about what to do if a system is down—as the FEPI application program contains the rules.

### 5.1.2 Scatter/Gather example (finance)

A customer rings up a bank (or finance house) to request details of their account balance. In order to provide this figure, a terminal operator has to know either the account number, or the customer's name and address.

If the customer simply gives their name and address, the terminal operator has to use some sort of lookup transaction to determine the account number. However, while the customer is in contact with the bank, there is an opportunity to introduce the customer to any additional services that may be appropriate. Thus, what is required is a method of assessing whether any services are appropriate while the account balance is being determined.

The bank already has CICS transactions that determine the suitability of a customer for new services, but they run via operator keying at a real terminal. Customers are not prepared to wait for the terminal operator to go (slowly) through all the required actions to determine suitability for these services.

FEPI can be used to run all the service suitabilities while the account balance is being determined, and without any keying by the terminal operator. The crucial thing is that the service suitability transactions, which already exist, are unchanged, but are now used in a new fashion.

Therefore, the following actions occur:

1. Use the customer's name and address to point to a personal record.
2. Start a CICS transaction that obtains the account balance (the scattering transaction).
3. Start any CICS transactions (scattered transactions) as required to determine service applicability (one per potential service).
4. A panel is presented by the scattering transaction to the terminal operator showing the account balance.
5. The panel is updated with yes/no indicators showing the suitability of the customer for new services (gathering the responses of the scattered transactions).

This technique of using FEPI to emulate many existing transactions in parallel with each other is a use of Scatter/Gather. The transaction that determines the account balance scatters the transactions that determine the service applicability. The balance transaction then gathers the responses, and displays the results on a single panel.

Consequently, use of Scatter/Gather has:

- Removed terminal operator keying.
- Introduced parallelism to reduce response time.
- Added new function without changing existing function.
- Joined together existing functions into a new seamless whole.

### 5.1.3 Conclusion

FEPI's Scatter/Gather techniques can permit a significant degree of multiprocessing to be done in background mode. This allows a reduction in response time by using parallel processing, as well as an improvement in quality due to the passing of data between the background and foreground tasks.

The crucial point is that *FEPI emulation does not always involve the end user.* You have facilities to run the emulation in whatever fashion you care to design.

# CHAPTER 6 Use of FEPI's asynchronous facilities

**GUIDANCE**

This chapter introduces the asynchronous facilities of FEPI. These facilities are unique within the EXEC CICS language.

## 6.1 Conversations and tasks

When communicating using CICS MRO or LU6.2 facilities, the Conversation ends at the end-of-task. The Conversation dies with the CICS task. FEPI Conversations, however, can continue over an end-of-task. FEPI Conversations can (and should) spread over many CICS tasks.

Therefore, FEPI Conversations can be designed in a full pseudo-conversational basis. These facilities are (partially) controlled by options on the `EXEC CICS FEPI FREE` command (see Sec. 27.8 and Chapter 36).

When a Conversation is continued in another CICS task, the partner system does not know that a CICS task-switch has occurred. As far as the partner is concerned, the 'operator' is just having a think about what to do next.

## 6.2 `EXEC CICS FEPI STARTs`

When coding FEPI pseudo-conversational transactions, you want a transaction started to process a flow from the partner system. In other words, you end the first transaction just after sending a flow to the partner system, and continue processing in a new transaction which is initiated when the partner system responds. This process is controlled by the `EXEC CICS FEPI START` command (see Sec. 27.9 and Chapter 35). Figure 6.1 shows this arrangement.

The use of `EXEC CICS FEPI START` (as an alternative to `EXEC CICS FEPI FREE`) permits a full pseudo-conversational operation of FEPI. This will be most useful for Passthrough applications, with one transaction handling terminal to FEPI (MAPIN) and the other FEPI to terminal (MAPOUT). See Chapter 49 for the tricks of this technique.

Use of `EXEC CICS FEPI START` is not restricted to Passthrough applications. The order application discussed in Chapter 5 could use them to transfer the data.

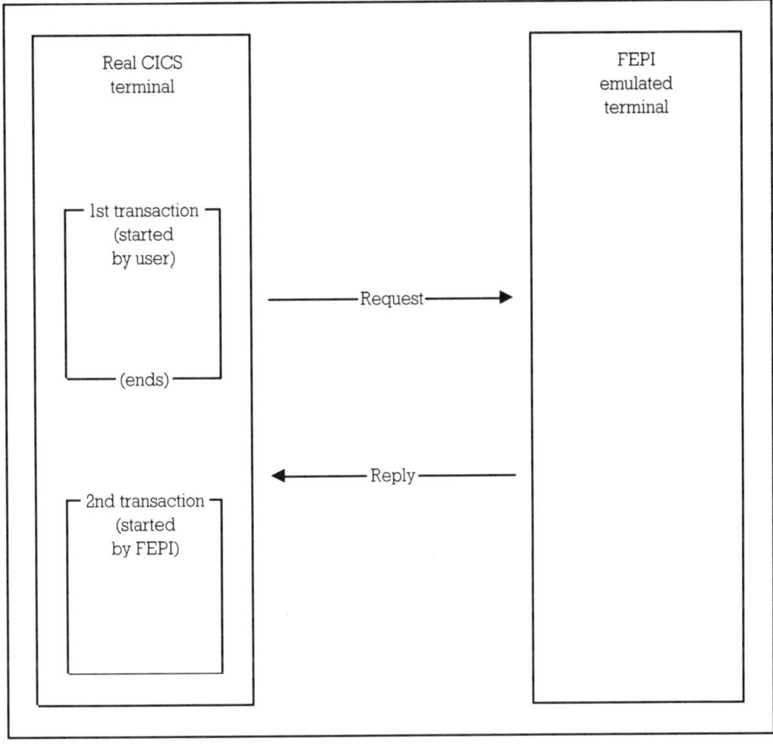


**Figure 6.1** Asynchronous FEPI usage

## 6.3 CICS resource constraints

CICS will only run about 500 active transactions (due to below-the-line storage requirements), but FEPI will cope with many more Connections than this. Consequently, if you have, say, 1000 FEPI Connections, you cannot be processing them all at once!

This large number of FEPI Conversations is therefore assessed by using the FEPI asynchronous facilities. These permit the maximal use of CICS resources while awaiting for partner systems to respond. You can further use TASKCLASS facilities to restrict resource usage.

You should design your FEPI transactions on a MAPIN and MAPOUT basis, using the techniques discussed in Chapter 49 for Passthrough applications. If processing Coded applications (using Formatted access), TIMEOUT (see Chapters 7 and 34) might be more appropriate.

# CHAPTER 7 Use of Timeouts

**GUIDANCE**

This chapter introduces the FEPI facilities used to ensure that events complete within a given interval.

## 7.1 Description

When you have sent a flow to the partner system, you do an `EXEC CICS FEPI RECEIVE` to get hold of the reply. However, as things stand, you will wait forever for this to happen. This is rather boring, as the program is incapable of doing anything else in the interval. What is needed is a method of terminating the operation after an interval, and reissuing it later to see if the reply has been generated.

FEPI provides `TIMEOUT` options on commands that can wait for things to happen. If an event does not complete in the specified interval, then the `EXEC CICS FEPI` command completes with an indication that the request timed out. You can then reissue the request later, or take some sort of remedial action in the meantime.

However, do not think that use of `TIMEOUT` is merely a way of cutting short waits. `TIMEOUT` provides a very flexible method of permitting multiple emulations within a single CICS task. You should use this design technique when full asynchronous operation is not required.

In this case (i.e., when not carrying out a full asynchronous operation), each request has a minimal `TIMEOUT` setting, and a polling operation is done to collect the information from partners.

### 7.1.1 Timeouts on EXEC CICS FEPI ALLOCATEs

The TIMEOUT setting on the EXEC CICS FEPI ALLOCATE command permits a notification that there are not enough Connections in the Pool to satisfy all requests. To continue, you can use the FEPI Dynamic Resource Definition facilities (see Chapters 13 and 48) to increase the bandwidth to the partner system.

Additionally, use of TIMEOUT permits the FEPI application program to notify the end user that the FEPI emulation is being delayed due to path constraints. This facility is not provided on the EXEC CICS ALLOCATE commands for MRO and LU6.2 Connections. For these access methods, if a free session is not available, the command either waits forever (i.e., until the transaction is cancelled) or returns immediately. EXEC CICS FEPI ALLOCATE permits a user-specified delay.

A detailed description of TIMEOUT usage can be found in Chapter 34.

### 7.1.2 Timeouts on EXEC CICS FEPI RECEIVEs

The TIMEOUT parameter on the EXEC CICS FEPI RECEIVE permits a user-specified interval in which the partner is given the opportunity to respond. If the partner does not reply in the interval, the EXEC CICS FEPI RECEIVE is ended with an indication of the timeout (the command will complete immediately if a flow from the partner has occurred).

As the Receive has not actually happened, it can be reissued (with a different timeout if desired) to get the flow when the partner system actually responds.

If the partner system fails, then a TIMEOUT will be ended, but the indication will not be Timeout, but session failure. Therefore, the EXEC CICS FEPI RECEIVE (with or without a TIMEOUT) will be ended if the partner system fails.

### 7.1.3 Timeouts on EXEC CICS FEPI STARTs

The TIMEOUT on the EXEC CICS FEPI START command says that you want the named transaction to be initiated after the given interval, whether or not the partner has responded. Consequently, you can guarantee that the STARTed transaction will get going after a set time. You get an indication in the Start Data (see Secs 35.1 and D.2) saying that the transaction was started due to a Timeout (or a session failure).

This facility is most useful when running a full asynchronous design, and you need to start the named transaction to process the fact that the partner has not responded in the expected interval.

# CHAPTER 8 Handlers

**GUIDANCE**

This chapter provides a brief introduction to the FEPI Handlers. They are fully documented in Chapter 44.

## 8.1 Introduction

FEPI provides facilities for transactions to be initiated to cope with special events. These transactions are called *Handlers*, and are fully discussed in Chapter 44.

The Handlers allow the processing of these events to be taken away from FEPI application programs and centralized in system-programmer-provided transactions. The Handlers can be viewed as a sort of Global User Exit, but they operate as transactions, not as part of the CICS nucleus.

The Handlers are specified on a Pool basis via the Propertyset attributes (see Chapter 16). The following events can trigger a Handler transaction:

- The *Bind* of a Connection generates the *Begin Session* Handler.
- The processing of an `EXEC CICS FEPI FREE` command will initiate the *End Session* (End of Conversation) Handler.
- The *Unbind* of a Connection generates the *End Session* (End of Connection) Handler.
- The receipt of data on a Connection from a partner when no FEPI application program is accessing the Connection will start the *Unsolicited Data* Handler.
- The receipt of sequence number data on an LU0 (SLUP) Connection will generate the *STSN* Handler.

The design decisions flowing from the use of these Handler transactions are fully discussed in Chapter 47.

CHAPTER 9

# FEPI Monitor Transient Data Queues

**GUIDANCE**

This chapter provides a brief introduction to the FEPI Monitor Transient Data Queues (TDQs).

## 9.1 FEPI Monitors

FEPI provides the ability to log information to TDQs when certain events occur. In contrast to the Handlers, the Monitors do not represent exit facilities, but rather a repository for types of failures.

The idea is that FEPI writes the failure information to a TDQ, which should have an associated Triggered Transaction. The Triggered Transaction should read the TDQ, extract the failure information, and act accordingly.

FEPI uses two types of TDQs for Monitors: Pool-specific TDQs (specified on the Propertyset for the Pool (see Sec. 16.2.5) and the CSZX Global TDQ.

The most important things notified by FEPI Monitors are *session failures*. When a FEPI Connection dies due to partner failure, this event is logged in a TDQ as well as being notified to the FEPI application program. Consequently, a centrally provided Monitor transaction can attempt to alleviate the situation, without relying on an individual FEPI program to do so.

CHAPTER 10

# FEPI Conversation types

**GUIDANCE**

This chapter describes the various styles of FEPI Conversations.

## 10.1 FEPI Conversations

There are various types of FEPI Conversations but, as all use FEPI Connections, they share some characteristics. However, there are interesting design issues in how you operate the Conversations, and it is these which are discussed in this chapter.

A FEPI *Conversation* runs over a FEPI *Connection*. The Conversation lasts between an `EXEC CICS FEPI ALLOCATE` (without `PASSCONVID`) and an `EXEC CICS FEPI FREE` (without the `PASS` parameter). Note that, unlike an LU6.2 or an MRO Conversation, a failure either to request a continuation of the Conversation in another task, or to end it, is treated an an error, and the underlying Connection will be terminated along with the Conversation.

Consequently, there are various types of Conversation, depending on how you arrange things. In addition to *Normal Conversations*, FEPI provides a *Temporary Conversation* for use in very specialized circumstances (which are mainly to do with LU0 Conversations, and are thus not covered in this book).

## 10.2 Normal FEPI Conversations

Use of a Normal FEPI Conversation is governed by the design of the overall FEPI Application. The following styles are possible:

- Single transaction Conversations
- Full asynchronous Conversations
- Handler Conversations

You should refer to Chapter 27 for a description of the `EXEC CICS FEPI` commands used to illustrate the techniques.

### 10.2.1 Single transaction Conversations

In this type of design, the FEPI Conversation lasts only for the duration of a single CICS transaction. You start the emulation with an EXEC CICS FEPI ALLOCATE without PASSCONVID, and end it with an EXEC CICS FEPI FREE HOLD.

This type of Conversation design is useful when you want to do only a small amount of work within the partner system, and are happy to emulate the whole sequence from partner signon to partner signoff.

As these type of Conversations reside within a single CICS Transaction, you may be limited in the number of concurrent conversations that CICS can support (see Sec. 6.3). Therefore, these single transaction Conversations should only be used in either a low-usage CICS system, or where the partner system will always respond rapidly.

### 10.2.2 Full asynchronous Conversations

The FEPI Conversations used in this design are *pass*ed from one CICS transaction to another. The Conversation is started via an EXEC CICS FEPI ALLOCATE (without PASSCONVID) and lasts until a final EXEC CICS FEPI FREE without PASS is specified. This latter command will be issued in a different CICS task to the allocate.

The FEPI Conversation is passed between one CICS transaction and another in one of two ways, depending on how you arrange for the subsequent transaction to be initiated. Either:

- EXEC CICS FEPI FREE PASS in the first transaction.
- Save the CONVID from the first transaction, and arrange for it to be known to the second transaction (usually in the COMMAREA passed to this second transaction).
- Issue an EXEC CICS FEPI ALLOCATE PASSCONVID to reuse the conversation in the second transaction.

Or:

- Issue an EXEC CICS FEPI START in the first transaction to start the named transaction when the partner responds.
- The partner responds and so FEPI initiates the named transaction.
- In this second transaction, issue an EXEC CICS FEPI ALLOCATE PASSCONVID to continue the conversation (the CONVID is part of the start data, see Sec. D.2).

If you choose the FEPI START method of asynchronous operation, then all the tedious copying of the CONVID is catered for. Alternatively, if you need to do your own transaction scheduling, then you must provide a way of copying the FEPI CONVID (and maybe protecting the Conversation from being illegally used by someone who knows the CONVID!).

### 10.2.3 Handler Conversations

Handler Conversations obey a similar, but slightly different, set of rules to normal FEPI Conversations. In particular, the actions the `EXEC CICS FEPI FREE` takes are different (see Chapter 36). However, the same rules apply for passing Conversations from a Handler transaction to another transaction. You can decide to continue a Handler in another CICS transaction (although this is not recommended, as it adds considerable complexity to the design), either manually via `EXEC CICS FEPI FREE PASS` or automatically via `EXEC CICS FEPI START` commands. The Handler processing is thereby extended over a sequence of CICS transactions, not just a single Handler transaction.

## **10.3** Temporary FEPI Conversations

Temporary FEPI Conversations are designed for client–server processes, whereby the partner system is the server, and the FEPI application program the client. The idea is that you send a single flow to the partner system, and get a single flow back (this mainly occurs in some types of LU0 emulation). These Temporary Conversations last only for the duration of this single request, and cannot be passed to other CICS transactions.

A Temporary Conversation does not go via the `EXEC CICS FEPI ALLOCATE` to `EXEC CICS FEPI FREE` sequence. Instead a variant of the `EXEC CICS FEPI CONVERSE` command with the `POOL` operand (and omitting the `CONVID` parameter) is used (see Secs 27.14 and 27.15).

Temporary conversations suffer from the disadvantage that there is no relationship between the end user running it and the partner systems' logonid. Consequently, the partner systems must trust that the invoking FEPI application program has done any relevant security processing. Similarly, a *Begin Session* Handler would normally be used to set up the partner system for temporary Conversation usage. *End Session* Handlers (End-of-Session) should also be used to tidy things up again.

Unless you have a good reason for using Temporary Conversations, I would recommend not using them. However, they can be very useful in some specific instances!

**P A R T 2**

# System definition and the SPI

**GUIDANCE**

This part of the book discusses the system programming (SPI) facilities of FEPI which are used to define, remove, and control FEPI resources.

The following topics are presented in this part of the book:

- FEPI resource concepts
- VTAM definitions for Nodes
- FEPI resource definition
- `EXEC CICS FEPI INSTALL/ADD`
- `EXEC CICS FEPI DISCARD/DELETE`
- Choosing the Propertyset options
- Resource definition examples
- Resource manipulation
- CEMT

The commands used to access FEPI (the API-type commands) are described in Chapter 27.

# CHAPTER 11 FEPI resource concepts

**GUIDANCE**

This chapter describes the resources FEPI uses to run its emulation. The way these resources are defined is contained in Chapter 13.

## 11.1 The FEPI resources

FEPI is a Terminal Emulator. To accomplish the emulation, therefore, you need a 'terminal' which is talking to a partner 'system'. The pseudo-terminals used for the emulation are called *Nodes*. The partner systems to which the emulation is running are called *Targets*. The combination of a Target and a Node represents a path to the partner system, and is called a *Connection*. FEPI uses Connections to run emulations which are called *Conversations*.

Therefore, Virtual Terminals called Nodes talk to partner systems called Targets, with the paths called Connections. A Conversation is made over the Connection to perform the emulation.

However, you do not need just one path to a partner system, you need lots. Therefore, FEPI provides an object to group the Connections called a *Pool*. The contents of a Pool represent the bandwidth of paths to the partner system. When you start a Conversation, you obtain usage of a Connection (a path) by accessing the Pool.

FEPI will operate the emulation using either LU2 (3270) or LU0 (SLUP) protocols. Consequently, there must be a method of relating the protocol to the Connection. This is done at the Pool level. Each Pool has a set of attributes associated with it called a *Propertyset*.

The Propertyset defines the attributes of the Pool, and all the Connections contained therein. (Note, in the *CICS/ESA FEPI User's Guide* the Propertyset is called a 'Property Set'.) Pools can have identical attributes, and so share Propertysets.

To summarize, the FEPI resources are:

**Nodes** which define the Virtual Terminals to be used.
**Targets** which define the partner systems to be accessed.
**Connections** which are a Target–Node combination and represent an emulation path (and also a VTAM session).
**Propertysets** which define a set of attributes.
**Pools** which contain Connections, whose characteristics are defined by a Propertyset.
**Conversations** which represent active emulations running over Connections.

## 11.1.1 FEPI Nodes

FEPI Nodes represent the pseudo-terminals used for the emulation. The way they are defined is discussed in Sec. 14.2.4. However, a Node has an underlying VTAM definition. This definition is discussed in Chapter 12.

The name of the Node, which must be that defined to VTAM, becomes the LU name at the partner system. Consequently, the name of the Node is, essentially, the Terminal Id used by the partner system.

If running an emulation to CICS, the Terminal Id is usually (depending on naming conventions) obtained by the equivalent of `SUBSTR(LUname,4,4)`. Therefore, if you are using AutoInstall on the partner CICS system (and have not altered CICS's algorithm using the AutoInstall GLUE), a FEPI Node called `IYAERAH1` will create a terminal called `RAH1`.

FEPI reuses its Nodes. Therefore, you can use a given Node to communicate with many partner systems (Targets) at the same time. You do not need to create separate Nodes for separate Targets (unless you choose to do so). Consequently, when communicating with, say, four partner CICSs, you can have the same Terminal Id in each!

This reuse of the Nodes permits significant audit-trailing when running a complex set of emulations.

## 11.1.2 FEPI Targets

FEPI Targets represent the partner systems with which communication is being performed. See Sec. 14.2.3 for information on their definition.

The Target represents the `APPLID` of the partner system. No extra VTAM definition is required to use an existing `APPLID` for FEPI usage, provided that the `APPLID` is 'visible' to the MVS containing FEPI's CICS system.

Unlike Nodes, FEPI Targets can have a different name to that of the `APPLID`. This permits the use of a logical name for the partner, without exposing the underlying VTAM definition.

This name aliasing is important when communicating with a XRF capable system (see Chapter 60), or using CLSDST(PASS) processing (see Chapter 51). However, in more common circumstances, it is possible to request access to a given Target within a Pool, so it is important to use a name which will be unchanged when a network redefinition changes the underlying VTAM APPLID.

### 11.1.3 FEPI Propertysets

The FEPI Propertysets define a set of attributes for a Pool, and, hence, all the Connections within the Pool. A Propertyset defines which access method (LU2 or LU0) is to be used for the Connections within the Pool, together with things like the terminal type (colour or monochrome, screen size) for the Connections, and whether or not Handlers are to be used.

The command for defining the Propertysets is discussed in Sec. 14.2.1, and a discussion of all the attributes (and the design decisions behind the choices) in Chaper 16.

A given Propertyset can be used in many Pools, resulting in all the Pools having the same set of characteristics.

### 11.1.4 FEPI Pools

FEPI Pools represent a set of Connections (Target–Node pairs) having a common set of characteristics (defined by the Propertyset associated with the Pool). See Sec. 14.2.2 for information on the definition of Pools.

The FEPI Pool is the object upon which a Conversation is started. The `EXEC CICS FEPI ALLOCATE` command (see Secs. 27.2 and 29.2) names the Pool from which a Connection is to be used for the emulation. Consequently, the Pool should contain enough Connections to satisfy peak FEPI usage.

However, FEPI provides facilities to manage the number of Connections within the Pool (see Sec. 14.3) to provide Dynamic Resource Tuning (see Chapter 48).

Once the Pool has been defined using a Propertyset, you cannot amend these characteristics. If this is required, then the Pool will have to be deleted (see Sec. 15.2.4), and recreated using a different Propertyset.

### 11.1.5 FEPI Connections

A FEPI Connection is a Target–Node pair that represents a path to a partner system with a fixed 'Terminal Id'. Connections are defined in a different fashion to other FEPI resources, as related in Sec. 14.3.

The Target–Node combination only exists within a Pool, and so long as a given combination does not exist in more than one pool, the constituent Targets and Nodes can (and should) be active in other Pools.

The Connection represents the underlying VTAM session to the target system. However, no VTAM definitions are required to generate the Connection; it will 'automatically' be created (and deleted) depending on the VTAM status of the Target and the Node that combine to form it.

### 11.1.6 FEPI Conversations

FEPI Conversations are the emulations currently being run over the Connections. Conversations are not defined, but come into being when a Connection is grabbed by use of the `EXEC CICS FEPI ALLOCATE` command (see Sec. 27.2 and Chapter 29) and are ended by a particular sort of `EXEC CICS FEPI FREE` command (see Sec. 27.8 and Chapter 36).

There is one major difference between FEPI Conversations and CICS's MRO and LU6.2 Conversations. The LU6.2/MRO Conversations *do not* last over a CICS End of Transaction. *FEPI Conversations do last over the End of Transaction.* This unique feature permits full pseudo-conversational use of FEPI Resources (see Chapters 6 and 35). In addition to the sheer convenience of the facility, you will need to use these asynchronous FEPI facilities to overcome CICS resource constraints (see Chapter 49).

In conceptual terms, there are different sorts of FEPI Conversations. These are discussed in Chapter 10, but these types arise purely out of how the Conversations are used; the underlying principles are the same.

# CHAPTER 12 VTAM definitions for Nodes

**GUIDANCE**

This chapter discusses the VTAM definitions required for FEPI Nodes. If you are not familiar with 'SYS1.VTAMLST', or are uninterested in VTAM definitions, skip this chapter.

You should refer to the *VTAM Network Implementation Guide* or the *VTAM Definition Reference Manual* for information on VTAM definitions.

## 12.1 VTAM and FEPI nodes

The FEPI Node represents the pseudo-terminal used for the emulation, therefore, in VTAM terms, it forms a *Secondary LU*. Consequently, a Secondary LU has to be defined to VTAM for FEPI's use. The name of the Secondary LU is the name of the FEPI Node. This VTAM name is also called an *Application Minor Node* name.

The VTAM method of defining this entity involves the use of the `APPL` statement (do not confuse this with the Applid.)

The definition placed in 'SYS1.VTAMLST' is simple:

```
⟨node name⟩  APPL
```

### 12.1.1 VTAM's APPL statement

The simplest form of the `APPL` statement can be extended in two ways:

```
IYAEZM10 APPL   ACBNAME=NODEZM10
```

says that the FEPI Node called `NODEZM10` (which would generate a CICS Terminal Id of 'ZM10') has a network name of `IYAEZM10`. This usage permits FEPI to use a name somewhat divorced from the underlying network name.

The statement:

```
IYAEZP99 APPL   PRTCT=SECURED
```

says that the `IYAEZP99` node is password protected. When installing the Node via an `EXEC CICS FEPI INSTALL NODE` command (see Sec. 14.2.4) the password (`SECURED`) must be quoted in the `PASSWORD` field. If however, the

PASSWORD is not specified, or is incorrect, then FEPI will not be able to use the node.

### 12.1.2 VTAM Node Activation and Control

These VTAM APPL statements are placed within a member of the 'SYS1.VTAMLST' PDS, so they will only be activated if the owning *major* (VTAM) Node is active. This basically means that a

`V NET,ACT,ID=⟨member name⟩`

command must be issued to activate the FEPI Nodes to VTAM.

As the FEPI nodes are, therefore, VTAM objects, they may be controlled by VTAM commands. Consequently, a FEPI Node can be made unusable by a

`V NET,INACT,ID=⟨node name⟩`

command.

Similarly, a FEPI node can be *forced* unusable by a V NET,INACT, FORCE,ID=⟨node name⟩ command. This is useful if FEPI shutdown fails (see Sec. 59.1).

## 12.2 VTAM Session parameters

When a FEPI node is used in a FEPI Connection, the terminal type for the resulting VTAM session is taken from the DEVICE parameter of the Property-set used for the Pool containing the Connection. When the Connection is ACQUIRED (i.e., the session starts), FEPI uses the DEVICE parameter to generate the Bind used in creating the VTAM session. Table 12.1 shows which VTAM LOGMODE is used for the given device (this setting is not alterable).

**Table 12.1** FEPI DEVICE settings and VTAM LOGMODEs

| Device CVDA setting | VTAM LOGMODE used | Terminal type |
|---|---|---|
| T3278M2 | **D4A32782** | LU2 3278 (monochrome) Model 2 |
| T3278M3 | **D4A32783** | LU2 3278 (monochrome) Model 3 |
| T3278M4 | **D4A32784** | LU2 3278 (monochrome) Model 4 |
| T3278M5 | **D4A32785** | LU2 3278 (monochrome) Model 5 |
| T3279M2 | **SNX32702** | LU2 3279 (colour) Model 2 |
| T3279M3 | **SNX32703** | LU2 3279 (colour) Model 3 |
| T3279M4 | **SNX32704** | LU2 3279 (colour) Model 4 |
| T3279M5 | **SNX32705** | LU2 3279 (colour) Model 5 |
| TPS55M2 | **SNX32702** | LU2 PS/55 (Double Byte Character Set) Model 2 |
| TPS55M3 | **SNX32703** | LU2 PS/55 (Double Byte Character Set) Model 3 |
| TPS55M4 | **SNX32704** | LU2 PS/55 (Double Byte Character Set) Model 4 |
| LUP | **IBM3600** | LU0 (SLUP) |

These LOGMODE entries define various VTAM characteristics of the session. Therefore, if you are using the Node in different Pools, the given Node can be using many LOGMODEs at the same time. This means that the Node can represent a different screen size in different Pools (defined by the Pools `DEVICE` Propertyset parameter).

These LOGMODE entries are defined in the VTAM default LOGMODE table ISTINCLM. If you are content with the settings for the LOGMODEs in this table, then you need not amend your `APPL` statements for the Nodes. However, your VTAM configuration may have altered these default IBM-supplied LOGMODE characteristics, or the default table may not contain the required LOGMODEs, or you may want to use a special set of VTAM characteristics for FEPI usage. In these cases, you want the Node to use the LOGMODEs contained in a particular `MODETABLE`. To do this, simply quote the relevant `MODETAB` on the `APPL` statement:

```
IYAFAST1 APPL   MODETAB=⟨new MODETAB name⟩
```

If the specified `MODETAB` does not contain the required LOGMODE, then the default (ISTINCLM) is used by VTAM.

See Sec. 52.3 for information on FEPI's requirements for LU0 (SLUP) processing.

## 12.3 VTAM and FEPI Targets

Bear in mind that the VTAM Applid specified for the FEPI Target must be contactable from the VTAM of the MVS running the CICS system containing FEPI.

# CHAPTER 13 FEPI resource definition

**GUIDANCE**

This chapter discusses the concepts of FEPI resource definition. The actual commands are discussed in Chapters 14 and 15.
Crucial to an appreciation of how FEPI resource definition is implemented is the understanding that FEPI resources are *not* defined using either CICS Resource Definition Macro (RDM) or Resource Definition Online (RDO) facilities.

## 13.1 A general review of CICS resource definition

CICS Resources can be created using two methods:

- Resource Definition Macro (RDM)
- Resource Definition Online (RDO)

RDM involves the generation of tables (via assembler macros) which are then loaded as part of CICS initialization. An example of such a table is the Destination Control Table (DCT), which is used to define Transient Data Queues (TDQs). Resources defined using RDM are static for the duration of CICS—existing resources cannot be removed, and new ones cannot be added. This type of resource definition is now becoming obsolete.

RDO involves the creation of CICS resources via the CEDA transaction, which stores the resources in the CSD file. In addition to providing an online method of describing the resources, RDO permits the installation of new resources (and the Discarding of extant ones) during the CICS run. A special feature of RDO permits the AutoInstall of CICS resources (only terminals at the moment).

FEPI uses neither of these methods, opting instead for an API-based technique. For convenience's sake, the `EXEC CICS FEPI` commands associated with FEPI Resource Management and Definition are called *SPI-type commands*, while those for FEPI access are referred to as *API-type commands*.

## 13.2 FEPI Dynamic Resource Definition

All FEPI resources (Propertysets, Nodes, Targets, Pools, and Connections) are defined using `EXEC CICS FEPI INSTALL` or `EXEC CICS FEPI ADD` commands. They are removed using `EXEC CICS FEPI DISCARD` and `EXEC CICS FEPI DELETE` commands (or the CEMT equivalents).

The FEPI resource creation commands are described in Chapter 14, and those for FEPI resource removal in Chapter 15.

Consequently, FEPI resources are processed in a completely different fashion to the other (extant) CICS resources. The technique of using the SPI-type commands is called *Dynamic Resource Definition*. The use of dynamic definition techniques for FEPI resources permits significant opportunities for Resource Tuning, and these are discussed in Chapter 48.

FEPI was designed from the start to be completely flexible, and the developers were very motivated to provide facilities that both execute as rapidly as possible, and allow the maximum possible flexibility for you, the application programmer. Consequently, if there are situations where you need more (or less) FEPI resource, or need to be able to respond to external events (such as a partner failure), you can easily perform the required FEPI resource definition actions at any time. By using a command-driven technique for FEPI resource definition, you can do whatever is required under program control.

Regrettably, all good things have a drawback, and FEPI's is that you have to define your FEPI resources in a startup program, which is run from a transaction that is started from a PLT program. However, this approach has the great advantage that *you* have FEPI resources under your control, and so can react to things like the day of startup (do you need to install the same resources every day?).

### WHINGE, MUTTER, GRUMBLE

'Mutter, mutter, whinge' I hear you grumbling. Why invent a new way of installing resources?

It is all to do with the flexibility of the emulation. You want:

- The ability to reroute communication in case of failure.
- The ability to add bandwidth to provide peak-time capability.
- The ability to add new emulations to a 24-hour system.
- The ability to control requests in times of crises.
- The ability to define different resource characteristics to different classes of users.
- A programming interface for resource definition.

4FEPI's Dynamic Resource Definition techniques permit them all! Bandwidth, in particular, is discussed in Sec. 48.2.

## **13.3** Definition of FEPI resources

FEPI resource definition is in three parts:

- Enabling FEPI in the CICS system.
- Adding the action of resource definition to CICS system initialization.
- Installing the FEPI resources.

### 13.3.1 Enabling FEPI in CICS

To get FEPI going in the CICS System, simply code FEPI=YES in the SIT, or supply this via SYSIN. Do not forget that other CICS resources may have to be defined (such as Transient Data Queues for Handlers and Monitors, see Part 6) before the FEPI/CICS environment is complete.

### 13.3.2 CICS initialization

I recommend that you install your FEPI resources from a transaction initiated from a PLT program. Therefore, once CICS has initialized, the FEPI resources will be available for use (FEPI itself starts up just before the PLT is scanned):

- Write a PLT program which just contains an EXEC CICS START TRAN('fepi') INTERVAL(0) (you probably have this program already).
- In the 'fepi' transaction issue the EXEC CICS FEPI INSTALL/ADD commands to Install all the necessary FEPI resources.

A separate transaction is used from the PLT-running CICS transaction so that any failures will not affect other CICS facilities.

When you code the EXEC CICS FEPI INSTALL and EXEC CICS FEPI ADD commands (see Chapter 14) to install all your FEPI resources, you should consider the effect upon the network. If you are using Lists to define the resources, it is possible to flood VTAM with requests. Coding the resources as discrete commands permits VTAM to cope with the load. This is one of the reasons why I recommend that you avoid list processing.

### 13.3.3 Order of installing the FEPI resources

A full description of the EXEC CICS FEPI INSTALL and EXEC CICS FEPI ADD commands for installing FEPI resources is contained in Chapter 14, while the equivalent commands for removing FEPI resources are in Chapter 15.

I recommend that you install your FEPI resources in this order:

1. Propertysets
2. Pools
3. Nodes
4. Targets
5. Connections

Therefore:

- The first things to define are the Propertysets required to set the attributes for the Pools.
- Secondly, create the empty Pools whose attributes are defined by the Propertysets.
- Next, install the Nodes with ACQSTATUS(ACQUIRED) (see Sec. 14.2.4) so that these pseudo-terminals are activated in VTAM terms. If you avoid using a list, then you will not run the risk of flooding VTAM with '*OPEN ACB*' requests.

- Fourthly, define the Targets (the partner systems) for communication.
- Lastly, create the Connections by issuing `EXEC CICS FEPI ADD` commands with `ACQSTATUS(ACQUIRED)`. Again, beware of flooding VTAM with requests by using lists.

All these commands are placed in the program which is run by the transaction started from the PLT. Therefore, the FEPI resource installation can be tailored according to circumstance. For example, suppose that some Connections fail to start because the partner system is unavailable. You may want to route the FEPI emulations to a backup system. This is easily done by `EXEC CICS FEPI ADD`ing the alternative Target into the Pool.

The logic of this startup program is completely dependent on your FEPI design, but whatever is required can be done because of these Dynamic Resource Definition facilities.

Note that you will not be able to use the Nodes until the correct VTAM definitions (see Chaper 13) are active.

CHAPTER 14

# EXEC CICS FEPI INSTALL/ADD

**GUIDANCE**

This chapter discusses how you define the FEPI resources discussed in Chapters 11 and 13. What you define depends, to a certain extent, on the Propertyset definitions discussed in Chapter 16.

## 14.1 Introduction

All FEPI resources are defined using the SPI-type commands (as discussed in Chapter 13), which are listed in Sec. A.2. For information about using these commands to provide Dynamic Resource Definition, see the discussion in Chapter 48.

A FEPI resource is defined using an `EXEC CICS FEPI INSTALL` command, and is removed by an `EXEC CICS FEPI DISCARD` (however, this removal does not happen until all existing usage of the resource ends).

The contents of Pools are controlled via `EXEC CICS FEPI ADD` and `EXEC CICS FEPI DELETE` commands, but these operations do not affect the underlying FEPI Resources. See Sec. 14.3 and Sec. 15.3 respectively, for a description of these operations.

When the developers were designing these FEPI SPI-commands, we were very concerned with the number of commands that would have to be issued to create a reasonably interesting FEPI setup. Consequently, we provided some unusual facilities within the EXEC CICS language:

- The ability to define more than one FEPI resource in a command, by using lists.
- The provision (and duplication) of some basic actions on other commands.
- The provision of more than one way of achieving a given FEPI setup.

However, these facilities are all concerned with performance issues (mainly the length of startup for FEPI resources in the CICS system), and should not normally be used. The following sections document these facilities, but I recommend that they not be used. Nevertheless, do not hesitate to use them to create your FEPI setup, but be warned that performance benefits lead to design complexity to cope with command failure.

The CICS translator does not distinguish between the FEPI API-type and SPI-type commands. `XOPTS(FEPI)` enables the translator to process all `EXEC CICS FEPI` commands.

## 14.2 EXEC CICS FEPI INSTALL commands

The `EXEC CICS FEPI INSTALL` commands install FEPI Propertysets, Nodes, Targets, and Pools. The general formats of the installation commands are:

- `EXEC CICS FEPI INSTALL PROPERTYSET`
- `EXEC CICS FEPI INSTALL NODELIST`
- `EXEC CICS FEPI INSTALL TARGETLIST`
- `EXEC CICS FEPI INSTALL POOL`

These formats show that you can install more than one Target and Node at the same time. This list processing may be used for performance purposes, but it leads to the use of monitor transactions (see Chapter 47) to process errors in the list. I would advise against using the list options unless *very* necessary.

All the commands can take `NOHANDLE`, `RESP`, and `RESP2` parameters to enable Return Code processing. FEPI places in the `RESP2` parameter the Return Code for the command. All Return Codes are documented in Chaper 28.

You are *required* to define the Propertyset (which defines attributes and can be used by many Pools) before the Pool. The Targets and Nodes can be defined and inserted into a Pool in one operation (in which case the Pool must be defined before them), or defined and then inserted into the Pool later on. I would recommend adopting this latter course of defining the Targets and Nodes in separate steps, and then associating them with a Pool in a later command. Therefore, you should define your FEPI resources in this order:

1. The Propertyset
2. The Pool
3. Nodes
4. Targets
5. Associate Targets and Nodes to a Pool

### 14.2.1 EXEC CICS FEPI INSTALL PROPERTYSET

The first thing you have to do is define a Propertyset, so that definitions can be created for a Pool. The full layout of the command follows. (However, a full discussion of all the parameters is contained in Chapter 16.)

```
EXEC CICS FEPI INSTALL PROPERTYSET(char8)

[BEGINSESSION(char4)]
[CONTENTION(cvda)|LOSE|WIN]
[DEVICE(cvda)|T3278M2|T3278M3|T3278M4|T3278M5|
              T3279M2|T3279M3|T3279M4|T3279M5|
              TPS55M2|TPS55M3|TPS55M4|LUP]
[ENDSESSION(char4)]
[EXCEPTIONQ(char4)]
[FJOURNALNUM(fixed31)]
[FORMAT(cvda)|FORMATTED|DATASTREAM]
[INITIALDATA(cvda)|NOTINBOUND|INBOUND]
[MAXFLENGTH(fixed31)]
[MSGJRNL(cvda)|NOMSGJRNL|INPUT|OUTPUT|INOUT]
[STSN(char4)]
[UNSOLDATA(char4)|UNSOLDATACK(cvda)|NEGATIVE|POSITIVE]
```

Once the Propertyset has been successfully created, it can be used in a Pool definition. The Propertyset can be used in as many Pools as required.

After the Pool has been created with the Propertyset, the Propertyset can be removed (only if CICS EDSA is *really extremely* short; otherwise do not bother getting rid of it) with an `EXEC CICS FEPI DISCARD PROPERTYSET`(name) command. As the contents of the Propertyset are copied to the Pool, this removal completes immediately.

If the same-named Propertyset is recreated, then the attributes do not affect any existing Pools. They only take effect when a new Pool is defined. Therefore, be careful in interpreting the Propertyset name returned on an `EXEC CICS FEPI INQUIRE POOL` command, as the Propertyset could well have been removed and recreated (this is why all the Propertyset attributes are returned on Inquire Pool) in the meantime, or might even not be present.

### 14.2.2 EXEC CICS FEPI INSTALL POOL

Having defined the Propertyset to create a set of attributes, you then create a Pool using these attributes. The full command is:

```
EXEC CICS FEPI INSTALL POOL(char8)
                       PROPERTYSET(char8)

[NODELIST(char)     NODENUM(fixed31)]
[TARGETLIST(char)   TARGETNUM(fixed31)]
[ACQSTATUS(cvda)|ACQUIRED|RELEASED]
[SERVSTATUS(cvda)|INSERVICE|OUTSERVICE]
```

The `PROPERTYSET` parameter names the set of attributes that the Pool is to assume.

The basic installation of the Pool just uses:

```
EXEC CICS FEPI INSTALL POOL(char8)
                       PROPERTYSET(char8)
[SERVSTATUS(cvda)|INSERVICE|OUTSERVICE]
```

The other parameters involve the creation of Connections into the Pool at the same time as the Pool is created. In this case, the named existing Targets and Nodes are inserted into the Pool as if an `EXEC CICS FEPI ADD` had been coded, and the Connections' status set as required.

The `ACQSTATUS` and `SERVSTATUS` parameters control the status of the Connections being created. See Sec. 14.3 for their meanings. However, the `SERVSTATUS` parameter also controls whether or not the Pool is usable. If the Pool is `OUTSERVICE`, then no communication can be established over any Connections in the Pool until it is set to `INSERVICE`, via either a CEMT operation (see Chapter 19) or an `EXEC CICS FEPI SET POOL SERVSTATUS INSERVICE)` command (see Sec. 18.2.3). Setting a Pool to be `OUTSERVICE` neither stops any 'definitional' actions on the Pool (so that, for example, things can still can be `EXEC CICS FEPI ADD`ed to it), nor are existing active Conversations affected. The default setting is `SERVSTATUS(INSERVICE)`.

I do *not* recommend the creation of Connections be done in the same operation as the creation of the Pool, because this leads to the use of monitor transactions (see Chapter 47) to process errors. Although there may be good user-type performance reasons for doing this (perhaps if it is absolutely required that all Connections be available for use as soon as a Pool exists—but why would this be required anyway?), do *not* use the list options unless really necessary.

Note that you do not have to place both Targets and Nodes into the Pool; you can simply quote one of them. However, in this case, no Connections are actually created until both resource types are present in the Pool.

### 14.2.3 EXEC CICS FEPI INSTALL TARGETLIST

The syntax of the command for installing Targets (partner systems) looks like you are required to create more than one Target at one go:

```
EXEC CICS FEPI INSTALL
              TARGETLIST(char) TARGETNUM(fixed31)
              APPLLIST(char)

[SERVSTATUS(cvda)|INSERVICE|OUTSERVICE]
```

However, if creating only one Target, you simply specify `TARGETNUM(1)`.

The names of the Targets you are installing are contained in the `TARGETLIST` parameter. These elements are eight-byte names, and should not contain any nulls (X'00') or imbedded blanks (X'40').

The `TARGETLIST` parameter contains as many eight-byte names as there are specified in `TARGETNUM`. This list is not delimited in any way, and any contained blanks will be treated as right-side padding (which is acceptable) or imbedded spaces (which generate a List error to CSZX, see Chapter 46). Therefore a list of

```
'APPL1000APPL2---APPL3---'
```

is acceptable (where * is an X'00' null and - an X'40' blank), but

```
'APPL-4--APPL*5**APPL6'
```

fails due to nulls (`APPL5`), imbedded blanks (`APPL4`), and too short an element (`APPL6`).

The `APPLLIST` parameter links with the VTAM Applid of the partner system with which you desire communication (see Sec. 12.1.1). Like `TARGETLIST`, an individual entry is an eight-byte name, and there must be as many elements as there are Targets (i.e., `TARGETNUM`).

To communicate with a CICS/XRF system, the APPLLIST name must be the *Generic Applid* of the partner system—not the *Primary* or *Secondary Applid* (see Sec. 60.1.1). A similar principle applies to all partners which are XRF enabled.

When each Target has been created, it may either be available for use or not. This status is controlled by the SERVSTATUS parameter. The Target can either be INSERVICE (usable) or OUTSERVICE (not usable). This status can either be quoted on the command, or specified by a variable containing a CVDA. The default setting is for the Target to be INSERVICE.

If the Target is set to be OUTSERVICE, then no communication can be made to the partner until it is set to INSERVICE, via either a CEMT operation (see Chapter 19) or via an EXEC CICS FEPI SET TARGET SERVSTATUS INSERVICE) command (see Sec. 18.2.4). Setting a Target to be OUTSERVICE does not stop any 'definitional' actions on the Target (so that, for example, it still can be EXEC CICS FEPI ADDed to a Pool), but it does stop any existing active Conversations to the Target.

It is worth repeating that I do *not* recommend your using the list facilities of this command unless absolutely necessary.

### 14.2.4 EXEC CICS FEPI INSTALL NODELIST

The syntax of the command for installing Nodes (pseudo-terminals) looks like you are required to create more than one Node at one go:

```
EXEC CICS FEPI INSTALL
               NODELIST(char) NODENUM(fixed31)

[ACQSTATUS(cvda)|ACQUIRED|RELEASED]
[PASSWORDLIST(char)]
[SERVSTATUS(cvda)|INSERVICE|OUTSERVICE]
```

However, if creating only one Node, you simply specify NODENUM(1).

The names of the Nodes you are installing are contained in the NODELIST parameter. These elements are eight-byte names, and should not contain any nulls (X'00') or imbedded blanks (X'40').

The NODELIST parameter contains as many eight-byte names as there are specified in NODENUM. This list is not delimited in any way, and any imbedded blanks will be treated as right-side padding (which is acceptable) or imbedded spaces (which generate a list error to CSZX, see Chapter 46). Therefore a list of

```
'NODE1000NODE2---NODE3---'
```

is acceptable (where * is an X'00' null and - an X'40' blank), but

```
'NODE-4--NODE*5**NODE6'
```

fails due to nulls (NODE5), imbedded blanks (NODE4), and too short an element (NODE6).

The Node names are those of VTAM *Application Minor Nodes*, and are defined in VTAM's 'SYS1.VTAMLST' (see Chapter 12). They represent the names of the terminals being used for the emulation.

Each VTAM Application Minor Node name may, in the 'SYS1.VTAMLST' definition, be protected with a password (see Sec. 12.1.1). If so, then this password must be quoted in the PASSWORDLIST parameter. This is again a list, of NODENUM elements. When installing a list of Nodes, some with passwords and some without, then an element of eight-blanks must be quoted to pad the list for nonpassword-protected Nodes.

When each Node has been created, it may either be available for use or not. This status is controlled by the SERVSTATUS parameter. The Node can either be INSERVICE (usable) or OUTSERVICE (not usable). This status can either be quoted on the command, or specified by a variable containing a CVDA.

If the Node is set to be OUTSERVICE, then no communication can be made on the pseudo-terminal until it is set to INSERVICE, via either a CEMT operation (see Chapter 19) or via an EXEC CICS FEPI SET NODE SERVSTATUS (INSERVICE) command (see Sec. 18.2.2). Setting a Node to be OUTSERVICE neither stops any 'definitional' actions on the Node (so that, for example, it still can be EXEC CICS FEPI ADDed to a Pool), nor stops any existing active Conversations using the Node.

The ACQSTATUS parameter (specified either statically or dynamically via a variable containing a CVDA) controls whether or not the underlying VTAM ACB is opened. If the ACQSTATUS is ACQUIRED, then the ACB is open, and so the Node is active in VTAM terms. When ACQSTATUS is RELEASED, then the pseudo-terminal is not active in VTAM terms.

Setting the Node to ACQSTATUS(RELEASED) will stop all Connections using the Node, as the VTAM ACB is closed, and so the pseudo-terminal is unavailable, and any Active Conversations using the Node will be ended. The default setting is for the Node to be INSERVICE ACQUIRED.

It is worth repeating that I do *not* recommend you using the list facilities of this command unless absolutely necessary. Indeed, if using a large list with ACQSTATUS(ACQUIRED), you may flood VTAM with requests which could cause network errors.

## 14.3 EXEC CICS FEPI ADD command

The EXEC CICS FEPI ADD command inserts Connections into a Pool. A Connection is a Target–Node pair within a Pool. The same Target–Node pair cannot exist in more than one Pool, but the same Target or Node can appear in any number of Pools, as long as they always generate unique Target–Node pairs.

The format of the EXEC CICS FEPI ADD command is:

```
EXEC CICS FEPI ADD
            POOL(char8)

[NODELIST(char)   NODENUM(fixed31)]
[TARGETLIST(char) TARGETNUM(fixed31)]

[ACQSTATUS(cvda)|ACQUIRED|RELEASED]
[SERVSTATUS(cvda)|INSERVICE|OUTSERVICE]
```

The command can take NOHANDLE, RESP, and RESP2 parameters to enable Return Code processing. FEPI places in the RESP2 parameter the Return Code for the command. All Return Codes are documented in Chapter 28.

The action of the command is to create NODENUM*TARGETNUM connections in the named Pool. If any of the Target–Node pairs already exist in the Pool, then errors are recorded in the Pool-specific Transient Data Queue (see Chapter 45) if it exists.

Either a single FEPI Connection can be added to the Pool (NODENUM(1) and TARGETNUM(1)), or as many as desired. The TARGETLIST and NODELIST parameters contain the list (or single name) of the relevant resources. These lists are in the same format as for the EXEC CICS FEPI INSTALL commands.

The Connections which are created have their status set to that required by the SERVSTATUS and ACQSTATUS parameters (or their static equivalents). If neither is quoted, the default setting for the Connections is INSERVICE ACQUIRED. The status of other existing Connections within the Pool are not altered.

When each Connection has been created, it may either be available for use or not. This status is controlled by the SERVSTATUS parameter. The Connection can either be INSERVICE (usable) or OUTSERVICE (not usable). This status can either be quoted on the command, or specified by a variable containing a CVDA.

If the Connection is set to be OUTSERVICE, then no communication can be made on the Connection until it is set to INSERVICE, via either a CEMT operation (see Chapter 19) or an EXEC CICS FEPI SET CONNECTION SERVSTATUS(INSERVICE) command (see Sec. 18.2.1). Setting a Connection to be OUTSERVICE neither stops it from being removed from the Pool, nor does it affect the existing Conversation (if any) using the Connection.

The ACQSTATUS parameter (specified either statically or dynamically via a variable containing a CVDA) controls whether or not the Connection is *Bound* in VTAM terms. If the ACQSTATUS is ACQUIRED, then the Connection is *Bound* and so communication can flow over it. When ACQSTATUS is RELEASED, the Connection is *Unbound*, and cannot immediately be used for communication. When using a large list with ACQSTATUS(ACQUIRED), you may flood VTAM with these *Bind* requests, which could cause network errors. The ACQSTATUS of the Connection can be altered via either an EXEC CICS FEPI SET CONNECTION command (see Sec. 18.2.1) or the CEMT equivalent (see Chapter 19).

However, the transition between RELEASED and ACQUIRED is dynamic. When the Connection is used and it has ACQSTATUS(RELEASED), then the Connection will be *Bound*, and so its status will become ACQSTATUS (ACQUIRED). This is discussed in Sec. 29.2.

The transition between ACQUIRED and RELEASED can occur either via CEMT use (see Chapter 19), a coded EXEC CICS FEPI SET CONNECTION ACQSTATUS(RELEASED) command (see Sec. 18.2.1), or via the use of an EXEC CICS FEPI FREE RELEASE/FORCE (see Sec. 27.8).

The act of Binding and Unbinding will schedule the Begin Session Handler (see Sec. 44.1) on the *Bind* (transition from `ACQSTATUS(RELEASED)` to `ACQSTATUS(ACQUIRED)`) and the End Session (End of Connection) Handler (see Sec. 44.2.2) on the *Unbind* (transition from `ACQSTATUS(ACQUIRED)` to `ACQSTATUS(RELEASED)`).

When using this command, I recommend that you `EXEC CICS FEPI ADD NODE`s to the Pool before an EXEC CICS FEPI ADD TARGET to the Pool. This is because you actually create the Connections when both the Targets and Nodes are placed in the Pool. Thus, if the Pool already contains a single Target, adding another one will double the number of Connections. Consequently, it is easier to control the initial setup (and thus the number of Connections) for a Pool by creating a set of Nodes (pseudo-terminals) and then doing a single action (adding a single Target) to create many Connections.

Things start to become complicated when you supply both Nodes and Targets in the same command, as you cannot easily determine what is left in the Pool if a failure occurs. Therefore:

- Create an empty Pool
- Add all the required Nodes to the Pool (preferably without using a list).
- Add all the required Targets to the Pool (most preferably by not using a list) to create the Connections, specifying `INSERVICE ACQUIRED`.

# CHAPTER 15 EXEC CICS FEPI DISCARD/DELETE

**GUIDANCE**

This chapter discusses the way FEPI resources are removed from the system.

## 15.1 Introduction

All FEPI resources are removed from the CICS system by using the `EXEC CICS FEPI DISCARD` command or, for Connections, the `EXEC CICS FEPI DELETE` command.

FEPI resources behave in a different manner to other CICS resources. When the `EXEC CICS FEPI DISCARD` command is executed for a FEPI resource, it completes immediately. The actual removal of the FEPI resource will occur as soon as the FEPI resource is not in use. The removal will occur either immediately if there is no usage or as soon as a usage count drops to zero. Other CICS resources refuse a deletion request if something is using them—FEPI resources accept the request for later actioning. This delayed `DISCARD`ing does not permit new uses of the FEPI resource, but allows existing usages to continue to a 'logical' end point. Once all extant usages have ended, then the FEPI resource is actually removed.

FEPI Nodes and Targets can be removed using lists. In contrast to the advice given in Chapter 14 about using Lists, `EXEC CICS FEPI DISCARD` operations *are* suitable for List usage because of this delayed action. This is because you are not concerned with 'definitional' errors—all that ought to go wrong is an attempt to discard an unknown resource. This should not concern you unduly, but if it does, then the CSZX Monitor (see Chapter 46) can be used to detect this failure. `DFHSZ` messages are produced to record in the FEPI log (CSZL) that a removal request will be actioned later. See Sec. 59.1 for the use of these commands during a Normal CICS Shutdown.

All the commands can take NOHANDLE, RESP, and RESP2 parameters to enable Return Code processing. FEPI places in the RESP2 parameter the Return Code for the command. All Return Codes are documented in Chapter 28.

## 15.2 EXEC CICS FEPI DISCARD commands

The following EXEC CICS FEPI DISCARD commands are used to remove FEPI resources from the CICS system:

- EXEC CICS FEPI DISCARD PROPERTYSET
- EXEC CICS FEPI DISCARD NODELIST
- EXEC CICS FEPI DISCARD TARGETLIST
- EXEC CICS FEPI DISCARD POOL

### 15.2.1 EXEC CICS FEPI DISCARD PROPERTYSET

The format of this command is:

```
EXEC CICS FEPI DISCARD
            PROPERTYSET(char8)
```

You just supply the name of the Propertyset that you wish to remove. Note that the Propertyset has to exist only for the duration of an EXEC CICS FEPI INSTALL POOL command. The values defined in the Propertyset are copied into the Pool definition.

However, it is not worth removing the Propertyset definitions from the system for CICS EDSA storage considerations—the space used is trivial. You should only think about discarding the Propertyset if you wish to reuse the name (and so define another set of attributes), or if there are other reasons for removing the name (perhaps for security purposes).

### 15.2.2 EXEC CICS FEPI DISCARD NODELIST

The format of this command is:

```
EXEC CICS FEPI DISCARD
            NODELIST(char) NODENUM(fixed31)
```

You supply a list (which may be of one element) of eight-byte Node names that you wish to remove, and give the number of elements in NODENUM.

A Node is not actually deleted until all Active Connections using the Node are ended. To stop any more new uses of the Node in the meantime, it is set to SERVSTATUS(OUTSERVICE).

### 15.2.3 EXEC CICS FEPI DISCARD TARGETLIST

The format of this command is:

```
EXEC CICS FEPI DISCARD
            TARGETLIST(char) TARGETNUM(fixed31)
```

You supply a list (which may be of one element) of eight-byte Target names that you wish to remove, and give the number of elements in TARGETNUM.

A Target is not actually deleted until all Active Connections communicating with the Target (partner system) have ended. To stop any more new uses of the Target in the meantime, it is set to SERVSTATUS(OUTSERVICE).

### 15.2.4 EXEC CICS FEPI DISCARD POOL

The format of this command is:

```
EXEC CICS FEPI DISCARD
              POOL(char8)
```

You just supply the name of the Pool that you wish to remove.

The Pool is not actually removed until all the Connections contained therein have also been removed. To stop any new use of the Pool in the meantime, it is set to SERVSTATUS(OUTSERVICE).

All the nonactive Connections in the Pool are immediately removed (it is only the Target–Node pairs that are removed, the actual Nodes and Targets (which can be present in other Pools) are not removed by this command), while the others are set to SERVSTATUS(OUTSERVICE) to prevent any new usage. When the active Conversations within the Pool end, their underlying Connections are removed. This process continues until all the Connections have disappeared, and then the Pool is removed.

## 15.3 EXEC CICS FEPI DELETE command

The EXEC CICS FEPI DELETE command is used to remove Connections (Target–Node pairs) from a Pool:

```
EXEC CICS FEPI DELETE
              POOL(char8)

[NODELIST(char)    NODENUM(fixed31)]
[TARGETLIST(char)  TARGETNUM(fixed31)]
```

The command completes immediately, and so the associated Connections are removed asynchronously.

The NODENUM*TARGETNUM Connections are removed from the named Pool. This removal occurs immediately if the Connection is not in use, or as soon as the Active Conversation using the Connection ends.

The Target–Node Pairs requested for removal are a combination of the eight-byte names specified in list format via the TARGETLIST and NODELIST parameters, so a single Connection is removed with 'NODELIST(name1) TARGETLIST(name1) NODENUM(1) TARGETNUM(1)'.

To stop a new usage of a Connection, it is set to SERVSTATUS (OUTSERVICE). This status change (and Connection removal) does not affect the underlying Targets and Nodes, it only affects the combinations which form the Connections.

# CHAPTER 16 Choosing the Propertyset options

**GUIDANCE**

This chapter documents all the attributes present on a FEPI Propertyset. You should refer to:

- Section 14.2.1 for usage in Propertyset definitions.
- Section 18.3.4 for usage on Propertyset inquiries.
- Section 18.3.5 for usage on Pool inquiries.

## 16.1 Introduction

The Propertyset definitions control the operation of Connections within a Pool. Consequently, how the Propertyset is defined affects how the Connections work, and thus the design of your FEPI application. This chapter describes all the settings, and comments on how they relate to application design.

The Propertyset attributes (underlines show `EXEC CICS FEPI INSTALL PROPERTYSET` command defaults) are:

```
BEGINSESSION(char4)
CONTENTION(cvda)|LOSE|WIN
DEVICE(cvda)|T3278M2|T3278M3|T3278M4|T3278M5|
             T3279M2|T3279M3|T3279M4|T3279M5|
             TPS55M2|TPS55M3|TPS55M4|LUP
ENDSESSION(char4)
EXCEPTIONQ(char4)
FJOURNALNUM(fixed31)
FORMAT(cvda)|FORMATTED|DATASTREAM
INITIALDATA(cvda)|NOTINBOUND|INBOUND
MAXFLENGTH(fixed31)
MSGJRNL(cvda)|NOMSGJRNL|INPUT|OUTPUT|INOUT
STSN(char4)
UNSOLDATA(char4)|UNSOLDATACK(cvda)|NEGATIVE|POSITIVE
```

(Underlined defaults: LOSE, T3278M2, FORMATTED, NOTINBOUND, NOMSGJRNL, NEGATIVE.)

Some parameters have CVDA variable alternatives to a coded setting on the `EXEC CICS FEPI INSTALL PROPERTYSET` command. However, on all other commands, the relevant CVDA is always returned in the variable.

### 16.1.1 Propertyset attribute types

The Propertyset attributes can be grouped into the following categories:

DEVICE ATTRIBUTES

- `DEVICE` (Sec. 16.2.3)

DATA HANDLING

- `CONTENTION` (Sec. 16.2.2)
- `FORMAT` (Sec. 16.2.7)
- `MAXFLENGTH` (Sec. 16.2.9)

SESSION MANAGEMENT

- `BEGINSESSION` (Sec. 16.2.1)
- `ENDSESSION` (Sec. 16.2.4)
- `INITIALDATA` (Sec. 16.2.8)
- `STSN` (Sec. 16.2.11)

UNEXPECTED EVENTS

- `EXCEPTIONQ` (Sec. 16.2.5)
- `UNSOLDATA` (Sec. 16.2.12)
- `UNSOLDATACK` (Sec. 16.2.12)

JOURNALLING

- `FJOURNALNUM` (Sec. 16.2.6)
- `MSGJRNL` (Sec. 16.2.10)

## 16.2 Propertyset attributes

### 16.2.1 BEGINSESSION

The BEGINSESSION parameter names the Handler transaction which will be scheduled for Begin Session Processing. (See Sec. 44.1). The named transaction will be initiated as a nonterminal transaction as soon as a Connection within the Pool starts (is '*Bound*' in VTAM terms).

If the Begin Session Handler is not required, then either omit the parameter on the EXEC CICS FEPI INSTALL PROPERTYSET command, or supply a name of '    ' (four blanks).

FEPI does not check to see that the transaction is defined to CICS, or that it will run locally.

### 16.2.2 CONTENTION

CONTENTION *only* specifies how an EXEC CICS FEPI SEND command (or the send part of an EXEC CICS FEPI CONVERSE) will work when either end of a Connection is capable of sending data, and there has been a flow of data from the partner which has not yet been EXEC CICS FEPI RECEIVEd. (In VTAM terms, this is a flow from the partner with *Begin Bracket* which has not been processed.)

If CONTENTION(WIN) is specified, then the send command will succeed. The pending data will be flushed, and the partner sent a VTAM *Negative Response* to tell it that FEPI did not receive the data.

CONTENTION(LOSE) is the default, and says that in this situation the send will fail, and an EXEC CICS FEPI RECEIVE has to be issued to clear the pending data before any other processing can occur. This position may commonly arise when communicating to IMS running Nonresponse mode transactions. In CICS terms, this is when nonterminal transactions are used to process requests, which then queue data back to a terminal in a 'random' fashion. Therefore, there will be circumstances when the FEPI pseudo-terminal's screen is not doing anything. Consequently, either the user (the FEPI application program) or the system (CICS/IMS) is entitled to grab the screen, and put some data upon it. This is called being in the *Contention State*.

When in Contention State, the CONTENTION attribute says who grabs the terminal. If you (the FEPI application program) want to overrule CICS/IMS, then use CONTENTION(WIN). If you want to know that the partner system has not grabbed the terminal underneath you, then use CONTENTION(LOSE), which forces the FEPI application to process the data sent from the partner system while in Contention State. The default setting is CONTENTION(LOSE), which forces all data sent from the partner system to be processed.

Only consider using CONTENTION(WIN) if you are running a passthrough application (see Chapter 4) to a partner where data sent to the partner can be accepted while some processing is occurring.

If running IMS nonresponse mode transactions, you have a choice to make. Use CONTENTION(WIN) to be able to send new IMS transactions at any time, and rely on the *Negative Response* sent when overruling an IMS flow (to get IMS's MFS to resend the flow). I would recommend using CONTENTION(LOSE) so you can detect when MFS has sent data in this situation.

### 16.2.3 DEVICE

The DEVICE parameter specifies the type of terminal and the access method used for all the Connections within the Pool. You can only specify particular terminal types (colour or monochrome, and model number) and not any generally permitted combination of row and screen size. Similarly, if using the LU0 (SLUP) access method, the concept of terminal type does not occur. If DEVICE is not specified on the EXEC CICS FEPI INSTALL PROPERTYSET command, then T3278M2 is assumed. Table 16.1 on page 52 shows the permitted options.

The definitions noted in Table 16.1 apply to all the Connections in the Pool. Once the DEVICE is set, then it cannot be changed. You have to use a colour (or DBCS) definition to be able to use the 3270 colour and Extended Attribute Bytes (field validation, must complete, etc.) in the flows to/from the partner system (see Chapter 20 for general information on the 3270 Datastream).

### 16.2.4 ENDSESSION

The ENDSESSION parameter names the Handler Transaction which will be scheduled for both End of Conversation and End of Connection Processing. See Sec. 44.2 for details. The named transaction will be initiated as a nonterminal transaction just before either the Conversation is ended, or the Connection is terminated. If the End Session Handler is not required, then either omit the parameter on the EXEC CICS FEPI INSTALL PROPERTYSET command, or supply a name of '    ' (four blanks).

FEPI does not check to see that the transaction is defined to CICS, or that it will run locally.

**Table 16.1** DEVICE settings

| CVDA or option | Format | Colour, Monochrome or Double Byte Character Set (DBCS) | Terminal type |
|---|---|---|---|
| T3278M2 | LU2 (3270) | Monochrome | 3278 Model 2 |
| T3278M3 | LU2 (3270) | Monochrome | 3278 Model 3 |
| T3278M4 | LU2 (3270) | Monochrome | 3278 Model 4 |
| T3278M5 | LU2 (3270) | Monochrome | 3278 Model 5 |
| T3279M2 | LU2 (3270) | Colour | 3279 Model 2B |
| T3279M3 | LU2 (3270) | Colour | 3279 Model 3C |
| T3279M4 | LU2 (3270) | Colour | 3279 Model 4D |
| T3279M5 | LU2 (3270) | Colour | 3279 Model 5D |
| TPS55M2 | LU2 (3270) | DBCS | PS/55, 24 lines |
| TPS55M3 | LU2 (3270) | DBCS | PS/55, 32 lines |
| TPS55M4 | LU2 (3270) | DBCS | PS/55, 43 lines |
| LUP | LU0 (SLUP) | | |

### 16.2.5 EXCEPTIONQ

The EXCEPTIONQ names the Pool-Specific Transient Data Queue (TDQ) used for logging certain events. The named TDQ should have an associated Triggered Transaction. This Monitor transaction should process the events. See Chapter 45 for details of this processing.

If no errors are to be logged to the Pool-Specific TDQ, then either omit the EXCEPTIONQ parameter, or specify a TDQ name of '    ' (four blanks). If the named TDQ does not exist, or is defined as being recoverable, then processing proceeds as if the EXCEPTIONQ were not specified.

### 16.2.6 FJOURNALNUM

FJOURNALNUM names the CICS journal file that is to be used to journal FEPI flows. The type of records journalled is under the control of the MSGJRNL attribute (see Sec. 16.2.10).

FEPI will not journal to the System Log, so FJOURNALNMUM(1) is not allowed. If FJOURNALNUM is omitted, or FJOURNALNUM(0) specified, then no journalling will occur.

### 16.2.7 FORMAT

The FORMAT parameter defines the data access mode for all the Connections within the Pool. If DEVICE(LUP) is specified, then FORMAT is not allowed (as its settings only apply to LU2 Connections).

`DEVICE(FORMATTED)` says that the Pool will contain Connections which will be used only for Formatted LU2 Conversations. `DEVICE(DATASTREAM)` says that the Pool will contain Connections which will be used only for Datastream Conversations. The programming of the emulation is completely different for Formatted and Datastream Conversations. This is discussed in Chapter 3.

If `FORMAT` is not specified and the Pool contains LU2-type Connections (i.e., `DEVICE` is not `LUP`), then Formatted is assumed.

### 16.2.8 INITIALDATA

**WARNING**

I think that the default setting of this parameter is not suitable for normal use.

The `INITIALDATA` parameter indicates how FEPI is to process the first flow from the partner system when a Connection is Acquired (see Sec. 18.1.1).

If the partner system is going to send an introductory flow (such as a signon panel) you can decide either to route this to a Begin Session Handler (see Sec. 44.1) or to process it as Unsolicited Data (see Sec. 16.2.12). To route the flow to the Begin Session Handler code `INITIALDATA(INBOUND)`. Specify `INITIALDATA(NOTINBOUND)` to process the flow as Unsolicited Data.

However, if the partner will not send a start-of-day flow, you do not want the Begin Session Handler (if one is being used) to wait for its arrival. In this case, code `INITIALDATA(NOTINBOUND)`, and the Begin Session Handler initiation will occur immediately the Connection is established.

The Begin Session Handler does not have to process the data, in which case so long as `INITIALDATA(INBOUND)` is specified, the reception of the flow can be postponed until the first usage of the Connection (this is discussed in Sec. 29.2.5).

Additionally, if `INITIALDATA(NOTINBOUND)` is specified, and there actually is a start-of-day flow, so long as the Begin Session Handler is active, it can issue an `EXEC CICS FEPI RECEIVE` command and wait for the flow to occur itself.

To summarize:

- Partner sends a Start-of-Day flow
  - Want to process it in a Begin Session Handler? Specify `INITIALDATA(INBOUND)`, and code an `EXEC CICS FEPI RECEIVE` in the Handler.
  - Want to process it in an Unsolicited Data Session Handler? Specify `INITIALDATA(NOTINBOUND)` and do not use a Begin Session Handler.
  - Want to process it in the first FEPI transaction to use the Connection?

- Specify `INITIALDATA(INBOUND)` and either no Begin Session Handler, or else that the Begin Session Handler does not issue an `EXEC CICS FEPI RECEIVE`.

- Partner does not send a Start-of-Day flow
  - Specify `INITIALDATA(NOTINBOUND)`.

IMS partners always send an Initial Flow, and CICS partners usually do (unless you have turned it off). However, the default setting is `INITIALDATA (NOTINBOUND)`, so you should always specify `INITIALDATA(INBOUND)` on the Propertyset (even if this is the only attribute you actually code!).

See Chapter 42 for information on first flows which are not panels.

I would always recommend specifying `INITIALDATA(INBOUND)` if the partner system will send an initial Start-of-Day flow. You can process it within either the Begin Session Handler or an application program as best suits your design.

> **RECOMMENDATION**
>
> You should always quote the `INITIALDATA` parameter, as the default setting of `NOTINBOUND` is not normally what you want.

### 16.2.9 MAXFLENGTH

The `MAXFLENGTH` parameter defines the maximum length of data that can be processed in one FEPI operation. It can be used to improve CICS storage usage (perhaps at the expense of extra FEPI commands). The permitted settings are in the range 128–1048576 inclusive. If omitted, `MAXFLENGTH(4096)` is used.

The use of this parameter on Formatted Conversations means that extra `EXEC CICS FEPI SEND` or `RECEIVE` commands may have to be used to process the required Data. Therefore, the `MAXFLENGTH` setting should be the largest you reasonably expect to use (if proceeding on a screen buffer basis, then the minimum setting should be the screen size, but it is best to allow four times the screen size).

If doing Datastream processing, then setting `MAXFLENGTH` to be too small will drastically affect your ability to send the correct 3270 Datastream to the partner system. Upon receiving data, you can use the `REMFLENGTH` parameter (see `REMFLENGTH`, Sec. 27.7) to obtain more data than `MAXFLENGTH` specifies.

I recommend that you set `MAXFLENGTH` to be at least four times the screen size for Formatted Pools, and as big as the maximum possible data flow for Datastream Pools. In any case, as the storage is above the line, it does not really matter if you overspecify the length, and it is better to have a too large area than a too small one.

> **WARNING**
>
> If `MAXFLENGTH` is set too small, then data will be mysteriously lost!

### 16.2.10 MSGJRNL

The MSGJRNL parameter indicates which type of FEPI records are to be journalled in the CICS journal specified by FJOURNALNUM (see Sec. 16.2.6).

The following types of flow can be journalled (see Chapter 56 for processing details):

| | |
|---|---|
| NOMSGJRNL | No FEPI records are to be journalled. |
| INPUT | FEPI Inbound records are to be journalled. |
| OUTPUT | FEPI Outbound records are to be journalled. |
| INOUT | Both FEPI Inbound and Outbound records are to be journalled. |

If MSGJRNL is not specified, then the default of NOMSGJRNL applies, and no FEPI records will be journalled irrespective of the FJOURNALNUM parameter. Similarly, FJOURNALNUM(0) will prevent any journalling, whatever the MSGJRNL setting.

### 16.2.11 STSN

The STSN parameter names the Handler transaction which will be scheduled for LU0 (SLUP) message resynchronization. The use of LU0 is outside the scope of this book, but see Sec. 44.4 and Chapter 52 for details. The specific setting rules follow those for the other Handlers.

### 16.2.12 UNSOLDATA and UNSOLDATACK

The UNSOLDATA parameter names the Handler transaction which will run nonterminal when Unsolicited Data flows on a Connection with the Pool. See Sec. 44.3 for details, and Chapter 24 for a definition of Unsolicited Data. FEPI does not check to see that the transaction is defined to CICS, or that it will run locally.

If the Unsolicited Data Handler is not required, then either omit the parameter on the EXEC CICS FEPI INSTALL PROPERTYSET command, or supply a name of '    ' (four blanks). In this case, the Unsolicited Data will be processed according to the UNSOLDATACK attribute.

UNSOLDATACK(NEGATIVE) says that, as no Unsolicited Data Handler is being used, a VTAM *Negative Response* will be sent to the partner that sent the Unsolicited Data, and the flow lost.

UNSOLDATACK(POSITIVE) says that FEPI will accept the flow from the partner, responding *positively* to it, and then discard the flow. These actions will continue until the partner stops sending data (signified by an SNA *End Bracket* indicator being received).

If you are not using an Unsolicited Data Handler to cope with flows in this circumstance (i.e., receipt of Unsolicited Data), you should consider very carefully a specification of UNSOLDATACK(POSITIVE). If this is used, the partner system is fully entitled to think that the 'terminal operator' has received the screen and will respond correctly to it. However, as FEPI loses the flow, this action will never occur. Thus, the application running in the partner system will fail.

Similarly, if the partner system receives a *Negative Response* due to the specification of UNSOLDATACK(NEGATIVE), it can legitimately decide to retry sending the flow. This could lead to looping errors in the partner system.

Therefore:

- Specify an UNSOLDATA Handler to receive the Unsolicited Data and process it yourself (even if you simply ignore the data).
- Specify UNSOLDATACK(POSITIVE) to simply lose the flow, without informing the partner system that it has been lost.
- Specify UNSOLDATACK(NEGATIVE) to let the partner know that the flow has not been accepted.

I recommend that an Unsolicited Data Handler is *always* provided to cope with Unsolicited Data.

# CHAPTER 17 Resource definition examples

**GUIDANCE**

This chapter shows some fragments of FEPI resource definition:

- Standard Pool
- Creating the Pool and Connections at the same time
- Pool Connections not Bound until use
- Pool containing usable and unusable Connections

## 17.1 Standard Pool

```
EXEC CICS FEPI INSTALL PROPERTYSET(=CL8'Y1')
                 DEVICE(DFHVALUE(T3279M2))
                 FORMAT(DFHVALUE(FORMATTED))
                 INITIALDATA(DFHVALUE(INBOUND))
                 BEGINSESSION(=CL4'HABS')
                 ENDSESSION(=CL4'HAES')
                 UNSOLDATA(=CL4'HAUN')
                 EXCEPTIONQ(=CL4'TDEX')

EXEC CICS FEPI INSTALL POOL(=CL8'P1')
                       PROPERTYSET(=CL8'Y1')

EXEC CICS FEPI INSTALL TARGETLIST(=CL8'T1')
                       APPLLIST(=CL8'RAHXRF11')
                       TARGETNUM(1)
                       INSERVICE

EXEC CICS FEPI INSTALL NODELIST(=CL16'N11     N12     ')
                       NODENUM(2)

EXEC CICS FEPI ADD POOL(=CL8'P1')
                   TARGETLIST(=CL8'T1')
                   TARGETNUM(1)
                   NODELIST(=CL16'N1     N12')
                   NODENUM(2)
                   INSERVICE
                   ACQUIRED
```

## **17.2** Creating the Pool and Connections at the same time

```
EXEC CICS FEPI INSTALL PROPERTYSET(=CL8'Y2')
                DEVICE(DFHVALUE(T3279M2))
                FORMAT(DFHVALUE(FORMATTED))
                INITIALDATA(DFHVALUE(INBOUND))
                BEGINSESSION(=CL4'HABS')
                ENDSESSION(=CL4'HAES')
                UNSOLDATA(=CL4'HAUN')
                EXCEPTIONQ(=CL4'TDEX')

EXEC CICS FEPI INSTALL TARGETLIST(=CL8'T2')
                       APPLLIST(=CL8'RAHXRF21')
                       TARGETNUM(1)
                       INSERVICE

EXEC CICS FEPI INSTALL NODELIST(=CL16'N21     N22     ')
                       NODENUM(2)

EXEC CICS FEPI INSTALL POOL(=CL8'P2')
                       PROPERTYSET(=CL8'Y2')
                       TARGETLIST(=CL8'T2')
                       TARGETNUM(1)
                       NODELIST(=CL16'N21     N22')
                       NODENUM(2)
                       INSERVICE
                       ACQUIRED
```

## **17.3** Pool Connections not Bound until use

```
EXEC CICS FEPI INSTALL PROPERTYSET(=CL8'Y4')
                       DEVICE(DFHVALUE(T3278M5))
                       FORMAT(DFHVALUE(FORMATTED))
                       INITALDATA(DFHVALUE(INBOUND))
                       MSGJRNL(DFHVALUE(INOUT))
                       FJOURNALNUM(2)

EXEC CICS FEPI INSTALL TARGETLIST(=CL8'T4')
                       APPLLIST(=CL8'RAHDFH41')
                       TARGETNUM(1)
                       INSERVICE

EXEC CICS FEPI INSTALL NODELIST(=CL16'N41     N42     ')
                       NODENUM(2)

EXEC CICS FEPI INSTALL POOL(=CL8'P4')
                       PROPERTYSET(=CL8'Y4')
                       TARGETLIST(=CL8'T4')
                       TARGETNUM(1)
                       INSERVICE

EXEC CICS FEPI ADD POOL(=CL8'P4')
                   NODELIST(=CL16'N41     N42')
                   NODENUM(2)
                   INSERVICE
                   RELEASED
```

## 17.4 Pool containing usable and unusable Connections

```
EXEC CICS FEPI INSTALL PROPERTYSET(=CL8'Y3')
                       DEVICE(DFHVALUE(T3278M2))
                       FORMAT(DFHVALUE(DATASTREAM))
                       INITIALDATA(DFHVALUE(NOTINBOUND))
                       UNSOLDATACK(DFHVALUE(NEGATIVE))

EXEC CICS FEPI INSTALL TARGETLIST(=CL8'T31')
                       APPLLIST(=CL8'RAHXRF31')
                       TARGETNUM(1)
                       INSERVICE

EXEC CICS FEPI INSTALL TARGETLIST(=CL8'T32')
                       APPLLIST(=CL8'RAHBAK32')
                       TARGETNUM(1)
                       INSERVICE

EXEC CICS FEPI INSTALL NODELIST(=CL16'N31     N32     ')
                       NODENUM(2)

EXEC CICS FEPI INSTALL POOL(=CL8'P3')
                       PROPERTYSET(=CL8'Y3')
                       TARGETLIST(=CL8'T31')
                       TARGETNUM(1)
                       NODELIST(=CL16'N31     N32')
                       NODENUM(2)
                       INSERVICE
                       ACQUIRED

EXEC CICS FEPI ADD POOL(=CL8'P3')
                   TARGETLIST(=CL8'T32')
                   TARGETNUM(1)
                   OUTSERVICE
                   ACQSTATUS(DFHVALUE(RELEASED))
```

# CHAPTER 18 Resource manipulation

**GUIDANCE**

This chapter discusses FEPI's facilities for altering and obtaining the status of resources, which revolve around the ACQSTATUS and SERVSTATUS operands.

## 18.1 Introduction

The FEPI resources (which have been installed as in Chapter 14) can have their status manipulated using EXEC CICS FEPI SET commands, or their CEMT equivalents (see Chapter 19). The only settings that can be manipulated in this fashion are the ACQSTATUS and SERVSTATUS settings. List processing is available on some of the SET commands. More function is provided on the EXEC CICS FEPI INQUIRE commands, where attributes etc. for the resource can be queried.

Each FEPI resource (with the exception of the Propertysets) has a 64-byte area called USERDATA into which any data can be placed. A discussion of Userdata and its usage can be found in Chapter 50. USERDATA is particularly useful when CLSDST(PASS) processing is being used (see Chapter 51).

All the EXEC CICS FEPI INQUIRE commands can either operate upon a given resource, or be used in browse mode. This is discussed in Secs 18.5 and 18.6.

### 18.1.1 Status transitions

The ACQSTATUS and SERVSTATUS settings show the current state of the resource. However, FEPI resources also know that a transition is in progress.

When a resource is changed from an active (INSERVICE/ACQUIRED) state to an inactive (OUTSERVICE/RELEASED) one, the transition may not complete immediately. If the FEPI resource is involved with an Active Conversation, the transition from active to inactive will be delayed until this involvement has ceased. While waiting for the transition to complete, the current state will be shown as pending inactive (GOINGOUT/RELEASING). A similar arrangement applies to FEPI resources that involve VTAM interactions on the inactive to active transition. While waiting for VTAM to complete processing, the current state will be shown as pending active (ACQUIRING).

### 18.1.2 Resource Status

The status transitions are:

- ACQSTATUS (for Nodes and Connections only)
  RELEASED to ACQUIRED: start usage of the underlying VTAM resource.
  ACQUIRED to RELEASED: stop usage of the underlying VTAM resource.
- SERVSTATUS
  OUTSERVICE to INSERVICE: to permit usage of the FEPI resource.
  INSERVICE to OUTSERVICE: to stop usage of the FEPI resource.

The current states are:

| | |
|---|---|
| ACQSTATUS | |
| ACQUIRED | The resource is active in VTAM terms, and so available for Communications. |
| RELEASED | The resource is inactive in VTAM terms, and so unavailable for Communications. |
| ACQUIRING | The resource has been set to ACQUIRED, and the underlying VTAM resource is initiating. |
| RELEASING | The resource has been set to RELEASED, and the underlying VTAM resource is quiescing. |
| SERVSTATUS | |
| INSERVICE | The resource is available for use. |
| OUTSERVICE | The resource is unavailable for use. |
| GOINGOUT | The resource has been set to OUTSERVICE, but is still being used by an Active Connection. |

## 18.2 EXEC CICS FEPI SET commands

The EXEC CICS FEPI SET commands are used to:

- Change the ACQSTATUS for FEPI Nodes and Connections.
- Change the SERVSTATUS for FEPI Nodes, Targets, Pools, and Connections.
- Set the USERDATA area for FEPI Nodes, Targets, Pools, and Connections.

There are no alterable attributes for the FEPI Propertysets.

The FEPI resources can be specified in either list or single-element format. However, the use of lists leads to all the 'usual' list error-processing problems. For all these commands, list errors are sent to the CSZX Global Transient Data Queue with an event code of SETFAIL. I would always recommend *not* using the list facilities for this reason.

### 18.2.1 EXEC CICS FEPI SET CONNECTION

The format of the EXEC CICS FEPI SET CONNECTION command is:

```
EXEC CICS FEPI SET CONNECTION
                   TARGET(char8)
                        |TARGETLIST(char) TARGETNUM(fixed31)
                   NODE(char8)
                        |NODELIST(char)   NODENUM(fixed31)

[ACQSTATUS(cvda)|ACQUIRED|RELEASED]
[SERVSTATUS(cvda)|INSERVICE|OUTSERVICE]
[USERDATA(char64)]
```

A FEPI Connection is a Target–Node pair that exists in only one Pool (see Sec. 11.1.5). Consequently, the Connection is identified by the provision of both a Target and a Node.

You can operate on a given Connection either by use of the TARGET and NODE parameters, or by using the list alternatives with TARGETNUM(1) and NODENUM(1). If the list format is used, then TARGETNUM*NODENUM Connections are processed.

The list operands are specified in exactly the same way as for the other lists (no imbedded blanks, eight-byte elements), and errors resulting from list operations are logged to the CSZX Global TDQ with an event code of SETFAIL (see Chapter 46).

### 18.2.2 EXEC CICS FEPI SET NODE

The format of the EXEC CICS FEPI SET NODE command is:

```
EXEC CICS FEPI SET
               NODE(char8)
                   |NODELIST(char)  NODENUM(fixed31)

[ACQSTATUS(cvda)|ACQUIRED|RELEASED]
[SERVSTATUS(cvda)|INSERVICE|OUTSERVICE]
[USERDATA(char64)]
```

You can operate on a given Node either by use of the NODE parameter, or by using the list alternative with NODENUM(1).

The list operand is specified in exactly the same way as for the other lists (no imbedded blanks, eight-byte elements), and errors resulting from list operations are logged to the CSZX Global TDQ with an event code of SETFAIL (see Chapter 46).

### 18.2.3 EXEC CICS FEPI SET POOL

The format of the EXEC CICS FEPI SET POOL command is:

```
EXEC CICS FEPI SET
               POOL(char8)
                   |POOLLIST(char)  POOLNUM(fixed31)

[SERVSTATUS(cvda)|INSERVICE|OUTSERVICE]
[USERDATA(char64)]
```

You can operate on a given Pool either by use of the POOL parameter, or by using the list alternative with POOLNUM(1).

The list operand is specified in exactly the same way as for the other lists (no imbedded blanks, eight-byte elements), and errors resulting from list operations are logged to the CSZX Global TDQ with an event code of SETFAIL (see Chapter 46).

### 18.2.4 EXEC CICS FEPI SET TARGET

The format of the EXEC CICS FEPI SET TARGET command is:

```
EXEC CICS FEPI SET
               TARGET(char8)
                   |TARGETLIST(char) TARGETNUM(fixed31)

[SERVSTATUS(cvda)|INSERVICE|OUTSERVICE]
[USERDATA(char64)]
```

You can operate on a given Target either by use of the TARGET parameter, or by using the list alternative with TARGETNUM(1).

The list operand is specified in exactly the same way as for the other lists (no imbedded blanks, eight-byte elements), and errors resulting from list operations are logged to the CSZX Global TDQ with an event code of SETFAIL (see Chapter 46).

## 18.3 EXEC CICS FEPI INQUIRE commands

The EXEC CICS FEPI INQUIRE commands return information about FEPI resources. This information includes attributes set at installation time, as well as various dynamic settings.

The information may be obtained for a given quoted resource, or by browse operations (see Secs 18.5 and 18.6). List operations are not available for the EXEC CICS FEPI INQUIRE commands, as browses are provided instead, and selective operations (like returning all Inservice resources) are not supported (but can be done via CEMT, see Chapter 19).

In the discussion of the attributes returned for each EXEC CICS FEPI INQUIRE command, you should refer to the EXEC CICS FEPI INSTALL or EXEC CICS FEPI SET commands for information on the parameters which can be quoted there. The following discussions will only dwell on new information which is returned.

### 18.3.1 EXEC CICS FEPI INQUIRE CONNECTION

The format of the EXEC CICS FEPI INQUIRE CONNECTION command is:

```
EXEC CICS FEPI INQUIRE CONNECTION
                       NODE(char8)  TARGET(char8)

[ACQNUM(fixed31)]
[ACQSTATUS(cvda)]
[CONVNUM(fixed31)]
[INSTLSTATUS(cvda)]
[LASTACQCODE(fixed31)]
[POOL(char8)]
[SERVSTATUS(cvda)]
[STATE(cvda)]
[USERDATA(char64)]
[WAITCONVNUM(fixed31)]
```

The Connection (Target–Node pair) is specified by quoting the name of the Target and Node that together form the Connection.

ACQNUM
This is a statistics field that returns the number of times the Connection has been acquired.

ACQSTATUS
This shows the VTAM status of the Connection. See Sec. 18.1.2.

CONVNUM
This is a statistics field that returns the number of times the Connection has been EXEC CICS FEPI ALLOCATEd (i.e., the number of Conversations that have used the Connection).

`INSTLSTATUS`
This field returns a CVDA that shows whether or not the Connection is in the process of being discarded (if it actually has been discarded, the Connection will not exist!).

`INSTALLED` shows that the Connection is in a Pool which has the title `INSTLSTATUS(INSTALLED)`, is not itself being discarded, and is available for use (which use depends on the `ACQSTATUS` and `SERVSTATUS` settings).

`NOTINSTALLED` shows that the Connection is currently being removed; either because it was explicitly discarded via an `EXEC CICS FEPI DELETE` command, or the Pool to which it belongs is being discarded by an `EXEC CICS FEPI DISCARD POOL` command.

`LASTACQCODE`
This field returns the VTAM *Sense Code* that results from the last attempt to Acquire the Connection. The act of Acquiring the Connection generates a VTAM *Bind* which flows to the partner system. If this Bind is rejected, or VTAM does not send it, or something unexpected happens, the Return Code is placed in this field (which will be X'00000000' if the Connection has successfully Acquired). You should consult the *VTAM Messages and Codes Manual* or the *SNA Formats Manual* to discover the meaning of the Sense Code.

On a failure to Acquire, a Transient Data Queue record will be written to the Pool-Specific TDQ, if defined, to record the failure (see Chapter 45). FEPI will also attempt to retry the act of acquisition (usually at 1 minute intervals for 30 retries).

`POOL`
This field shows in which Pool the Connection resides.

`SERVSTATUS`
This shows the usability status of the Connection. See Sec. 18.1.2.

`STATE`
The `STATE` field returns a CVDA which shows what position the Conversation running over the Connection has reached. The possible settings are:

| | |
|---|---|
| `APPLICATION` | A normal FEPI application task owns the conversation. |
| `BEGINSESSION` | A Begin Session Handler owns the conversation. |
| `FREE` | An End Session (End of Conversation) Handler owns the conversation. |
| `NOCONV` | No conversation is active on the connection. |
| `PENDBEGIN` | A Begin Session Handler has been scheduled. |
| `PENDDATA` | FEPI is waiting for inbound data, following a `EXEC CICS FEPI START` request. |
| `PENDFREE` | An End Session (End of Conversation) Handler has been scheduled. |
| `PENDPASS` | The conversation is 'unowned' following a `EXEC CICS FEPI FREE PASS` command. |
| `PENDRELEASE` | An End Session (End of Connection) Handler has been scheduled. |

| | |
|---|---|
| PENDSTART | Inbound data has arrived, so a EXEC CICS FEPI START transaction has been scheduled. |
| PENDSTSN | An STSN Handler has been scheduled. |
| PENDUNSOL | An Unsolicited Data Handler has been scheduled. |
| RELEASE | An End Session (End of Connection) Handler owns the conversation. |
| STSN | A STSN Handler owns the conversation. |
| UNSOLDATA | An Unsolicited Data Handler task owns the conversation. |

The PEND states indicate that the Connection is not actually owned by a CICS Transaction, FEPI is waiting for one to run and grab the Connection by issuing an EXEC CICS FEPI ALLOCATE PASSCONVID command.

If the PEND state appears for an undue length of time, it may be that CICS has purged the transaction that was due to grab the Connection. In this case, to clear the state (and so allow the Connection to be reused), you should use EXEC CICS FEPI SET CONNECTION ACQSTATUS(RELEASED) and then EXEC CICS FEPI SET CONNECTION ACQSTATUS(ACQUIRED) (or the CEMT equivalents, see Chapter 19) to recycle the Connection (see Sec. 18.2.1). However, if things are just running slowly, you will erroneously break the Conversation by taking this action, so be careful!

USERDATA
This field shows the contents of the user supplied data field; it is the only way of obtaining the data which was set on a preceding EXEC CICS FEPI SET CONNECTION USERDATA( ) command.

WAITCONVNUM
This field shows how many Conversations are waiting to use the Connection (i.e., the number of waiting EXEC CICS FEPI ALLOCATE commands). Note that WAITCONVNUM applies to all the Connections in the Pool, so this number really says that for the Pool which contains the Connection, there are WAITCONVNUM allocates queuing up (although as you can EXEC CICS FEPI ALLOCATE to a given Target within the Pool, you should interpret WAITCONVNUM on a Target basis).

### 18.3.2 EXEC CICS FEPI INQUIRE NODE

The format of the EXEC CICS FEPI INQUIRE NODE command is:

```
EXEC CICS FEPI INQUIRE
               NODE(char8)

[ACQNUM(fixed31)]
[ACQSTATUS(cvda)]
[INSTLSTATUS(cvda)]
[LASTACQCODE(fixed31)]
[SERVSTATUS(cvda)]
[USERDATA(char64)]
```

ACQNUM
This is a statistics field that returns the number of times the Node has been acquired.

ACQSTATUS
This shows the VTAM status of the ACB representing the Node. See Sec. 18.1.2.

INSTLSTATUS
This field returns a CVDA that shows whether or not the Node is in the process of being discarded. (If it actually has been discarded, the Node will not exist!).

INSTALLED shows that the Node is not being discarded, and is available for use (which use depends on the ACQSTATUS and SERVSTATUS settings).

NOTINSTALLED shows that the Node is currently being removed because it was explicitly discarded via an EXEC CICS FEPI DISCARD NODELIST command. The actual removal occurs when all current usages of the Node have ended.

LASTACQCODE
This field returns the VTAM *Return Code* that results from the last attempt to Acquire the Node. The act of Acquiring the Node generates a VTAM *open* of the ACB which represents the Node. If this *open* is rejected, or something unexpected happens, the *Return Code* is placed in this field (which will be X'00000000' if the Node has successfully acquired). You should consult the *VTAM Messages and Codes Manual* or the *VTAM Programming Manual* to discover the meaning of the Sense Code.

On a failure to acquire, a Transient Data Queue record will be written to the Pool-specific TDQ, if defined, to record the failure (see Chapter 45). FEPI will also attempt to retry the act of acquisition (usually at 1 minute intervals for 30 retries).

SERVSTATUS
This shows the usability status of the Connection. See Sec. 18.1.2.

USERDATA
This field shows the contents of the user supplied data field; it is the only way of obtaining the data which was set on a preceding EXEC CICS FEPI SET NODE USERDATA( ) command.

### 18.3.3 EXEC CICS FEPI INQUIRE TARGET

The format of the EXEC CICS FEPI INQUIRE TARGET command is:

```
EXEC CICS FEPI INQUIRE
               TARGET(char8)

[APPL(char8)]
[INSTLSTATUS(cvda)]
[SERVSTATUS(cvda)]
[USERDATA(char64)]
```

APPL
The APPL parameter returns the Applid of the partner system (see Sec. 14.2.3).

INSTLSTATUS
This field returns a CVDA that shows whether or not the Target is in the process of being discarded. (If it actually has been discarded, the Target will not exist!)

INSTALLED shows that the Target is not being discarded, and is available for use (which use depends on the SERVSTATUS settings). NOTINSTALLED shows that the Target is currently being removed because it was explicitly discarded via an EXEC CICS FEPI DISCARD TARGETLIST command. The actual removal occurs when all current usages of the Target have ended.

SERVSTATUS
This shows the usability status of the Target. See Sec. 18.1.2.

USERDATA
This field shows the contents of the user supplied data field; it is the only way of obtaining the data which was set on a preceding EXEC CICS FEPI SET TARGET USERDATA( ) command.

### 18.3.4 EXEC CICS FEPI INQUIRE PROPERTYSET

The format of the EXEC CICS FEPI INQUIRE PROPERTYSET command is:

```
EXEC CICS FEPI INQUIRE
               PROPERTYSET(char8)

[BEGINSESSION(char4)]
[CONTENTION(cvda)]
[DEVICE(cvda)]
[ENDSESSION(char4)]
[EXCEPTIONQ(char4)]
[FJOURNALNUM(fixed31)]
[FORMAT(cvda)]
[INITIALDATA(cvda)]
[MAXFLENGTH(fixed31)]
[MSGJRNL(cvda)]
[STSN(char4)]
[UNSOLDATA(char4)]
[UNSOLDATACK(cvda)]
```

The contents of all the returned parameters are discussed in Chapter 16.

### 18.3.5 EXEC CICS FEPI INQUIRE POOL

The format of the EXEC CICS FEPI INQUIRE POOL command is:

```
EXEC CICS FEPI INQUIRE
               POOL(char8)

[INSTLSTATUS(cvda)]
[PROPERTYSET(char8)]
[SERVSTATUS(cvda)]
[USERDATA(char64)]

[BEGINSESSION(char4)]
[CONTENTION(cvda)]
[DEVICE(cvda)]
[ENDSESSION(char4)]
[EXCEPTIONQ(char4)]
[FJOURNALNUM(fixed31)]
[FORMAT(cvda)]
[INITIALDATA(cvda)]
[MAXFLENGTH(fixed31)]
[MSGJRNL(cvda)]
[STSN(char4)]
[UNSOLDATA(char4)]
[UNSOLDATACK(cvda)]
[WAITCONVNUM(fixed31)]
```

Other than described below, the parameters relate to the attributes set by the Pool from the corresponding Propertyset. See Chapter 16 for details.

`INSTLSTATUS`
This field returns a CVDA that shows whether or not the Pool is in the process of being discarded. (If it actually has been discarded, the Pool will not exist!)

`INSTALLED` shows that the Pool is not being discarded, and is available for use (which use depends on the `SERVSTATUS` settings).

`NOTINSTALLED` shows that the Pool is currently being removed because it was explicitly discarded via an `EXEC CICS FEPI DISCARD POOL` command. The actual removal occurs when all current usages of the Pool (i.e., the Active Connections) have ended.

`PROPERTYSET`
This shows the name of the Propertyset that was used to define the attributes for the Pool. Note that the Propertyset could no longer exist, or have been redefined since the Pool was created. This is why all the Propertyset attributes are returned on the `EXEC CICS FEPI INQUIRE POOL`.

`SERVSTATUS`
This shows the usability status of the Pool. See Sec. 18.1.2.

`USERDATA`
This field shows the contents of the user supplied data field; it is the only way of obtaining the data which was set on a preceding `EXEC CICS FEPI SET POOL USERDATA()` command.

`WAITCONVNUM`
This field shows how many Conversations are waiting to use a Connection within the Pool (i.e., the number of waiting `EXEC CICS FEPI ALLOCATE` commands).

## 18.4 Browsing FEPI resources

All FEPI Resources may be browsed in the usual manner for CICS resources.

## 18.5 Browsing FEPI Nodes, Targets, Pools, and Propertysets

The browsing of Nodes, Targets, Pools, and Propertysets follows the usual rules for CICS resources: You issue:

- `EXEC CICS FEPI INQUIRE` ⟨resource⟩ `START`
- `EXEC CICS FEPI INQUIRE` ⟨resource name⟩ `NEXT`
- `EXEC CICS FEPI INQUIRE` ⟨resource⟩ `END`

where <resource> is:

- `NODE` or
- `TARGET` or
- `POOL` or
- `PROPERTYSET`

and ⟨resource name⟩ is:

- NODE(name) or
- TARGET(name) or
- POOL(name) or
- PROPERTYSET(name)

The attributes returned on the NEXT operation are those described for the basic EXEC CICS FEPI INQUIRE commands as described in Sec. 18.3.

## 18.6 Browsing FEPI Connections

The browsing of FEPI Connections follow a different set of rules from a browse of other FEPI resources:

```
EXEC CICS FEPI INQUIRE CONNECTION START
```

. . . to start the browse of Connections

```
EXEC CICS FEPI INQUIRE CONNECTION NEXTNODE|NEXTTARGET
```

⟨Inquire Connection's attributes⟩
. . . to obtain attributes

```
EXEC CICS FEPI INQUIRE CONNECTION END
```

. . . to end the browse of Connections

You can browse the Connections in either Node order or Target order. You control this by specifying either NEXTNODE or NEXTTARGET instead of a simple NEXT.

If NEXTNODE is used then you obtain:

- The next Node for the current Target or
- The first Node for the next Target (having reached the end of the Nodes for the previous Target).

If NEXTTARGET is used then you obtain:

- The next Target for the current Node or
- The first Target for the next Node (having reached the end of the Targets for the previous Node).

In both cases, the returned NODE and TARGET parameters denote the Connection (Target–Node pair) returned.

CHAPTER 19

# CEMT

| GUIDANCE |
|---|
| This chapter outlines the CEMT commands available for FEPI. |

## 19.1 Introduction

FEPI provides CEMT facilities for the manipulation of FEPI resources. The actual implementation of the underlying operations is via the equivalent SPI-type commands.

Table 19.1 shows the CEMT operations available, and their `EXEC CICS FEPI FEPI` equivalents.

## 19.2 CEMT usage

The normal CEMT rules apply to FEPI's use of CEMT. All FEPI resources can be inquired upon, and the usual rules for searching apply. Consequently, wild-card matching can be used on resource names, and selection can be done on the settings. Therefore, `CEMT I FEN(A*) ACQU` will display all the FEPI nodes starting with 'A' that are Acquired.

All FEPI resources (apart from Propertysets) can have their `SERVSTATUS` and/or `ACQSTATUS` settings changed by overkeying the fields with INSE/OUTS or ACQU/RELE in the usual CEMT fashion.

All FEPI resources (apart from Connections) can be discarded by entering 'D' in the left-hand side column.

**Table 19.1** FEPI CEMT operands

| CEMT command | EXEC CICS FEPI equivalent | Settings |
|---|---|---|
| D **FEN**ODE | DISCARD NODE | |
| D **FEPO**OL | DISCARD POOL | |
| D **FEPR**OPSET | DISCARD PROPERTYSET | |
| D **FET**ARGET | DISCARD TARGET | |
| I **FEC**ONNECTION | INQUIRE CONNECTION | ■ POOL<br>■ STATE<br>■ WAIT<br>■ LASTACQCODE<br>■ **INST**alled \| **NOTI**nstalled<br>■ **INSE**ervice \| **OUTS**ervice<br>■ **ACQU**ired \| **RELE**eased |
| I **FEN**ODE | INQUIRE NODE | ■ LASTACQCODE<br>■ **INST**alled \| **NOTI**nstalled<br>■ **INSE**rvice \| **OUTS**ervice<br>■ **ACQU**ired \| **RELE**eased |
| I **FEP**OOL | INQUIRE POOL | ■ DEVICE<br>■ WAITCONVNUM<br>■ **INST**alled \| **NOTI**nstalled<br>■ **INSE**rvice \| **OUTS**ervice |
| I **FEP**ROPSET | INQUIRE PROPERTYSET | |
| I **FET**ARGET | INQUIRE TARGET | ■ APPL<br>■ **INST**alled \| **NOTI**nstalled<br>■ **INSE**rvice \| **OUTS**ervice |
| S **FEC**ONNECTION | SET CONNECTION | ■ **INSE**rvice \| **OUTS**ervice<br>■ **ACQU**ired \| **RELE**eased |
| S **FEN**ODE | SET NODE | ■ **INSE**rvice \| **OUTS**ervice<br>■ **ACQU**ired \| **RELE**eased |
| S **FEP**OOL | SET POOL | ■ **INSE**rvice \| **OUTS**ervice |
| S **FET**ARGET | SET TARGET | ■ **INSE**rvice \| **OUTS**ervice |

*Note:* FEPI's CEMT settings are all four characters long.

## 19.3 CEMT examples

The following sections show some of the CEMT screens.

### 19.3.1 PROPERTYSETS

FEPI Propertysets do not support set operations. The main purpose of the display is to allow a CEMT DISCARD operation.

### CEMT INQUIRE FEPROPSET

```
I FEPROP
STATUS:  RESULTS
 Fepr(YMARY07 )
 Fepr(YMARY08 )
 Fepr(YMARY19 )
 Fepr(YMARY20 )
 Fepr(YRAH1   )
```

### CEMT INQUIRE FEPROPSET discarding

```
  I FEPROP
  STATUS:  RESULTS
   Fepr(YMARY07 )
   Fepr(YMARY08 )
   Fepr(YMARY19 )
d  Fepr(YMARY20 )
   Fepr(YRAH1   )
```

## 19.3.2 NODES

FEPI Nodes can have their INSErvice/OUTService and/or ACQUired/RELEased status' changed by overkeying the displayed fields. They can also be discarded. The `LACQ` field shows the VTAM OPEN ACB error code (see Sec. 18.3.2) which (if not X'00000000') shows why the Node could not acquire. A message shows that an operation for the Node is in progress.

### CEMT INQUIRE FENODE

```
I FENODE
STATUS:  RESULTS - OVERTYPE TO MODIFY
 Feno(IYAEZM40) Inst Inse Rele Lacq(X'0000005A')
 Feno(IYAEZM41) Inst Inse Rele Lacq(X'0000005A')
 Feno(IYAEZM42) Inst Inse Rele Lacq(X'0000005A')
 Feno(IYAEZM43) Inst Inse Rele Lacq(X'0000005A')
 Feno(IYAEZM49) Inst Inse Rele Lacq(X'0000005A')
 Feno(IYAHZC40) Inst Inse Acqu Lacq(X'00000000')
 Feno(IYAHZC41) Inst Inse Acqu Lacq(X'00000000')
 Feno(IYAHZC42) Inst Inse Acqu Lacq(X'00000000')
 Feno(IYAHZC46) Inst Inse Acqu Lacq(X'00000000')
```

### CEMT INQUIRE FENODE acquisition

```
I FENODE
STATUS:  RESULTS - OVERTYPE TO MODIFY
 Feno(IYAEZM40) Inst Inse Rele Lacq(X'0000005A')
 Feno(IYAEZM41) Inst Inse ACQU Lacq(X'0000005A')
 Feno(IYAEZM42) Inst Inse Rele Lacq(X'0000005A')
 Feno(IYAEZM43) Inst Inse Rele Lacq(X'0000005A')
 Feno(IYAEZM49) Inst Inse Rele Lacq(X'0000005A')
 Feno(IYAHZC40) Inst Inse Acqu Lacq(X'00000000')
 Feno(IYAHZC41) Inst Inse Acqu Lacq(X'00000000')
 Feno(IYAHZC42) Inst Inse Acqu Lacq(X'00000000')
 Feno(IYAHZC46) Inst Inse Acqu Lacq(X'00000000')
```

```
I FENODE
STATUS:  RESULTS - OVERTYPE TO MODIFY
 Feno(IYAEZM40) Inst Inse Rele Lacq(X'0000005A')
 Feno(IYAEZM41) Inst Inse Rele Lacq(X'0000005A') BEING ACQUIRED
 Feno(IYAEZM42) Inst Inse Rele Lacq(X'0000005A')
 Feno(IYAEZM43) Inst Inse Rele Lacq(X'0000005A')
 Feno(IYAEZM49) Inst Inse Rele Lacq(X'0000005A')
 Feno(IYAHZC40) Inst Inse Acqu Lacq(X'00000000')
 Feno(IYAHZC41) Inst Inse Acqu Lacq(X'00000000')
 Feno(IYAHZC42) Inst Inse Acqu Lacq(X'00000000')
 Feno(IYAHZC46) Inst Inse Acqu Lacq(X'00000000')
```

### 19.3.3 TARGETS

FEPI Targets can have their INSErvice/OUTService status changed by over-keying the displayed field. They can also be discarded.

#### CEMT INQUIRE FET

```
I FET
STATUS:  RESULTS - OVERTYPE TO MODIFY
 Feta(IGJZVAMP) Appl(IGJZVAMP) Inst Inse
 Feta(IMSDC3  ) Appl(IMSDC3  ) Inst Inse
 Feta(IYAHZCE6) Appl(IYAHZCE6) Inst Inse
 Feta(IYAHZCV6) Appl(IYAHZCV6) Inst Inse
 Feta(MARY07  ) Appl(MARY07  ) Inst Inse
 Feta(MARY08  ) Appl(MARY08  ) Inst Inse
 Feta(MARY19  ) Appl(MARY19  ) Inst Inse
 Feta(MARY20  ) Appl(MARY20  ) Inst Inse
 Feta(RAHXRF3 ) Appl(RAHXRF3 ) Inst Inse
 Feta(RAHXRF4 ) Appl(RAHXRF4 ) Inst Inse
```

### 19.3.4 POOLS

FEPI Pools can have their INSErvice/OUTService status changed by overkeying the displayed field. They can be also be discarded. The DEVI field shows the `DEVICE` setting for the Pool's terminal type. The WAIT field shows how many Conversations are waiting within the Pool (see Sec. 18.3.5)

#### CEMT INQUIRE FEPOOL

```
I FEPOOL
STATUS:  RESULTS - OVERTYPE TO MODIFY
 Fepo(PMARY07 ) Inst Inse Devi(T3278M2 ) Wait(00000)
 Fepo(PMARY08 ) Inst Inse Devi(T3278M3 ) Wait(00000)
 Fepo(PMARY19 ) Inst Inse Devi(T3278M4 ) Wait(00000)
 Fepo(PMARY20 ) Inst Inse Devi(T3278M5 ) Wait(00000)
 Fepo(PX3     ) Inst Inse Devi(T3278M2 ) Wait(00000)
 Fepo(PX4     ) Inst Inse Devi(T3278M2 ) Wait(00000)
 Fepo(P1      ) Inst Inse Devi(T3278M2 ) Wait(00000)
 Fepo(P1D     ) Inst Inse Devi(T3278M2 ) Wait(00000)
 Fepo(P2      ) Inst Inse Devi(T3278M2 ) Wait(00000)
 Fepo(P2D     ) Inst Inse Devi(T3278M2 ) Wait(00000)
 Fepo(P3      ) Inst Inse Devi(T3278M2 ) Wait(00000)
 Fepo(P4      ) Inst Inse Devi(T3278M2 ) Wait(00000)
 Fepo(P5      ) Inst Inse Devi(LUP     ) Wait(00000)
 Fepo(P6      ) Inst Inse Devi(T3278M2 ) Wait(00000)
```

### 19.3.5 CONNECTIONS

FEPI Connections can have their INSErvice/OUTService and/or their ACQUired/RELEased status changed by overkeying the displayed fields. They cannot be discarded. The `Lacq` field shows a VTAM sense code (see Sec. 18.3.1) which (if not X'00000000') shows why the Connection failed to acquire. The `State` field shows what the Conversation running on the connection is currently doing (see `STATE` in Sec. 18.3.1). The `Wait` field shows how many queued allocates could be satisfied by the Connection (see `WAITCONVNUM` in Sec. 18.3.1). The message shows that an operation for the Connection is in progress.

## CEMT INQUIRE FECONN

```
I FECONN
STATUS:  RESULTS - OVERTYPE TO MODIFY
 Node(IYAEZM42) Targ(IYAHZCE6) Pool(P1      ) Inst Inse Rele BEING ACQUIRED
    Stat(NOCONV      ) Wait(00000) Lacq(X'00000000')
 Node(IYAEZM44) Targ(IYAHZCE6) Pool(P2      ) Inst Inse Rele BEING ACQUIRED
    Stat(NOCONV      ) Wait(00000) Lacq(X'00000000')
 Node(IYAEZM45) Targ(IYAHZCE6) Pool(P2      ) Inst Inse Rele BEING ACQUIRED
    Stat(NOCONV      ) Wait(00000) Lacq(X'00000000')
 Node(IYAEZM46) Targ(IYAHZCE6) Pool(P1D     ) Inst Inse Rele
    Stat(NOCONV      ) Wait(00000) Lacq(X'00000000')
 Node(IYAEZM47) Targ(IYAHZCE6) Pool(P1D     ) Inst Inse Rele
    Stat(NOCONV      ) Wait(00000) Lacq(X'00000000')
 Node(IYAEZM48) Targ(IYAHZCE6) Pool(P1D     ) Inst Inse Acqu
    Stat(BEGINSESSION) Wait(00000) Lacq(X'00000000')
 Node(IYAEZM49) Targ(IYAHZCE6) Pool(P1D     ) Inst Inse Rele
    Stat(NOCONV      ) Wait(00000) Lacq(X'00000000')
 Node(IYAHZC40) Targ(IYAHZCE6) Pool(P1      ) Inst Inse Acqu
    Stat(APPLICATION ) Wait(00000) Lacq(X'00000000')
 Node(IYAHZC41) Targ(IYAHZCE6) Pool(P1      ) Inst Inse Acqu
    Stat(PENDSTART   ) Wait(00000) Lacq(X'00000000')
```

# PART 3

# Application programming techniques and the API

**GUIDANCE**

This part of the book describes the commands used for FEPI application programming. The discussion is contained in the following sections:

- Introduction to 3270 Datastream
- Terminal emulation and what is on the screen
- Scatter/Gather techniques
- Knowing when you have got all that you need
- The difference between Unexpected and Unsolicited input
- IMS partners
- FEPI command sequences
- Full description of the API-type commands
- EIBRESP2 codes and what to do with them

# CHAPTER 20 Introduction to 3270 Datastream

**GUIDANCE**

This chapter introduces the 3270 Datastream and the VTAM concepts that you need to run a FEPI emulation.

A more detailed understanding of 3270 is required for FEPI Datastream Conversations, and this is provided in Chapter 37.

The *IBM 3270 Data Stream Programming Reference* manual provides a full description of the 3270 protocol.

## 20.1 Introduction to 3270

A 3270 Datastream consists of a sequence of characters consisting of *Attribute* Bytes and *Data* Bytes. The Attribute Bytes precede Data Bytes, and set the format of the following Data.

A *field* is conventionally taken to start at an Attribute Byte, and continue up to, but not including, the following Attribute Byte. Consequently, a field consists of an area of the screen, preceded by an Attribute Byte. The Attribute Byte (which occupies one screen position) sets the format for the data. The field can be updatable/static, displayed in normal/highlight, etc., all under the influence of the Attribute Byte.

However, 3270 supports Colour displays, so the 3270 Datastream also supports *Extended Attribute* Bytes that define the Colour for the field (and things like Underline or Blink). Extended Attributes provide the mechanism whereby a field on the screen has to be 'filled in' or 'entered'.

The layout of the field on the screen is controlled by 3270 *orders*. These orders say that a following field is to start at a given position on the screen. Unfortunately, this screen position is expressed in a peculiar code, and moreover, there are potentially three codes! When running a FEPI Formatted Conversation, this coding is all taken care of by FEPI, but when running a FEPI Datastream Conversation, you have to worry about it (as discussed in Sec. 40.1).

An extension to the 3270 Datastream is support for 3290 panels (and suchlike devices). The 3290 can be configured so that it is running several partitions on the same screen. Each of these partitions is updated separately, and so the 3270 Datastream supports the concept of partition selection.

Partition selection works via 3270 *Structured Fields*. Structured Fields provide an alternative to the 'basic' 3270 Datastream described earlier. Again, FEPI takes care of all of this for you when running Formatted Conversations. See Chapters 38 and 39 for information on Structured Field processing and FEPI Datastream Conversations.

### 20.1.1 Query Structured Field

A special sort of 3270 Structured Field is the *Query*. A *Query Structured Field* is sent from a host to a terminal in order for the host to find out what sort of terminal it is talking to. The terminal responds to a Query Structured Field by building a 3270 sequence that describes itself (containing things like screen size and colour support).

The Query Structured Field flow will usually be the first flow sent from a partner system after the terminal has been connected to the partner system (but it can also be sent from within an application program). If the Connection is running Formatted Conversations, then FEPI responds appropriately. If running a Datastream Conversation, then you have to cope with this response yourself. The way this is done is discussed in Chapter 38.

The processing of the first flow on a Datastream Conversation (which may be this Query Structured Field) has an impact on the design of the Begin Session Handler (see Sec. 44.1).

In general, an IMS partner does not send a Query Structured Field. A CICS partner will issue this query, but this is controllable. I recommend that the CICS `TYPETERM` for the FEPI 'terminal' contain `QUERY(NO)` to prevent a Query Structured Field flowing.

When a FEPI Connection is running a Formatted Conversation (see Sec. 3.1.1), FEPI will automatically respond to these Structured Field Queries according to the `DEVICE` setting on the owning Propertyset (see Sec. 16.2.3).

## **20.2** 3270 and VTAM indicators

When VTAM sends a 3270 Datastream, it chops the flow into various pieces. Each of these pieces is called a *Request Unit* (RU). A collection of RUs is called a *Chain*.

FEPI's receive commands complete as soon as a Chain is fully received from the partner (some of the commands can extend or reduce this period). However, the receipt of a whole Chain does not mean that all the data from the partner has been received. It *might* be all the flow, or it *might not*. This is the major problem when running any sort of 3270 emulator (not specially FEPI), as you do not get any positive indication that the partner system is not going to send any more data.

Things are not quite as bad as this, because VTAM supplies some indicators to assist in this process. However, it is always up to the partner system as to how it uses them. CICS and IMS partners both use these indicators, but in different ways; this is discussed in Chapter 37. These VTAM indicators are *Change Direction* (CD) and *End Bracket* (EB).

### 20.2.1 CD

If the partner system fully obeys the LU2 rules (CICS does), it will always send the CD on the last Chain that it sends to the terminal. The idea is that the end which has the CD has permission to send a flow. Therefore, the host tells the terminal that it has finished sending a 3270 datastream by putting the CD on the last flow it makes. Consequently, if the `EXEC CICS FEPI RECEIVE` command notes the occurrence of a CD in the `ENDSTATUS` field (see Secs 27.6 and 27.7), you know that you have all the data the partner is going to send. In the reverse direction, FEPI always puts the CD on its flow.

Partner systems which fully support the CD convention are very much easier to emulate with FEPI, simply because you have this firm indication that all the data from the partner has been obtained.

Unfortunately, IMS does not use the CD convention (see Sec. 25.1.4), so it is more difficult emulating IMS transactions with FEPI than it is emulating CICS transactions.

### 20.2.2 EB

The EB says that one end of the conversation is never going to send any more data. In VTAM terms, a sequence of flows between a terminal and a host is called a *Bracket*.

When the sequence of flows ends, the EB flows. At this point, either the host or the terminal can decide to send data, and both ends are in *Contention State*. The `CONTENTION` parameter on the Pool's Propertyset (see Sec. 16.2.2) controls how FEPI works while in Contention State. Thus, if the FEPI Receive command gets an EB, it could assume that no more data is to flow from the partner. Alas, this assumption may not be valid. Some partner systems (like IMS) may always send each chunk of data with an EB indicator. Consequently, use of the EB to detect all the data from the partner is not always possible. In situations where both a CD and a EB could flow, EB is the indicator that wins.

When communicating to a CICS partner, the EB will be placed on the last flow from the CICS transaction (that is, on the flow caused by the highest-level `EXEC CICS RETURN` command). Intermediate flows will have the CD. Therefore, if the partner CICS system is running a conversational transaction, the CD will flow. If it is running a pseudo-conversational transaction, the EB will flow.

# CHAPTER 21 Terminal emulation and what is on the screen

**GUIDANCE**

This chapter emphasizes that you must know what is on the emulated terminal's 'screen' at all times. Chapter 23 discusses how you determine that the 'screen' is complete, and Chapter 24 discusses problems with accuracy.

## 21.1 Knowledge of the position

When running an emulation (not necessary a FEPI Conversation), at all times you have to know what is the position of the underlying object. The concept of position covers such things as whether or not the partner system can accept input, and what the partner thinks is on the 'screen'.

If the 'screen' within the partner system differs from what your FEPI application program thinks is the display, your emulation will fail—possibly horribly. Therefore, you must:

- Know what is on the screen.
- Know where you are in a sequence of emulations.
- Know if you have not received all of a panel from the partner.
- Know whose turn it is to send data.

If you get any of these decisions wrong, the FEPI emulation will fail.

### 21.1.1 First flows

Once you have initiated a transaction within the partner system, knowing where you are becomes more straightforward. However, when you initially contact the partner system, you do not know what is likely to happen.

When you first make contact with the partner system (when a Connection is *Bound* in VTAM terms, or Acquired in FEPI terms), it will respond as if the 'terminal' has been switched on.

Chapter 38 discusses what needs to be done if (like CICS), the partner system sends a 3270 'Query Structured Field' flow. However, you cannot rely on the system either always sending the flow, or never sending the flow if it is capable of so doing. How you respond to this flow depends on whether or not you are running within a Begin Session Handler (see Sec. 44.1).

### 21.1.2 Signons

Having disposed of a (potential) Query Structured Field flow, you should then deal with the 'Start-of-Day' panel sent from the partner system. This panel will probably require the terminal 'operator' to sign on to the system, therefore, your FEPI emulation will have to fill in (at least) a logonid and a password. This is difficult to accomplish within a Begin Session Handler, but is not simple anyway. The problem arises as to how you get hold of the logonid and password.

If the FEPI application program is running at a terminal, then the currently signed on userid can easily be obtained via an `EXEC CICS ASSIGN USERID` command. However, there are no facilities within CICS (or RACF for that matter) to obtain a password (for obvious security reasons). Thus, you have to provide it yourself.

Your design should consider acquiring the password using these techniques:

- If you are running your own CICS signon transaction for the FEPI CICS System, you could consider saving away the provided password when the operator signs on. *This is a security exposure.*
- Alternatively, you may not need to sign on to the partner system with a password if your application design can ensure that the partner system trusts that access to it via FEPI emulated terminals have been authorized within your FEPI application program. This may be the case if the partner system application is 'read only', and so may only require a signon (without password) for access.
- You could consider using RACF (or equivalent External Security Manager) exits and use temporary time-sensitive passwords to sign on the partner system.
- Mimicking a PC-based method that supplies passwords collected from a workstation operator to a host.
- If all else fails, you may need to request the real end user to respecify their password whenever a FEPI Connection is Bound (as detected by the `SESSNSTATUS` operand on the `EXEC CICS FEPI ALLOCATE` command (see Sec. 29.2.5).

### 21.1.3 Signoffs

Having signed on a user to a Connection, you should remember to sign off before the `EXEC CICS FEPI FREE` (without the `PASS` keyword) command or else the partner system will still think the previous user is signed on when another CICS transaction comes to use the Connection.

### 21.1.4 Asynchronous operation

If you are using the full asynchronous facilities for your emulation (see Chapters 6 and 35), you need to track carefully where you are in the MAPIN/MAPOUT cycle.

In addition, you have to make a decision as to when you drop out of the cycle (perhaps when a given screen appears) and in what state you then leave the emulated terminal. This depends on how you are running the emulation and your FEPI application design.

### 21.1.5 Contention State

If you are using `CONTENTION(LOSE)` (see Sec. 16.2.2) on the Connection, then what you think of the Send State for the Connection may be overtaken by events. In this case, your `EXEC CICS FEPI SEND` will fail because the partner system has sent a flow which requires `EXEC CICS FEPI RECEIVE`ing before the data can be sent. When you have obtained the flow from the partner, you could well find that what you were going to send is inappropriate.

Your FEPI application design has to consider carefully the effect of the `CONTENTION` settings.

# CHAPTER 22 Scatter/Gather techniques

**GUIDANCE**

This chapter briefly describes the things to think about when running Scatter/Gather emulations. The concepts behind Scatter/Gather are discussed in Chapter 5.

## 22.1 Overview

A Scatter/Gather FEPI application design has the following attributes:

- A single request (maybe from a transaction in the FEPI CICS System) generates (scatters) multiple FEPI emulations (scattered).
- These multiple scattered FEPI emulations run in parallel.
- All these scattered emulations have to end before the single scattering request completes.

When a FEPI application design involves the gathering of data from more than one source, you are using Scatter/Gather techniques.

### 22.1.1. Sequential scatter/gather

A special case of Scatter/Gather is where you are doing multiple FEPI Conversations, but in a sequential manner. This is not really scatter/gather, as it fails the parallel attribute. However, there may be cases where some of the operations have to be performed in an ordered fashion.

## 22.2 Scattering the emulations

In order to initiate the multiple scattered FEPI emulations, you arrange for each scattered FEPI emulation to run as a separate CICS transaction. In this way, you get parallel operation, and so the quickest response.

The drawback in using multiple scattered transactions is that, in a heavily used CICS System, other transactions may monopolize the CPU, so your set does not get the service it requires, and so the required answer comes back after a longer than expected time. If this is the case, you may well decide to remove the parallelism, so that at least a consistent response time for the scattered emulation is obtained.

When you EXEC CICS START the transactions which run the multiple scattered emulations, you should do an EXEC CICS SYNCPOINT to ensure that the Transactions are started as soon as possible. (This is not strictly speaking necessary, but I always think it is a good thing to do to ensure that transactions are initiated.)

The application program that scatters the FEPI transactions should be coded to take account of the possibility that one of the scattered transactions will fail.

The scatterer can use all of the standard CICS facilities to detect completion of the scattered transactions. The use of EXEC CICS WAIT EVENT is probably the best alternative to a looping test of completion.

## 22.3 The scattered transactions

The scattered transactions know what task they have to perform, and what data they are required to return. However, these transactions must take care to protect themselves against abends or CEMT cancellations.

As the transactions have been scattered to get various pieces of data, the scatterer will not complete until all of the scattered transactions complete. If one of them fails, then the set will not be complete, and so things will hang. Consequently, the scattered transactions must use EXEC CICS HANDLE ABENDs to protect against failure. Similarly, they must protect against CEMT cancellation within FEPI processing by checking for EIBRESP2s like 10, 12 or 18 (see Sec. 28.1).

## 22.4 Returning the scattered transactions' data

When the scattered FEPI emulation transactions finish their actions, they will return some data (even if it is only to say successfully ended). There are lots of techniques for collecting the data from the scattered transactions. Here are some of them.

### 22.4.1 Via a shared storage area

The scattering transaction can obtain a shared storage area (via EXEC CICS GETMAIN SHARED) and pass its address into the scattered transactions via their Start Data.

Each scattered transaction updates the area to show that it started and completed/failed, together with the returned data. Each scattered transaction knows the layout of the shared area.

When the scattering transaction detects that all the scattered transactions have ended (by looking at the shared area status flags), it uses the collected data. The shared area must not be freemained until it is positively known that all the scattered transactions have ended. An early freemain will result in a Storage Violation.

### 22.4.2 Via temporary storage

Each of the scattered transactions can update a Temporary Storage Queue (TSQ) record with its status and data. The name of the TSQ, and record number, are passed into the scattered transactions via their Start Data.

Alternatively, each scattered transaction can be allocated its own TSQ for data, and the scattering transaction uses the existence of the TSQ to show that the individual scattered transaction has completed. The name of the TSQ is passed to the scattered transactions via their Start Data.

## **22.5** Gathering the data

Once the scattered transactions have completed, their returned information is extracted, manipulated, and returned to the invoker of the Scatter/Gather sequence by the scatterer. However, the Gather process must take steps to handle events like the abending or cancellation of one of the scattered transactions. The gatherer should take a view about what interval is normally required for the scattered transactions to complete, and if they all do not finish in this interval decide not to wait for them all. But, if you terminate the gathering operation, you have to consider how to recover from a too zealous termination. It may just be that the partner system is a bit slow, not that a scattered transaction has failed.

## **22.6** Scattered updates

If the scattered transactions are doing updates, you should very carefully consider how Syncpointing and recovery are to be accomplished. As each scattered transaction is complete within itself, each of the scattered transactions will have updated a database independently of what the others were doing. Thus, you must consider how to back-out all the scattered transactions if this becomes necessary. This is not a trivial task.

If you know about Advanced Transaction Models, then this is the problem of Compensation.

CHAPTER 23

# Knowing when you have all that you need

**GUIDANCE**

This chapter outlines some techniques that you could use to know when you have received a whole panel from the partner system.

VTAM aspects of this problem are discussed in Chapter 20.

## 23.1 The problem

There is a general problem with 3270 emulation: you cannot be sure when the partner system has sent everything it is going to send. 3270 Datastreams have an ability to update any part of the terminal's screen at any time. Therefore, the updating of the bottom right-hand side of the screen does not mean that the whole screen has been received; it *might*, or it *might not*. It depends on how the partner system is generating the datastream. Therefore, while running a FEPI emulation, you *have* to know when the partner system has sent all the data it is going to send. Only with this information can you design your FEPI application program.

The use of VTAM indicators as discussed in Chapter 20 may provide you with some assistance.

If you run into problems in this arena, you will need to run a VTAM I/O trace (using GTF). Use of IPCS will show what the flows actually are (together with the VTAM indicators), and so you can work out where the logic of the FEPI application program has failed. Alternatively, if communicating to a CICS partner, you can get the partner CICS' terminal control trace to show partially what is going on.

### 23.1.1 BMS maps

If you are running an emulation to a CICS partner which is using BMS maps to generate panels, then BMS does not send the whole panel in one lump. BMS tends to send the constant parts of the panel first, and then the variable parts. Therefore, you cannot rely on a constant indicator appearing on the 'screen' to deduce that all the panel has been received.

### 23.1.2 CICS partners

As discussed in Chapter 20, CICS uses the VTAM CD protocol. Therefore, if you keeping doing `EXEC CICS FEPI RECEIVE` commands until either a CD or an EB is obtained (shown by the `ENDSTATUS` parameter), you will have obtained all of the flow. The FEPI Formatted Receive commands (see Sec. 27.6) may require a repetition of the command until either the EB or CD arrives, whereas the Datastream Receives have the flexibility to wait for either one of the indications before ending (see Sec. 27.7).

### 23.1.3 IMS Partners

Unlike CICS partners, IMS partners do not use the CD convention (see Sec. 25.1.4). IMS sends flows via Message Formatting Services (MFS). If MFS is appropriately configured, you should be able to arrange that the whole panel is sent in one lump. If this is so, then a single Receive command will obtain the panel. However, if this is not possible, then you have to resort to your judgement about panel completion for MFS. The only advice I can offer is always to put a `TIMEOUT` on the `EXEC CICS FEPI RECEIVE` and use a delay to indicate that nothing else is going to arrive.

### 23.1.4 The `EXEC CICS FEPI CONVERSE` commands

Knowing when all the flow has been obtained is more difficult when using the `EXEC CICS FEPI CONVERSE FORMATTED` and `EXEC CICS FEPI CONVERSE DATASTREAM` commands. This is because you only have one chance to obtain the data. This is why I recommend *avoiding* the use of the `EXEC CICS FEPI CONVERSE` commands, and prefer utilizing separate `EXEC CICS FEPI SEND` and `EXEC CICS FEPI RECEIVE` commands.

## **23.2** General warning

**WARNING**

When using FEPI Datastream facilities, coding to take account of the `ENDSTATUS` parameter is conceptually obvious. However, you must also take notice of `ENDSTATUS` on FEPI Formatted Conversations. If a keystroke emulation does not respond as it should, you may not have obtained all the flow from the partner in a single `EXEC CICS FEPI RECEIVE FORMATTED` command.

*You must keep* `EXEC CICS FEPI RECEIVE FORMATTED`*ing until* `ENDSTATUS` *returns* `EB` *or* `CD`.

CHAPTER

# 24 The difference between Unexpected and Unsolicited input

**GUIDANCE**

When running a FEPI emulation, you *must* be aware of the conceptual differences between *Unexpected* and *Unsolicited data*. This chapter describes the difference between the two.

## 24.1 Things are not what they seem!

When you are running your emulation, you have to be aware of what is on the screen. The importance of this is thoroughly discussed in Chapter 21. However, there will come a circumstance when the FEPI emulation breaks down because what is on the virtual screen is not what your FEPI application program thinks is there.

The problems are:

- How do you recognize the circumstance?
- How do you cope with it?

Within the FEPI environment, there is a distinction as to how the screen mismatch occurs:

**Unexpected data** is where something odd suddenly appears in the middle of a FEPI Conversation.

**Unsolicited data** occurs when the partner system decides to send a panel on a FEPI Connection that is not being used by a FEPI Conversation.

Therefore, the crucial difference between Unexpected and Unsolicited Data is whether or not there is a FEPI Conversation running at the time.

## 24.2 Unsolicited data

Unsolicited data occurs when the partner system sends data to its FEPI (emulated) terminal of its own accord. There is no FEPI Conversation running on the Connection at the time the partner has sent the flow.

This is not to say that Unsolicited data occurs when there is an inactive Conversation suspended on the Connection (for example, when an `EXEC CICS FEPI START`ed transaction is due to be run when a flow occurs). In this case, the flow is *Unexpected* data, not Unsolicited data.

Thus, Unsolicited data is that which arrives when the Connection is not being used by a FEPI Conversation.

### 24.2.1 Processing the Unsolicited data

How you process the Unsolicited data is controlled by the `UNSOLDATA` and `UNSOLDATACK` parameters (see Sec. 16.2.12) for the Propertyset which was used to define the Pool in which the Connection resides.

The choice of actions when Unsolicited data arrives is to:

- Accept it, and start the Unsolicited Data Handler (see Sec.44.3) to process the flow (`UNSOLDATA` is used).
- Lose the flow, but let the partner system think it was displayed (via `UNSOLDATACK(POSITIVE)`).
- Reject the flow altogether (via `UNSOLDATACK(NEGATIVE)`).

If you reject the flow, then you do not know what the partner system will do, and in what state it left the emulated terminal.

If you lose the flow, but let the partner system think it was displayed, you also do not know what is now on the terminal's 'screen'. Additionally, you do not know what the partner was expecting you to do when the Unsolicited data was displayed. This could easily lead to the terminal being locked.

Accepting the data and processing it within an Unsolicited Data Handler provides the FEPI application with a mechanism for looking at the flow and taking a reasonable action.

Of all the alternatives, I *strongly* recommend using the Unsolicited Data Handler to process the Unsolicited data in a controlled fashion.

#### ACTIONS FOR DATASTREAM CONVERSATIONS

If you are running a Datastream Conversation, you are probably running a passthrough scenario. As the Connection is not currently running a Conversation, there is no real end user to shunt the panel to for processing.

Therefore, you should analyse the message sent by the partner in the Unsolicited Data Handler. In all probability, it will be some sort of broadcast message. In this case, you have to hope that the transaction that caused the broadcast to appear on the screen saved away the current image before intruding. If things are well behaved in this manner, the Unsolicited Data Handler only needs to reply with something like CLEAR or ENTER to restore the previous screen image.

Some FEPI application designs can use the Unsolicited Data Handler to cope with asynchronous flows. In this case, your design routes or processes the Unsolicited data in whatever manner is deemed appropriate.

If you cannot decide what to do with the Unsolicited data, then you can simply `EXEC CICS FEPI FREE RELEASE` (see Chapter 36) the Conversation, and so end the Connection. If this is done, your FEPI application design will have determined how the 'first flow' is to be processed, and so you can decide whether or not to restart the FEPI Connection by doing an `EXEC CICS FEPI SET CONNECTION ACQSTATUS(ACQUIRED)` within the Unsolicited Data

Handler, or wait until FEPI decides to reacquire the Connection when a subsequent Conversation uses the same.

### ACTIONS FOR FORMATTED CONVERSATIONS

When Unsolicited data arrives for a Formatted Connection, things are more complicated than for a Datastream Connection. This is because the Unsolicited data may have only updated part of the screen. Thus, it may be difficult to determine exactly where (or if) the Unsolicited data has corrupted the screen.

However, the actions to be taken are exactly the same as for Datastream Connections: you have to decide whether or not a simple Enter/Clear response is appropriate, or if a complicated sequence is required, or if simply dropping the Connection is acceptable.

## 24.3 Unexpected data

Unexpected data is much more difficult to detect than Unsolicited data. Conceptually, you know when you have Unsolicited data, because the Unsolicited Data Handler is invoked to process it. There are no equivalent facilities for Unexpected data.

Unexpected data arises because the partner responds in a fashion other than normal. The most common occurrence is when the partner system's transaction has abended, so producing a DFH (or DFS) message instead of the expected panel.

Detecting an abend message may be quite easy—you simply scan the `EXEC CICS FEPI RECEIVE`d data for something starting 'DFH'. However, what you do when you detect this is another matter.

Unexpected data may not be as obvious as an abend message. It may be that the partner system has changed its panels and the FEPI application program is ignorant of this change. Therefore, your prime assumption of knowing what the emulated screen is fails, and so things will stop working (in varying degrees of obviousness!).

In general, there is no coherent advice I can give about detecting Unexpected data. It all depends on how your FEPI application program works. The easiest scenario is running a Datastream Passthrough emulation. In this case, you do not care whether or not there is Unexpected data, as you simply display it to the real end user's terminal and let the operator respond appropriately.

At the most extreme, you could check the position of every field returned from the partner against what you expect. This is terribly tedious, and slows things down enormously. I would recommend scanning your received data for occurrences of 'DFH' (or 'DFS') error messages, but otherwise assume everything is as expected.

However, as always, you may need to be more sophisticated than this within logic which is processing 'first flows' (like a Begin Session Handler). If your partner system is running some sort of bulletin-board as a Communication pipe for signed-on terminals, you will have to know how to cope with its display techniques in order to permit usage of the Connection.

# CHAPTER 25 IMS partners

**GUIDANCE**

This chapter outlines some of the things that CICS programmers should be aware of when communicating with IMS. However, the information presented is very selective, and just covers enough IMS concepts to permit a CICS programmer to run an IMS transaction via FEPI emulation.

If you do not understand any of the terminology used in this chapter, you are not IMS knowledgeable! You should look at the IMS programming documentation for enlightenment.

IMS does not behave like CICS! This truism should be borne in mind by CICS programmers when communicating with IMS. You must involve IMS programmers when designing a FEPI emulation to IMS if you are not familiar with IMS.

In particular, you should understand how IMS uses Message Formatting Services (MFS) to send and receive data, and bear in mind the difference between a CICS Conversation and an IMS Conversation. See also Chapter 54 for more information on IMS Conversations, and Sec. 16.2.2 for how the Propertyset `CONTENTION` parameter should be set for IMS partners.

## 25.1 IMS message protocols

### 25.1.1 Unsolicited and Unexpected data

The definitions of Unexpected and Unsolicited data are documented in Chapter 24. When running an LU2 Conversation, MFS will send a flow only in response to a request from a terminal. Thus, MFS will not unilaterally send a flow from the terminal without the terminal 'requesting' it. The 'request' is simply any flow to MFS from the terminal. Consequently, the concept of Unsolicited data does not occur in the same fashion as for communication to a CICS partner.

However, the possibility still exists for Unsolicited data, because you could `EXEC CICS FEPI FREE HOLD` the Conversation immediately after `EXEC CICS FEPI SEND`ing a flow to IMS. Consequently, although the possibilities for Unsolicited data are reduced with IMS, the opportunities for Unexpected data are enhanced. As MFS can elect to send any queued data for the terminal, it is possible that MFS will send a panel that is not that which was expected. This is especially true when running IMS nonresponse mode transactions (see Chapter 54).

### 25.1.2 IMS transactions

IMS transactions behave in a different fashion to CICS transactions. It is possible for an IMS transaction to be scheduled at the terminal either by use of the `/SET` command, or by placing information in the SPA. (Putting something like this in the SPA is the equivalent of doing an `EXEC CICS RETURN NEXTTRAN()`.)

You should be aware of the consequences of IMS's usage of the SPA for IMS transaction continuation, because it may cause unexpected information to appear on the FEPI emulated terminal.

### 25.1.3 MFS paging

I hope that you are not trying to run a FEPI emulation on an IMS transaction that uses either logical or physical paging. Use of these IMS techniques adds considerably to the complexity of the FEPI application program, and you *must* know what is going on, and why it is happening.

You must know whether or not a page is automatically deleted from the MFS Message Queue when MFS receives the next input flow for the 'terminal'. Similarly, you should know whether or not `PA1` is required to obtain more pages from the MFS queue.

### 25.1.4 VTAM indicators

Chapter 20 explains how IMS uses the VTAM EB indicators. When MFS sends a message, it does so when the terminal has sent a flow. Consequently, MFS will not use the CD indicators. Instead, MFS will always send a message to the terminal with an EB.

## 25.2 Session acquisition

Unlike CICS, IMS will always send a 'first flow' message. On the plus side, it will never send any 3270 Structured Field Queries (see Sec. 20.1.1). However, MFS is very capable of sending more than one panel for the 'first flow'. This is because MFS will log (in CICS terms, journal) messages that have not successfully been delivered to the terminal. Consequently, MFS can deliver panels that were left over from a previous use of the FEPI Connection.

Let me explain this more explicitly. If you end the Connection (by setting it to `ACQSTATUS(RELEASED)` or whatever), and MFS attempts to send a flow to that terminal in the meantime, the panel will actually be delivered to the 'terminal' when FEPI restarts the Connection. This happens because IMS transactions do not actually run at a terminal. They are all executed in background mode (using BMPs), with the terminal association only being done via MFS. It does not matter to the IMS Conversation that the invoking terminal is not active, it does the necessary regardless. It is only when a panel is to be delivered does the matter of the accessibility of the terminal become an issue.

If MFS sends multiple panels in this 'Start-of-Day' processing, then the FEPI application program has to decide what to do with them. In general, because the FEPI emulation that caused the flow to be generated has ended, the necessary action may just be to lose it. However, you have to tell MFS that the panel has been received and processed. This is usually done by sending either a PA1 or a Clear.

## 25.3 Session termination

When a FEPI Connection to an IMS system is about to be ended, you should ensure that MFS is tidied up. This will prevent any panels from being queued in the manner described in Sec. 25.2. In particular, you must ensure that any IMS Conversations 'owning' the Connection's terminal have ended (so preventing MFS from queuing any more output to the emulated terminal). You should also ensure that MFS is not holding any queued output for the terminal.

## 25.4 Message logging

When MFS delivers a message, it is tagged with VTAM indicators that require a VTAM response to indicate that FEPI has successfully received and processed the message (the equivalent facility within CICS is message protection, as specified on `TYPETERM`s). Chapter 53 shows how you cope with this, but this section (briefly) outlines how MFS works with messages. I am using the word 'message' rather than 'flow', because this is what MFS processes. You can consider an MFS message to be a panel's flow.

MFS logs (journals) all messages sent from MFS to a terminal. This is done so that the message can be resent if the terminal thinks it has been corrupted, or if the network fails to deliver it (because of a Session Outage or the terminal being switched off).

MFS will consider a message to have been successfully delivered to the terminal (and found acceptable) if a subsequent flow arrives from the terminal. When this happens, MFS unlogs the message and forgets all about it. This acknowledgement can also be actioned through a special flow from the terminal involving only VTAM indicators.

In FEPI terms, you acknowledge a previous panel by `EXEC CICS FEPI SEND`ing something on the Connection. FEPI knows if the partner (MFS in this case) wants some VTAM response indicators and, if so, puts them on the front of the `EXEC CICS FEPI SEND`ed flow. Alternatively, you can transmit the VTAM indicators manually using an `EXEC CICS FEPI ISSUE` command (see Sec. 27.13 and Chapter 53). This command is also used to reject the flow. Rejecting the flow will probably cause MFS to resend the message.

If the FEPI Connection is ended before the acknowledgement of a prior message has been received by MFS, the message will be represented during 'first flow' processing as described in Sec. 25.2.

## 25.5 IMS conversational transactions

IMS conversational transactions run in background mode, sending and receiving messages via MFS. Therefore, if you think that you are running a FEPI Conversation to an IMS nonconversational transaction, but actually communicating with an IMS conversational transaction, your emulation will fail. This is because the IMS conversational transaction 'owns' the FEPI Conversation's terminal until it decides to release it. Therefore, a subsequent use of the FEPI Connection will actually be communicating to the (background) IMS conversational transaction, and not that the new FEPI application program thought it invoked. Therefore, things will go horribly wrong.

Unfortunately, there is no way of knowing within the FEPI application program whether the IMS transaction is IMS conversational or not. If you suspect that an IMS conversational transaction has grabbed the FEPI Connection, you could issue the IMS `/EXIT` command to force it off, so releasing the MFS terminal, and thus the FEPI Conversation, for other use.

CHAPTER 26

# FEPI command sequences

**GUIDANCE**

This chapter outlines the command sequences that you use to run a FEPI emulation. A detailed description of all the commands is contained in Chapter 27.

## 26.1 General command sequence

As discussed in Chapter 23, you have to know when the partner system has sent all the information that it is going to send. Consequently, you have to be aware of the ENDSTATUS field and what it means for your FEPI emulation.

Figure 26.1 (page 96) shows the general sequence of commands for a Formatted Conversation, and Fig. 26.2 (page 97) shows the sequence for a Datastream Conversation.

## 26.2 Command overview

The simplest sequence of FEPI commands involves simply sending a flow to the partner system, and receiving the response. Figure 26.3 (page 98) shows this sequence.

Figures 26.4 and 26.5 (page 98) show the sequences involved for an asynchronous design.

Figure 26.6 (page 99) shows an example of a Multiple Attentioned Keystroke Send.

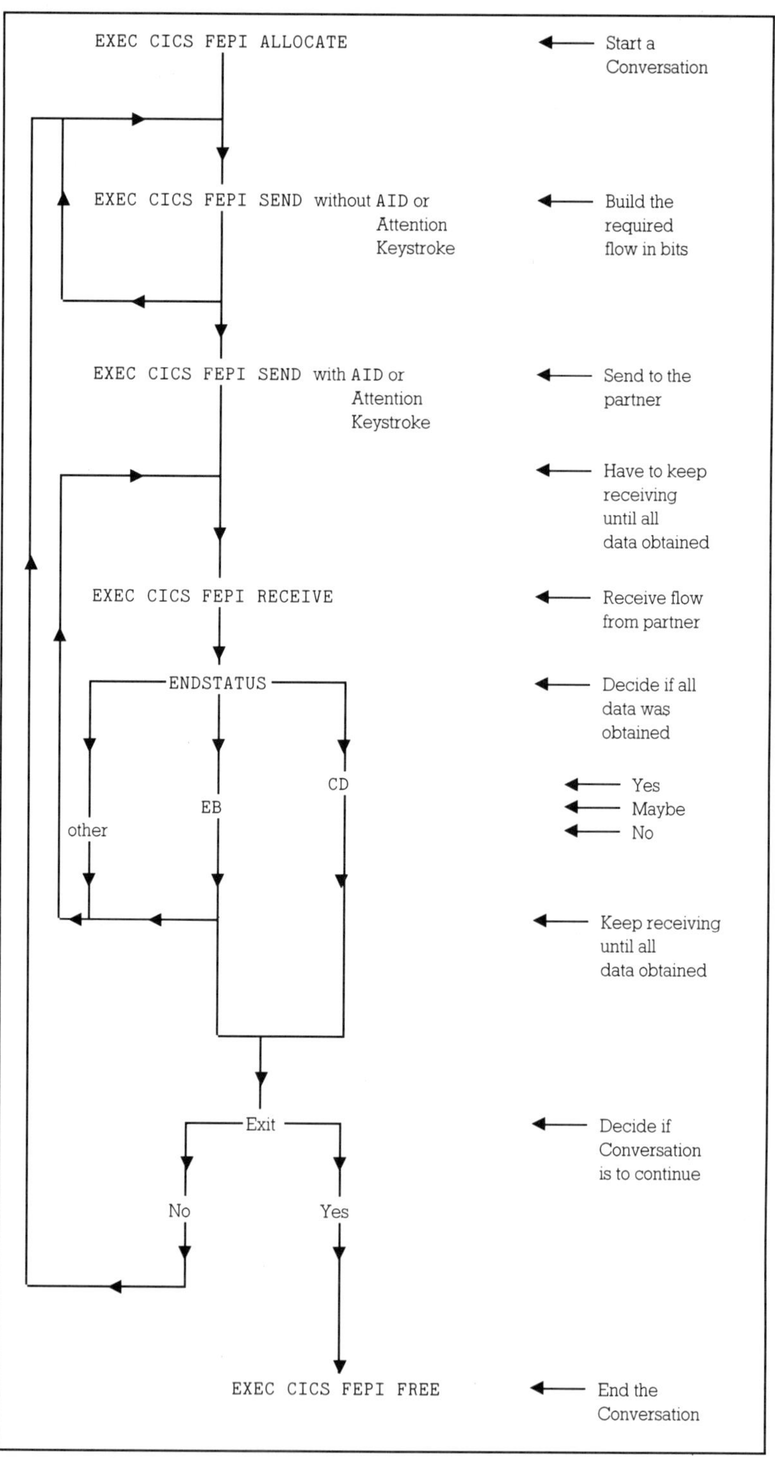


**Figure 26.1** Formatted command sequence

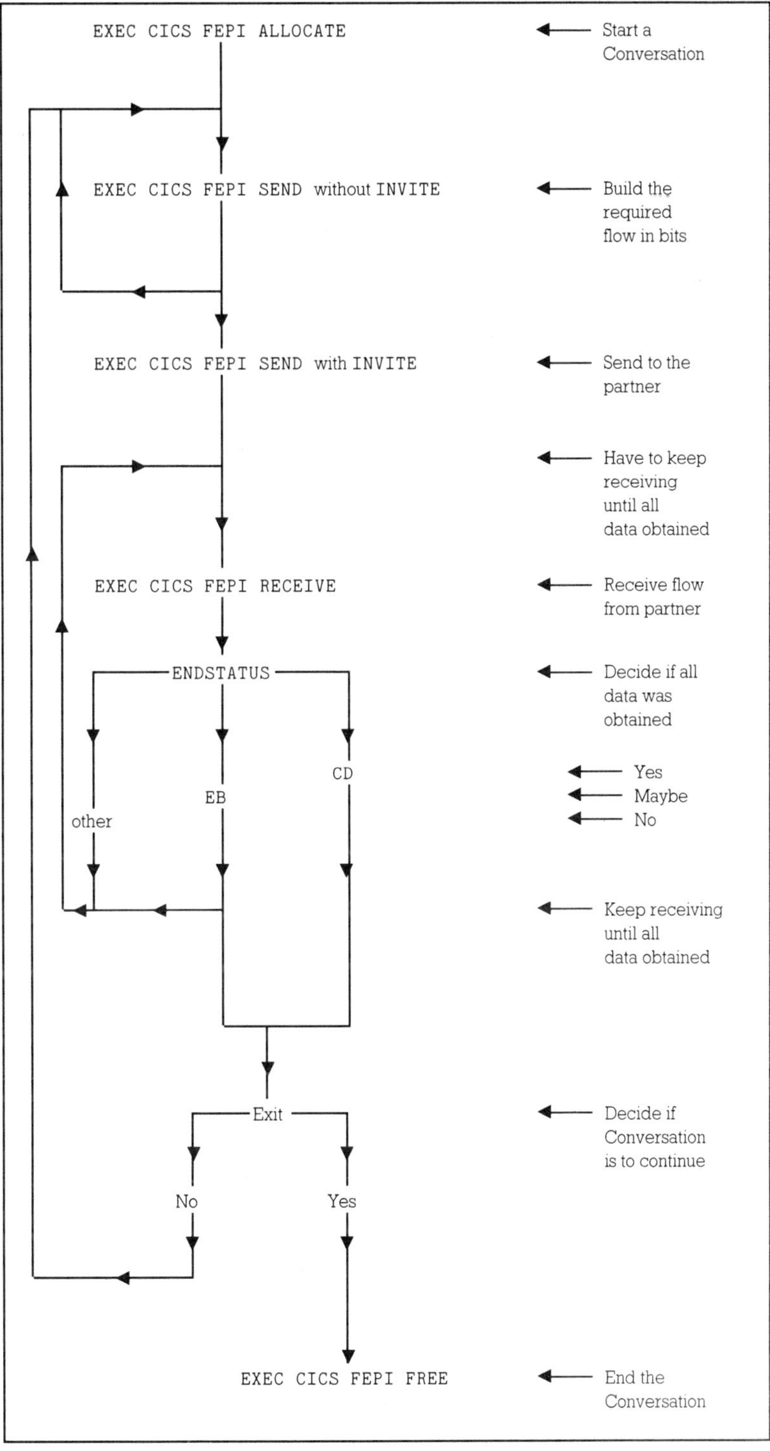


**Figure 26.2** Datastream command sequence

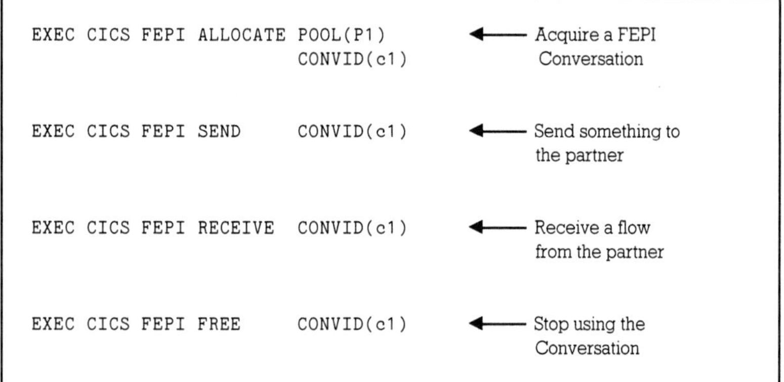


**Figure 26.3** Simple FEPI command sequence

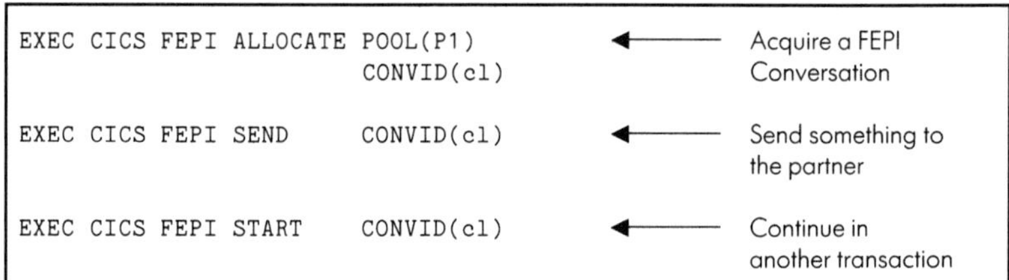


**Figure 26.4** Asynchronous FEPI command sequence—sending

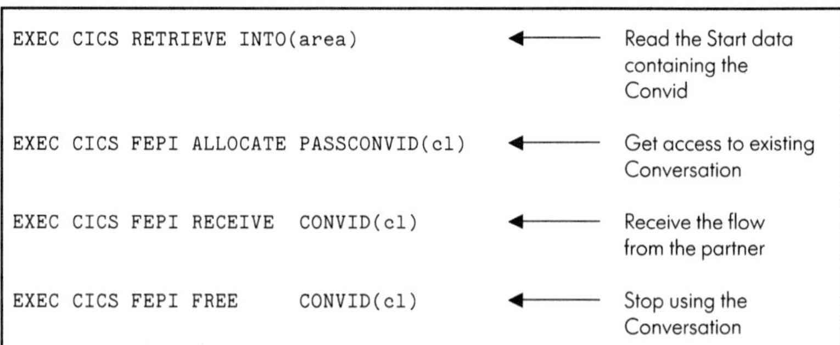


**Figure 26.5** Asynchronous FEPI command sequence—receiving

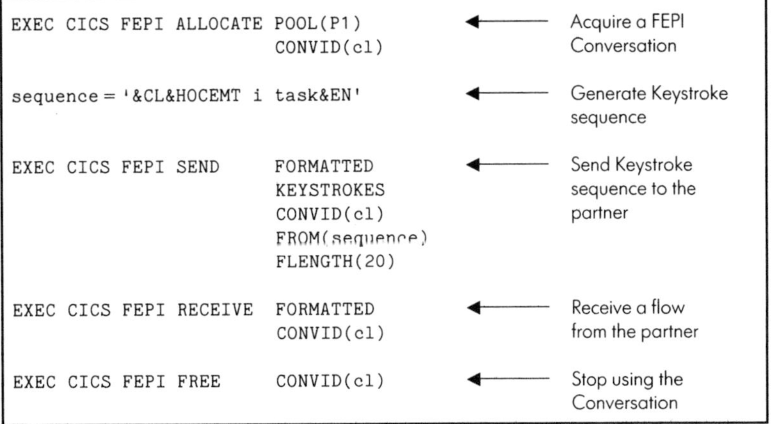


**Figure 26.6** Multiple Attentioned Keystroke Send

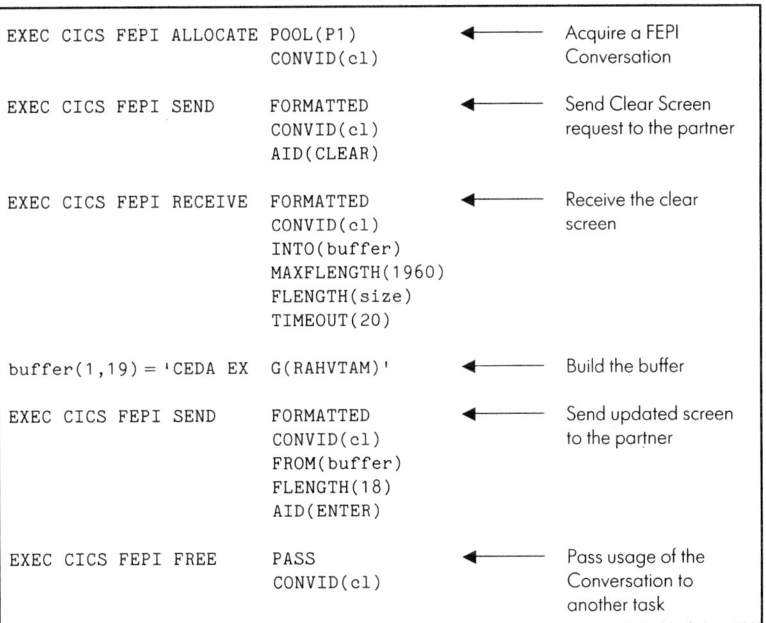


**Figure 26.7** Formatted Buffer Send

Figure 26.7 shows an example of a Buffered Send.

Figure 26.8 shows an example of a Formatted Buffer Receive operation.

Figure 26.9 shows an example of a Formatted Field Receive.

Figure 26.10 shows the general case for a Datastream Conversation.

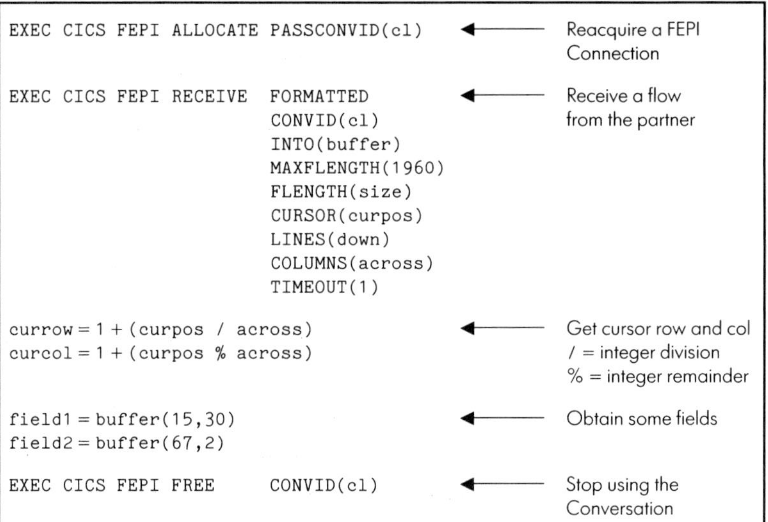

```
EXEC CICS FEPI ALLOCATE PASSCONVID(cl)     <----  Reacquire a FEPI
                                                  Connection

EXEC CICS FEPI RECEIVE  FORMATTED          <----  Receive a flow
                        CONVID(cl)                from the partner
                        INTO(buffer)
                        MAXFLENGTH(1960)
                        FLENGTH(size)
                        CURSOR(curpos)
                        LINES(down)
                        COLUMNS(across)
                        TIMEOUT(1)

currow = 1 + (curpos / across)             <----  Get cursor row and col
curcol = 1 + (curpos % across)                    / = integer division
                                                  % = integer remainder

field1 = buffer(15,30)                     <----  Obtain some fields
field2 = buffer(67,2)

EXEC CICS FEPI FREE     CONVID(cl)         <----  Stop using the
                                                  Conversation
```

**Figure 26.8** A Formatted Buffer Receive

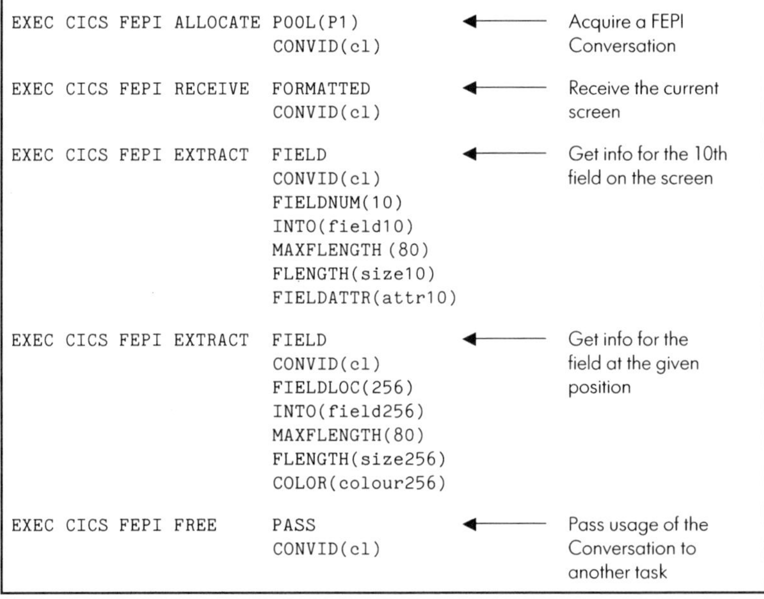

```
EXEC CICS FEPI ALLOCATE POOL(P1)           <----  Acquire a FEPI
                        CONVID(cl)                Conversation

EXEC CICS FEPI RECEIVE  FORMATTED          <----  Receive the current
                        CONVID(cl)                screen

EXEC CICS FEPI EXTRACT  FIELD              <----  Get info for the 10th
                        CONVID(cl)                field on the screen
                        FIELDNUM(10)
                        INTO(field10)
                        MAXFLENGTH (80)
                        FLENGTH(size10)
                        FIELDATTR(attr10)

EXEC CICS FEPI EXTRACT  FIELD              <----  Get info for the
                        CONVID(cl)                field at the given
                        FIELDLOC(256)             position
                        INTO(field256)
                        MAXFLENGTH(80)
                        FLENGTH(size256)
                        COLOR(colour256)

EXEC CICS FEPI FREE     PASS               <----  Pass usage of the
                        CONVID(cl)                Conversation to
                                                  another task
```

**Figure 26.9** Formatted Field Receive

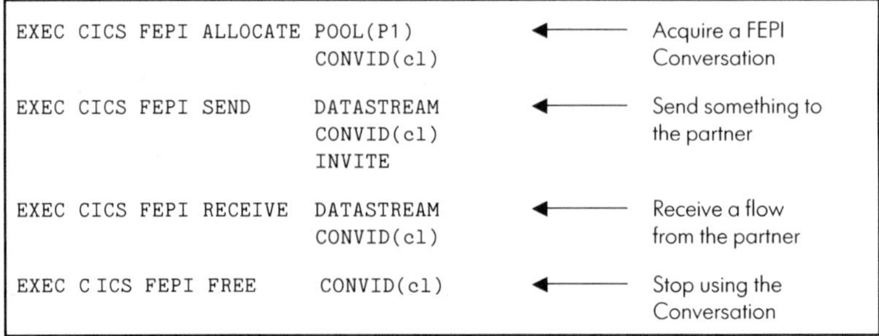

```
EXEC CICS FEPI ALLOCATE POOL(P1)           <----  Acquire a FEPI
                        CONVID(cl)                Conversation

EXEC CICS FEPI SEND     DATASTREAM         <----  Send something to
                        CONVID(cl)                the partner
                        INVITE

EXEC CICS FEPI RECEIVE  DATASTREAM         <----  Receive a flow
                        CONVID(cl)                from the partner

EXEC CICS FEPI FREE     CONVID(cl)         <----  Stop using the
                                                  Conversation
```

**Figure 26.10** General FEPI Datastream command sequence

# CHAPTER 27 Full description of the API-type commands

**GUIDANCE**

This chapter documents the FEPI API-type commands.

The following commands are discussed:

- EXEC CICS FEPI ALLOCATE a new Conversation
- EXEC CICS FEPI ALLOCATE an existing Conversation
- EXEC CICS FEPI SEND Formatted
- EXEC CICS FEPI SEND Datastream
- EXEC CICS FEPI RECEIVE Formatted
- EXEC CICS FEPI RECEIVE Datastream
- EXEC CICS FEPI FREE a Conversation
- EXEC CICS FEPI START a new FEPI Transaction
- EXEC CICS FEPI EXTRACT Conversation details
- EXEC CICS FEPI EXTRACT STSN Sequence Numbers
- EXEC CICS FEPI ISSUE SNA Responses
- EXEC CICS FEPI CONVERSE Formatted
- EXEC CICS FEPI CONVERSE Datastream
- EXEC CICS FEPI AP NOOP
- EXEC CICS FEPI SP NOOP

The SPI-type commands used to manipulate FEPI resources are discussed in Part 2

## 27.1 Introduction

All `EXEC CICS FEPI` commands are enabled by the `XOPTS(FEPI)` translator option. The FEPI API commands which operate on Formatted and Datastream Conversations are described separately. Also, the `EXEC CICS FEPI CONVERSE` commands are not extensively discussed, as they are a joining of the appropriate `EXEC CICS FEPI SEND` and `EXEC CICS FEPI RECEIVE` commands.

### 27.1.1 Return Codes

All the commands can take `NOHANDLE`, `RESP`, and `RESP2` parameters to enable Return Code processing. FEPI places in the `RESP2` parameter the Return Code for the command. All Return Codes are documented in Chapter 28.

## **27.2** EXEC CICS FEPI ALLOCATE a new Conversation

The format of an EXEC CICS FEPI ALLOCATE command to start a FEPI Conversation is:

```
EXEC CICS FEPI ALLOCATE
               POOL(char8)

[TARGET(char8)]
[TIMEOUT(fixed31)]

CONVID(char8)

[SEQNUMIN(fixed31)]
[SEQNUMOUT(fixed31)]

[SESSNSTATUS(cvda)]
```

The operation of this command is discussed in Chapter 29 for both Formatted and Datastream Conversations.

POOL
The POOL parameter names the Pool out of which a FEPI Connection is to be used to run the Conversation.

CONVID
The CONVID returns a handle to the FEPI Conversation that was started when the command completed. It must be saved away and quoted on each subsequent FEPI command for the Conversation.

TARGET
If you want to use a Connection to a given Target from within the Pool, quote its name in TARGET.

TIMEOUT
If you want the action of Acquiring the Connection to wait forever until a Connection within the Pool becomes free, omit the TIMEOUT parameter. If TIMEOUT is specified, then the command will wait for the specified number of seconds for a Connection to become available for use. If one is not usable after this interval, the EXEC CICS FEPI ALLOCATE command completes without gaining access to a Connection.

SESSNSTATUS
When the Connection is obtained for use by the Conversation, the Connection is either newly VTAM Bound or was already Bound. This is indicated by SESSNSTATUS which returns a CVDA as follows:

| | |
|---|---|
| NEWSESSION | says that the Connection was newly Bound (in FEPI terms 'Acquired') for the Connection. |
| OLDSESSION | says that the Connection was not newly Acquired for the Conversation. |

SESSNSTATUS is useful for Handling 'first flows' as described in Secs 44.1 and 44.3, and Chapter 21.

SEQNUMIN and SEQNUMOUT
These fields return STSN sequence numbers for LU0 (SLUP) Conversations.

## 27.3 EXEC CICS FEPI ALLOCATE an existing Conversation

The format of the EXEC CICS FEPI ALLOCATE command to reuse an existing FEPI Conversation is as follows:

```
EXEC CICS FEPI ALLOCATE
                      PASSCONVID(char8)
```

The operation of this command for resuming usage of a FEPI Conversation is discussed in Sec. 29.3 and Chapter 6.

PASSCONVID
PASSCONVID is used to specify the Convid for the FEPI Conversation which is being resumed.

## 27.4 EXEC CICS FEPI SEND Formatted

The format of the EXEC CICS FEPI SEND command used to transmit formatted data to the partner is as follows:

```
EXEC CICS FEPI SEND FORMATTED
                        CONVID(char8)

FROM(char)  [FLENGTH(fixed31)]

{AID(char1)  [CURSOR(fixed31)]
  |KEYSTROKES  [ESCAPE(char1)]}
```

The operation of this command is discussed in Chapters 30 and 31.

CONVID
CONVID names the FEPI Conversation for the operation.

FROM
The FROM parameter specifies the flow to be sent to the partner system. The use of the KEYSTROKE parameter (or not) controls the way FEPI processes the area.

FLENGTH
FLENGTH states the length of the FROM data area.

AID and CURSOR
AID and CURSOR are only valid for Formatted Buffer access. The AID parameter says that the formatted virtual terminal's screen contents are to be sent to the partner system with the quoted Attention key having been pressed. CURSOR can be used to specify where the cursor is on the screen when the AID key is pressed. If omitted, the cursor stays where it was on the previous Receive.

The values for AID are contained in the DFHAID copybook, and CURSOR starts at 0 for the top left-hand corner of the screen.

KEYSTROKES and ESCAPE
KEYSTROKES says that the FROM area is in Keystroke format. If omitted, the area is in Buffer format. Use of ESCAPE changes the '&' character used to prefix a Keystroke Escape sequence to that specified.

## 27.5 EXEC CICS FEPI SEND Datastream

The format of the EXEC CICS FEPI SEND command used to transmit Datastream data to the partner is as follows:

```
EXEC CICS FEPI SEND DATASTREAM
                    CONVID(char8)

FROM(char)  [FLENGTH(fixed31)]
[FMH]
[INVITE]

[SEQNUMIN(fixed31)]
[SEQNUMOUT(fixed31)]
```

CONVID
CONVID names the FEPI Conversation for the operation.

FROM
The FROM parameter specifies the flow to be sent to the partner system.

FLENGTH
FLENGTH states the length of the FROM data area.

INVITE
Usage of INVITE adds the CD (see Sec. 20.2.1) to the FROM data sent to the partner system, indicating that the FEPI Application program will next do a Receive operation.

If INVITE is not quoted, then the FROM data is sent to the partner system without the CD. Thus, another Send will be done on the Conversation.

FMH
Usage of FMH says that the FROM data contains an FMH.

SEQNUMIN and SEQNUMOUT
For LU0 (SLUP) Conversations only, these fields return the new STSN sequence numbers resulting from the Send operation.

## 27.6 EXEC CICS FEPI RECEIVE Formatted

The format of the EXEC CICS FEPI RECEIVE command to obtain data from the partner system over a FEPI formatted Conversation is as follows:

```
EXEC CICS FEPI RECEIVE FORMATTED
                       CONVID(char8)
[MAXFLENGTH(fixed31)]
[TIMEOUT(fixed31)]

[ALARMSTATUS(cvda)]
[COLUMNS(fixed31)]
[CURSOR(fixed31)]
[ENDSTATUS(cvda)]
[FIELDS(fixed31)]
[INTO(char)]  [FLENGTH(fixed31)]
[LINES(fixed31)]
[RESPSTATUS(cvda)]
```

The operation of this command is described in Chapter 32.

| **WARNING** |
|---|
| A single EXEC CICS FEPI RECEIVE FORMATTED command may not get all of the partner's flow. See Chapter 23 and *always* use the parameter ENDSTATUS. |

CONVID

CONVID names the FEPI Conversation for the operation.

TIMEOUT

If TIMEOUT is omitted, the command waits forever until the partner responds. If TIMEOUT is quoted, then if the partner does not respond in the given interval, the command will complete anyway.

MAXFLENGTH

MAXFLENGTH specifies the length of the area specified by the INTO parameter. It sets the maximum length of data that can be received.

INTO

INTO specifies an area into which FEPI puts the data received from the partner. If omitted, then the data is still received, but EXEC CICS FEPI EXTRACT FIELD commands must be used to determine the screen layout.

FLENGTH

FLENGTH says how much data FEPI placed into the INTO area.

LINES and COLUMNS

You can choose to be informed of the size of the emulated screen. This rectangle is described by the LINES and COLUMNS parameters (starting at 1).

FIELDS

FIELDS returns the number of fields upon the emulated screen.

CURSOR

CURSOR returns the placement of the cursor upon the screen. The returned number starts at 0 for the top left-hand corner of the screen.

ALARMSTATUS

ALARMSTATUS returns a CVDA indicating whether or not the alarm 'sounded' when the 'terminal' received the flow.

ALARM The terminal buzzed.
NOALARM The terminal stayed silent.

ENDSTATUS

ENDSTATUS says why the Receive command completed. It returns a CVDA showing the VTAM information which caused the completion as follows:

EB An EB caused completion.
CD A CD caused completion.
LIC The command completed when a full Chain was received. No EB or CD was present.

See Chapter 21 for an explanation of this field and its usage.

RESPSTATUS
RESPSTATUS returns a CVDA saying what VTAM response is required by the partner system to acknowledge FEPI's receipt of the flow. See Chapter 53 and Sec. 27.13.

| | |
|---|---|
| NONE | No VTAM response is required. |
| DEFRESP1 | A DR1 is required to acknowledge the flow. |
| DEFRESP2 | A DR2 is required to acknowledge the flow. |
| DEFRESP3 | A DR1 and a DR2 are required to acknowledge the flow. |

## 27.7 EXEC CICS FEPI RECEIVE Datastream

The format of the EXEC CICS FEPI RECEIVE command to obtain data from the partner system over a FEPI Datastream Conversation is as follows:

```
EXEC CICS FEPI RECEIVE DATASTREAM
                       CONVID(char8)
[MAXFLENGTH(fixed31)]
[TIMEOUT(fixed31)]
[CHAIN|RU|UNTILCDEB]

[ENDSTATUS(cvda)]
[FMHSTATUS(cvda)]
[INTO(char)]  [FLENGTH(fixed31)]
[REMFLENGTH(fixed31)]
[RESPSTATUS(cvda)]
[SEQNUMIN(fixed31)]
[SEQNUMOUT(fixed31)]
```

CONVID
CONVID names the FEPI Conversation for the operation.

TIMEOUT
If TIMEOUT is omitted, the command waits forever until the partner responds. If TIMEOUT is quoted, then if the partner does not respond in the given number of seconds, the command will complete anyway.

MAXFLENGTH
MAXFLENGTH says how long is the area specified in the INTO parameter. It sets the maximum length of the data that can be received. The length of the excess data may be available in the REMFLENGTH parameter.

INTO
INTO specifies an area into which FEPI puts the data received from the partner.

FLENGTH
FLENGTH says how much data FEPI placed into the INTO area.

CHAIN, RU and UNTILCDEB
These parameters control when the command is to terminate. In other words, it controls how many VTAM RUs are to be processed. See Sec. 37.1.4 for more information.

| | |
|---|---|
| RU | The command completes as soon as a single VTAM RU has been received. |
| CHAIN | The command completes as soon as a full VTAM Chain has been received from the partner. |
| UNTILCDEB | The command will not complete until a chain containing either a VTAM CD or an EB has been received. |

CHAIN is the preferred (and default) setting.

REMFLENGTH

REMFLENGTH only has a meaning if the ENDSTATUS parameter returns the MORE CVDA. REMFLENGTH says that the INTO area was not big enough to return all the data that could have been received. 0 is returned if there is no more data to receive. If a nonzero value is returned, then another EXEC CICS FEPI RECEIVE DATASTREAM must be executed to obtain the remaining part of the flow.

Note that REMFLENGTH does not necessarily return all the data to be received. It depends on whether or not the network has delivered all the flow. Therefore, ENDSTATUS should be consulted along with REMFLENGTH.

FMH

The FMH parameter returns a CVDA saying whether or not the received data contained an FMH:

| | |
|---|---|
| FMH | The data contained an FMH. |
| NOFMH | The data did not contain an FMH. |

ENDSTATUS

ENDSTATUS says why the Receive command completed. It returns a CVDA showing the VTAM information which caused completion as follows:

| | |
|---|---|
| MORE | Command completion was caused by the INTO area being too small to receive all the data. |
| EB | An EB caused completion. |
| CD | A CD caused completion. |
| LIC | Completion was caused by the reception of a full Chain of data. |
| RU | The command completed when a single RU was received. |

See Chapter 20 for an explanation of this field and its usage.

RESPSTATUS

RESPSTATUS returns a CVDA saying what VTAM response is required by the partner system to acknowledge FEPI's receipt of the flow. See Chapter 53 and Sec. 27.13.

| | |
|---|---|
| NONE | No VTAM response is required. |
| DEFRESP1 | A DR1 is required to acknowledge the flow. |
| DEFRESP2 | A DR2 is required to acknowledge the flow. |
| DEFRESP3 | A DR1 and a DR2 are required to acknowledge the flow. |

SEQNUMIN and SEQNUMOUT
For LU0 (SLUP) Conversations only, these fields return the new STSN sequence numbers resulting from the send operation.

## 27.8 EXEC CICS FEPI FREE a Conversation

The format of the EXEC CICS FEPI FREE command used to end a FEPI Conversation is as follows:

```
EXEC CICS FEPI FREE
                  CONVID(char8)

[HOLD|RELEASE|FORCE|PASS]
```

The operation of this command, for both Formatted and Datastream Conversations is described in Chapter 36. The End Session Handler (End of Conversation see Sec. 47.1.4) will be started if appropriate.

CONVID
CONVID names the FEPI Conversation for the operation.

HOLD, RELEASE, FORCE and PASS
The parameters state how the Conversation and the underlying Connection are to be treated when the named Conversation is ended. The actions of each parameter depend upon where the command is issued, but in general:

- HOLD — End the current Conversation, and keep the underlying Connection Acquired (HOLD is the default option).
- PASS — The FEPI Conversation is to be resumed in another CICS transaction.
- RELEASE — End the current FEPI Conversation, but Release the underlying FEPI Connection.
- FORCE — End the current FEPI Conversation, and stop the underlying FEPI Connection.

## 27.9 EXEC CICS FEPI START a new FEPI Transaction

The format of the EXEC CICS FEPI START command used to continue a FEPI Conversation in a new CICS task is as follows:

```
EXEC CICS FEPI START
                  CONVID(char8)

TRANSID(char4)
[TERMID(char4)]
[USERDATA(char)[FLENGTH(fixed31)]]
[TIMEOUT(fixed31)]
```

The operation of this command, for both Formatted and Datastream Conversations is described in Chapter 35.

CONVID
CONVID names the FEPI Conversation for the operation.

TRANSID and TERMID

The TRANSID parameter names the CICS transaction that is to be started when a flow is received from the partner system. The transaction will be started at the TERMID terminal, or in background mode if TERMID is omitted (or set to four blanks or X'00000000').

TIMEOUT

If the TIMEOUT parameter is specified, the named transaction will be started after the given number of seconds whether or not the partner has responded. If TIMEOUT is omitted, then the transaction will not get started until the partner responds (which may be never).

USERDATA and FLENGTH

USERDATA and FLENGTH can be used to pass data to the new transaction. Up to 128 bytes can be passed.

## 27.10 EXEC CICS FEPI EXTRACT Field

The format of the EXEC CICS FEPI EXTRACT FIELD command used to query a FEPI Formatted Conversation's emulated screen is as follows:

```
EXEC CICS FEPI EXTRACT FIELD
                        CONVID(char8)

FIELDLOC(fixed31)|FIELDNUM(fixed31)
[MAXFLENGTH(fixed31)]

[BACKGROUND(char1)]
[COLOR(char1)]
[FIELDATTR(char1)]
[HILIGHT(char1)]
[INPUTCONTROL(char1)]
[INTO(char)]  [FLENGTH(fixed31)]
[MDT(cvda)]
[OUTLINE(char1)]
[POSITION(fixed31)]
[PROTECT(cvda)]
[PS(char1)]
[SIZE(fixed31)]
[TRANSPARENCY(char1)]
[VALIDATION(char1)]
```

The operation of this command, for Formatted Conversations only, is described in Chapter 33.

CONVID

CONVID names the FEPI Conversation for the operation.

FIELDLOC and FIELDNUM

The field for querying is specified either by its position using FIELDLOC (starting from 0 for the top left-hand corner of the screen) or by the number of the field upon the screen with FIELDNUM.

INTO, FLENGTH and MAXFLENGTH

The contents of the named field can be returned in the INTO area. The size of this area is specified via MAXFLENGTH, and after the command completes the size of the field is returned in FLENGTH.

POSITION
The named field's position on the screen can be returned in POSITION. This starts at 0 for the top left-hand corner of the screen.

PROTECT
The PROTECT field returns a CVDA saying whether or not the field is updatable:

PROTECTED The field is not updatable.
UNPROTECTED The field is updatable.

MDT
The MDT field returns a CVDA saying whether or not the field has been updated (i.e., the Modified Data Tag for the field is set):

MDT The field has been updated.
NOMDT The field has not been updated.

FIELDATTR
FIELDATTR returns the 3270 Attribute Byte for the field. The settings are described in the DFHBMSCA copybook.

SIZE
SIZE returns the length of the field (excluding the Attribute byte).

COLOR
COLOR returns the (foreground) colour of the field. The settings are described in the DFHBMSCA copybook.

BACKGROUND
BACKGROUND returns the background colour for the field. The settings are described in the DFHBMSCA copybook.

HILIGHT
HILIGHT returns the 3270 Extended Attribute Byte for the field. The settings are described in the DFHBMSCA copybook.

PS
PS returns the number of the Programmed Symbol Set used to display the field.

VALIDATION
VALIDATION returns the 3270 Field Validation Attribute for the field. The settings are described in the DFHBMSCA copybook.

OUTLINE
OUTLINE returns the 3270 Field Outline setting the field. The settings are described in the DFHBMSCA copybook.

TRANSPARENCY
TRANSPARENCY returns the 3270 Transparency option for the field. The settings are described in the DFHBMSCA copybook.

INPUTCONTROL

INPUTCONTROL returns the Double Byte Character control attribute of the field. The settings are described in the DFHBMSCA copybook.

## 27.11 EXEC CICS FEPI EXTRACT Conversation details

The format of the EXEC CICS FEPI EXTRACT CONV command used to determine details of the FEPI Connection running the FEPI Conversation is as follows:

```
EXEC CICS FEPI EXTRACT CONV
                         CONVID(char8)

[DEVICE(cvda)]
[FORMAT(cvda)]
[NODE(char8)]
[POOL(char8)]
[SENSEDATA(fixed31)]
[TARGET(char8)]
```

CONVID

CONVID names the FEPI Conversation for the operation.

DEVICE

DEVICE returns a CVDA indicating what device type the Conversation is emulating. The settings are as for the DEVICE parameter used on the EXEC CICS FEPI INSTALL PROPERTYSET, and are documented in Table 16.1.

POOL, NODE and TARGET

POOL names the Pool in which the Connection running the Conversation resides. TARGET and NODE name the FEPI Resources that make up the Connection.

FORMAT

FORMAT returns a CVDA which says what FEPI access technique is being used for the Conversation:

| | |
|---|---|
| FORMATTED | The Connection is running a FEPI Formatted Conversation. |
| DATASTREAM | The Connection is running a FEPI Datastream Conversation. |

SENSEDATA

The SENSEDATA field returns the VTAM Sense Code associated with the last EXEC CICS FEPI SEND, EXEC CICS FEPI RECEIVE or EXEC CICS FEPI CONVERSE command. It represents the VTAM Return Code for the operation. If X'00000000' is returned, then the command successfully completed.

## 27.12 EXEC CICS FEPI EXTRACT STSN Sequence Numbers

The format of the EXEC CICS FEPI EXTRACT STSN command used to determine LU0 (SLUP) sequence numbers is as follows:

```
EXEC CICS FEPI EXTRACT STSN
                         CONVID(char8)

[SEQNUMIN(fixed31)]
[SEQNUMOUT(fixed31)]
[STSNSTATUS(cvda)]
```

This command is briefly discussed in Chapter 52.

`CONVID`
`CONVID` names the FEPI Conversation for the operation.

`SEQNUMIN` and `SEQNUMOUT`
`SEQNUMIN` and `SEQNUMOUT` return the current STSN sequence numbers for the LU0 Conversation.

`STSNSTATUS`
`STSNSTATUS` returns a CVDA which returns the current LU0 sequence number's *Test and Set* status. The CVDAs are:

| | |
|---|---|
| `NOSTSN` | No *Set* or *Test and Set* has been issued. |
| `STSNSET` | A *Set* sequence number has been issued. |
| `STSNTEST` | A *Test and Set* sequence number has been issued. |

## 27.13 EXEC CICS FEPI ISSUE SNA Responses

The format of the `EXEC CICS FEPI ISSUE` command used to transmit SNA responses is as follows:

```
EXEC CICS FEPI ISSUE
                CONVID(char8)

CONTROL(cvda)
[SENSEDATA(fixed31)]
[VALUE(cvda)]
```

The SNA responses required are dependent upon what the partner system is expecting, and how you design your FEPI Conversation. This is briefly discussed in Chapter 53. See the *SNA Formats Manual* and *VTAM Messages and Codes Manual* for details of these flows and their contents.

The operation of the `EXEC CICS FEPI ISSUE` command is mostly applicable only to the very low-level FEPI Datastream accesses. If you do not understand the terms, you should not be using the command!

`CONVID`
`CONVID` names the FEPI Conversation for the operation.

`CONTROL`
The `CONTROL` parameter is set to a CVDA that specifies what type of SNA flow is to be sent. Therefore, `CONTROL` determines the operation of the `EXEC CICS FEPI ISSUE` command. The permitted CVDAs (and so the type of flow transmitted) are:

| | |
|---|---|
| `NORMALRESP` | (valid for all types of conversations) requests that an SNA *Normal Response* is to be transmitted. The actual response is specified by the `VALUE` CVDA. |
| `EXCEPTRESP` | (valid for all types of conversations) requests that an SNA *Exception Response* is to be transmitted. The actual response is specified by the `SENSEDATA` field, and the type of exception response by the `VALUE` CVDA. |

| | |
|---|---|
| `ATTENTION` | (valid for all types of Conversations) requests that an SNA *Attention* command is transmitted. This is a SNA Signal command (X'00010000'). |
| `LUSTAT` | (valid for all types of conversations) requests that an SNA *LUSTAT* be transmitted to the partner. The Sense Data placed in the *LUSTAT* is specified by the `SENSEDATA` parameter. |
| `CANCEL` | (valid only for Datastream Conversations) requests that an SNA *Cancel* command is transmitted. |
| `STSN` | (valid only for an LU0 conversation) requests that an SNA *Set and Test* sequence number command be transmitted. |
| `RTR` | (valid only for an LU0 conversation) requests that an SNA *Ready to Receive* command be transmitted. |

`SENSEDATA`

The `SENSEDATA` parameter is used to provide the Sense Data if the flow to be transmitted is either an Exception Response or a LUSTAT (as specified by the `CONTROL` parameter).

`VALUE`

The `VALUE` CVDA specifies the actual response sent if the flow is a Normal Response, an Exception response, or a STSN request (as specified by the `CONTROL` CVDA). The following CVDAs can be specified:

For `NORMALRESP` and `EXCEPTIONRESP`:

| | |
|---|---|
| `DEFRESP1OR2` | Transmit a DR1 or a DR2 as appropriate. |
| `DEFRESP1` | Transmit a DR1. |
| `DEFRESP2` | Transmit a DR2. |
| `DEFRESP3` | Transmit a DR1 and a DR2. |

For STSN only:

| | |
|---|---|
| `POSITIVE` | Transmit a STSN Positive Response. |
| `NEGATIVE` | Transmit a STSN Negative Response. |
| `DEFRESP2` | Transmit a DR2 |
| `DEFRESP3` | Transmit a DR1 and a DR2. |
| `INVALID` | Transmit a STSN *Response not Valid*. This has the side-effect of releasing the FEPI Connection. |
| `RESET` | Transmit an STSN *Reset*. This has the side-effect of releasing the FEPI Connection. |

## 27.14 EXEC CICS FEPI CONVERSE Formatted

The format of the EXEC CICS FEPI CONVERSE FORMATTED command is as follows:

```
EXEC CICS FEPI CONVERSE FORMATTED

CONVID(char8)
  |{POOL(char8)    [TARGET(char8)]}

FROM(char)       [FROMFLENGTH(fixed31)]
{AID(char1)      [FROMCURSOR(fixed31)]
  |KEYSTROKES    [ESCAPE(char1)]}

[MAXFLENGTH(fixed31)]
[TIMEOUT(fixed31)]

[ALARMSTATUS(cvda)]
[ENDSTATUS(cvda)]
[FIELDS(fixed31)]
[INTO(char)]         [TOFLENGTH(fixed31)]
[LINES(fixed31)]     [COLUMNS(fixed31)]
[RESPSTATUS(cvda)]
[TOCURSOR(fixed31)]
```

See Secs 27.4 and 27.6 for details of the parameters on this command. Note that the relevant FLENGTH parameters have been renamed FROMFLENGTH and TOFLENGTH for the Send and Receive parts of the command.

The use of a Temporary Conversation (see Sec. 10.3) is set by quoting the POOL parameter rather than the CONVID parameter.

I do *not* recommend using this command; you should issue the EXEC CICS FEPI SEND FORMATTED and EXEC CICS FEPI RECEIVE FORMATTED separately (see Sec. 23.1.4). In particular, carefully consider whether the fact that the command completes on the first Chain to be received is the real completion point (see Chapter 23).

## 27.15 EXEC CICS FEPI CONVERSE Datastream

The format of the EXEC CICS FEPI CONVERSE DATASTREAM command is as follows:

```
EXEC CICS FEPI CONVERSE DATASTREAM

CONVID(char8)
  |{POOL(char8)   [TARGET(char8)]}

FROM(char)   [FROMFLENGTH(fixed31)]
[MAXFLENGTH(fixed31)]
[TIMEOUT(fixed31)]
[CHAIN|RU|UNTILCDEB]
[FMH]

[ENDSTATUS(cvda)]
[FMHSTATUS(cvda)]
[INTO(char)]   [TOFLENGTH(fixed31)]
[REMFLENGTH(fixed31)]
[RESPSTATUS(cvda)]
[SEQNUMIN(fixed31)]
[SEQNUMOUT(fixed31)]
```

See Secs 27.5 and 27.7 for details of the parameters on this command. Note that the relevant FLENGTH parameters have been renamed FROMFLENGTH and TOFLENGTH for the Send and Receive parts of the command.

The use of a temporary conversation (see Sec. 10.3) is set by quoting the POOL parameter rather than the CONVID parameter.

I do *not* recommend using this command; you should issue the EXEC CICS FEPI SEND DATASTREAM and EXEC CICS FEPI RECEIVE DATASTREAM separately (see Sec. 23.1.4).

In particular, carefully consider the choice of CHAIN, RU, and UNTILCDEB—the default of CHAIN may require further EXEC CICS FEPI RECEIVE DATASTREAM commands to obtain all the flow (see Chapter 23); however, use of UNTILCDEB may lead to processing errors.

## 27.16 EXEC CICS FEPI AP NOOP

The format of the EXEC CICS FEPI AP NOOP command, which does nothing but check that FEPI is available, is as follows:

```
EXEC CICS FEPI AP NOOP
```

## 27.17 EXEC CICS FEPI SP NOOP

The format of the EXEC CICS FEPI SP NOOP command, which does nothing but check that the current user can issue FEPI SPI-type commands, is as follows:

```
EXEC CICS FEPI SP NOOP
```

CHAPTER

# 28 EIBRESP2 codes and what to do with them

**GUIDANCE**

This chapter details all the Return Codes that FEPI uses. A more convenient list is provided in Appendix C.

FEPI provides Return Codes via the `EIBRESP` and `EIBRESP2` fields on all the `EXEC CICS FEPI` commands. The usual condition generated upon an error is `INVREQ`, but sometimes `END`, `ILLOGIC` or `NOTAUTH` can be returned. Like any other condition, these conditions can be trapped using an `EXEC CICS HANDLE CONDITION()` command, but I recommend that the more general use of quoting `RESP()` and `RESP2()` on each individual command be used to trap errors.

Each return Code has a name, defined in the following copybooks:

**DFHSZAPA** Assembler Programs

**DFHSZAPC** C Programs

**DFHSZAPO** Cobol Programs (a '_' is a '-')

**DFHSZAPP** PL/1 Programs (a '_' is a '-')

Table 28.1 shows where all the EIBRESP2s are documented.

**Table 28.1** Location of full EIBRESP2 descriptions

| RC (EIBRESP2) | Condition (EIBRESP) | Described in section | RC name |
|---|---|---|---|
| 0 | | 28.1 | DFHSZ_RESPX_OK |
| 1 | ILLOGIC | 28.11 | DFHSZ_RESPS_SEQ_BROWSE |
| 2 | END | 28.11 | DFHSZ_RESPS_END_BROWSE |
| 10 | INVREQ | 28.1 | DFHSZ_RESPX_BYPASS |
| 11 | INVREQ | 28.1 | DFHSZ_RESPX_NO_FEPI |
| 12 | INVREQ | 28.1 | DFHSZ_RESPX_SHUTDOWN |
| 13 | INVREQ | 28.1 | DFHSZ_RESPX_OUT_FEPI |
| 14 | INVREQ | 28.1 | DFHSZ_RESPX_BUSY |
| 15 | INVREQ | 28.1 | DFHSZ_RESPX_UNK_COMMAND |
| 16 | INVREQ | 28.1 | DFHSZ_RESPX_ERR_INTERNAL |
| 17 | INVREQ | 28.1 | DFHSZ_RESPX_BUSYEXIT |
| 18 | INVREQ | 28.1 | DFHSZ_RESPX_OPSYS |
| 30 | INVREQ | 28.5 | DFHSZ_RESPA_UNK_POOL |
| 31 | INVREQ | 28.5 | DFHSZ_RESPA_OUT_POOL |
| 32 | INVREQ | 28.5 | DFHSZ_RESPA_UNK_TARGET |
| 33 | INVREQ | 28.5 | DFHSZ_RESPA_OUT_TARGET |
| 34 | INVREQ | 28.5 | DFHSZ_RESPA_REQ_TARGET |
| 35 | INVREQ | 28.5 | DFHSZ_RESPA_BAD_POOL |
| 36 | INVREQ | 28.5 | DFHSZ_RESPA_NOSESSION |
| 40 | INVREQ | 28.6 | DFHSZ_RESPA_INV_FROMLEN |
| 41 | INVREQ | 28.6 | DFHSZ_RESPA_INV_ESCAPE |
| 50 | INVREQ | 28.6 | DFHSZ_RESPA_INBOUNDDATA |
| 51 | INVREQ | 28.6 | DFHSZ_RESPA_INV_AID |
| 52 | INVREQ | 28.6 | DFHSZ_RESPA_INV_CURSOR |
| 53 | INVREQ | 28.6 | DFHSZ_RESPA_INV_CODE |
| 54 | INVREQ | 28.6 | DFHSZ_RESPA_INV_ATTR |
| 55 | INVREQ | 28.6 | DFHSZ_RESPA_INV_KEYESC |
| 56 | INVREQ | 28.6 | DFHSZ_RESPA_ERR_VALIDATION |
| 57 | INVREQ | 28.6 | DFHSZ_RESPA_INPUTINHIBIT |
| 58 | INVREQ | 28.6 | DFHSZ_RESPA_ERR_SEND |
| 59 | INVREQ | 28.6 | DFHSZ_RESPA_ERR_DBCS |
| 60 | INVREQ | 28.7 | DFHSZ_RESPA_INV_MAXLEN |
| 61 | INVREQ | 28.7 | DFHSZ_RESPA_INV_STARTLEN |
| 62 | INVREQ | 28.7 | DFHSZ_RESPA_INV_TRANSID |
| 63 | INVREQ | 28.7 | DFHSZ_RESPA_INV_TERMID |
| 70 | INVREQ | 28.7 | DFHSZ_RESPA_INV_FIELD |
| 71 | INVREQ | 28.7 | DFHSZ_RESPA_ERR_RECEIVE |
| 80 | INVREQ | 28.8 | DFHSZ_RESPA_INV_CONTROL |
| 81 | INVREQ | 28.8 | DFHSZ_RESPA_INV_VALUE |
| 82 | INVREQ | 28.8 | DFHSZ_RESPA_BAD_SENSEDATA |
| 90 | INVREQ | 28.8 | DFHSZ_RESPA_BAD_DEFRESP |
| 91 | INVREQ | 28.8 | DFHSZ_RESPA_NOT_RESPONSE |
| 92 | INVREQ | 28.8 | DFHSZ_RESPA_NOT_POSITIVE |
| 93 | INVREQ | 28.8 | DFHSZ_RESPA_NOT_STSN |
| 94 | INVREQ | 28.8 | DFHSZ_RESPA_NOT_STSNRESP |
| 95 | INVREQ | 28.8 | DFHSZ_RESPA_BAD_CONTROL |
| 100 | NOTAUTH | 28.9 | DFHSZ_RESPS_NOTAUTH |
| 110 | INVREQ | 28.9 | DFHSZ_RESPS_INV_SERV |
| 111 | INVREQ | 28.9 | DFHSZ_RESPS_INV_ACQ |
| 115 | INVREQ | 28.9 | DFHSZ_RESPS_UNK_POOL |
| 116 | INVREQ | 28.9 | DFHSZ_RESPS_UNK_TARGET |
| 117 | INVREQ | 28.9 | DFHSZ_RESPS_UNK_NODE |
| 118 | INVREQ | 28.9 | DFHSZ_RESPS_UNK_CONN |
| 119 | INVREQ | 28.9 | DFHSZ_RESPS_ERR_LIST |
| 130 | INVREQ | 28.9 | DFHSZ_RESPS_INV_TARGETNUM |
| 131 | INVREQ | 28.9 | DFHSZ_RESPS_INV_NODENUM |
| 132 | INVREQ | 28.9 | DFHSZ_RESPS_INV_POOLNUM |

**Table 28.1** Location of full EIBRESP2 descriptions—*cont.*

| RC (EIBRESP2) | Condition (EIBRESP) | Described in section | RC name |
|---|---|---|---|
| 140 | INVREQ | 28.10 | DFHSZ_RESPI_INV_DEVICE |
| 141 | INVREQ | 28.10 | DFHSZ_RESPI_INV_CONTENTION |
| 142 | INVREQ | 28.10 | DFHSZ_RESPI_INV_INITLDATA |
| 143 | INVREQ | 28.10 | DFHSZ_RESPI_INV_UNSOLACK |
| 144 | INVREQ | 28.10 | DFHSZ_RESPI_INV_MSGJRNL |
| 150 | INVREQ | 28.10 | DFHSZ_RESPI_INV_FORMAT |
| 153 | INVREQ | 28.10 | DFHSZ_RESPI_INV_STSN |
| 154 | INVREQ | 28.10 | DFHSZ_RESPI_INV_BEGINSESS |
| 155 | INVREQ | 28.10 | DFHSZ_RESPI_INV_UNSOLDATA |
| 156 | INVREQ | 28.10 | DFHSZ_RESPI_INV_EXCEPTIONQ |
| 157 | INVREQ | 28.10 | DFHSZ_RESPI_INV_JOURNAL |
| 158 | INVREQ | 28.10 | DFHSZ_RESPI_INV_MAXLEN |
| 159 | INVREQ | 28.10 | DFHSZ_RESPI_INV_ENDSESS |
| 160 | INVREQ | 28.10 | DFHSZ_RESPI_INV_PROPSET |
| 162 | INVREQ | 28.10 | DFHSZ_RESPI_INV_POOL |
| 163 | INVREQ | 28.10 | DFHSZ_RESPI_INV_NODE |
| 164 | INVREQ | 28.10 | DFHSZ_RESPI_INV_TARGET |
| 167 | INVREQ | 28.10 | DFHSZ_RESPI_INV_APPL |
| 170 | INVREQ | 28.10 | DFHSZ_RESPI_DUP_PROPSET |
| 171 | INVREQ | 28.10 | DFHSZ_RESPI_UNK_PROPSET |
| 172 | INVREQ | 28.10 | DFHSZ_RESPI_DUP_POOL |
| 173 | INVREQ | 28.10 | DFHSZ_RESPI_DUP_NODE |
| 174 | INVREQ | 28.10 | DFHSZ_RESPI_DUP_TARGET |
| 175 | INVREQ | 28.10 | DFHSZ_RESPI_DUP_CONN |
| 176 | INVREQ | 28.10 | DFHSZ_RESPI_ERR_OPENNODE |
| 177 | INVREQ | 28.10 | DFHSZ_RESPI_DUP_APPL |
| 210 | INVREQ | 28.2 | DFHSZ_RESPA_BAD_PARMP |
| 211 | INVREQ | 28.2 | DFHSZ_RESPA_BAD_PARM2 |
| 212 | INVREQ | 28.2 | DFHSZ_RESPA_BAD_DATAFMT |
| 213 | INVREQ | 28.2 | DFHSZ_RESPA_TIMEOUT |
| 214 | INVREQ | 28.2 | DFHSZ_RESPA_FREECONV |
| 215 | INVREQ | 28.2 | DFHSZ_RESPA_LOSTSESSION |
| 216 | INVREQ | 28.2 | DFHSZ_RESPA_ERR_LASTSEND |
| 220 | INVREQ | 28.3 | DFHSZ_RESPA_SEQ_SEND |
| 221 | INVREQ | 28.3 | DFHSZ_RESPA_SEQ_RECEIVE |
| 223 | INVREQ | 28.3 | DFHSZ_RESPA_SEQ_START |
| 224 | INVREQ | 28.3 | DFHSZ_RESPA_NOT_ISSUEFREE |
| 230 | INVREQ | 28.4 | DFHSZ_RESPA_RCV_CLEAR |
| 231 | INVREQ | 28.4 | DFHSZ_RESPA_RCV_CANCEL |
| 232 | INVREQ | 28.4 | DFHSZ_RESPA_RCV_CHASE |
| 233 | INVREQ | 28.4 | DFHSZ_RESPA_RCV_EXCEPTRESP |
| 234 | INVREQ | 28.4 | DFHSZ_RESPA_RCV_EXCEPTREQ |
| 240 | INVREQ | 28.2 | DFHSZ_RESPA_UNK_CONVID |
| 241 | INVREQ | 28.2 | DFHSZ_RESPA_INV_TIMEOUT |

## 28.1 Universal errors

These Errors can be detected on all `EXEC CICS FEPI` commands.

**0** The command has successfully completed without any errors.

**10 (INVREQ)** The `EXEC CICS FEPI` command has not been executed because the XSZBRQ Global User Exit has rejected the request (see Chapter 57). This response means, therefore, that your systems programmers have intervened in FEPI processing to stop the command.

**11 (INVREQ)** Return Code 11 should not occur during normal processing. It indicates that you are trying to run a `EXEC CICS FEPI` command without FEPI being installed in the CICS system.

This means either that the SIT (or override) parameter `FEPI=YES` has not been specified, or (somewhat unusually) FEPI has not been installed in the system at all!

**12 (INVREQ)** This response indicates that the CICS system you are running in is undergoing a *normal* (i.e. warm) shutdown. The command has successfully completed. Therefore, you can take some action to quiesce the partners' Nodes (like doing signoff transactions) so that all loose ends are tidied up. However, there is nothing forcing you to do this action, but politeness costs nothing! Remember that the CICS shutdown will not proceed until all the active conversations have ended (see Chapter 59).

**13 (INVREQ)** FEPI has *abended* (which, of course, will never happen!). As FEPI operates somewhat independently of the rest of CICS, it is possible that FEPI can abend without crunching the rest of CICS (which is why you were able to issue the command anyway). You can use this Return Code to send a message to the end user saying that links are down, but there should be a DFHSZ4199E message on the MVS console announcing that FEPI has failed.

**14 (INVREQ)** FEPI has not accepted the request, as either FEPI is too busy to accept it, or there is not enough CICS EDSA available to process the request. Consequently, this Return Code indicates either that FEPI is in a CPU loop, or that there is a CICS Short On Storage Condition. If CICS has not purged the current transaction during Storage Stall recovery, then you should consider reissuing the request.

**15 (INVREQ)** A logic error has occurred. The EXEC CICS layers have presented to FEPI an unknown command (see Appendix E for details of known Command Codes). This may have been generated by the erroneous intervention of a Global User Exit involved with EXEC CICS processing.

**16 (INVREQ)** Not a lot of assistance can be given for this Return Code, as it indicates some sort of undetermined error.

**17 (INVREQ)** In common with the processing done by other parts of the CICS nucleus when doing Global User Exit (GLUE) processing, FEPI will copy various bits of information to build a GLUE parameter list. This copying involves obtaining some storage, and it is this GETMAIN which has failed. Consequently, the request has failed, and CICS is probably in a Short On Storage Condition. If CICS has not purged the current transaction, then consider reissuing the request (however, it could be the after-call GLUE that failed, so the request may have been processed).

**18 (INVREQ)** This Return Code indicates that the request has failed due to operator or System action. This means that either CICS has decided to purge the current transaction during Stall Conditions, or someone has Force Purged the transaction via CEMT.

## 28.2 General API errors

The errors are not specific to any particular command, but usually indicate that some sort of system-wide event has occurred.

**210 (INVREQ)** The use of the current command is not allowed on LU0 (SLUP) Connections. Some of the API-type commands are only valid for LU2 Connections (like `EXEC CICS FEPI CONVERSE FORMATTED`), so using them on LU0 (SLUP) Connections is rejected.

**211 (INVREQ)** The use of the current command is not allowed on LU2 Connections. Some of the API-type commands are only valid for LU0 (SLUP) Connections (like `EXEC CICS FEPI EXTRACT STSN`), so using them on LU2 Connections is rejected.

**212 (INVREQ)** You are attempting to issue Datastream commands on a Connection which is defined (in the associated Propertyset for the owning Pool) as being Formatted (or vice versa).

**213 (INVREQ)** The current command specified the Timeout parameter, and the required operation did not complete in the specified interval. Depending on the command being processed, the request may be retried:

- For an `EXEC CICS FEPI ALLOCATE` there was not an available Connection to Acquire. This may indicate a FEPI resource shortage, and you could consider defining a few more Connections in the Pool to alleviate this condition. See EIBRESP2(36) for more information.
- For an `EXEC CICS FEPI RECEIVE` or an `EXEC CICS FEPI CONVERSE`, the partner system has not responded in the specified interval. This would indicate that the partner is either processing slower than expected, or that it is in a stall situation. The `EXEC CICS FEPI RECEIVE` could be reissued with a different Timeout setting to see which is the case.
- For an `EXEC CICS FEPI START` the partner system has not responded within the interval (the partner has not abended because this will trigger the transaction), so FEPI started the transaction anyway. This is a different situation to a Receive Timeout, because another transaction has started, so an 'automatic' use of an `EXEC CICS FEPI RECEIVE` to await the response may not be appropriate.

**214 (INVREQ)** The use of `EXEC CICS FEPI START` or `EXEC CICS FEPI FREE PASS` was rejected because CICS was shutting down. This is very similar to EIBRESP2(12), but is raised during the attempt to initiate asynchronous processing, and so the Connection has been `EXEC CICS FEPI FREE RELEASEd` instead. This means that the Connection is no longer valid for the current task.

**215 (INVREQ)** The session to the partner system has been lost. This probably means that the partner system has abended (but it could mean that the MVS or Network operator has issued a `V NET,INACT,FORCE` command on the session to break it). A Transient Data Queue record will also be written to CSZX to log this event, so that a Monitor program can have the opportunity to take some actions.

**216 (INVREQ)** FEPI is highly optimized for speed. This means that FEPI does not wait until a flow reaches the partner system before allowing the application program to do other things. Consequently, VTAM may reject the data sent, but this response will not be returned to the application program until much later. EIBRESP2(216) indicates that VTAM has rejected a prior send, and the current command is the earliest opportunity to let on about it. I would recommend that the current connection is `EXEC CICS FEPI FREE RELEASE`d when this occurs.

**240 (INVREQ)** This error code can be returned on all of the API-type commands. It indicates that the supplied Convid is invalid. This could mean that the Convid is corrupt, or that the Conversation represented by a valid Convid is not owned by the current task. Additionally, this response is returned if an attempt is made to access the Connection after an `EXEC CICS FEPI FREE` has been performed.

**241 (INVREQ)** The value of a Timeout is invalid. This usually means that the delay is negative.

## 28.3 Sequence errors

These errors are returned to indicate that an invalid sequence of Commands has been issued. Therefore, they indicate that a programming or logic error has occurred.

**220 (INVREQ)** An `EXEC CICS FEPI SEND` or an `EXEC CICS FEPI CONVERSE` has been issued after an `EXEC CICS FEPI SEND INVITE` without a prior `EXEC CICS FEPI RECEIVE`. In other words, you are trying to do a second Send without obtaining the response to the first one.

**221 (INVREQ)** An `EXEC CICS FEPI RECEIVE` is not allowed at this point in the Conversation. An example of this will occur if the `EXEC CICS FEPI RECEIVE` is issued after an `EXEC CICS FEPI SEN4` without the `INVITE` option.

**223 (INVREQ)** An `EXEC CICS FEPI START` is not allowed at this point in the Conversation. An example of this will occur if the `EXEC CICS FEPI START` is issued after an `EXEC CICS FEPI SEND` without the `INVITE` option. In general, an `EXEC CICS FEPI START` can only be issued where a single `EXEC CICS FEPI RECEIVE` is appropriate.

**224 (INVREQ)** This error code shows that only an `EXEC CICS FEPI ISSUE` or an `EXEC CICS FEPI FREE` command can be issued at this point in the Conversation. This sequence error usually means that the partner system is trying to stop the conversation, so it should be ended by the application program.

## 28.4 Datastream errors

These responses indicate that some VTAM control flows have been received. What they mean is dependant upon the partner system, and no general advice can be given as to how to proceed. You should consult VTAM documentation for further information.

**230 (INVREQ)** An SNA CLEAR flow has been received.

**231 (INVREQ)** An SNA CANCEL flow has been received.

**232 (INVREQ)** An SNA CHASE flow has been received.

**233 (INVREQ)** An EXCEPTION RESPONSE has been received from the partner. This can commonly occur when communicating with IMS partners, and usually means that IMS has rejected the previous flow (and commonly proceeds a DFS message).

**234 (INVREQ)** An Exception Request has been received from the partner.

## 28.5 Allocation errors

These errors are raised from an `EXEC CICS FEPI ALLOCATE` command (whether explicit or implied by the use of Temporary Conversations).

**30 (INVREQ)** The name quoted in the Pool parameter is not known.

**31 (INVREQ)** The supplied Pool is Out of Service, and so cannot be accessed.

**32 (INVREQ)** The name quoted in the Target parameter is not known.

**33 (INVREQ)** The supplied Target is Out of Service, and so cannot be accessed.

**34 (INVREQ)** The Target parameter is required, but was not specified.

**35 (INVREQ)** The Pool specified for the Temporary Conversation (see Sec. 10.3) cannot be used for Temporary Conversations. This is because the defining Propertyset has specified the term `CONTENTION(LOSE)` or it has `INITIALDATA(INBOUND)` without a Begin Session Handler (see Chapter 16 for information on Propertyset settings).

**36 (INVREQ)** The `EXEC CICS FEPI ALLOCATE` failed because the Pool did not contain an available Connection (in other words they were all in use and/or set out of service). If the command specified `TIMEOUT`, then EIBRESP2(36) is not returned, as 213 is returned instead. The request could be retried after a delay, as a Connection could have become available. Alternatively, some more Connections could be defined.

## 28.6 Send errors

The errors in this section are generated by an invalid `EXEC CICS FEPI SEND` command. However, they can also arise due to processing of the Send component of an `EXEC CICS FEPI CONVERSE` command. While most of the errors apply only to Formatted Conversations, some apply to Datastream ones as well.

**40 (INVREQ)** The `FLENGTH` (or `FROMFLENGTH` on a converse) parameter is invalid:

- The value is either 0 or negative.
- The value given is greater than the maximum size specified for the Pool containing the Conversation. This maximum size is set by the `MAXFLENGTH` value for the Propertyset which defines the attributes of the owning pool (see Sec. 16.2.9).

**41 (INVREQ)** The value given in the `ESCAPE` parameter is invalid. It must be in the range of X'40' to X'FE'.

**50 (INVREQ)** An attempt was made to Send a flow to the partner, but the partner had already sent some data which is waiting to be received, and CONTENTION(LOSE) was specified in the Propertyset for the Pool containing the Conversation. See Sec. 16.2.2 for details of the Contention parameter.

If the Propertyset had specified CONTENTION(WIN), then the Send would have succeeded.

**51 (INVREQ)** The value given in the AID parameter is invalid. The permitted settings are those used for BMS operation, and are specified in the DFHAID copybook.

**52 (INVREQ)** The value given by the CURSOR parameter is invalid. This parameter is specified as an offset from the top left-hand corner of the screen, so this error means that the value given was either negative or beyond the bottom right-hand corner of the screen.

**53 (INVREQ)** The data supplied via the FROM parameter is invalid. This means that you are trying to Send noncharacter data on a Formatted Conversation.

**54 (INVREQ)** An invalid attempt was made to update FEPI's Formatted data buffer. This means that, for example, you are trying to update a protected field.

**55 (INVREQ)** An invalid Keystroke Escape sequence was detected. All the Keystroke Escape sequences start with & (or the Escape character) and are two bytes long. See Appendix G for the allowed sequences.

**56 (INVREQ)** Data sent to FEPI's Formatted data buffer failed a Field Validation check. The 3270 Field Validation Attribute Bytes specify options like Mandatory Fill or Mandatory Enter, but the supplied data for the field failed this type of check.

**57 (INVREQ)** Data sent to FEPI's Formatted data buffer via a Keystroke sequence was rejected because the Input Inhibited 'light' is on. This is usually caused by a previous attempt to write to a protected field, and the reset 'key' was not pressed to clear it.

**58 (INVREQ)** This indicates some sort of FEPI/VTAM logic error, as VTAM has not accepted the VTAM Send operation. Your best bet is to retry the operation.

**59 (INVREQ)** You are operating over a Formatted conversation, but an attempt was made to send invalid Double Byte Character Set data.

## 28.7 Receive/Start errors

These errors are generated on either an EXEC CICS FEPI RECEIVE (or the Receive part of an EXEC CICS FEPI CONVERSE), an EXEC CICS FEPI EXTRACT, or an EXEC CICS FEPI START command.

**60 (INVREQ)** The MAXFLENGTH parameter is invalid. This is because it is either negative, or it is more than the MAXFLENGTH setting on the Propertyset that defined the Pool containing the current Conversation.

**61 (INVREQ)** The FLENGTH parameter is invalid. The permitted settings for USERDATA length are 0 to 128 inclusive.

**62 (INVREQ)** The value of the TRANSID specified is invalid. This does not mean that the specified transaction is incorrect (FEPI does not check for its existence), only that it contains nonpermitted characters (like an embedded space).

**63 (INVREQ)** The value of the TERMID specified is invalid. This does not mean that the specified terminal is absent (FEPI does not check for its existence), only that it contains nonpermitted characters (like an embedded space).

**70 (INVREQ)** The field for the EXEC CICS FEPI EXTRACT FIELD specified via the FIELDLOC or FIELDNUM parameters is invalid. This means that either the field number is not on the screen (FIELDNUM), or the position is off the screen (FIELDLOC).

**71 (INVREQ)** This indicates a logic error. FEPI issued a VTAM *RECEIVE* operation, but VTAM rejected the request. Try reissuing the command.

## 28.8 Issue errors

These errors are detected when processing an EXEC CICS FEPI ISSUE command. They relate to either some sort of state check (FEPI cannot do what you asked at the current point in the Conversation) or format error. You should refer to VTAM manuals for more information.

**80 (INVREQ)** The CVDA specified in the CONTROL parameter is invalid.

**81 (INVREQ)** The VALUE parameter is invalid.

- The CVDA specified is not valid.
- VALUE is specified when it is not required.
- VALUE is required but not supplied.
- The CVDA specified is not permitted with the given CONTROL parameter.

**82 (INVREQ)** The SENSEDATA parameter is invalid.

- SENSEDATA is specified when it is not required.
- SENSEDATA is required but not supplied.

**90 (INVREQ)** The previous EXEC CICS FEPI RECEIVE (or *converse*) completed with the RESPSTATUS parameter notifying that the partner has requested a response to the flow. The EXEC CICS FEPI ISSUE command was sending the response, but the value supplied in the VALUE was not permitted for the prior RESPSTATUS. In other words, the response did not match that required.

**91 (INVREQ)** The CVDA specified in the CONTROL parameter is not permitted at this point in the Conversation. Only NORMALRESP or EXECPTRESP are permitted.

**92 (INVREQ)** At this point in the Conversation, you are required to Send a positive response, so the requested response is rejected (this usually occurs only for LU0 (SLUP) processing).

**93 (INVREQ)** The CVDA specified in the CONTROL parameter is not permitted at this point in the Conversation. Only STSN is permitted.

**94 (INVREQ)** The CVDA specified in the CONTROL parameter is not permitted at this point in the Conversation. Only NORMALRESP or STSN are permitted.

**95 (INVREQ)** The CVDA specified in the CONTROL parameter is not permitted at this point in the Conversation.

## 28.9 General errors on the SPI-type commands

These errors can occur on any FEPI SPI-type command. They usually relate to a bad parameter setting.

**100 (NOTAUTH)** All the FEPI SPI-type commands undergo a general security authorization, which this task has failed (browses require Read authority, while the other SPI-commands usually require Update authority). See Chapter 55 for details.

**110 (INVREQ)** The CVDA supplied in the SERVSTATUS parameter is invalid. The permitted CVDAs are INSERVICE and OUTSERVICE (but NOTAPPLIC is also accepted if SERVSTATUS is an optional parameter on the current command).

**111 (INVREQ)** The CVDA supplied in the ACQSTATUS parameter is invalid. The permitted CVDAs are ACQUIRED and RELEASED (but NOTAPPLIC is also accepted if ACQSTATUS is an optional parameter on the current command).

**115 (INVREQ)** The POOL specified is not known.

**116 (INVREQ)** The TARGET specified is not known.

**117 (INVREQ)** The NODE specified is not known.

**118 (INVREQ)** The supplied Connection is not known. The given Target and Node are both known to FEPI, but their combination (to form a Connection) is not present in any Pool.

**119 (INVREQ)** The current request failed for one of the items in the list. Some of the SPI commands (like the INSTALLs) take operands which are lists of names, and the operation failed for one (or more) of these items. Depending on the command being processed, some TDQ records may well be produced which will identify the failing item.

**130 (INVREQ)** The value specified in the TARGETNUM parameter is invalid. This usually means that it is negative, zero, or greater than 256.

**131 (INVREQ)** The value specified in the NODENUM parameter is invalid. This usually means that it is negative, zero, or greater than 256.

**132 (INVREQ)** The value specified in the POOLNUM parameter is invalid. This usually means that it is negative, zero, or greater than 256.

## 28.10 Install errors

These errors relate to the INSTALL commands for FEPI. These are mainly errors in a Propertyset definition, but they also record attempts to make duplicate definitions.

**140 (INVREQ)** The DEVICE CVDA parameter on the EXEC CICS FEPI INSTALL PROPERTYSET command is invalid (see Sec. 16.2.3).

The permitted CVDAs are T3278M2, T3278M3, T3278M4, T3278M5 (for monochrome terminals), T3279M2, T3279M3, T3278M4, T3279M5 (for colour boxes), TPS55M2, TPS55M3, TPS55M4 (for Double Byte Character Set displays), and LUP (for SLUP devices).

**141 (INVREQ)** The CONTENTION CVDA parameter on the EXEC CICS FEPI INSTALL PROPERTYSET command is invalid (see Sec. 16.2.2).

The permitted CVDAs are LOSE and WIN.

**142 (INVREQ)** The INITIALDATA CVDA parameter on the EXEC CICS FEPI INSTALL PROPERTYSET command is invalid (see Sec. 16.2.8).

The permitted CVDAs are INBOUND and NOTINBOUND.

**143 (INVREQ)** The UNSOLDATACK CVDA parameter on the EXEC CICS FEPI INSTALL PROPERTYSET command is invalid (see Sec. 16.2.12).

The permitted CVDAs are NEGATIVE and POSITIVE.

**144 (INVREQ)** The MSGJRNL CVDA parameter on the EXEC CICS FEPI INSTALL PROPERTYSET command is invalid (see Sec. 16.2.10).

The permitted CVDAs are NOMSGJRNL, INPUT, OUTPUT and INOUT.

**150 (INVREQ)** The FORMAT CVDA parameter on the EXEC CICS FEPI INSTALL PROPERTYSET command is invalid (see Sec. 16.2.7).

The permitted CVDAs are FORMATTED and DATASTREAM, but this error will also be raised if the setting is inappropriate for the given device (such as DEVICE(SLUP) with FORMAT(FORMATTED)).

**153 (INVREQ)** The STSN parameter on the EXEC CICS FEPI INSTALL PROPERTYSET command is invalid (see Sec. 16.2.11).

FEPI does not check the STSN transaction name to see that it exists, only that it is not formatted incorrectly (such as not containing any imbedded blanks).

**154 (INVREQ)** The BEGINSESSION parameter on the EXEC CICS FEPI INSTALL PROPERTYSET command is invalid (see Sec. 16.2.1).

FEPI does not check the BEGINSESSION transaction name to see that it exists, only that it is not formatted incorrectly (such as not containing any imbedded blanks).

**155 (INVREQ)** The UNSOLDATA parameter on the EXEC CICS FEPI INSTALL PROPERTYSET command is invalid (see Sec. 16.2.12).

FEPI does not check the UNSOLDATA transaction name to see that it exists, only that it is not formatted incorrectly (such as not containing any imbedded blanks).

**156 (INVREQ)** The EXCEPTIONQ parameter on the EXEC CICS FEPI INSTALL PROPERTYSET command is invalid (see Sec. 16.2.5).

FEPI does not check the EXCEPTIONQ TDQ name to see that it exists, only that it is not formatted incorrectly (such as not containing any imbedded blanks).

**157 (INVREQ)** The FJOURNALNUM parameter on EXEC CICS FEPI INSTALL PROPERTYSET is invalid (see Sec. 16.2.6).

The permitted values are 0 (indicating no journalling) or greater than 1 (the system journal cannot be specified). FEPI does not check to see if the specified journal exists.

**158 (INVREQ)** The MAXFLENGTH parameter on the EXEC CICS FEPI INSTALL PROPERTYSET command is invalid (see Sec. 16.2.9).

The permitted values are in the range 128 to 1048576.

**159 (INVREQ)** The ENDSESSION parameter on EXEC CICS FEPI INSTALL PROPERTYSET is invalid (see Sec. 16.2.4).

FEPI does not check the ENDSESSION transaction name to see that it exists, only that it is not formatted incorrectly (such as not containing any imbedded blanks).

**160 (INVREQ)** The PROPERTYSET parameter is invalid as it contains things like imbedded blanks.

**162 (INVREQ)** The POOL/POOLLIST parameter is invalid as it contains things like imbedded blanks.

**163 (INVREQ)** The NODE/NODELIST parameter is invalid as it contains things like imbedded blanks.

**164 (INVREQ)** The TARGET/TARGETLIST parameter is invalid as it contains things like imbedded blanks.

**167 (INVREQ)** The APPLLIST parameter is invalid as it contains things like imbedded blanks.

**170 (INVREQ)** The EXEC CICS FEPI INSTALL PROPERTYSET failed as the Propertyset already exists.

**171 (INVREQ)** The EXEC CICS FEPI INSTALL POOL/POOLLIST failed as the Propertyset is not known.

**172 (INVREQ)** The EXEC CICS FEPI INSTALL POOL/POOLLIST failed as the Pool already exists. If there is more than one item in the POOLLIST, then EIBRESP2(119) is returned instead of this error, with a Transient Data Queue record indicating which item failed.

**173 (INVREQ)** The EXEC CICS FEPI INSTALL NODE/NODELIST failed as the Node already exists. If there is more than one item in the NODELIST, then EIBRESP2(119) is returned instead of this error, with a Transient Data Queue record indicating which item failed.

**174 (INVREQ)** The EXEC CICS FEPI INSTALL TARGET/TARGETLIST failed as the Node already exists. If there is more than one item in the TARGETLIST, then EIBRESP2(119) is returned instead of this error, with a Transient Data Queue record indicating which item failed.

**175 (INVREQ)** The EXEC CICS FEPI ADD failed as the Connection (called Target–Node pair) already exists.

**176 (INVREQ)** The Acquisition of the Node failed because VTAM failed to *open* the Node (see Chapter 12). The failure code is available in the SENSECODE field on the EXEC CICS FEPI INQUIRE NODE command.

**177 (INVREQ)** The EXEC CICS FEPI INSTALL NODE/NODELIST failed as the APPL (or APPLLIST item) is already defined in another Target. If there is more than one item in the NODELIST, then EIBRESP2(119) is returned instead of this error, with a Transient Data Queue record indicating which item failed.

## 28.11 Browse errors

These errors are generated during a browse operation. They are exactly the same as those for all the other EXEC CICS browse commands.

**1 (ILLOGIC)** The browse operation failed because:

- The START browse of the FEPI resource failed as a browse was already in progress for the current task.
- The NEXT or END operation failed as a browse was not in progress for the FEPI resource by the current task.

**2 (END)** The NEXT operation 'failed' as all the FEPI resource definitions have been scanned.

# PART 4

# Formatted programming

**GUIDANCE**

This part contains information on the Formatted facilities of FEPI. However, the information relating to Conversation initiation and termination are equally applicable to Datastream access.
The following topics are discussed in this part of the book:

- EXEC CICS FEPI ALLOCATE options
- Sending with Keystrokes
- Sending with Buffers
- Receiving with Buffers
- Receiving with Fields
- The effect of Receive TIMEOUT usage
- EXEC CICS FEPI START and asynchronous operation
- EXEC CICS FEPI FREE

The art of a FEPI application program is that *it must, at all times, think like a human operator.*

# CHAPTER 29 EXEC CICS FEPI ALLOCATE options

**GUIDANCE**

This chapter describes the operation of the EXEC CICS FEPI ALLOCATE command, and how this is used to initiate FEPI Conversations. The information is equally applicable to Datastream access as well as Formatted access.

## 29.1 Starting a FEPI Conversation

A FEPI Conversation may be started in either of two ways (excluding Temporary Conversations which are rather odd, see Sec. 10.3):

- Manually, within a FEPI application program
- Automatically, by the initiation of a Handler (see Sec. 43.1.1)

The manual initiation of a Conversation is performed by the execution of an EXEC CICS FEPI ALLOCATE command, without the PASSCONVID operation.

When a Handler starts a Conversation, the Handler program does not need to initiate the Conversation, so the command EXEC CICS FEPI ALLOCATE PASSCONVID( ) is executed to *use* the Conversation. Therefore, the initiation of a FEPI Conversation in a Handler is exactly the same as the resumption of a Conversation.

The detailed description of the EXEC CICS FEPI ALLOCATE command is contained in Secs 27.2 and 27.3.

## 29.2 EXEC CICS FEPI ALLOCATEing a new FEPI Conversation

To start a new FEPI Conversation, the following EXEC CICS FEPI ALLOCATE command must be issued:

```
EXEC CICS FEPI ALLOCATE
              POOL(char8)

[TARGET(char8)]
[TIMEOUT(fixed31)]

CONVID(char8)
[SEQNUMIN(fixed31)]
[SEQNUMOUT(fixed31)]
[SESSNSTATUS(cvda)]
```

You generate the Conversation by obtaining a Connection from the named Pool. The Pool is the basic object upon which you Allocate.

### 29.2.1 Timeouts

If there are no inactive Connections in the Pool, then the command will wait for the TIMEOUT(*n*) interval (in seconds) for one to become unused. If one does not become available in this period, then the command completes with an EIBRESP2 indicating that Timeout occurred (213). If TIMEOUT is not specified (or is set to 0), then the command will wait indefinitely until a Connection becomes available.

You should always use TIMEOUT on the EXEC CICS FEPI ALLOCATE command, as this gives you the opportunity to take some sort of remedial action if there are not enough Connections available for (peak time) usage. Some techniques for altering the number of Connections are discussed in Chapter 48. However, doing Dynamic Resource Definition is not the only reason for using TIMEOUT. You could consider using a Timeout as an indication that transactions are hogging the Connections, and so this may mean that the partner system is not responding as quickly as usual. This may give you an early warning of network or system problems.

### 29.2.2 The Convid

When the EXEC CICS FEPI ALLOCATE successfully completes you have obtained a FEPI Connection, and started a FEPI Conversation over it. The command returns a key in the CONVID parameter. This Convid must be saved away, and quoted on all subsequent FEPI commands which access the Conversation.

The Convid is a 'randomish' number, and cannot directly be used to identify the underlying Connection (this is performed by the EXEC CICS FEPI EXTRACT CONV command). If you are doing Conversation management, you should consider saving the Convid in the USERDATA for the underlying Connection (see Chapter 61).

Once the Convid has been generated by the EXEC CICS FEPI ALLOCATE command, it is locked to the owning CICS task. No two CICS tasks (transactions) can be using the same Convid. (Note that this condition precludes any fancy monitoring transactions, which know the Convid, from looking at what is going on.) This locking prevents any use of the Conversation by another task, so preserving the integrity of the emulation. If another task is to use the Conversation, the Convid must be made known to the second task, and the Conversation is EXEC CICS FEPI FREE PASSed (see Chapter 36) or EXEC CICS FEPI STARTed (see Chapter 35) so that the second transaction can use the Conversation.

### 29.2.3 Target selection

When you EXEC CICS FEPI ALLOCATE, you obtain the use of an inactive Connection to run the Conversation. All Connections in the Pool are eligible for use. This is fine if your Pool contains only one Target, because all the Connections route to the same partner system. You do not have any control over which Node is selected; FEPI works on the basis that all Nodes are equivalent (you get round this by using Convid management).

The idea of having multiple Targets within a Pool stems from the idea that a single partner may be too slow to process the anticipated workload. Consequently, you may need two (or more) systems to provide an adequate response time. You do not care to which Target you are running the emulation, because the same facilities are available in both. Consequently, when you `EXEC CICS FEPI ALLOCATE` into a Pool with multiple targets, then you do not know with which partner system you will be communicating.

### DESIGN ISSUES

This is all well and good, but sometimes you might want to treat the two (or more) partners on some sort of priority basis. You could have VTAM-defined the paths to one system to be quicker than to the other. Consequently, one Target in the Pool can be used for high-priority requests, while the other is for normal accesses. In this situation, use two Pools, each containing a single Target.

However, as an alternative to using two Pools, you can select which Target within the Pool you want to use. The drawback of this method is that you have to expose the Target names to the FEPI application program, which may lead to maintenance problems. This selection of Target within the Pool is achieved by the use of the `TARGET` parameter.

An alternative design could be that the Pool contains two (or more) Targets, and you want to access them in priority order. For example, you have a local system containing the required transactions to be emulated, but it is severely resource constrained, and so can cope with only a small number of Connections. If all these Connections are in use, you have to resort to using a remoter system, which adds to the response time. As the two systems are equivalent, you have decided to put both Targets in the same Pool. Now, you sometimes do not particularly care how long the emulation takes (say, during slack times), so you simply allocate at the Pool level, and take pot luck as to which system you use. However, during peak hour (or running the emulation via a high-priority CICS transaction) you need to use the local system if at all possible. In this case, you would first attempt to `EXEC CICS FEPI ALLOCATE POOL() TARGET` (local) `TIMEOUT(1)`, and if this failed reissue the command without the Target (so that you might still pick up a local session if another transaction ended in the meantime).

In general, I would recommend that you do not mix Targets in a given Pool and access them in this fashion.

### 29.2.4 Order of Connection usage

When Allocating a Conversation, FEPI scans the Connections within the Pool to select a suitable path. The priority for selection is the first Conversation that meets the following criteria (see Sec. 18.1.2 for information on the status):

- A Connection that is not running a Conversation (and associated with the given Target, if this is supplied) and has `SERVSTATUS(INSERVICE)` and `ACQSTATUS(ACQUIRED)`, or
- A Connection that is not running a Conversation (and associated with the given Target, if this is supplied) and has `SERVSTATUS(INSERVICE)` and `ACQSTATUS(RELEASED)`.

If a Connection meeting these criteria is not found, then FEPI will wait for one second before rescanning. When the `TIMEOUT` interval has elapsed and a suitable Connection has not been found, the `EXEC CICS FEPI ALLOCATE` command will terminate.

If FEPI selects a Connection with `ACQSTATUS(RELEASED)`, it means that the Connection is *Unbound* in VTAM terms. Therefore, FEPI will *Bind* the Connection, changing the status to `ACQSTATUS(ACQUIRED)`. This will result in the partner system receiving notification that a 'terminal' has been switched on, and will also trigger a Begin Session Handler (see Sec. 44.1) if one has been defined for the Pool. Therefore, the use of a Released Connection generates a lot more processing than an Acquired one, so you should ensure that all the Connections have `ACQSTATUS(ACQUIRED)` when created to avoid this delay. However, if you are defining the Connections using lists, then you must beware of flooding VTAM with requests.

However, an interesting question is: 'What is the order of the Connections within the Pool, and can this be influenced?'

Naturally, this is a rhetorical question, to hint that you can influence the order of the Connections. Section 14.3 describes the way connections are generated using the `EXEC CICS FEPI ADD` command. I have not placed this discussion of Connection ordering within that section, as I thought that this would be of more interest to the application programmer.

When you `EXEC CICS FEPI ADD` either a Target or a Node into a Pool, then the Connections are generated. Therefore, the order of adding the Nodes and Targets to the Pool determines the order of the Connections. So, if you have defined some Nodes in VTAM terms to have a quicker service than others, you want these Connections to be first in the list. Thus, place the Target in the Pool first, then the 'quick' Nodes, and then the 'slow' Nodes. This will result in a Connections list with the quicker Nodes being available before the slower ones (assuming they are all Acquired or all Released).

Similarly, if the Pool contains multiple Targets, and you want one Target to be used first, you should first place all the Nodes in the Pool, then the first Target, and finally the second Target. This will result in a list with the Connections for the first Target coming before those for the second Target.

I must caution that this is the way things work at the moment. There is no guarantee that this will be maintained. Additionally, relying on this ordering within the Pool for performance purposes does not fill me with a great degree of glee. I recommend that if you really need to do this sort of ordering, you should use separate Pools.

### 29.2.5 How the Connection started

When the `EXEC CICS FEPI ALLOCATE` selects a Connection, it may (as described in Sec. 29.2.4) select a Connection that has not been used before. Thus, the Connection has to be *bound* in VTAM terms.

When a FEPI Connection is *bound*, the operation of the `INITIALDATA` and `BEGINSESSION` parameters for the Pool's Propertyset (see Chapter 16) come into play. If you are not using a Begin Session Handler (see Sec. 44.1) then you may have to do 'first flow' processing on the Connection (because the partner system's terminal has just been 'switched on', and it will usually send a Start-of-Day screen). The way you are notified of this is via the SESSNSTATUS parameter.

SESSNSTATUS returns a CVDA of either NEWSESSION or OLDSESSION. If OLDSESSION is returned, then either the Connection was already Acquired when you Allocated it, or it was Acquired, and a Begin Session Handler was run. In any case, you do not have to worry about first flow considerations. NEWSESSION says that the Connection was Acquired for the (new) FEPI Conversation, and no Begin Session Handler was used. Therefore, you should process the Start-of-Day flows in the application program. Consequently, SESSNSTATUS must be used where no Begin Session Handler is used, to allow a FEPI application program to distinguish between FEPI Connection startup types.

## 29.3 EXEC CICS FEPI ALLOCATEing an existing FEPI Conversation

You use an existing FEPI Conversation in one of three ways:

- In an EXEC CICS FEPI STARTed transaction.
- In a Handler transaction.
- Because a prior transaction has EXEC CICS FEPI FREE PASSed the Conversation.

In all these cases a prior function (whether it be FEPI internally or a FEPI application program) has started the FEPI Conversation, and you are now (re)gaining access to it.

To gain access to the FEPI Conversation, you need to know its CONVID. In the case of a Handler or an EXEC CICS FEPI STARTed transaction, this is provided via the Start Data (see Sec. D.2) which has to be EXEC CICS RETRIEVEd. If manually passing the Convid (via EXEC CICS FEPI FREE PASS) you have to arrange the knowledge of the Convid yourself (usually via a COMMAREA).

Once you know the Convid, you use the alternative form of the EXEC CICS FEPI ALLOCATE command to gain access to the Conversation:

```
EXEC CICS FEPI ALLOCATE
               PASSCONVID(char8)
```

Quoting the Convid in the PASSCONVID parameter is all that is required to reuse the FEPI Conversation.

Once the FEPI Conversation has been reacquired, then access proceeds as normal on it. The partner system does not know that its 'terminal' is being run from a different CICS transaction.

# CHAPTER 30 Sending with Keystrokes

**GUIDANCE**

This chapter outlines the techniques for a FEPI Formatted Conversation to send a flow to the partner system via Keystroke operations.

The alternative method for sending Formatted Conversational data using Buffer operations is discussed in Chapter 31.

## 30.1 Overview

FEPI Formatted Conversations (see Chapter 3 for the difference between a FEPI Formatted Conversation and one running Datastream) are defined by Connections that appear in a Pool whose Propertyset specifies FORMAT(FORMATTED) (see Sec. 16.2.7).

The idea behind Formatted access is that FEPI provides as much assistance as possible, so that all the complexities of 3270 protocols are hidden. Consequently, Formatted Conversations provide two ways of sending data to the partner system:

- By specifying a sequence of keys that mimic the action of a 'real' terminal user, or
- By treating the screen as a buffer, and filling it in.

*Keystroke* access provides the former facility; Buffer techniques are discussed in Chapter 31. Note that Keystroke techniques and Buffer techniques for sending formatted data to the partner system are not mutually exclusive, and can be mixed (as long as you do not do anything too silly!).

## 30.2 Keystroke concepts

As the Keystroke facilities mimic the keys pressed by a 'real' end user, Keystroke facilities are applicable only to data that is sent from the FEPI application program to the partner system.

Conceptually, there are the following types of keys:

- Keys that move the cursor (things like Home, Newline, or Cursor Left),

- Keys that alter the screen state (things like Insert or Reset),
- Keys that send the screen (keys like PF3 or Clear), called *attention keys*,
- Keys that just update the screen (like A or 6).

As keystroke access is mimicking the keys pressed, the normal 'letter' keys can be easily specified; you just quote the letter or number as normal. However, a technique must be provided so that the other types of keys (which do 3270-specific operations) can be mimicked. Keystroke access uses the '&' character to denote that the next two characters denote a 3270-specific key press (this & can be changed). These two are called *escape sequences*.

When FEPI encounters one of the *Attention* keys (like Enter, PF1, Clear, PA1, or Cursor Select), the sequence of keys is translated into a 3270 Datastream and sent to the partner system. This translation involves the knowledge of the underlying panel (which was previously sent from the partner system) so that the correct 3270 Datastream can be generated. When the partner responds to the keystrokes, FEPI updates its knowledge of the underlying panel. The FEPI application program gains access to the partner's flow by the techniques discussed in Chapers 32 and 33.

## 30.2.1 The escape sequences

FEPI keystroke access supports the following two-byte escape sequences. Each sequence is preceeded by the '&' character (see Sec. 30.3 for how to change the & to something else).

CURSOR KEYS

**&Bn** Backtab, *n* times

**&Dn** Cursor down, *n* times

**&HO** Home

**&Ln** Cursor left, *n* times

**&Nn** Newline, *n* times

**&Rn** Cursor right, *n* times

**&Tn** Tab, *n* times

**&Un** Cursor up, *n* times

(*Note*: $n = 1...9$)

SPECIAL KEYS

**&DL** Delete

**&DU** DUP

**&EF** Erase end-of-field

**&EI** Erase input

**&ES** Escape character

**&FM** Field mark

**&IN** Insert

**&MS** Start secure Magnetic Strip Reader (MSR)

**&RS** Reset

**&SI** Shift in

**&SO** Shift out

ATTENTION KEYS

**&AT** Attention

**&An** PA*n* (*n* = 1...3)

**&CL** Clear

**&CS** Cursor Select (light pen)

**&EN** Enter

**&ME** End secure MSR

**&nn** **PF***nn* (*nn* = 01...24; a leading 0 must be specified)

## 30.3 The FEPI Keystroke command

You tell FEPI that you are sending Keystroke data to the partner system by using the KEYSTROKE parameter on the EXEC CICS FEPI SEND FORMATTED command (or the equivalent EXEC CICS FEPI CONVERSE FORMATTED command). A full description of these commands is provided in Secs 27.4 and 27.14 (although I do not recommend using the EXEC CICS FEPI CONVERSE FORMATTED command as explained in Sec. 23.1.4).

The layout of the FEPI keystroke send command is:

```
EXEC CICS FEPI SEND FORMATTED KEYSTROKES
                    CONVID(char8)

                    FROM(char)  FLENGTH(fixed31)
                    [ESCAPE(char1)]
```

The KEYSTROKE parameter says that the string specified in FROM is not in Buffer format, but is a sequence of Keystrokes. The Escape Prefix character (defaulting to &) can be changed by specifying the required byte in the ESCAPE parameter.

If the & character is used as a 'normal' key press, then you *must* change the Escape character to something not present in the string (I find that '|' is suitably rare). However, you can get the Escape character into the keystroke sequence by use of &ES if really necessary.

All the Escape sequences are two bytes long. FEPI will check the Escape sequences. However, this check operates *between* Attention keys. Therefore, if using multiple Attention keys (see Sec. 30.4.2) you will get communication with the partner system before the error is detected.

## **30.4** Keystroke techniques

### 30.4.1 Starting from a known point

When specifying the Keystroke string, you must be aware of the underlying screen 'display'. Only with this knowledge is it possible to send the correct sequence of key presses to achieve your goal. Therefore, you should always aim to start a Keystroke sequence from a known point. The best way to do this is to send a Clear key followed by a Home key to position the cursor at the top left-hand side of the 'screen'. Therefore, you could expect to start a sequence with: `'&CL&HO'`.

However, sending a Clear key may not be the most suitable action to return to a fixed point. It all depends on what the partner system is running (or not) at the FEPI emulated terminal. In some situations, Clear is most definitely not the thing to do!

### 30.4.2 Multiple Attentions

FEPI permits the specification of multiple Attentions in a Keystroke sequence. For example, the following sequence brings up the CECI variable panel:

```
'&CL&HOceci&EN&05'
```

When FEPI detects multiple Attentions, the following processing occurs:

1. FEPI detects the first Attention key, builds the 3270 Datastream from its underlying screen image (updated by the preceding Keystrokes), and sends it to the partner system.
2. Now, as there are more keys to be processed, FEPI will wait until the partner system has responded (in VTAM terms, this wait ends when a flow is received with either an End Bracket or a Change Direction).
3. FEPI now updates its internal screen image, and then processes the next lot of Keystrokes until another Attention key is found.
4. If this Attention key is at the end of the Keystroke sequence, then the conversion occurs and the flow is sent to the partner. At this point, the `EXEC CICS FEPI SEND FORMATTED KEYSTROKES` command completes, without waiting for the partner system to respond.

Therefore, if you have multiple Attention keys in your Keystroke sequence, you lose all knowledge of the intermediate panels that the partner system will return. You are relying on the fact that the partner system sends what you expected it to. If this is the case, then everything is fine, and your Keystroke sequence will give you the expected result. However, if the partner system decides to respond in an unexpected fashion (such as a broadcast message or a transaction abend), you do not get any indication of this, and so your Keystroke sequence will fail.

Unfortunately, in this circumstance, you will have to investigate why the emulation failed, and so recover from it. You will detect the problem either when you attempt to update a non-existent field (perhaps by something like trying to put 16 characters into a 4 byte field) or when FEPI rejects your Keystroke sequence because the 'Input Inhibited' light is on.

Investigation, and resolution, of these types of problems are difficult. Therefore, I do *not* recommend using multiple Attentions in a Keystroke sequence unless you are very sure that nothing untoward can occur in the middle of the sequence.

### 30.4.3 Keystrokes without Attention keys

When assembling your Keystroke sequence, you do not have to provide an Attention key for each `EXEC CICS FEPI SEND FORMATTED KEYSTROKES` command. If you omit an Attention key, FEPI merely updates its internal copy of the emulated terminal with your key presses. At the end of this operation, the virtual cursor will be positioned wherever it has ended up.

Therefore, if you are building a sequence using multiple Keystroke sequences, it is advisable to start each sequence with the Home key so that you know where the cursor is, and then to use Tab operations to position the cursor at the appropriate field for update.

Remember, that at some stage, you have to specify an Attention key to get the flow sent to the partner.

## **30.5** Keystroke errors

When using Keystroke access techniques, you have to be aware of the underlying screen image (that FEPI is tracking). Thus, the most common Keystroke errors result from a mismatch between what the FEPI application program thinks is on the screen, and what FEPI knows is on the screen.

A common error is an attempt to `EXEC CICS FEPI SEND FORMATTED KEYSTROKES` after a previous `EXEC CICS FEPI SEND FORMATTED KEYSTROKES` containing an Attention key. If a send contains an Attention key, then the next command to be issued must be an `EXEC CICS FEPI RECEIVE FORMATTED`. This confusion arises because of the ability to send multiple Attention keys in a single command. However, using multiple Attention keys is a special FEPI facility, and is not generally applicable.

However, there are a few 3270 protocol errors to be considered:

- FEPI has detected that you have turned the 'Input Inhibited' light on, and refuses to accept any data.
- You are using the Shift Escape sequences to emulate Double Byte Character Set input, and somehow have broken the DBCS rules.
- The underlying panel uses 3270 Extended Attributes (like 'Must Fill' or 'Must Enter') and the Keystroke sequence has failed the check.

These errors will all cause the command `EXEC CICS FEPI SEND FORMATTED KEYSTROKES` to fail (but note that, if using multiple Attentions, these errors may not be detected until a flow has been sent to the partner and the partner has responded).

Other errors involve the FEPI Conversation itself:

- Bad command sequencing (such as doing a Send when one was not expected).
- Problems involving `CONTENTION(LOSE)` on the Pool's Propertyset (see Sec. 16.2.2).

For both of these error categories, you probably have a bad FEPI application design. All I can suggest is that you examine your code, and remove any Keystroke sequences using multiple Attentions (for at least you will know where the problem has occurred).

# CHAPTER 31 Sending with Buffers

**GUIDANCE**

This chapter discusses the method of sending Formatted data using a screen image buffer. The alternative method for sending Formatted data via Keystrokes is discussed in Chapter 30.

Refer to Chapter 32 for information about obtaining the buffer.

## 31.1 Buffer concepts

When you send Formatted data using a Buffer you simply update an area which represents the fields contained on the emulated screen. This Buffer does not contain any 3270 Attribute Bytes (these are held internally under-the-covers by FEPI), but an Attribute Byte still occupies a single position in the Buffer.

When you update the buffer, you simply 'fill-in-the-blanks' by replacing the data for a field in the relevant place for it in the buffer. When the buffer is given to FEPI via an `EXEC CICS FEPI SEND FORMATTED` command (without the specification of the `KEYSTROKES` parameter) FEPI updates its internal copies of the screen, setting the Attribute bytes accordingly.

When giving the buffer to FEPI, you can either simply elect for the internal copy of the screen to be updated or ask for the partner to be sent the updated copy of the screen. When you send the flow to the partner, you specify which Attention key is used to send the screen.

As with all FEPI Formatted Conversations' functions, you must know the contents of the screen in order to update it. However, you can use the techniques discussed in Chapter 33 to discover the layout.

### 31.1.1 Obtaining the Buffer

The screen image Buffer used to update the screen is usually obtained from the prior execution of an `EXEC CICS FEPI RECEIVE FORMATTED` command. See Chapter 32 for details of this command.

## 31.2 The EXEC CICS FEPI SEND command for Formatted Buffer usage

The full description of the EXEC CICS FEPI SEND FORMATTED command for buffer usage is described in Sec. 27.4. However, it basically consists of:

```
EXEC CICS FEPI SEND FORMATTED
                    CONVID(char8)
                    FROM(char)   [FLENGTH(fixed31)]
                    AID(char1)   [CURSOR(fixed31)]
```

The data specified in the FROM parameter is the screen image Buffer containing updated (and unchanged) fields.

You do not have to supply the whole buffer. If you are interested in updating say, only the first two lines of an emulated 3278 Model 2, you would use a 160-byte area (and specify this via FLENGTH(160)).

If the AID parameter is not specified, then the contents of the supplied buffer are simply used to update the FEPI internal copy of the emulated terminal's display. When AID is specified, the contents of this screen are translated into a 3270 Datastream and sent to the partner system. The AID byte (specified using the values from the DFHAID copybook) details the attention key which the end user would have pressed to send the screen.

### 31.2.1 Attribute Byte processing

If you have obtained the buffer via the command EXEC CICS FEPI RECEIVE FORMATTED, then the Attribute Bytes will be represented in the buffer as X'FF's. In general, you do not specify Attribute Bytes for the fields you update. This is because you have no control over them (in exactly the same way you do not have any control over real Attribute Bytes on a terminal). If you change a field so that the field's buffer contents are different from FEPI's internal memory of the field, then FEPI notes that you have changed the field, and sets the preceding Attribute Byte accordingly.

However, FEPI does provide you with a method of setting the MDT for a field without altering the field contents. To do this, set the Attribute Byte to X'01'. The setting of X'01' is the only setting in Attribute Byte's position that FEPI recognizes.

### 31.2.2 Protected and Unprotected fields

When you build the buffer, you have to supply the whole of the screen fields. Therefore, you have to supply the contents of both Protected and Unprotected fields. If you have obtained the buffer from an EXEC CICS FEPI RECEIVE FORMATTED command, then these fields will be correctly set. An attempt to change a Protected field will result in an error.

### 31.2.3 The cursor position

If you wish to set the cursor position explicitly when the flow is sent to the partner system, then you can quote it using the CURSOR field. If this is not used, the position set when the previous EXEC CICS FEPI RECEIVE FORMATTED is used.

## 31.3 Buffer example

Consider that you are running an emulation of a 3270 Model 2 terminal. The first line of the screen consists in part of the fields shown in Fig. 31.1. The assembler DSECT applicable to this line is shown in Fig. 31.2:

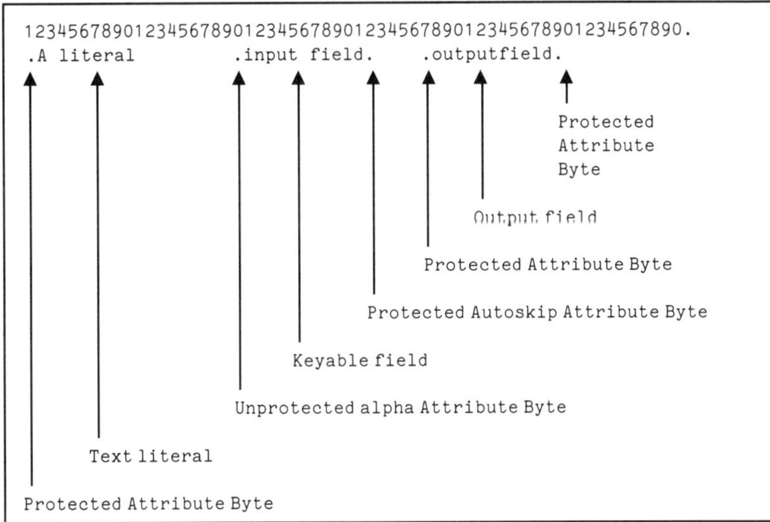


**Figure 31.1** Example 3270 screen showing Attribute Bytes

```
LINE01   DS  CL80
         ORG LINE01
ATR01    DS  XL1
LIT01    DS  CL18
ATR02    DS  XL1
INP02    DS  CL11
ATR02S   DS  XL1
PAD03    DS  XL4
ATR04    DS  XL1
OUT04    DS  CL12
ATR04S   DS  XL1
         ORG *
```

**Figure 31.1** Structure mapping

Thus, having received the buffer from an EXEC CICS FEPI RECEIVE FORMATTED command, it is simply updated with:

```
MVC INP02,=CL11'abcdefghijk'
```

and sent to the partner system with:

```
EXEC CICS FEPI SEND FORMATTED CONVID(...)
                    FROM(LINE01)
                    FLENGTH(80)
                    AID(ENTER)
```

# CHAPTER 32 Receiving with Buffers

**GUIDANCE**

This chapter details how you receive data over FEPI Formatted conversations using Buffers. An alternative method which returns data on a field-by-field basis is discussed in Chapter 33.

The FEPI Formatted Conversation's Buffer thus received is used in the formatted send operations, as discussed in Chapter 31.

## 32.1 Concepts

When you have sent a flow over a FEPI Formatted Conversation to a partner, you obtain the panel sent by the partner (in response to the flow) by doing an `EXEC CICS FEPI RECEIVE FORMATTED` command. This command waits for a flow from the partner system and then returns (Timeout facilities are available as discussed in Chapter 34). Section 32.3 discusses exactly what a completion means, and how you cope with it.

When you are issuing the `EXEC CICS FEPI RECEIVE FORMATTED` command, you can choose whether or not you want a Buffer containing an image of the screen to be returned. If you do not choose this option, then the contents of the screen must be obtained using the techniques discussed in Chapter 33.

Having obtained the flow from the partner, you reply to the partner by building a flow either using Keystrokes (see Chapter 30) or updating the buffer (see Chapter 31). In both cases, you have to know the layout of the screen. Chapter 33 discusses how you might find out what this is if you do not know, or if the partner has sent something that is unexpected.

## 32.2 The EXEC CICS FEPI RECEIVE FORMATTED command

The layout of the EXEC CICS FEPI RECEIVE command for Formatted Conversations is:

```
EXEC CICS FEPI RECEIVE FORMATTED
                           CONVID(char8)

[INTO(char)]   [FLENGTH(fixed31)]

[MAXFLENGTH(fixed31)]
[TIMEOUT(fixed31)]
[ALARMSTATUS(cvda)]
[COLUMNS(fixed31)]
[CURSOR(fixed31)]
[ENDSTATUS(cvda)]
[FIELDS(fixed31)]
[LINES(fixed31)]
[RESPSTATUS(cvda)]
```

### 32.2.1 Buffer reception

To obtain a Buffer representing the screen image (with Attribute Bytes noted as X'FF's), quote the INTO parameter. If you are only interested in the top part of the screen, then the length of the buffer can be specified via MAXFLENGTH. If MAXFLENGTH is not supplied, then the MAXFLENGTH setting on the Pool's Propertyset (see Sec. 16.2.9) is assumed.

If you choose to request only a partial screen image Buffer, then the rest of the screen information is lost. In this case, if you wish to find out the remaining contents of the screen, you have to use the EXEC CICS FEPI EXTRACT FIELD techniques discussed in Chapter 33.

In general, you should always receive all of the screen, so you must know what size of the Buffer is required to receive it all (i.e., the MAXFLENGTH setting for the Pool). If you need to provide a degree of terminal-type independence, an EXEC CICS FEPI INQUIRE POOL command (see Sec. 18.3.5) can be used to determine the required value. If you rely on the Pool's MAXFLENGTH defaulting on the EXEC CICS FEPI RECEIVE FORMATTED command, then you must ensure that the buffer is big enough. If it is not, then you will start getting CICS storage violations!

### 32.2.2 Screen parameters

As an aid to manipulating the screen Buffer, you can request the actual dimensions of the screen to be returned in the LINES and COLUMNS fields. You can then use these values to access the Buffer in array format.

The number of fields on the screen is likewise returned in the FIELDS parameter. You can use this parameter in scanning through the Buffer (if you are using one) for fields starting with X'FF' Attribute Bytes, or to determine the last field number for use with EXEC CICS FEPI EXTRACT FIELD commands (see Chapter 33).

The number of fields on the screen may be different to the number sent by the partner. This can occur if Datastream compression is in force (whereby, for example, adjacent protected fields are merged into one). The only thing I can say about this is to advise that Datastream compression software is not used for FEPI communication, and that you code application programs to access the buffer on a positional basis, not a field number basis.

The current cursor location is provided in the `CURSOR` parameter (the top left-hand corner is 0). You can use this position in combination with the `LINES` and `COLUMNS` fields to obtain the row/column position of the cursor.

If you are interested in knowing whether or not the emulated terminal 'beeped' when the flow was received, then use the `ALARMSTATUS` parameter to find out.

## 32.3 Knowing when you have everything

When you issue an `EXEC CICS FEPI RECEIVE FORMATTED` command (whether or not you are obtaining the screen image in a buffer), it completes as soon as any flow is received from the partner system. In VTAM terms, the command completes on *End of Chain* (see Chapter 23 and Sec. 37.1).

You determine what VTAM indicator was received on the chain by reference to the CVDA returned in the `ENDSTATUS` parameter. You should use this setting, together with an understanding of how the partner uses these VTAM indicators, to determine when the partner system has sent all that it is going to send.

If you determine that the partner system is going to send more data, then simply reissue the `EXEC CICS FEPI RECEIVE FORMATTED` command. When it completes, the returned Buffer will contain the union of the first flow and all subsequent ones. If you get this reception decision wrong, your `EXEC CICS FEPI RECEIVE FORMATTED` command will wait forever for a non-existent flow. Therefore, I recommend that you *always* quote a `TIMEOUT` setting on the command to remove this possibility.

### 32.3.1 CICS usage

Provided that you have set the terminal control RU sizes correctly in the partner CICS system, CICS will usually send a panel in three pieces: the (constant) header, the (constant) trailer, and the (variable) middle part. However, CICS will usually send a VTAM Change Direction (CD) Indicator on the last of these flows.

Therefore, you should keep issuing `EXEC CICS FEPI RECEIVE FORMATTED` commands until `ENDSTATUS` returns `CD`. When this is obtained, you know that all of the panel has been received. Alternatively, issue the first `EXEC CICS FEPI RECEIVE FORMATTED` without a `TIMEOUT` parameter, and then issue lots of `EXEC CICS FEPI RECEIVE FORMATTED TIMEOUT(1)` commands until they Timeout, indicating that the partner has sent everything.

### 32.3.2 IMS usage

IMS uses MFS to send its panels. Providing certain IMS buffers are set correctly, MFS tends to send everything in one lump with a VTAM End Bracket (EB) indicator.

Therefore, you should keep issuing `EXEC CICS FEPI RECEIVE FORMATTED` commands until `ENDSTATUS` returns `EB`. When this is obtained, then you know that all of the panel has been received. Alternatively, issue the first `EXEC CICS FEPI RECEIVE FORMATTED` without a `TIMEOUT` parameter, and then issue lots of `EXEC CICS FEPI RECEIVE FORMATTED TIMEOUT(1)s` until they Timeout, indicating that MFS has sent everything.

## 32.4 VTAM responses

The `RESPSTATUS` parameter shows what VTAM response is required to be forwarded to the partner system to show that the FEPI application has received the flow, and found it acceptable. See Chapter 53 for usage of this parameter. In general, you do not need to worry about `RESPSTATUS`, and you normally do not quote it upon the `EXEC CICS FEPI RECEIVE FORMATTED` command.

## 32.5 Obtaining Attribute Bytes and field information

If you need to determine the Attributes associated with a field, use the `EXEC CICS FEPI EXTRACT FIELD` command as described in Chapter 33. In fact, these `EXEC CICS FEPI EXTRACT FIELD` commands can be issued not only after an `EXEC CICS FEPI RECEIVE FORMATTED` command (with or without Buffer usage), but also at any time during a FEPI Formatted Conversation to determine the underlying FEPI image of the screen.

CHAPTER

# 33 Receiving with Fields

**GUIDANCE**

This chapter details the way individual field data is obtained for FEPI Formatted Conversations. Although these facilities provide an alternative way of processing a panel from the partner system to that using Buffer techniques (see Chapter 32), the command can be issued at any time during a Formatted Conversation.

## 33.1 Field concepts

FEPI Formatted Conversations work by FEPI maintaining internal representations of the emulated terminal's screen. FEPI implements the 3270 Datastream as defined in the *IBM 3270 Data Stream Programming Reference* manual.

Each field on the screen has an associated set of attributes. Some of these are physically transmitted with the 3270 flow sent from the partner, but some are generated from the context (such as a previous attribute byte). FEPI also maintains details about each field such as its length and contents.

All these field details can be obtained by use of the `EXEC CICS FEPI EXTRACT FIELD` command (which is provided only for Formatted Conversations). The command can be issued at any time during a FEPI Formatted Conversation, and the results are always up to date. This means that if the `EXEC CICS FEPI EXTRACT FIELD` is issued after an `EXEC CICS FEPI SEND FORMATTED` which does not result in a transmission, the returned information has been updated with the contents of the send.

The field for the `EXEC CICS FEPI EXTRACT FIELD` operation can be specified by either its screen position (in offset terms from the top left-hand corner) or its number on the screen. The quoted position may refer to any part of the field, not merely to the position of the Attribute Byte. Consequently, repeated use of `EXEC CICS FEPI EXTRACT FIELD` commands can be used to browse the screen, and so determine its layout if this is not known by the FEPI application program.

The number of fields on the screen may be different to the number sent by the partner. This can occur if Datastream compression is in force (whereby, for example, adjacent protected fields are merged into one). The only thing I can say about this is to advise that Datastream compression software is not used for FEPI communication. The application program should be aware of the possibility of field numbers 'randomly' changing.

## 33.2 The EXEC CICS FEPI EXTRACT FIELD command

The layout of the EXEC CICS FEPI EXTRACT FIELD command is:

```
EXEC CICS FEPI EXTRACT FIELD
                CONVID(char8)
                FIELDLOC(fixed31) FIELDNUM(fixed31)
[INTO(char)]  [FLENGTH(fixed31)]
[MAXFLENGTH(fixed31)]
[BACKGROUND(char1)]
[COLOR(char1)]
[FIELDATTR(char1)]
[HILIGHT(char1)]
[INPUTCONTROL(char1)]
[MDT(cvda)]
[OUTLINE(char1)]
[POSITION(fixed31)]
[PROTECT(cvda)]
[PS(char1)]
[SIZE(fixed31)]
[TRANSPARENCY(char1)]
[VALIDATION(char1)]
```

### 33.2.1 Specifying the field of interest

The field you wish to inquire upon is selected by either its position on the screen (starting from 0 at the top left-hand corner) or its field number (starting from 1 at the top left-hand corner of the screen). If specifying the field via FIELDLOC, the location need not be that of the field's Attribute Byte. FEPI knows where the ruling Attribute Byte is located, and so can return the relevant details. When specifying the number of the field on the screen, using FIELDNUM, the last field ends at the bottom right-hand corner of the screen, whether or not an Attribute Byte is in that position. The total number of fields on the screen can be determined by use of the FIELDS parameter on the prior EXEC CICS FEPI RECEIVE FORMATTED command.

#### BROWSING THE SCREEN

If you need to determine the full layout of the screen, then you can easily browse the screen by using EXEC CICS FEPI EXTRACT FIELD FIELDNUM(n) within a loop. When EIBRESP2(70) is returned, you have run off the end of the screen.

#### THE ACTUAL FIELD POSITION

For each field on the screen, the POSITION parameter returns the offset (starting from 0 at the top left-hand corner of the screen) of the first data byte (not the Attribute Byte) of the field.

#### THE SIZE OF THE FIELD

The size of the specified field is returned on the SIZE field. This length excludes the Attribute Byte.

### 33.2.2 Obtaining the field's contents

The INTO parameter will return the contents of the field. You quote the size of the area into which the field's contents are to be placed via the MAXFLENGTH parameter. When the EXEC CICS FEPI EXTRACT FIELD completes, the FLENGTH parameter contains the actual length of the data returned in INTO. If MAXFLENGTH is smaller than the actual field, then as much of the field is returned as possible.

Therefore, if you want to ensure that you obtain all the contents of the field, the worst case is an Unformatted screen. Thus, the size of the INTO field should be the MAXFLENGTH setting for the Pool (see Sec. 16.2.9). This setting can be obtained via an EXEC CICS FEPI INQUIRE POOL command (see Sec. 18.3.5) (and if required, the name of the Pool from an EXEC CICS FEPI EXTRACT CONV command, see Sec. 27.11).

As an alternative, you could issue two EXEC CICS FEPI EXTRACT FIELD commands, the first specifying the SIZE parameter. This returns the size of the field (excluding the Attribute Byte). The second invocation can be used to ensure that the INTO field is big enough for the information.

### 33.2.3 Obtaining the Attribute Bytes

All the attributes for a field can be obtained via the various parameters on the EXEC CICS FEPI EXTRACT FIELD command. The attribute settings (like colour and highlighting) are not interpreted. The standard BMS copybook DFHBMSCA contains the interpretations. However, all the attributes are documented in the *IBM 3270 Data Stream Programming Reference Manual.*

CHAPTER

# 34 The effect of Receive TIMEOUT usage

**GUIDANCE**

This chapter discusses the operation of the `TIMEOUT` parameter for `EXEC CICS FEPI RECEIVE` processing. The information in this chapter is applicable to both Formatted and Datastream access.

The operation of Timeout on the `EXEC CICS FEPI ALLOCATE` command is discussed in Sec. 29.2.1, and that for the `EXEC CICS FEPI START` command in Chapter 35.

The specification of `TIMEOUT(n)` on an `EXEC CICS FEPI RECEIVE` command (or the Receive part of an `EXEC CICS FEPI CONVERSE)` permits the command to terminate before a flow is obtained from the partner system.

If the flow from the partner has not arrived when the `EXEC CICS FEPI RECEIVE` command is executed, then FEPI will wait for the number of seconds specified in the `TIMEOUT` parameter for the flow to arrive. If the flow does not arrive in the interval, then the command will terminate with a Timeout indication (EIBRESP2=213).

If `TIMEOUT` is not specified on the command (or is set to 0), the `EXEC CICS FEPI RECEIVE` will wait forever for the flow to happen.

## 34.1 Recovering from a Timeout

If the `EXEC CICS FEPI RECEIVE` has timed out, then the partner has not sent a flow within the given interval. This leads to the question about what to do next. You should first consider simply reissuing the `EXEC CICS FEPI RECEIVE` command. A Timeout does not affect the operation of a subsequent `EXEC CICS FEPI RECEIVE` which succeeds in obtaining the flow from the partner system.

If you are running the FEPI Conversation with separate `EXEC CICS FEPI SEND` and `EXEC CICS FEPI RECEIVE` commands, then you already have an interval for the partner to respond to the Send request before the Receive gets issued. You may well choose to design your FEPI application so that you are doing additional processing in this interval. Therefore, you might take the view that if the partner has not responded within one second of the `EXEC CICS FEPI RECEIVE` being issued, there is a problem. However, it could simply be that the partner system, or the network, is a bit slow.

Consequently, your application program has to decide whether or not it is worth reissuing the `EXEC CICS FEPI RECEIVE` with another Timeout, issuing a full `EXEC CICS FEPI RECEIVE` and waiting until the partner responds (not really recommended), or doing error processing.

I would *always* recommend that you choose a suitable `TIMEOUT(n)` for the `EXEC CICS FEPI RECEIVE` operation. 'Suitable' means thinking about the worst case for partner response time (at peak loadings). Thus, if the partner does not respond in this interval you can assume that an error has occurred, and act accordingly.

Another design would be to use polling techniques, and issue as many `EXEC CICS FEPI RECEIVE TIMEOUT(1)`s as are required to get the flow from the partner. The advantage of using lots of small interval Receives is that you are allowing the CICS task scheduler to give service to the transaction, and that you have the opportunity to stop the Receives after a decent quantity.

If your FEPI application design is using asynchronous techniques, then a Timeout in the Receive operation should be processed by the transaction `EXEC CICS START`ing itself in order to reissue the Receive operation. If the partner fails during an `EXEC CICS FEPI RECEIVE` operation, then the Receive command will immediately terminate with an error (EIBRESP2(215)).

## 34.2 Unsolicited Data Handler's first Receive

When an Unsolicited Data Handler is scheduled, the first `EXEC CICS FEPI RECEIVE` will not require the specification of a `TIMEOUT`, because the circumstance which generated the Unsolicited Data Handler will ensure the relevant flow has occurred. However, just to be on the safe side, you could use `TIMEOUT(1)`, and then use a Timeout failure to raise an error.

## 34.3 EXEC CICS FEPI STARTed transaction's first Receive

A transaction that is `EXEC CICS FEPI START`ed will be initiated in several ways:

- A Timeout expired without a flow from the partner.
- The partner failed.
- Data arrived from the partner system.

The reason why the transaction started is obtained from the `EXEC CICS RETRIEVE`d Start Data (see Sec. D.2).

You should ensure that the first `EXEC CICS FEPI RECEIVE` does contain a `TIMEOUT(1)` parameter to ensure that an internal application logic failure does not cause the transaction to wait forever if the Receive is erroneously executed when the transaction has not started due to a data flow from the partner.

## 34.4 The Begin Session Handler's first Receive

If you are coding a generic Begin Session Handler, you can use the `TIMEOUT` parameter to avoid consideration of the `INITIALDATA` parameter (see Sec. 16.2.8) for the Pool. If the Begin Session Handler is involved when the first flow occurs, then the first `EXEC CICS FEPI RECEIVE` should complete immediately. However, if the Begin Session Handler is invoked without waiting for the first flow, then specification of `TIMEOUT(1)` should be used to prevent the Begin Session Handler from an eternal wait. Therefore, to be on the safe side, use `TIMEOUT(1)` on the first `EXEC CICS FEPI RECEIVE`.

CHAPTER

# 35 EXEC CICS FEPI START and asynchronous operation

**GUIDANCE**

This chapter discusses the operation of the EXEC CICS FEPI START command. The chapter is equally applicable to Formatted access and Datastream access.

The EXEC CICS FEPI START command requests the continuation of the FEPI Conversation in another CICS transaction. The subsequent transaction is to be initiated when the partner responds. Once the EXEC CICS FEPI START command has been issued, the FEPI Conversation is not available for use in the issuing transaction.

The format of the EXEC CICS FEPI START command is:

```
EXEC CICS FEPI START
               CONVID(char8)

TRANSID(char4)
[TERMID(char4)]

[USERDATA(char) [FLENGTH(fixed31)]]

[TIMEOUT(fixed31)]
```

The named transaction will start (either at the specified terminal or in background mode) when the partner responds (to a prior EXEC CICS FEPI SEND) or fails. If TIMEOUT is specified, then the transaction will start after the requested interval, even if the partner has not sent a flow.

If TIMEOUT is not specified (or set to 0), then the transaction will not be initiated until either the partner fails or a flow arrives. If the EXEC CICS FEPI START is issued when there is a flow which could be EXEC CICS FEPI RECEIVEd, then the transaction will start immediately.

## 35.1 What the started transaction should do

When the EXEC CICS FEPI STARTed transaction is initiated, Start Data is provided by FEPI to let the transaction know why it got going. The layout of this Start Data is described in Sec. D.2.

This Start Data has to be obtained via an EXEC CICS RETRIEVE command. If you do not get the Start Data, then the usual CICS rules for transaction initiation apply, and the transaction will be initiated another five times (or until the Start Data is obtained).

The EVENTTYPE field in the Start Data contains a CVDA which describes why the transaction was started:

**DATA** A flow arrived from the partner (the expected event).

**SESSIONLOST** The partner failed while awaiting a flow.

**TIMEOUT** A flow did not arrive in the specified interval.

The CONVID for the FEPI Conversation that is being continued in the new transaction is obtained from the CONVID field in the Start Data.

You should obtain use of the FEPI Connection in the EXEC CICS FEPI STARTed transaction by quoting the Convid in an EXEC CICS FEPI ALLOCATE PASSCONVID(convid) command. Once this has been done, all the usual FEPI commands and operations are available for use.

If, for some reason, the FEPI Conversation is not EXEC CICS FEPI ALLOCATE PASSCONVIDied, then the FEPI Connection will hang forever. This can be detected via CEMT I FECONN, which shows a state of PENDSTART (PENDDATA is shown in the interval before the initiation of the EXEC CICS FEPI STARTed transaction). The Connection can only be reused by recycling it using ACQSTATUS(RELEASED) and then ACQSTATUS(ACQUIRED) (see Chapter 19).

### 35.1.1 Detecting that FEPI initated the transaction

You can tell if FEPI initiated the transaction by use of the EXEC CICS ASSIGN STARTCODE command. This returns 'SZ' if FEPI initiated the transaction. I recommend that you *always* check the STARTCODE, so that you can cope with any unexpected initiations. This STARTCODE will also be returned within Handler transactions.

# CHAPTER 36 EXEC CICS FEPI FREE

**GUIDANCE**

This chapter discusses the EXEC CICS FEPI FREE command, and how the options on it control FEPI Connections. The description is applicable to both Formatted and Datastream accesses.

## 36.1 Concepts

When a FEPI application program wants to give up usage of a Conversation, it can issue either an EXEC CICS FEPI START command (described in Chapter 35) or an EXEC CICS FEPI FREE command. The EXEC CICS FEPI FREE command says not only that the FEPI application program is giving up usage of the FEPI Conversation, but also that the underlying FEPI Connection is to be manipulated. The format of the EXEC CICS FEPI FREE command is:

```
EXEC CICS FEPI FREE
[HOLD|RELEASE|FORCE|PASS]
CONVID(char8)
```

The various options (HOLD, RELEASE, FORCE, and PASS) control the disposition of the FEPI Conversation named in the CONVID parameter and the status of the underlying Connection.

## 36.2 Free options

The action of the parameters depend on where the EXEC CICS FEPI FREE is issued. Table 36.1 gives a detailed description of the positions, but can be generalized to:

**HOLD** End the current Conversation, and keep the underlying Connection acquired (HOLD is the default option).

**PASS** The FEPI Conversation is to be resumed in another CICS transaction.

**RELEASE** End the current FEPI Conversation, but RELEASE the underlying FEPI Connection.

**FORCE** End the current FEPI Conversation, and STOP the underlying FEPI Connection

**Table 36.1** EXEC CICS FEPI FREE options

| EXEC CICS FEPI FREE option | Application program | Begin Session Handler | End Session Handler | Unsolicited Data Handler | STSN Handler |
|---|---|---|---|---|---|
| HOLD (default) | The Conversation is ended. The underlying Connection is unchanged. | The Begin Session Conversation is ended. The underlying Connection is unchanged. Application programming use of the Connection can proceed. | The End Session Conversation is ended. If CICS shutdown is proceeding, the underlying Connection is released, otherwise it is unchanged. | The Unsolicited Data Conversation is ended. The underlying Connection is unchanged. | The STSN Conversation is ended. The underlying Connection is unchanged. Application programming use of the Connection can proceed. |
| PASS | The Conversation is maintained for use in another CICS transaction. The underlying Connection is unchanged. However, during CICS shutdown, this setting results in the Connection being released. | | | | |
| RELEASE | The Conversation is ended. The underlying Connection is released (with usage of the End Session (End of Connection) Handler, if defined). | The Begin Session Conversation is ended. The underlying Connection is released (with usage of the End Session (End of Connection) Handler, if defined). Application programming usage of the Connection is not permitted. | The End Session Conversation is ended. The underlying Connection is released. | The Unsolicited Data Conversation is ended. The underlying Connection is released (with usage of the End Session (End of Connection) Handler, if defined). | The STSN Conversation is ended. The underlying Connection is released (with usage of the End Session (End of Connection) Handler, if defined). Application programming usage of the Connection is not permitted. |
| FORCE | The Conversation is ended. The underlying Connection is stopped. | | | | |

### 36.2.1 Application programming usage

The operation of the EXEC CICS FEPI FREE options within a FEPI application program is as follows:

**HOLD** The current Conversation is ended, and the underlying Connection kept Acquired (HOLD is the default option).

Once the FEPI Conversation is EXEC CICS FEPI FREE HOLDed, then the Conversation no longer exists. The underlying Connection can be reused by another Conversation.

**PASS** The FEPI Conversation is to be resumed in another CICS transaction.

The CONVID is being manually supplied to the subsequent transaction.

**RELEASE** End the current FEPI Conversation, but Release the underlying FEPI Connection.

This option is like `HOLD`, but the underlying Connection is released. Consequently, when the Connection is next used, the Begin Session Handler (if defined) will be initiated.

**FORCE** End the current FEPI Conversation, and stop the underlying FEPI Connection.

This is a *hard stop* for the Connection. It should be used only when you wish to emulate a 'pulling the plug' on the partner system's 'terminal'.

## 36.2.2 Begin Session Handler usage

The operation of the `EXEC CICS FEPI FREE` options within a Begin Session Handler is as follows:

**HOLD** The Begin Session Conversation is ended, and the underlying Connection kept Acquired (`HOLD` is the default option).

As the Begin Session Conversation has ended, this permits the `EXEC CICS FEPI ALLOCATE` command to complete (if this caused the Begin Session Handler to be initiated).

**PASS** The FEPI Conversation is to be resumed in another CICS transaction.

The `CONVID` is being manually supplied to the subsequent transaction.

**RELEASE** End the Begin Session Conversation, but Release the underlying FEPI Connection.

This option is like `HOLD`, but the underlying Connection is released. Consequently, when the Connection is next used, another Begin Session Handler will be initiated. Hence, a FEPI application program's `EXEC CICS FEPI ALLOCATE`'s processing will attempt to select another Connection.

**FORCE** End the Begin Session Conversation, and stop the underlying FEPI Connection.

This is a *hard stop* for the Connection. It should be used only when you wish to emulate a 'pulling the plug' on the partner system's 'terminal'.

## 36.2.3 End Session Handler usage

The operation of the `EXEC CICS FEPI FREE` options within an End Session Handler is as follows:

**HOLD** The current Conversation is ended, and the underlying Connection kept Acquired (`HOLD` is the default option).

However, if the End Session Handler is executing during CICS shutdown, the Connection will be Released (and thus deleted).

**PASS** The FEPI Conversation is to be resumed in another CICS transaction.

The `CONVID` is being manually supplied to the subsequent transaction. This operation is not permitted during CICS shutdown processing.

**RELEASE** End the current FEPI Conversation, but Release the underlying FEPI Connection.

If the End Session Handler is running during CICS shutdown, this will result in the Connection being deleted.

**FORCE** End the current FEPI Conversation, and stop the underlying FEPI Connection.

This is a *hard stop* for the Connection. It should be used only when you wish to emulate a 'pulling the plug' on the partner system's 'terminal'.

### 36.2.4 Unsolicited Data Handler usage

The operation of the `EXEC CICS FEPI FREE` options within an Unsolicited Data Handler is as follows:

**HOLD** The Unsolicited Data Conversation is ended, and the underlying Connection kept Acquired (`HOLD` is the default option).

**PASS** The FEPI Conversation is to be resumed in another CICS transaction.

The `CONVID` is being manually supplied to the subsequent transaction.

**RELEASE** End the Unsolicited Data Conversation, but Release the underlying FEPI Connection.

This option is like `HOLD`, but the underlying Connection is released. This should stop the partner system sending any more data.

**FORCE** End the Unsolicited Data Conversation, and stop the underlying FEPI Connection.

This is a *hard stop* for the Connection. It should be used only when you wish to emulate a 'pulling the plug' on the partner system's 'terminal'. This is a harder way of not getting any more Unsolicited Data than doing a `RELEASE.`

### 36.2.5 STSN Handler usage

The operation of the `EXEC CICS FEPI FREE` options within an STSN Handler is as follows:

**HOLD** The STSN Conversation is ended, and the underlying Connection kept Acquired (`HOLD` is the default option).

This permits normal FEPI application programming usage of the LU0 (SLUP) Connection.

**PASS** The FEPI Conversation is to be resumed in another CICS transaction.

The CONVID is being manually supplied to the subsequent transaction.

**RELEASE** End the STSN Conversation, but Release the underlying FEPI Connection.

This option is like HOLD, but the underlying Connection is released. Consequently, no further application program usage of the Connection is permitted.

**FORCE** End the STSN Conversation, and stop the underlying FEPI Connection.

This is a *hard stop* for the Connection. It should be used only when you wish to emulate a 'pulling the plug' on the partner system's 'terminal'.

# PART 5

# Datastream programming

**GUIDANCE**

This part of the book contains information about FEPI Datastream programming. The information is aimed at Passthrough programs.

The following topics are discussed in this part of the book:

- 3270 Datastreams and VTAM
- Structured Fields
- The EXEC CICS Terminal Control API for FEPI Passthrough operations
- Datastream programming considerations
- Datastream programming techniques
- Passthrough program

CHAPTER

# 37 3270 Datastreams and VTAM

**GUIDANCE**

This chapter contains background information on 3270 Datastreams and VTAM processing. It extends the description given in Chapter 20.

You should refer to these books for more information:

- *SNA Formats Manual*
- *VTAM Programming Manual*
- *IBM 3270 Data Stream Programming Reference*

## 37.1 VTAM flows

When a terminal sends a flow to a host, VTAM may parcel the flow up into various items (so VTAM may send a flow of 500 bytes in two 250-byte parts). Each of these parts is called a *Request Unit* (RU), together they form a *Chain*. The `EXEC CICS FEPI RECEIVE DATASTREAM` command can choose to Receive either each individual RU, or the whole Chain. However, for normal 3270 devices, a single RU is usually sufficient to contain a single Chain.

### 37.1.1 SNA RU indicators

Each RU carries (as part of its header information) indicators as to its position in the chain (see the *SNA Formats Manual* for details). These indicators are not directly available to FEPI application programs, but can be inferred from the `ENDSTATUS` CVDA returned on the command `EXEC CICS FEPI RECEIVE DATASTREAM RU()`:

| RU Chain indicator | `ENDSTATUS` CVDA setting |
|---|---|
| **First in Chain** | `RU`, on the first RU obtained |
| **Middle in Chain** | `RU`, on a subsequent RU |
| **Last in Chain** | `LIC` |

The `LIC` CVDA will only be obtained if the `CD` or `EB` indicators are not present. The layout of the `EXEC CICS FEPI RECEIVE DATASTREAM` command is described in Sec. 27.7.

FEPI does not provide the ability to transmit an individual RU; it only provides access at the RU level to received data.

### 37.1.2 SNA Chains

The SNA Chain (consisting of one or more RUs) represents a chunk of data sent to or from a device. Whenever an `EXEC CICS FEPI SEND DATASTREAM` is executed, a Chain is transmitted to the partner system. The `EXEC CICS FEPI RECEIVE DATASTREAM` command takes the `CHAIN` option to obtain a whole Chain's worth of data at one go (this Chain may consist of one or more RUs), with all the component RUs joined together. The individual RUs making up the Chain are not distinguishable (this is an advantage!).

The Chain is formatted according to the 3270 Protocol:

- For FEPI Inbound data (that is EXEC CICS FEPI RECEIVE DATASTREAMed), the Chain may contain:
  - A Single Byte Command Code identifying the operation to be done on the 'terminal'. This is always present, and is the first byte in the Chain.
  - A Single Byte Write Control Character, controlling things like Keyboard Unlocking and the Alarm.
  - Structured Field Data.
  - 'Normal' 3270 Attribute Bytes, Orders, and data.
- For FEPI Outbound Data (that is `EXEC CICS FEPI SEND DATASTREAM`ed), the Chain consists of:
  - A single byte identifying the AID (PF key) used to send the data from the terminal to FEPI.
  - Two bytes showing the current cursor position (encoded in 12-bit format).
  - 3270 Attribute Bytes, Orders, and data

The great majority of the code involved at the FEPI Datastream level involves manipulating these flows.

If you choose to process Inbound data at the RU level, then the first RU to be obtained will contain the Single Byte Control Code which determines how the following flow(s) is (are) to be processed.

### 37.1.3 Brackets

SNA Chains flow between the 'terminal' and the 'host' within an SNA *Bracket.* If the two ends are not currently in communication, then they are *Out of Bracket*, and in *Contention State*. While in Contention State, each side may decide to send a flow. If both sides attempt to communicate at the same time whilst in Contention State, then some rules determine which side wins the race. In FEPI terms, this is controlled by the `CONTENTION` parameter on the Propertyset for the owning Pool (see Sec. 16.2.2).

Each Chain may either continue the Bracket, or End it. The CVDA returned in the ENDSTATUS parameter of the `EXEC CICS FEPI RECEIVE DATASTREAM` shows whether or not the Chain ended the Bracket.

| ENDSTATUS CVDA | SNA MEANING |
|---|---|
| **EB** | The Chain ended the Bracket, so the partner will not send any more data. |
| **CD** | The Chain did not end the Bracket, but it is now the FEPI application program's turn to send a flow to the partner system. |
| **LIC** | The partner system will send some more data within the bracket |

Chapter 23 outlines how these indicators relate to the FEPI application program's processing. In particular, the EB and CD indicators are vital evidence in determining whether or not all of the partner's data has been obtained.

Brackets start to become important only when the partner can send data at any moment, and so this flow may occur against the 'logical' state of the communication. When an EXEC CICS FEPI SEND is issued outside of a bracket, then FEPI attempts to start the Bracket. If the partner has sent some data which is waiting to be received, the CONTENTION setting on the Pool's Propertyset (see Sec. 16.2.2) determines whether or not the EXEC CICS FEPI SEND succeeds or is rejected.

### 37.1.4 EXEC CICS FEPI RECEIVE DATASTREAM options

The EXEC CICS FEPI RECEIVE DATASTREAM command (see Sec. 27.7) will terminate according to the RU, CHAIN or UNTILCDEB options.

#### UNTILCDEB

The UNTILCDEB option will obtain multiple Chains. This might, at first sight, appear to be the ideal option for Datastream programming. However, the problem is that you cannot distinguish between the various Chains. Each of these Chains starts with a Command Code which determines what the FEPI application program should do with the Chain.

Therefore, in general, obtaining Multiple Chains is not terribly helpful. The exception is when you are not going to send the data onto a real terminal. When obtaining the data merely to scan it, you do not need to process the individual Command Codes and so you can obtain all the Chains together. However, if you then decide that, after all, you need to transmit the data to a terminal, you cannot do so, as there is no way of breaking up the data into the individual chunks starting with the Command Code. Therefore, I recommend *not* using the UNTILCDEB option on any EXEC CICS FEPI RECEIVE DATASTREAM command.

#### RU

It is not helpful to process the data on a RU basis, as you have to build up the set of RUs to make the complete flow to the terminal. Therefore, the EXEC CICS FEPI RECEIVE DATASTREAM RU command should not normally be used.

#### CHAIN

The CHAIN option is the one to use on most (if not all) EXEC CICS FEPI RECEIVE DATASTREAM commands. It provides the whole flow, controlled by the first byte (the Command Code).

## 37.2 3270 Command Codes for FEPI Inbound data

The first byte of a Chain obtained by the `EXEC CICS FEPI RECEIVE DATASTREAM CHAIN` consists of a Command Code. These Command Codes are documented in the *IBM 3270 Data Stream Programming Reference*. Each of these Command Codes results in different processing in the FEPI application program. These techniques are discussed in Sec. 41. 2.
The defined Command Codes for Inbound data are:

| COMMAND CODE | ACTION |
|---|---|
| **X'F1'** | Write |
| **X'F5'** | Erase Write |
| **X'7E'** | Erase Write Alternate |
| **X'F3'** | Write Structured Field |
| **X'F2'** | Read Buffer |
| **X'F6'** | Read Modified |
| **X'6E'** | Read Modified All |
| **X'6F'** | Erase All Unprotected |

### WRITE
The Write Command is used to format and display the screen of a 'real' terminal. Multiple Write commands will overwrite the screen on a field-by-field basis. The Write Command is the 'normal' mode of operation.

### ERASE WRITE
The Erase Write Command is similar to the Write Command, except that the screen is first cleared before the display is built. Therefore, multiple Erase Write Commands will lose all the data apart from that sent on the last command. The Erase Write Command is usually sent when the host system has lost (or does not know) what is currently on the screen, and so needs to clear it before a new panel is displayed.

### ERASE WRITE ALTERNATE
This command is similar to the Erase Write Command, except that the screen is switched into its alternate size before the panel is built. There is no direct `EXEC CICS` Terminal Control Command which generates this 3270 Command Code.

### WRITE STRUCTURED FIELD
This command shows that the following data is not in the 'usual' 3270 format, but in 3270 Structured Field Format. This layout is discussed in Chapter 38.

### READ BUFFER
The Read Buffer Command does not send data to the terminal; rather, it requests that the terminal return its current display. Therefore, when this command is sent to the terminal, a reply will be generated.

### READ MODIFIED
The Read Modified Command works like the Read Buffer Command, except that all of the screen is not returned. Instead, only those fields which would be sent when an AID key is pressed (those fields whose Modified Data Tag has been set via either Attribute Byte or field usage) are returned. Therefore, if a Clear, PA1, PA2 or PA3 key was used, no field data is sent.

### READ MODIFIED ALL

The Read Modified All Command works like the Read Buffer Command, except that all of the screen is not returned. Instead, only those fields that have been keyed (those whose Modified Data Tag has been set via either Attribute Byte or field usage) are returned. The fields are returned no matter what AID key was used. There are no `EXEC CICS` Terminal Control Commands which generate this Command Code.

### ERASE ALL UNPROTECTED

The Erase All Unprotected Command works like the Erase Write Command, except that it clears only Unprotected Fields, not the whole screen. There are no `EXEC CICS` Terminal Control Commands which generate this Command Code.

## **37.3** Write Control Character for FEPI Inbound data

After the Write, Erase Write, Erase Write Alternate, and Erase All Unprotected command codes, the second byte of the 3270 Inbound Data Stream is the Write Control Character (WCC). The WCC controls things like Keyboard Unlock, and sounding the alarm. In general, if running a Passthrough program, this should be saved for further usage.

## **37.4** 3270 Data format for FEPI Outbound data

The FEPI 3270 Outbound data format (i.e. that `EXEC CICS FEPI SEND DATASTREAM`ed) consists of the 'normal' 3270 datastream proceeded by a three-byte prefix:

- A single byte showing the AID key pressed (or that no AID is present!).
- Two bytes showing the cursor position in 12-bit format (see Sec. 37.4.1 and Chapter 42).

### 37.4.1 12-bit cursor position

3270 Devices use either a 12-bit, 14-bit, or 16-bit format for the cursor position. However, the 14- and 16-bit implementations are device dependent. All devices will accept a 12-bit cursor position, and so this is the format that the FEPI application program must use.

The Cursor position obtained in `EIBCPOSN` (16-bit) has to be converted into 12-bit format before it is `EXEC CICS FEPI SEND DATASTREAM`ed to the partner system. Thus, a format of B'abcdefgh ijklmnop' has to turn into B'01efghij 00klmnop', and then be turned into a printable format. Section 42.6 gives a code fragment to do this.

# CHAPTER 38 Structured Fields

**GUIDANCE**

This chapter discusses some of the implications of 3270 Structured Fields upon FEPI Datastream processing. The *IBM 3270 Data Stream Programming Reference* describes these fields.

## 38.1 Overview

3270 Structured Fields provide an alternative method of generating a display. This processing was introduced to support multipartitioned displays (like the 3290 panel), but this datastream has now been extended to support other 3270 functions. In particular, Structured Fields are used by CICS Terminal Control to determine the characteristics of a Terminal. CICS sends a *Structured Field Query* when it initially contacts the terminal, in order to determine screen size, colour support, etc. This operation is under the control of the `QUERY` parameter of the terminal's `TYPETERM`, and so the query can be prevented from flowing by specifying `QUERY(NO)`. IMS does not use this function.

Structured Fields do not flow in the same Chain as a 'normal' 3270 Datastream; this applies to both FEPI Inbound and FEPI Outbound processing.

When consulting the *IBM 3270 Data Stream Programming Reference*, remember that FEPI Inbound equates to 3270 Outbound, and FEPI Outbound is 3270 Inbound.

## 38.2 FEPI Inbound Structured Fields

FEPI Structured Field Inbound flows are identified by the X'F3' Command Code. A WCC (the second byte) is not present for a Structured Field Command.

After the Structured Field Command code, there follows a set of Structured Field elements. These elements follow a fixed format of X'llllcc...', where llll is a two-byte length of element (including itself), and cc is the one-byte operation. Most elements contain a subcode indicating a particular operation flavour.

Some of the Structured Field Operations are:

| OPERATION | ID |
|---|---|
| **X'40'** | The element contains a 3270 Datastream |
| **X'01'** | The operation is a Read (a subcode of X'02' indicates a Read Partition Query). |

If you are running a Passthrough program, you use the `STRFIELD` variants of the CICS Terminal Control Commands (see Chaper 39) to send Structured Field Data to a 'real' terminal. However, you have to scan the Structured Field elements themselves in order to take the correct actions for a Read operation. This is in contrast to the normal 3270 Datastream, where the Command Code is solely used to determine the Terminal Control operations performed.

## 38.3 FEPI Outbound Structured Fields

FEPI Outbound Structured Fields follow the same format as for FEPI Inbound flows. The flow is preceded by X'88' to indicate the following information is in Structured Field format, not normal 3270 format. Following this pseudo-AID byte there is no cursor position information. Instead, a series of Structured Field elements immediately follow the X'88' AID byte (the layout is the same as for FEPI Inbound).

If you are running a Passthrough program, then CICS Terminal Control Commands will supply information in the Structured Field format, and all you have to do is prefix it with the X'88' before you `EXEC CICS FEPI SEND DATASTREAM` it to the partner system.

However, if you are not running a Passthrough program, or there is no real end-user terminal to send a flow to, you will have to format a suitable response to Structured Field data. In particular, you may have to do this for a Structured Field Query (when processing it in a Handler transaction, for example).

You should take care to issue a reply to each FEPI Inbound Structured Field element that requires one. If you do not know the correct answer, then return a default reply, but *be sure* you do reply. If CICS Sends a Structured Field Query to your FEPI application program, then CICS expects a reply. If this reply is not forthcoming, then the CICS terminal is locked. If you do not know exactly the characteristics of a real terminal, you should reply with a null (the Structured Field is X'000481FF"), indicating that the emulated terminal does not support any 3270 functions other than the base set.

CHAPTER 39

# The EXEC CICS Terminal Control API for FEPI Passthrough operations

**GUIDANCE**

This chapter outlines how the CICS Terminal Control API is used for FEPI Passthrough operations. You should consult the *CICS/ESA Application Programming Reference Book* for full details.

## 39.1 EXEC CICS RECEIVE

The EXEC CICS RECEIVE command is used both to receive data from a terminal in the normal course of events, and to initiate Read Buffer operations.

If you are running a Passthrough program, then you should EXEC CICS RECEIVE the flow three bytes into the buffer (so that you can insert the three-byte prefix). Use the FLENGTH parameter to avoid converting CICS halfword lengths to FEPI's fullword lengths. You should ensure that the buffer is big enough to cope with all the 3270 Datastream.

The BUFFER option says that you want to read all the contents of the screen, not wait for the user to press an AID key. This option is used to perform the 'Read Buffer' operation.

The ASIS option is used to perform a 'Read Modified' operation (this is the same option used to perform a usual Receive operation). CICS terminal control does not provide a method of generating the 'Read Modified All' operation, a 'Read Buffer' should be done instead.

## 39.2 EXEC CICS SEND

The EXEC CICS SEND command is used to send a 3270 Datastream to the terminal. If the datastream is composed of Structured Fields, then the STRFIELD option should be specified.

If the screen is to be cleared before the datastream is placed on the panel, use the ERASE option (the 3270 Erase Write Command). If ERASE is omitted, then the datastream is added to the existing display (the 3270 Write Command).

The CTLCHAR parameter should specify the Write Control Code (the second byte of a FEPI Inbound Datastream) which controls the sounding of the alarm and the unlocking of the keyboard.

## 39.3 EXEC CICS CONVERSE

In general, you should not use the EXEC CICS CONVERSE command to communicate with a real terminal. If you do so, then you are running a CICS conversational program, which will tie up CICS resources unnecessarily.

However, you *must* use an EXEC CICS CONVERSE STRFIELD in order to process a Structured Field Query Command at the terminal. The *CICS/ESA Application Programming Reference Book* explicitly states that if you are asking a terminal to supply its characteristics via a Structured Field Query operation, you have to use the EXEC CICS CONVERSE STRFIELD command.

# CHAPTER 40 Datastream programming considerations

## GUIDANCE

This chapter outlines some of the considerations applicable to FEPI Datastream programming. However, Formatted programming techniques are also relevant.

## 40.1 3270 orders

When you are running a FEPI Datastream Conversation which is not a Passthrough Conversation, you must be aware of all aspects of the 3270 Datastream as described in *IBM 3270 Data Stream Programming Reference*. In particular, you must take account of the fact that a subsequent element may overwrite, or otherwise modify, a preceding element.

The FEPI application program must be able to cope with all the following 3270 Orders in the FEPI Inbound (3270 Outbound) Datastream:

| CODE | 3270 ORDER |
|---|---|
| **X'1D'** | Start Field (SF) |
| **X'29'** | Start Field Extended (SFE) |
| **X'11'** | Set Buffer Address (SBA) |
| **X'28'** | Set Attribute (SA) |
| **X'2C'** | Modify Field (MF) |
| **X'13'** | Insert Cursor (IC) |
| **X'05'** | Program Tab (PT) |
| **X'3C'** | Repeat to Address (RA) |
| **X'12'** | Erase Unprotected to Address (EUA) |
| **X'08'** | Graphic Escape (GE) |

On a FEPI Outbound Datastream (3270 Inbound) only SF, SFE, SBA, SA and GE codes will be present.

### 40.1.1 3270 order descriptions

You should consult the *IBM 3270 Data Stream Programming Reference* for full details of 3270 Orders.

#### START FIELD (SF)

SF indicates the start of a 3270 Field. The next byte will be an Attribute Byte.

#### START FIELD EXTENDED (SFE)

The SFE is an alternative method of defining a field to the SF order. The format of the SFE is as follows:

- A single byte defining the number of definitions that follow.
- A two-byte definition consisting of a Attribute Type and an Attribute setting.

The SFE order is used where background colour definition is used, or where 3270 Extended Attributes like 'Underline' or 'Must Fill' are present.

#### SET BUFFER ADDRESS (SBA)

The SBA order defines a position on the display for the following field. It is followed by a two-byte position. The position can be specified as either a 12-bit or a 14-bit position (if no other action is taken). The 14-bit position is in format B'00cdefgh ijklmnop' (from a 16-bit position of B'abcdefgh ijklmnop').

#### SET ATTRIBUTE (SA)

The Set Attribute order is followed by a two-byte pair defining an Attribute and its setting. This attribute is then assumed for all following fields, unless it is explicitly overridden. The SA command is most commonly used to set colour.

#### MODIFY FIELD (MF)

The layout of the MF order is exactly the same as that for SFE. However, the MF order updates the settings for the current field without altering its contents.

#### INSERT CURSOR (IC)

IC is a single-byte order that positions the cursor at the current position. If a Datastream contains multiple IC orders, then the last one determines the cursor position.

#### PROGRAM TAB (PT)

PT is a single-byte Order that updates the current position to that of the start of the next unprotected field.

#### REPEAT TO ADDRESS (RA)

The RA order takes a two-byte position, and a single character. This single character is repeated on the screen from the current position to the given position. The specification of the end address follows the rules for SBA processing. Note that if operating in Double Byte Character Set mode, this single character is not one byte long!

#### ERASE UNPROTECTED TO ADDRESS (EUA)

EUA takes a two-byte cursor position, formatted according to the SBA rules. The EUA order overwrites all Unprotected Fields on the display from the current position to the given position with nulls (X'00').

### GRAPHIC ESCAPE (GE)

The GE order allows the selection of characters from an alternate character set supported by the display (for example, the APL character set).

## 40.2 3270 format control orders

The 3270 Format Control Orders are embedded within the 3270 Datastream, and provide special field display options:

| CODE | 3270 FORMAT |
|---|---|
| **X'00'** | A Null (NUL) |
| **X'3F'** | Substitute (SUB) |
| **X'1C'** | Duplicate (DUP) |
| **X'1E'** | Field Mark (FM) |
| **X'0C'** | Form Feed (FF) |
| **X'0D'** | Carriage Return (CR) |
| **X'15'** | New Line (NL) |
| **X'19'** | End of Medium (EM) |
| **X'FF'** | Eight Ones (EO) |
| **X'0F'** | Shift In (SI) to Double Byte Character Set mode |
| **X'0E'** | Shift Out (SO) of Double Byte Character Set mode |

These Format Control Codes are mainly concerned with 3270 printer operation. However, a FEPI application program may have to cope with the DUP and FM bytes, as these can be entered from the keyboard (but are not often used). Note that these control codes are different when operating in DBCS mode.

## 40.3 3270 Attribute Bytes

The 3270 Attribute Bytes, defining a Field to be Protected/Unprotected, Alpha/Numeric, Normal/Non-display/Intensified, MDT On/Off are those used within BMS processing, and so will be familiar to you without any further explanation.

## 40.4 3270 Extended Attribute Bytes

The 3270 Extended Attribute bytes are as follows:

| CODE | 3270 EXTENDED ATTRIBUTE |
|---|---|
| **X'00'** | Reset Attributes |
| **X'C0'** | Field Attribute |
| **X'C1'** | Field Validation |
| **X'C2'** | Field Outlining |
| **X'41'** | Extended Highlighting |
| **X'42'** | Foreground Colour |
| **X'43'** | Character Set |
| **X'45'** | Background Colour |
| **X'46'** | Transparency |

These control codes are followed (except for reset) by a single byte defining the setting.

## 40.5 Datastream errors

If you build a 3270 Datastream incorrectly, the fault will not be detected on the `EXEC CICS FEPI SEND DATASTREAM` command. The error will be reported on a subsequent `EXEC CICS FEPI` command—not necessarily the next one. This is because FEPI does not wait for the partner to validate a flow before permitting another `EXEC CICS FEPI` command. Therefore, if you have a complicated application design, it may be difficult to detect upon which flow the error occurred.

The fact that a badly formatted flow was detected will be notified via the 216 Return Code. The `EXEC CICS FEPI EXTRACT CONVID` command (see Sec. 27.1) should then be used to get the Error Code in the `SENSEDATA` field. The Sense Code may well indicate the error, but equally may simply reiterate the fact that a badly formatted flow was rejected by the partner system.

When this occurs, you should proceed on the assumption that the whole of the partner system's display was corrupted, and rebuild it all on the subsequent flow.

## 40.6 Asynchronous processing

All the techniques used in Formatted programming are available for Datastream programming:

- Timeouts (see Chapter 34)
- Asynchronous operation (see Chapter 35)
- Free processing (see Chapter 36)

The design issues for FEPI Formatted programming are similarly relevant to FEPI Datastream programming.

# CHAPTER 41 Datastream programming techniques

**GUIDANCE**

This chapter outlines techniques for FEPI Datastream Conversations by considering a Passthrough program. A sample Passthrough program using these techniques is contained in Chapter 42.

## 41.2 Datastream techniques

The design of a FEPI Datastream program follows that for a Formatted program; the difference arises in how the flows to and from the partner system are processed.

The heart of a FEPI Datastream program is concerned with the recognition of 3270 Command Codes (see Sec. 37.2) which control how the 3270 Orders (see Chapter 40) and 3270 Attribute Bytes determine a display's format. The most direct relationship is where a FEPI application program is running a Passthrough application. In this case, the 3270 Command Codes relate directly to an `EXEC CICS` Terminal Control Command.

## 41.2 3270 Command Codes and EXEC CICS Terminal Control Commands

The 3270 Command Codes are:

| COMMAND CODE | ACTION |
|---|---|
| **X'F1'** | Write |
| **X'F5'** | Erase Write |
| √ **X'7E'** | Erase Write Alternate |
| **X'F3'** | Write Structured Field |
| **X'F2'** | Read Buffer |
| **X'F6'** | Read Modified |
| **X'6E'** | Read Modified All |
| √ **X'6F'** | Erase All Unprotected |

## 41.2.1 EXEC CICS Terminal Control Commands for Writes

### SUPPORTED OPERATIONS

The Write and Erase Write Commands can be directly translated into EXEC CICS Terminal Control Commands. However, the Erase Write Alternate and Erase All Unprotected Commands do not have any direct CICS Terminal Control Equivalent.

Data is sent to the *Principal Facility* to a CICS Transaction via the EXEC CICS Terminal Control Commands:

- The Write command should be processed via an EXEC CICS SEND command without the specification of the ERASE option.
- The Erase Write command should be processed via an EXEC CICS SEND ERASE command.

The Erase Write command would normally be expected to be the First operation of a group of CICS Terminal Control Commands. It is very unusual for this 3270 Command to be imbedded within a sequence. The Write Command is the most common operation to be done for communications.

For both of these Command Codes, the CTLCHAR field on the EXEC CICS SEND command must be supplied. This parameter should contain the WCC (controlling Alarm and Keyboard Unlock) for the operation. If running a Passthrough program, the required setting will be found in the FEPI Inbound Datastream immediately after the 3270 Command Code. Consequently, the data actually EXEC CICS SENDed will commence immediately after the WCC (i.e., from the third byte of the FEPI Inbound Datastream).

You may consider buffering up the data for an EXEC CICS SEND in order to reduce network traffic. However, I would not normally recommend doing this. A FEPI application program running a Passthrough operation should normally exactly emulate the flows. Doing a buffering operation destroys this correspondence. However, if you decide to do this buffering, you should take care to handle the conditions where an Erase Write Command occurs in the middle of a flow (and thus discard all previous instructions).

You must be able to decide when it is time for the FEPI partner system to stop supplying 3270 data, and so the time for the real terminal to start supplying data. This decision may be easier for a FEPI Datastream Conversation than for a FEPI Formatted conversation because you have the ability to scan the flow before onward transmission. Therefore, you have the ability to detect that a given termination condition has occurred, and use this circumstance to terminate the passthrough operation.

You may therefore design a Passthrough application that leaves the FEPI emulated screen in a given state for further usage. Such a technique is useful when managing Convids (see Chapter 61).

### UNSUPPORTED COMMANDS

The CICS Terminal Control API does not provide a method of processing Erase Write Alternate and Erase All Unprotected Commands.

ERASE WRITE ALTERNATE

The CICS usage of alternate screen sizes is controlled by an option on the TRANSACTION definition for the currently executing Transaction. Therefore, CICS assumes that the principal facility is always going to operate in normal size or alternate size for the life of a transaction. This provides a problem for running a passthrough emulation to a partner that changes screen size according to circumstance.

The way round this problem is to set the real terminal into its alternate screen size via the TRANSACTION setting. However, this is not entirely satisfactory, as the screen will not format properly while the partner system thinks its terminal is in normal mode. To get the real terminal back to normal setting (but still in its alternate size as far as CICS Terminal Control is concerned), you should issue the Structure Field Erase/Reset Command (not an Erase Alternate command) using an EXEC CICS SEND STRFIELD operation. The required Structured field flow is X'00040300' to set the screen to its normal size. Thus, when the Erase Write Alternate is detected, insert a X'000403FF" Structured Field flow before the following datastream, and treat this datastream as if it were on an Erase Write Command.

Note that the sample Passthrough program in Chapter 42 does not adopt this technique. It assumes that the real terminal's screen is big enough to cope with all the data, and so treats the Erase Write Alternate as an Erase Write Command.

ERASE ALL UNPROTECTED

There is no direct method of getting CICS to EXEC CICS SEND an Erase All Unprotected Command to a real terminal. The sample program in Chapter 42 treats this command as being equivalent to an Erase Write Command. This may well be an adequate operation.

However, you may well decide that a more proper action is required. In this case, you should treat the following data as a Write command, but precede this operation with a Structured Field flow that performs the required erasing on keyable fields.

This flow is sent with an EXEC CICS SEND STRFIELD command data of X'000840006F00ffff', where ffff is the end position from the Erase All Unprotected Command. However, in general, the Erase All Unprotected Command is so rarely sent that I would not bother adding this complexity to your FEPI program.

## 41.2.2 EXEC CICS Terminal Control Commands for Reads

### SUPPORTED OPERATIONS

The Read Buffer Command is supported via the EXEC CICS RECEIVE BUFFER ASIS command. The Read Modified Command is supported via the EXEC CICS RECEIVE ASIS command without the BUFFER option.

### UNSUPPORTED OPERATIONS

The Read Modified All Command is not supported by the CICS Terminal Control API. However, as the information returned is a subset of that for the Read Buffer Command, use of the EXEC CICS RECEIVE BUFFER ASIS will be a suitable substitute.

### 41.2.3 THE EXEC CICS Commands for Structured Fields

The Write Structured Field Command is processed by issuing an `EXEC CICS SEND STRFIELD` operation. The exception is for a Structured Field Query, which *has* to be processed via an `EXEC CICS CONVERSE STRFIELD` operation. The reason for this is that the Structured Field Query operation returns information relating to what the real terminal will support.

It is not easy to detect a Structured Field Query operation. It may be imbedded deep with other Structured Field operations. Therefore, when a Write Structure Field Command is detected, the following Datastream should be scanned to see if the query operation is present. The layout of a Structured Field Query element is X'llll01FF02...' or a X'llll01FF03...' (where llll is the element length).

The sample program in Chapter 42 does not distinguish between the various types of Read Operation actioned by a Structured Field request. This is the correct thing to do, as there is no point doing different things for basically the same operation.

## **41.3** FEPI Outbound operations

Generating a Datastream to `EXEC CICS FEPI SEND` to the partner system for a Passthrough operation is easy. You just stick on a three-byte prefix to the data obtained from an `EXEC CICS RECEIVE` command.

This three-byte prefix consists of the AID key pressed on the terminal (which is obtained from `EIBAID`) together with a two-byte cursor position (obtained from `EIBCPOSN`). However, this cursor position has to be translated from the 16-bit EIB format into the 12-bit format supported by the 3270 architecture. The conversion is B'abcdefgh ijklmnop' to B'00efghij 00klmnop' and then translated into a printable format. Section 42.6 shows how this is done.

If you are generating the Datastream manually, then you have to be aware of the possibility of generating an incorrect Datastream. This error will not be detected on the `EXEC CICS FEPI SEND DATASTREAM` command, but on a subsequent command. The Sense Code available from an EXEC CICS FEPI EXTRACT CONV command may not indicate where the error occurred. Unfortunately, the only way of determining the error is to examine the Datastream manually!

CHAPTER

# 42 Passthrough program

**GUIDANCE**

This chapter presents an assembler FEPI Passthrough program, using the Datastream techniques discussed in this part of the book. The code is presented in fragments, together with a commentary on the contents.

In general, all the FEPI commands are assumed to have worked. This is to prevent cluttering up the logic of the program. In real life, you must check the results of each `EXEC CICS FEPI` command.

Similarly, this code runs as a Conversational program at a CICS terminal to highlight the logic involved. In practice, this program would run in a fully asynchronous mode.

## 42.1 Headers

```
*ASM XOPTS(FEPI)
         TITLE 'PASS FEPI Passthrough Program'
* ■■■■■■■■■■■■■■■■■■■■■■■■■■■■■■■■■■■■■■■■■■■■■■■■■■■■■■■■■■■■■■■■■■■■
* ■                                                                    ■
* ■     PASS     : Example FEPI Passthrough Program                    ■
* ■     ■■■■                                                           ■
* ■                                                                    ■
* ■     Example Program showing FEPI Passthrough techniques,           ■
* ■             stops when the User keys PF15.                         ■
* ■                                                                    ■
* ■                                                                    ■
* ■     Register Usage :                                               ■
* ■     ■■■■■■■■■■■■■■■■                                               ■
* ■                                                                    ■
* ■         R0   →                                                     ■
* ■         R1   →                                                     ■
* ■         R2   →   Data Buffer                                       ■
* ■         R3   →                                                     ■
* ■         R4   →                                                     ■
* ■         R5   →                                                     ■
* ■         R0   →                                                     ■
* ■         R7   →   1st link reg                                      ■
* ■         R8   →   Base 1                                            ■
* ■         R9   →   Base 2                                            ■
* ■         R18  →   DFHEISTG                                          ■
* ■         R11  →   EIB                                               ■
* ■         R12  →                                                     ■
* ■         R13  →                                                     ■
* ■         R14  →                                                     ■
* ■         R15  →                                                     ■
* ■                                                                    ■
* ■■■■■■■■■■■■■■■■■■■■■■■■■■■■■■■■■■■■■■■■■■■■■■■■■■■■■■■■■■■■■■■■■■■■
*
*        SPACE 2
*        EJECT
*        SPACE 2
*
* ■■■■■■■■■■■■■■■■■■■■■■■■■■■■■■■■■■■■■■■■■■■■■■■■■■■■■■■■■■■■■■■■■■■■
* ■                FEPI Dsects                                         ■
* ■■■■■■■■■■■■■■■■■■■■■■■■■■■■■■■■■■■■■■■■■■■■■■■■■■■■■■■■■■■■■■■■■■■■
*
         SPACE 2
         COPY  DFHSZAPA                      FEPI Constants etc.
         COPY  DFHAID                        Attention Key names etc.
         SPACE 2
         EJECT
```

There is not very much to say about this fragment. It just shows that `XOPTS(FEPI)` has to be quoted to get the program to compile with `EXEC CICS FEPI` commands.

`DFHSZAPA` is a copybook containing names for all the FEPI Return Codes, etc., while `DFHAID` provides names for Attention Keys, etc.

## 42.2 Variables

```
*
*■■■■■■■■■■■■■■■■■■■■■■■■■■■■■■■■■■■■■■■■■■■■■■■■■■■■■■■■■■■■■■■■■■■■■■■
* ■                      Variables                                        ■
*■■■■■■■■■■■■■■■■■■■■■■■■■■■■■■■■■■■■■■■■■■■■■■■■■■■■■■■■■■■■■■■■■■■■■■■
*
         SPACE 2
DFHEISTG DSECT
         SPACE 2
EISSTART DS    0H                          Start of EIS
         SPACE 2
         DS    0F
PMAPIN   DS    AL4                         MAPIN  Area address
RMAPIN   DS    AL4                                Return address
MILEN    DS    F                                  Data length
MILENH   DS    H                                  Data length (H)
         SPACE 2
         DS    0F
PMAPOUT  DS    AL4                         MAPOUT Area address
PMAPOUT  DS    AL4                                Return address
MOEND    DS    F                                  ENDSTATUS
MOLEN    DS    F                                  Data Length
MOLENH   DS    H                                  Data Length (H)
MOLENH1  DS    H                                  Data Length (H)-1
MOLENH2  DS    H                                  Data Length (H)-2
CONTROL  DS    XL1                                First flow char
INVITER  DS    CL1                                CD/EB flag
CTLCHAR  DS    XL1                                CTLCHAR
         SPACE 2
         DS    0F
CONVID   DS    XL8                         The CONVID
RESP     DS    F                           EIBRESP
RESP2    DS    F                           EIBRESP2
CURPOOL  DS    CL8                         CONVID's attributes
CURNODE  DS    CL8
CURTARG  DS    CL8
         SPACE 2
WCAID    DS    XL1                         GenWCC -Aid
WCCUR    DS    XL2                                -Cursor pos
WCWCC    DS    XL3                                -generated WCC
         SPACE 1
EISEND   DS    0H
         SPACE 2
*
*■■■■■■■■■■■■■■■■■■■■■■■■■■■■■■■■■■■■■■■■■■■■■■■■■■■■■■■■■■■■■■■■■■■■■■■
* ■                      Constants (place at the end of the program)     ■
*■■■■■■■■■■■■■■■■■■■■■■■■■■■■■■■■■■■■■■■■■■■■■■■■■■■■■■■■■■■■■■■■■■■■■■■
*
         SPACE 2
EISLEN   DC    Y(EISEND-EISSTART)          Length of EXEC Storage
LPOOL    DC    CL8'PRAH1   '               Pool used
         SPACE 1
STRREJL  DC    F'5'
STRREJ   DC    XL5'88000481FF'             Reject STRFIELD request
         SPACE 1
         DS    0F
LMAPIN   DC    F'6000'                     Buffer lengths
LMAPINH  DC    H'6000'
LMAPOUT  DC    F'6003'
LMAPOUTH DC    H'6003'
         SPACE 2
*
*                                          12bit Cursor trans Table
*
CURCONV  DC    CL64' ABCDEFGHIJ¢.<(+|&&JKLMNOPQR!$*);¬-/STUVWXYZ¦,%_>?0|
               123456789:#@''="'
*                                 Note && and '' are 1 char!
```

This fragment shows the variables and constants used for the Passthrough program. You should note that the double definition of certain buffer lengths (in fullword and halfword formats) is because of the difference in data lengths supported by the CICS Terminal Control and the FEPI APIs. Conversion between these formats occur intermittently in the code.

The CURCONV table is used in the translation of cursor positions into the 12-bit format. This conversion is done in the GENWCC routine, and is only required for the MAPIN of data from CICS to FEPI.

The STRREJ constant can be used to reject a Structured Field request. It is not used in this program.

## 42.3 Initialization

```
*
*■■■■■■■■■■■■■■■■■■■■■■■■■■■■■■■■■■■■■■■■■■■■■■■■■■■■■■■■■■■■■■■■■■■■■■
* ■                    Initialization                                   ■
*■■■■■■■■■■■■■■■■■■■■■■■■■■■■■■■■■■■■■■■■■■■■■■■■■■■■■■■■■■■■■■■■■■■■■■
*
         SPACE 2
PASS     DFHEIENT CODEREG=(R8,R9),                                      |
               DATAREG=(R10),                                           |
               EIBREG=(R11)
         SPACE 2
PASS     AMODE 31
PASS     RMODE ANY
         SPACE 2
         B     START
         SPACE 2
         DC    CL8'PASS    '
         DC    CL8'&SYSDATE'
         DC    CL8'&SYSTIME'
         SPACE 2
START     DS    0H
         SPACE 2
*
*■■■■■■■■■■■■■■■■■■■■■■■■■■■■■■■■■■■■■■■■■■■■■■■■■■■■■■■■■■■■■■■■■■■■■■
* ■    Grab the MAPIN and MAPOUT Areas                                  ■
*■■■■■■■■■■■■■■■■■■■■■■■■■■■■■■■■■■■■■■■■■■■■■■■■■■■■■■■■■■■■■■■■■■■■■■
*
         SPACE 2
         EXEC  CICS GETMAIN SET(R2)                                     |
                            FLENGTH(LMAPOUT)                            |
                            INITIMG(=XL1'00')
         SPACE 1
         ST    R2,PMAPIN
         SPACE 2
         EXEC  CICS GETMAIN SET(R2)                                     |
                            FLENGTH(LMAPOUT)                            |
                            INITIMG(=XL1'00')
         SPACE 1
         ST    R2,PMAPOUT
         SPACE 2
*
*■■■■■■■■■■■■■■■■■■■■■■■■■■■■■■■■■■■■■■■■■■■■■■■■■■■■■■■■■■■■■■■■■■■■■■
* ■                 ALLOCATE to the partner system                      ■
*■■■■■■■■■■■■■■■■■■■■■■■■■■■■■■■■■■■■■■■■■■■■■■■■■■■■■■■■■■■■■■■■■■■■■■
*
         SPACE 2
         EXEC   CICS FEPI ALLOCATE POOL(LPOOL)                          |
                                   CONVID(CONVID)                       |
                                   RESP(RESP)                           |
                                   RESP2(RESP2)
         SPACE 2
*
*■■■■■■■■■■■■■■■■■■■■■■■■■■■■■■■■■■■■■■■■■■■■■■■■■■■■■■■■■■■■■■■■■■■■■■
* ■                 Get hold of the CONVIDs attributes                  ■
*■■■■■■■■■■■■■■■■■■■■■■■■■■■■■■■■■■■■■■■■■■■■■■■■■■■■■■■■■■■■■■■■■■■■■■
*
         SPACE 2
         EXEC   CICS FEPI EXTRACT CONV                                  |
                                 CONVID(CONVID)                         |
                                 POOL(CURPOOL)                          |
                                 NODE(CURNODE)                          |
                                 TARGET(CURTARG)                        |
                                 RESP(RESP)                             |
                                 RESP2(RESP2)
```

After the standard command-level program initialization, two areas are obtained: one for the use of the MAPIN operation (CICS to FEPI) and the other for MAPOUT (FEPI to CICS). The areas are three bytes longer than the maximum screen size to accommodate building three-byte Write Control Characters (WCCs) in front of the flows. (I know that a WCC is only one byte long, and that the second two bytes are a cursor position, but I refer to them together for convenience.)

Later, I am going to build a WCC in front of the `PMAPIN` area, so I have obtained an area the size of the `PMAPOUT` area to cope with this, and left the logical size of the area to be the data size. Once these areas have been obtained, then the usual `EXEC CICS FEPI ALLOCATE` is performed to Acquire access to the partner system. The Pool does not have a Begin Session Handler, but assumes that a first flow will occur. I have omitted the logic to cater for this operation failing to avoid clutter.

I also find out exactly with what I am communicating to by issuing an `EXEC CICS FEPI EXTRACT CONVID` command.

## 42.4 Processing loop

```
*
*■■■■■■■■■■■■■■■■■■■■■■■■■■■■■■■■■■■■■■■■■■■■■■■■■■■■■■■■■■■■■■■■■■■■■
* ■           Loop until Exit Detected                                  ■
*■■■■■■■■■■■■■■■■■■■■■■■■■■■■■■■■■■■■■■■■■■■■■■■■■■■■■■■■■■■■■■■■■■■■■
*
         SPACE 2
MAPLOOP  DS    0H
         SPACE 2
         BAL   R7,MAPOUT
         SPACE 1
         BAL   R7,MAPIN
         SPACE 1
         B     MAPLOOP
         SPACE 2
         EJECT
         SPACE 2
```

This simple code loops forever, taking the input from the partner and sending it to the real terminal (`MAPOUT`) and then sending the data from the terminal to the partner system (`MAPIN`). Code is placed within the MAPIN routine to exit the loop when PF15 is pressed.

The `MAPOUT` routine is processed first so that the first-flow from the partner system is correctly processed. As there is no Begin Session Handler defined, the first-flow may be complex (and include Structured Field Queries).

## 42.5 MAPIN

```
*
*■■■■■■■■■■■■■■■■■■■■■■■■■■■■■■■■■■■■■■■■■■■■■■■■■■■■■■■■■■■■■■■■■■■■
* ■       MAPIN : Receive CICS Screen (PF15 exits) 1st 3 bytes WCC ■
*■■■■■■■■■■■■■■■■■■■■■■■■■■■■■■■■■■■■■■■■■■■■■■■■■■■■■■■■■■■■■■■■■■■■
*
         SPACE 2
MAPIN    DS    0H
         SPACE 2
MI0      DS    0H
         SPACE 2
         L     R2,PMAPIN                       Load Buffer address
         MVC   MILENH,LMAPINH                  Set  Buffer length
         SPACE 1
         EXEC  CICS RECEIVE INTO(3(,R2))                           |
                            LENGTH(MILENH)                         |
                            ASIS                                   |
                            RESP(RESP)                             |
                            RESP2(RESP2)
         SPACE 1
         CLI   EIBAID,X'C3'                   PF15 Keyed?
         BE    EXIT                            Yes-Quit
         SPACE 1
         LH    R15,MILENH                     Convert length
         LA    R15,3(,R15)                    Include WCC area len
         ST    R15,MILEN
         SPACE 2
MI1      DS    0H
         SPACE 2
         CLI   EIBAID,X'6C'                   Clear or PA keys
         BE    MI2                            Only send 1 byte down
         CLI   EIBAID,X'6E'                   PA1 PA2 PA3 Clear
         BE    MI2
         CLI   EIBAID,X'6B'
         BE    MI2
         CLI   EIBAID,X'6D'
         BE    MI2
         B     MI3
         SPACE 1
MI2      DS    0H
         SPACE 1
         MVC   0(1,R2),EIBAID                 Set single PA/Clear key
         MVC   MILEN,=F'1'
         B     MI4
         SPACE 1
MI3      DS    0H
         SPACE 1
         MVC   WCAID,EIBAID                   Get Key pressed
         MVC   WCCUR,EIBCPOSN                 Get Cursor position
         BAL   R7,GENWCC                      Generate the WCC
         SPACE 1
         MVC   0(3,R2),WCWCC                  Set the WCC
         B     MI4
         SPACE 2
MI4      DS    0H
         SPACE 2
         EXEC CICS FEPI SEND DATASTREAM                             |
                             CONVID(CONVID)                         |
                             FROM(0(,R2))                           |
                             FLENGTH(MILEN)                         |
                             INVITE                                 |
                             RESP(RESP)                             |
                             RESP2(RESP2)
         SPACE 2
MAPINX   DS    0H
         SPACE 2
         L     R15,RMAPIN                     Load return address
         BR    R15                            Return to caller
```

The `MAPIN` routine takes the data sent to CICS by the real end-user terminal, and sends it to the partner system via FEPI.

The first thing is to gather the data sent from the terminal. This is done by a native CICS Terminal Control Command, `EXEC CICS RECEIVE`. The data is received three bytes into the buffer, to allow for the fact that the first three bytes have to be converted into a WCC before onward transmission to FEPI (this is actually made up of a single byte representing the AID key pressed, and a two-byte cursor position, encoded in 12-bit format). Consequently, the length of data to be received uses the length-three values. You should ensure that the buffer is big enough to obtain all the possible flows from the terminal.

The PF key pressed on the terminal is available in `EIBAID`, and the current cursor position in `EIBCPOSN`.

This program assumes that PF15 is used to terminate the Passthrough operation. Thus, this is explicitly checked for in the code.

If the screen is to be sent to the partner system via FEPI, then the data length has to be increased to cope with the three-byte WCC prefix. If the user keyed CLEAR, PA1, PA2 or PA3, then there is no data to be sent to FEPI. Thus, the only thing to be sent is the AID key used, and no cursor position is required. Therefore, the data length is explicitly set to one for these keys. For clarity, I have not used the Attention key names within `DFHAID`; however, they should normally be used.

Before the terminal's data is sent to FEPI, the three-byte prefix is built via a call to the `GENWCC` routine, and placed in the unused front of the data buffer. Once the buffer has been updated with the three-byte WCC, it is then sent to FEPI via the `EXEC CICS FEPI SEND` datastream command. The `INVITE` option is used to tell the partner that the terminal is ready to accept a flow.

## 42.6 Generating a 12-bit cursor position

```
*
■■■■■■■■■■■■■■■■■■■■■■■■■■■■■■■■■■■■■■■■■■■■■■■■■■■■■■■■■■■■■■■■■■■■■■■■
* ■      GENWCC Routine - Generate a 12-bit WCC                          ■
■■■■■■■■■■■■■■■■■■■■■■■■■■■■■■■■■■■■■■■■■■■■■■■■■■■■■■■■■■■■■■■■■■■■■■■■
*
         SPACE 2
GENWCC   DS    0H
         SPACE 1
         MVC   WCWCC,=XL3'000000'             Clear the WCC Area
         MVC   WCWCC(1),WCAID                 Set the Aid Key
         SPACE 1
         MVC   WCWCC+2(1),WCCUR+1             set ???????? ijklmnop
         NI    WCWCC+2,B'00111111'            set ???????? 00klmnop
         XR    R14,R14
         ICM   R14,B'0011',WCCUR              abcdefgh ijklmnop
         SRL   R14,6                          000000ab cdefghij
         STC   R14,WCWCC+1                    set cdefghij 00klmnop
         NI    WCWCC+1,B'00111111'            set 00efghij 00klmnop
         OI    WCWCC+1,B'01000000'            set 01efghij 00klmnop
         SPACE 1
         XR    R14,R14                        Clear work regs
         XR    R15,R15
         ICM   R15,B'0011',WCCUR              Load Cursor address
         D     R14,=F'64'                     Get offsets rem/num
         SPACE 1
         LA    R1,CURCONV                     Address Conv table
         AR    R1,R15                         Point to char/num
         MVC   WCWCC+1(1),0(R1)               Save char
         SPACE 1
         LA    R1,CURCONV                     Address Conv table
         AR    R1,R14                         Point to char/rem
         MVC   WCWCC+2(1),0(R1)               Save char
         BR    R7
         SPACE 2
         EJECT
         SPACE 2
```

This routine generates the three-byte WCC for the data prefix required to precede flows sent via FEPI to the partner system. The first byte is the key pressed (the AID key), and bytes 2 and 3 are the 12-bit cursor position (generated from the 16-bit cursor position that CICS returns in `EIBCPOSN`).

The format of the 16-bit cursor position is B'abcdefgh ijklmnop', and the 12-bit format B'01efghij 00klmnop'. However, the bytes are then converted into a printable format (which is where the `CURCONV` conversation table comes in). Note that this conversion to printable format may not be necessary (some partners are more relaxed than others in this regard), but this should usually be done to ensure correct partner processing.

The logic first sets the bottom 12–16 bits into the required 12-bit format (the highest order 4 bits are lost—which does not matter as the 3270 architecture does not use them anyway for positional purposes). Then, the two bytes are converted into a printable format.

## 42.7 MAPOUT data reception

```
*
*■■■■■■■■■■■■■■■■■■■■■■■■■■■■■■■■■■■■■■■■■■■■■■■■■■■■■■■■■■■■■■■■■■■■■■
* ■       MAPOUT Routine : FEPI → CICS                                  ■
*■■■■■■■■■■■■■■■■■■■■■■■■■■■■■■■■■■■■■■■■■■■■■■■■■■■■■■■■■■■■■■■■■■■■■■
*
         SPACE 2
MAPOUT   DS    0H
         SPACE 1
         ST    R7,RMAPOUT                        Save return address
         SPACE 2
*
*■■■■■■■■■■■■■■■■■■■■■■■■■■■■■■■■■■■■■■■■■■■■■■■■■■■■■■■■■■■■■■■■■■■■■■
* ■      MAPOUT : Receive the Flow                                      ■
*■■■■■■■■■■■■■■■■■■■■■■■■■■■■■■■■■■■■■■■■■■■■■■■■■■■■■■■■■■■■■■■■■■■■■■
*
         SPACE 2
MOO      DS    0H
         SPACE 2
         L     R2,PMAPOUT                        Load Buffer address
         MVC   MOLEN,LMAPOUT                     Set  Buffer length
         SPACE 1
         EXEC  CICS FEPI RECEIVE DATASTREAM                          |
                                 CHAIN                               |
                                 CONVID(CONVID)                      |
                                 MAXFLENGTH(LMAPOUT)                 |
                                 INTO(0(,R2))                        |
                                 FLENGTH(MOLEN)                      |
                                 ENDSTATUS(MOEND)                    |
                                 TIMEOUT(1)                          |
                                 RESP(RESP)                          |
                                 RESP2(RESP2)
         SPACE 2
         CLC   RESP,DFHRESP(INVREQ)              Partner dead?
         BE    EXIT                               Yes, Exit
         SPACE 2
         L     R15,MOLEN                         Convert data length
         STH   R15,MOLENH
         SH    R15,=H'1'                         Set Offset parts
         STH   R15,MOLENH1
         SH    R15,=H'1'
         STH   R15,MOLENH2
         SPACE 1
         MVC   CONTROL,0(R2)                     Save control Character
         MVC   CTLCHAR,1(R2)                     Save CTL     Character
         SPACE 1
         CLC   MOEND,DFHVALUE(CD)                See if INVITE needed
         BE    MOOXY
         CLC   MOEND,DFHVALUE(EB)
         BE    MOOXY
         B     MOOXN
         SPACE 1
MOOXY    DS    0H
         SPACE 1
         MVI   INVITER,C'Y'
         B     MO1
         SPACE 1
MOOXN    DS    0H
         SPACE 1
         MVI   INVITER,C'N'
         B     MO1
```

The MAPOUT routine takes information sent from the partner system, and directs it to the real end-user terminal via standard CICS Terminal Control commands.

Of the possible options of the EXEC CICS FEPI RECEIVE DATASTREAM command, CHAIN is the most suitable choice. This is because you need to inspect the Command Code (the first byte of the flow) to determine what sort of flow the partner has sent. This first byte is saved in the CONTROL variable.

The second byte of the flow is (usually) the CTLCHAR used in the CICS Terminal Control Commands. Thus, it is saved away in the CTLCHAR variable.

You also need to know whether or not the partner system is going to send any more data. This example program is assumed to be talking to a CICS partner, so the CD/EB protocol can be used to detect the 'final' flow. If either a VTAM CD or an EB is received, then the partner is not going to send any more data, and it is time to let the real end-user key in some information. If neither a CD or an EB is received, then the partner system is going to send some more data. The INVITER variable is set accordingly.

Various data lengths, omitting the first two bytes of flow, are also determined.

In this simple program I have assumed that no immediate DRn response is required to the flow from the partner system. In practice, you should consider whether a RESPSTATUS needs to be processed on the EXEC CICS FEPI RECEIVE DATASTREAM command, so that an EXEC CICS FEPI ISSUE can be performed to immediately acknowledge flow reception from the partner.

## 42.8 Deciding what action to take

```
*
*■■■■■■■■■■■■■■■■■■■■■■■■■■■■■■■■■■■■■■■■■■■■■■■■■■■■■■■■■■■■■■■■■■■■■■
* ■      MAPOUT : Decide on Action to take                               ■
*■■■■■■■■■■■■■■■■■■■■■■■■■■■■■■■■■■■■■■■■■■■■■■■■■■■■■■■■■■■■■■■■■■■■■■
*
         SPACE 2
MO1      DS    0H
         SPACE 1
         CLI   CONTROL,X'F1'                 Write
         BE    MOA1
         CLI   CONTROL,X'F5'                 Erase Write
         BE    MOA2
         CLI   CONTROL,X'7E'                 Erase Write Alt
         BE    MOA3
         CLI   CONTROL,X'F3'                 Write Structured Field
         BE    MOA4
         CLI   CONTROL,X'F2'                 Read Buffer
         BE    MOA5
         CLI   CONTROL,X'F6'                 Read Modified
         BE    MOA6
         CLI   CONTROL,X'6E'                 Read Modified All
         BE    MOA7
         CLI   CONTROL,X'6F'                 Erase All Unprot
         BE    MOA8
         B     MOA9
         SPACE 2
         EJECT
         SPACE 2
```

The first byte of the flow from the partner system controls what is to be done with the flow. Consequently, the Passthrough program has to mimic these actions. This code fragment shows the possibilities. However, the CICS Terminal Control commands do not permit all these commands to be implemented (but these cases do not usually occur!).

## 42.9 Write

```
*
*■■■■■■■■■■■■■■■■■■■■■■■■■■■■■■■■■■■■■■■■■■■■■■■■■■■■■■■■■■■■■■■■■■■■
* ■      MAPOUT : Write : X'F1'                                        ■
*■■■■■■■■■■■■■■■■■■■■■■■■■■■■■■■■■■■■■■■■■■■■■■■■■■■■■■■■■■■■■■■■■■■■
*
         SPACE 2
MOA1     DS    0H
         SPACE 1
         CLI   INVITER,C'Y'                    INVITE needed?
         BE    MOA1I
         B     MOA1N
         SPACE 2
MOA1I    DS    0H
         SPACE 1
         LA    R3,2(,R2)                       Point to Data Byte
         SPACE 1
         EXEC  CICS SEND FROM(0(,R3))                                   |
                         LENGTH(MOLENH2)                                |
                         CTLCHAR(CTLCHAR)                               |
                         INVITE                                         |
                         RESP(RESP)                                     |
                         RESP2(RESP2)
         SPACE 2
         B     MOA1X
         SPACE 2
MOA1N    DS    0H
         SPACE 1
         LA    R3,2(,R2)                       Point to Data Byte
         SPACE 1
         EXEC  CICS SEND FROM(0(,R3))                                   |
                         LENGTH(MOLENH2)                                |
                         CTLCHAR(CTLCHAR)                               |
                         RESP(RESP)                                     |
                         RESP2(RESP2)
         SPACE 2
         B     MOA1X
         SPACE 2
MOA1X    DS    0H
         SPACE 1
         B     MO2
```

The Write operation simply sends the datastream to the real terminal. However, the INVITE option may, or may not, be present, so there has to be two EXEC CICS SENDs to cope with this circumstance.

The first byte of the datastream (the CONTROL character) is lost, as this is supplied within the EXEC CICS SEND processing. However, the CTLCHAR (the second byte of the flow) is specified in the CTLCHAR variable.

The great majority of the flows sent from the partner system will consist of this simple Write operation. However, the use of Erase Write is also common.

## **42.10** Erase Write

```
*
*■■■■■■■■■■■■■■■■■■■■■■■■■■■■■■■■■■■■■■■■■■■■■■■■■■■■■■■■■■■■■■■■■■■
* ■      MAPOUT : Erase Write : X'F5'                               ■
*■■■■■■■■■■■■■■■■■■■■■■■■■■■■■■■■■■■■■■■■■■■■■■■■■■■■■■■■■■■■■■■■■■■
*
         SPACE 2
MOA2     DS    0H
         SPACE 1
         CLI   INVITER,C'Y'                INVITE needed?
         BE    MOA2I
         B     MOA2N
         SPACE 2
MOA2I    DS    0H
         SPACE 1
         LA    R3,2(,R2)                   Point to Data Byte
         SPACE 1
         EXEC  CICS SEND FROM(0(,R3))                                  |
                         LENGTH(MOLENH2)                               |
                         CTLCHAR(CTLCHAR)                              |
                         ERASE                                         |
                         INVITE                                        |
                         RESP(RESP)                                    |
                         RESP2(RESP2)
         SPACE 2
         B     MOA2X
         SPACE 2
MOA2N    DS    0H
         SPACE 1
         LA    R3,2(,R2)                   Point to Data Byte
         SPACE 1
         EXEC  CICS SEND FROM(0(,R3))                                  |
                         LENGTH(MOLENH2)                               |
                         CTLCHAR(CTLCHAR)                              |
                         ERASE                                         |
                         RESP(RESP)                                    |
                         RESP2(RESP2)
         SPACE 2
         B     MOA2X
         SPACE 2
MOA2X    DS    0H
         SPACE 1
         B     MO2
```

The Erase Write command is processed similarly to the Write command, except that the `ERASE` option is specified on the `EXEC CICS SEND`s.

This command has the effect of clearing the screen before the data flow is written to it. Therefore, it will commonly occur on the first part of a flow from the partner, when the partner is not sure of what is currently on the screen.

## 42.11 Erase Write Alternate

```
*
*■■■■■■■■■■■■■■■■■■■■■■■■■■■■■■■■■■■■■■■■■■■■■■■■■■■■■■■■■■■■■■■■■■■■
* ■      MAPOUT : Erase Write Alt : X'7E'                              ■
*■■■■■■■■■■■■■■■■■■■■■■■■■■■■■■■■■■■■■■■■■■■■■■■■■■■■■■■■■■■■■■■■■■■■
*
         SPACE 2
MOA3     DS    0H
         SPACE 1
         CLI   INVITER,C'Y'                    INVITE needed?
         BE    MOA3I
         B     MOA3N
         SPACE 2
MOA3I    DS    0H
         SPACE 1
         LA    R3,2(,R2)                       Point to Data Byte
         SPACE 1
         EXEC  CICS SEND FROM(0(,R3))                              |
                         LENGTH(MOLENH2)                           |
                         CTLCHAR(CTLCHAR)                          |
                         ERASE                                     |
                         INVITE                                    |
                         RESP(RESP)                                |
                         RESP2(RESP2)
         SPACE 2
         B     MOA3X
         SPACE 2
MOA3N    DS    0H
         SPACE 1
         LA    R3,2(,R2)                       Point to Data Byte
         SPACE 1
         EXEC  CICS SEND FROM(0(,R3))                              |
                         LENGTH(MOLENH2)                           |
                         CTLCHAR(CTLCHAR)                          |
                         ERASE                                     |
                         RESP(RESP)                                |
                         RESP2(RESP2)
         SPACE 2
         B     MOA3X
         SPACE 2
MOA3X    DS    0H
         SPACE 1
         B     MO2
```

The Erase Write Alternate Command should switch the terminal into its alternate size, clear the screen, and then place the flow on the display. However, CICS does not support this switching (CICS sets the screen size on a transaction basis).

Fortunately, CICS and IMS partner systems do not usually attempt to switch screen sizes in mid-transaction, so this is not a problem. However, when communicating with some partners you may have to bear this in mind. This is because the screen size could change rather dynamically. (The solution to this is to use the CICS TRANSACTION definition to force the real terminal into the bigger alternate screen size for the Passthrough emulation).

Thus, as CICS does not support this operation, the code is exactly the same as for the Erase Write operation.

## 42.12 Write Structured Field selection

```
*
* ■■■■■■■■■■■■■■■■■■■■■■■■■■■■■■■■■■■■■■■■■■■■■■■■■■■■■■■■■■■■■■■■■■■
* ■      MAPOUT : Write SF    =X'F3' LLLL type                           ■
* ■■■■■■■■■■■■■■■■■■■■■■■■■■■■■■■■■■■■■■■■■■■■■■■■■■■■■■■■■■■■■■■■■■■
*
         SPACE 2
MOA4     DS    0H
         SPACE 2
*                                         You have to distinguish
*                                         between the 3 SF cases of
*                                          * Just SF to be sent to
*                                            the Terminal
*                                          * Query Partition data
*                                            with its XC CONVERSEd
*                                            to the terminal
*                                          * Normal SF fields which
*                                            want a PFkey response
*
         SPACE 1
         CLI   INVITER,C'Y'               INVITE needed?
         BE    MOA4I                        Yes - Read operations
         B     MOA4N                        No  - SEND operation
         SPACE 2
MOA4I    DS    0H
         SPACE 1
*                                         See if the INVITE is
*                                          due to a Read Partition
*                                          SF or a 'normal' CD
         SPACE 1
MOA4I1   DS    0H
         SPACE 1
         LA    R5,1(,R2)                  Set start of commands
         LR    R6,R5                      Point to end of SFs
         AH    R6,MOLENH1
         SPACE 1
MOA4I2   DS    0H
         SPACE 1
         CLI   2(R5),X'01'                Read Partition SF Command?
         BE    MOA4I4                      Yes - do a CONVERSE
         SPACE 1
MOA4I3   DS    0H
         SPACE 1
         AH    R5,8(,R5)                   No - Up to next STR Field
         CR    R5,R6                            At end of STR data?
         BNL   MOA4SI                            Yes - Normal Send
         B     MOA4I2                            No  - scan again
```

The Write Structured Field Command requires a most careful consideration. This is because the command can generate several different operations:

- The equivalent of the Write Command simply to send a flow to the terminal
- The equivalent of the Write Command to send a flow to the terminal with `INVITE` processing
- A request for the real terminal to describe itself via a Query Structured Field operation (which information has to be returned to the partner system)

Each of these operations has to be treated separately, as they result in different `EXEC CICS` commands. However, the logic to distinguish between the cases is not direct:

- If the `INVITE` condition was not detected, then the partner system is not expecting any data back from the flow. Therefore, this means that the flow is simply to be sent to the real end-user terminal.

- If the partner is expecting a reply, then you have to distinguish between these possibilities:
  - A data flow consisting of 3270 Structured Fields to be sent to the terminal which unlocks the terminal for end-user input.
  - The flow is a request for information about the characteristics of the terminal (a Query Partition Structured Field request), which are then returned to the partner. This typically occurs as the 'Start-of-Day' flow from a CICS partner.

Unfortunately, the only way of distinguishing between these cases is actually to scan the flow for the Query Partition Structured Field command. The layout of a Structured Field element is X'llllcc...', where llll is the length of the element, and cc is the operation. Therefore, as the Query Partition operation is X'01', each of the Structured Field elements is scanned, looking for this X'01' operation. If this is found, then a Structured Field Query is performed; if not, then the normal sequence is performed. Note that it is possible for the Query Partition operation to be imbedded within a flow, and you should *not* rely on the fact that the query is usually the first element in the Structured Field Sequence.

## 42.13 Write Structured Field operation

```
         SPACE 1
MOA414   DS       OH
         SPACE 2
*                                         Query CD Write SF command
         SPACE 1
         LA    R3,1(,R2)                  Point to STR Data
         L     R4,PMAPIN                  Load Return Buf addr
         MVI   0(R4),X'88'                Set STR Reply
         MVC   MILEN,LMAPIN               Set Buffer length
         SPACE 1
         EXEC CICS CONVERSE FROM(0(,R3))                              |
                            FROMLENGTH(MOLENH1)                       |
                            INTO(1(,R4))                              |
                            TOFLENGTH(MILEN)                          |
                            STRFIELD                                  |
                            RESP(RESP)                                |
                            RESP2(RESP2)
         SPACE 1
         EXEC CICS FEPI SEND DATASTREAM                               |
                             CONVID(CONVID)                           |
                             FROM(0(,R4))                             |
                             FLENGTH(MILEN)                           |
                             INVITE                                   |
                             RESP(RESP)                               |
                             RESP2(RESP2)
         SPACE 1
         MVI   INVITER,C'N'               Keep partner receiving
         SPACE 1
         B     MOA4X
         SPACE 2
MOA4SI   DS    OH
         SPACE 1
*                                         Normal CD Write SF command
         SPACE 1
         EXEC CICS SEND FROM(1(,R2))                                  |
                        LENGTH(MOLENH1)                               |
                        STRFIELD                                      |
                        INVITE                                        |
                        RESP(RESP)                                    |
                        RESP2(RESP2)                                  |
         SPACE 1
         B     MOA4X
         SPACE 2
         SPACE 2
MOA4N    DS    OH
         SPACE 1
*                                         Just a Write SF command
```

```
         SPACE 1
         EXEC CICS SEND FROM(1(,R2))
                        LENGTH(MOLENH1)
                        STRFIELD
                        RESP(RESP)
                        RESP2(RESP2)
         SPACE 1
         B     MOA4X
         SPACE 2
MOA4X    DS    0H
         SPACE 1
         B     MO2
         SPACE 2
```

This code fragment shows how the three types of Structured Field operations are to be processed:

- The most complex Structured Field Processing is where the partner has requested that the real end-user terminal supply details about itself. The only way CICS supports these operations is via the `EXEC CICS CONVERSE STRFIELD` command (you cannot separate this into an `EXEC CICS SEND STRFIELD` and a `EXEC CICS RECEIVE` operation).

  The reply to a Structured Field Query has an AID key of X'88', so this is set up in the reception area before the `EXEC CICS CONVERSE STRFIELD` is issued.

  Once the terminal has responded with the requested characteristics, this information is returned to the partner system via the `EXEC CICS FEPI SEND INVITE` command. The `INVITE` option is required to let the partner system know that no other Structured Field Query reply information is going to be sent.

  The `INVITER` flag is changed so that the MAPOUT operation is repeated, as it is still the partner's turn to send a flow.

  If you are running a Datastream program in background mode, then it is not possible to ask the terminal its characteristics. Therefore, you can either build up a suitable reply and return it directly (starting with the X'88'), or simply reply with a null. What you should *not* do is never reply. If CICS is the partner system, a wait state will result if no reply to the Structured Field Query is returned.

- If the Structured Field command means that the flow is to be sent to the real end-user terminal, which is then permitted to key in data, the `STRFIELD` format of the 'normal' `EXEC CICS SEND` command is used. There is no `CTLCHAR` to worry about, as this is contained within the Structured Field flow. The first byte of the data which was originally obtained is not transmitted (as this is the Structured Field indication which the `STRFIELD` option replaces). The `INVITE` option permits the end-user terminal to accept key presses in the normal fashion.

- The Structured Field data is to be sent to the real end-user terminal, but more data is to follow. Consequently, the layout of the `EXEC CICS SEND STRFIELD` command is the same as in the preceding example, but the `INVITE` option is omitted.

## 42.14 Read Buffer

```
*
*■■■■■■■■■■■■■■■■■■■■■■■■■■■■■■■■■■■■■■■■■■■■■■■■■■■■■■■■■■■■■■■■■■■■
* ■       MAPOUT : Read Buffer : X'F2'                                  ■
*■■■■■■■■■■■■■■■■■■■■■■■■■■■■■■■■■■■■■■■■■■■■■■■■■■■■■■■■■■■■■■■■■■■■
*
         SPACE 2
MOA5     DS    OH
         SPACE 1
         L     R2,PMAPIN                    Load Buffer address
         MVC   MILENH,LMAPINH               Set  Buffer length
         SPACE 1
         EXEC  CICS RECEIVE INTO(3(,R2))                              |
                            LENGTH(MILENH)                            |
                            ASIS                                      |
                            BUFFER                                    |
                            RESP(RESP)                                |
                            RESP2(RESP2)
         SPACE 2
         LH    R15,MILENH                   Convert length
         LA    R15,3(,R15)                  Include WCC area len
         ST    R15,MILEN
         SPACE 2
MOA51    DS    OH
         SPACE 2
         MVC   WCAID,EIBAID                 Get Key pressed
         MVC   WCCUR,EIBCPOSN               Get Cursor position
         BAL   R7,GENWCC                    Generate the WCC
         SPACE 1
         MVC   0(3,R2),WCWCC                Set the WCC
         SPACE 2
         CLI   INVITER,C'Y'                 INVITE needed?
         BE    MOA5I
         B     MOA5N
         SPACE 2
MOA5I    DS    OH
         SPACE 2
         EXEC  CICS FEPI SEND DATASTREAM                              |
                              CONVID(CONVID)                          |
                              FROM(0(,R2))                            |
                              FLENGTH(MILEN)                          |
                              INVITE                                  |
                              RESP(RESP)                              |
                              RESP2(RESP2)
         SPACE 1
         B     MOA5X
         SPACE 2
MOA5N    DS    OH
         SPACE 2
         EXEC  CICS FEPI SEND DATASTREAM                              |
                              CONVID(CONVID)                          |
                              FROM(0(,R2))                            |
                              FLENGTH(MILEN)                          |
                              RESP(RESP)                              |
                              RESP2(RESP2)
         SPACE 1
         B     MOA5X
         SPACE 2
MOA5X    DS    OH
         SPACE 1
         B     MO2
```

The Read Buffer Command requests that the real end-user terminal supply all the contents of its screen. Therefore, the current image is obtained via the `EXEC CICS RECEIVE BUFFER` command (`ASIS` is used to prevent any upper/lower case translation).

The data is returned three bytes into the area to allow the generation of the WCC prefix via the `GENWCC` routine used for `MAPIN` processing. In this case, the AID key (the first byte in the area) is the *last* PF key pressed. Thus, now PA1/2/3 and Clear keys return a cursor position and screen data.

## 42.15 Read Modified

```
*
*■■■■■■■■■■■■■■■■■■■■■■■■■■■■■■■■■■■■■■■■■■■■■■■■■■■■■■■■■■■■■■■■■■■■
* ■      MAPOUT : Read Modified : X'F6'                               ■
*■■■■■■■■■■■■■■■■■■■■■■■■■■■■■■■■■■■■■■■■■■■■■■■■■■■■■■■■■■■■■■■■■■■■
*
         SPACE 2
MOA6     DS    0H
         SPACE 1
         L     R2,PMAPIN                     Load Buffer address
         MVC   MILENH,LMAPINH                Set  Buffer length
         SPACE 1
         EXEC  CICS RECEIVE INTO(3(,R2))                             |
                              LENGTH(MILENH)                         |
                              ASIS                                   |
                              RESP(RESP)                             |
                              RESP2(RESP2)
         SPACE 2
         LH    R15,MILENH                    Convert length
         LA    R15,3(,R15)                   Include WCC area len
         ST    R15,MILEN
         SPACE 2
MOA61    DS    0H
         SPACE 2
         MVC   WCAID,EIBAID                  Get Key pressed
         MVC   WCCUR,EIBCPOSN                Get Cursor position
         BAL   R7,GENWCC                     Generate the WCC
         SPACE 1
         MVC   0(3,R2),WCWCC                 Set the WCC
         SPACE 2
         CLI   INVITER,C'Y'                  INVITE needed?
         BE    MOA6I
         B     MOA6N
         SPACE 2
MOA6I    DS    0H
         SPACE 2
         EXEC CICS FEPI SEND DATASTREAM                              |
                             CONVID(CONVID)                          |
                             FROM(0(,R2))                            |
                             FLENGTH(MILEN)                          |
                             INVITE                                  |
                             RESP(RESP)                              |
                             RESP2(RESP2)
         SPACE 1
         B     MOA6X
         SPACE 2
MOA6N    DS    0H
         SPACE 2
         EXEC CICS FEPI SEND DATASTREAM                              |
                             CONVID(CONVID)                          |
                             FROM(0(,R2))                            |
                             FLENGTH(MILEN)                          |
                             RESP(RESP)                              |
                             RESP2(RESP2)
         SPACE 1
         B     MOA6X
         SPACE 2
MOA6X    DS    0H
         SPACE 1
         B     MO2
```

The Read Modified Command asks the real terminal to return fields which have been updated (those whose MDT has been set). Therefore, the processing is similar to that for the Read Buffer operation, except that the `EXEC CICS RECEIVE` command omits the `BUFFER` option.

## 42.16 Read Modified All

```
*
*■■■■■■■■■■■■■■■■■■■■■■■■■■■■■■■■■■■■■■■■■■■■■■■■■■■■■■■■■■■■■■■■■■■■■
* ■      MAPOUT : Read Modified All : X'6E'                              ■
*■■■■■■■■■■■■■■■■■■■■■■■■■■■■■■■■■■■■■■■■■■■■■■■■■■■■■■■■■■■■■■■■■■■■■
*
         SPACE 2
MOA7     DS    OH
         SPACE 1
         L     R2,PMAPIN                         Load Buffer address
         MVC   MILENH,LMAPINH                    Set  Buffer length
         SPACE 1
         EXEC  CICS RECEIVE INTO(3(,R2))                              |
                           LENGTH(MILENH)                             |
                           BUFFER                                     |
                           ASIS                                       |
                           RESP(RESP)                                 |
                           RESP2(RESP2)
         SPACE 2
         LH    R15,MILENH                        Convert length
         LA    R15,3(,R15)                       Include WCC area len
         ST    R15,MILEN
         SPACE 2
MOA71    DS    OH
         SPACE 2
         MVC   WCAID,EIBAID                      Get Key pressed
         MVC   WCCUR,EIBCPOSN                    Get Cursor position
         BAL   R7,GENWCC                         Generate the WCC
         SPACE 1
         MVC   0(3,R2),WCWCC                     Set the WCC
         SPACE 2
         CLI   INVITER,C'Y'                      INVITE needed?
         BE    MOA7I
         B     MOA7N
         SPACE 2
MOA7I    DS    OH
         SPACE 2
         EXEC CICS FEPI SEND DATASTREAM                               |
                            CONVID(CONVID)                            |
                            FROM(0(,R2))                              |
                            FLENGTH(MILEN)                            |
                            INVITE                                    |
                            RESP(RESP)                                |
                            RESP2(RESP2)
         SPACE 1
         B     MOA7X
         SPACE 2
MOA7N    DS    OH
         SPACE 2
         EXEC CICS FEPI SEND DATASTREAM                               |
                            CONVID(CONVID)                            |
                            FROM(0(,R2))                              |
                            FLENGTH(MILEN)                            |
                            RESP(RESP)                                |
                            RESP2(RESP2)
         SPACE 1
         B     MOA7X
         SPACE 2
MOA7X    DS    OH
         SPACE 1
         B     MO2
```

The Read Modified All Command is another of those which CICS does not support. Therefore, it looks exactly the same as the Read Buffer operation. This lack of support does not really matter, as this command is very uncommon.

## 42.17 Erase All Unprotected

```
*
*■■■■■■■■■■■■■■■■■■■■■■■■■■■■■■■■■■■■■■■■■■■■■■■■■■■■■■■■■■■■■■■■■■■■
* ■      MAPOUT : Erase All Unprot : X'6F'                            ■
*■■■■■■■■■■■■■■■■■■■■■■■■■■■■■■■■■■■■■■■■■■■■■■■■■■■■■■■■■■■■■■■■■■■■
*
         SPACE 2
MOA8     DS    0H
         SPACE 1
         CLI   INVITER,C'Y'                  INVITE needed?
         BE    MOA8I
         B     MOA8N
         SPACE 2
MOA8I    DS    0H
         SPACE 1
         LA    R3,2(,R2)                     Point to Data Byte
         SPACE 1
         EXEC  CICS SEND FROM(0(,R3))                                 |
                         LENGTH(MOLENH2)                              |
                         CTLCHAR(CTLCHAR)                             |
                         ERASE|                                       |
                         INVITE                                       |
                         RESP(RESP)                                   |
                         RESP2(RESP2)
         SPACE 2
         B     MOA8X
         SPACE 2
MOA8N    DS    0H
         SPACE 1
         LA    R3,2(,R2)                     Point to Data Byte
         SPACE 1
         EXEC  CICS SEND FROM(0(,R3))                                 |
                         LENGTH(MOLENH2)                              |
                         CTLCHAR(CTLCHAR)                             |
                         ERASE|                                       |
                         RESP(RESP)                                   |
                         RESP2(RESP2)
         SPACE 2
         B     MOA8X
         SPACE 2
MOA8X    DS    0H
         SPACE 1
         B     MO2
```

The Erase All Unprotected Command clears all Unprotected fields (instead of the whole screen) before writing the flow to the screen. However, this is another operation that is not supported by CICS. Therefore, this fragment looks like the Erase Write operation.

## 42.18 Unknown command

```
*
*■■■■■■■■■■■■■■■■■■■■■■■■■■■■■■■■■■■■■■■■■■■■■■■■■■■■■■■■■■■■■■■■■■■■
* ■      MAPOUT : Unknown Command                                     ■
*■■■■■■■■■■■■■■■■■■■■■■■■■■■■■■■■■■■■■■■■■■■■■■■■■■■■■■■■■■■■■■■■■■■■
*
         SPACE 2
MOA9     DS    0H
         SPACE 1
         SPACE 2
MOA9X    DS    0H
         SPACE 1
         B     MO2
```

If the flow from the partner system does not start with one of the known Command Codes, this is a logic error. I have omitted error processing to avoid clutter, but I expect that you would issue an `EXEC CICS FEPI FREE FORCE` to 'switch off' the terminal.

## 42.19 MAPOUT End of processing

```
*
*■■■■■■■■■■■■■■■■■■■■■■■■■■■■■■■■■■■■■■■■■■■■■■■■■■■■■■■■■■■■■■■■■■■■
* ■      MAPOUT : End of Actions                                       ■
*■■■■■■■■■■■■■■■■■■■■■■■■■■■■■■■■■■■■■■■■■■■■■■■■■■■■■■■■■■■■■■■■■■■■
*
         SPACE 2
MO2      DS    OH
         SPACE 2
         CLI   INVITER,C'Y'                   Any more RUs?
         BNE   MOO                             Yes - keep going
         B     MAPOUTX                         No  - exit Mapout logic
         SPACE 2
*
*■■■■■■■■■■■■■■■■■■■■■■■■■■■■■■■■■■■■■■■■■■■■■■■■■■■■■■■■■■■■■■■■■■■■
* ■      MAPOUT : Return to caller                                     ■
*■■■■■■■■■■■■■■■■■■■■■■■■■■■■■■■■■■■■■■■■■■■■■■■■■■■■■■■■■■■■■■■■■■■■
*
         SPACE 2
MAPOUTX  DS    OH
         SPACE 1
         ST    R7,RMAPOUT                     Save return address
         SPACE 2
         L     R15,RMAPOUT                    Load return address
         BR    R15                            Return to caller
         EJECT
```

The `MAPOUT` routine has to know when it is time to stop receiving flows from the partner system, so that data can be received from the real end-user terminal. This is done by looking at the `INVITER` flag (which was changed for a Structured Field Query for just this purpose).

## 42.20 End of program

```
*
*■■■■■■■■■■■■■■■■■■■■■■■■■■■■■■■■■■■■■■■■■■■■■■■■■■■■■■■■■■■■■■■■■■■■
* ■      End of Logic - return to CICS                                 ■
*■■■■■■■■■■■■■■■■■■■■■■■■■■■■■■■■■■■■■■■■■■■■■■■■■■■■■■■■■■■■■■■■■■■■
*
         SPACE 2
EXIT     DS    OH
         SPACE 2
         EXEC  CICS FEPI FREE CONVID(CONVID)                           |
                              RELEASE                                  |
                              RESP(RESP)                               |
                              RESP2(RESP2)
         SPACE 2
         EXEC  CICS RETURN
         SPACE 2
         EJECT
         SPACE 2
*
*■■■■■■■■■■■■■■■■■■■■■■■■■■■■■■■■■■■■■■■■■■■■■■■■■■■■■■■■■■■■■■■■■■■■
* ■      Literals                                                      ■
*■■■■■■■■■■■■■■■■■■■■■■■■■■■■■■■■■■■■■■■■■■■■■■■■■■■■■■■■■■■■■■■■■■■■
*
         SPACE 2
         LTORG
         SPACE 2
         EJECT
         SPACE 2
*
■■■■■■■■■■■■■■■■■■■■■■■■■■■■■■■■■■■■■■■■■■■■■■■■■■■■■■■■■■■■■■■■■■■■■
* ■      End of program                                                ■
■■■■■■■■■■■■■■■■■■■■■■■■■■■■■■■■■■■■■■■■■■■■■■■■■■■■■■■■■■■■■■■■■■■■■
*
         SPACE 2
         END   PASS
```

When PF15 is pressed, the Passthrough program ends. The Connection is `EXEC CICS FEPI FREE RELEASE`d to prevent anyone else using the partner 'terminal' in case the end user does not do a signoff sequence.

PART 6

# The use of Monitors and Handlers

**GUIDANCE**

This part contains information about the FEPI Monitors and Handlers. They are optional, but recommended, facilities that present significant opportunities for recoverability and asynchronous operation.

The following topics are presented in this part of the book:

- Introduction to Handlers and Monitors
- Handler descriptions
- Pool-specific Monitors
- CSZX Monitors
- How to use Monitors and Handlers

CHAPTER 43

# Introduction to Handlers and Monitors

**GUIDANCE**

This chapter discusses the concepts behind the FEPI Handlers and Monitors, and describes how they are defined. See Chapter 47 for information about how (and if) to use them.

## 43.1 The Handler and Monitor transactions

A FEPI *Handler* or a *Monitor* are CICS transactions that are initiated when certain events occur. They are coded exactly like any other CICS transaction, and all the FEPI commands are available for use with them.

The Handler transactions are defined in the Propertyset, whereas the Monitor transactions are defined via the DCT. Consequently, whether or not they are initiated depends on the definitions used. If they are not defined, then FEPI does not worry about their absence.

Therefore, a Handler is directly initiated by FEPI when the given event occurs, but the Monitors are initiated via CICS Transient Data facilities. Consequently, the Monitor transaction can be either initiated via Transient Data Triggering or manually initiated via Interval Control. The Monitor program then reads the Transient Data Queue to get the information contained therein. Thus, the Monitor function need not be placed in a separate program to main-line processing, as it is keyed by TDQ records.

### 43.1.1 Defining the Handlers

As the Handlers and Monitors are merely CICS transactions, they must be defined by the usual CICS methods. Consequently, an RDO `TRANSACTION` and `PROGRAM` definition must exist for each Monitor and Handler (but there are no restrictions on sharing programs between the transactions, as `START` data gives the indication as to why the transaction got started). The transactions should be defined as local transactions, as FEPI does not support transaction routing or any sort of remote operation.

For the Monitor transaction, a DCT entry has to be made for the TDQ, and the Monitor transaction specified as the Triggered transaction. As all FEPI transactions have to run locally, you should ensure that no shipping is active. There is also an important thing to note about the recoverability of the TDQ—it *must* be defined as *nonrecoverable*. If the TDQ has any recoverability at all, FEPI will not write to the TDQ.

**EXPLANATION**

Why is there this recoverability restriction?

This is imposed because FEPI does not take any notice of Syncpoints, and, therefore, does not issue any `EXEC CICS SYNCPOINT` commands internally. Consequently, if the TDQ is defined as being recoverable, because there is never a Syncpoint, the data records will never be committed.

There are four Handlers:

- The *Begin Session* Handler
- The *End Session* Handler
- The *Unsolicited Data* Handler
- For SLUP (LU0) Communications only, the *STSN* Handler

They are defined via parameters on the `EXEC CICS FEPI INSTALL PROPERTYSET` command which sets the options for a Pool. Consequently, they apply for all the Connections defined within the Pool (see Chapter 16). There is no restriction about the transaction names being unique to a Pool. The following options on the Propertyset define the Handler transactions to be used (see Chapter 44 for when they are invoked by FEPI):

**BEGINSESSION** The Begin Session Handler transaction name

**ENDSESSION** The End Session Handler transaction name

**UNSOLDATA** The Unsolicited Data Handler transaction name (but beware interaction with the `UNSOLDATACK` parameter (see Sec. 16.2.12)

**STSN** The STSN Handler transaction name (applicable only to SLUP (LU0) Communications)

The FEPI Conversations used in the Handlers are accessed by the execution of an `EXEC CICS FEPI ALLOCATE PASSCONVID` command (see Sec. 27.3). The required `CONVID` is obtained from the Start Data supplied to the Handler (see Sec. D.2).

### 43.1.2 Defining the Monitors

There are two types of Monitor Transient Data Queues: *Pool-specific* and the *FEPI Global TDQ* (CSZX). If the relevant TDQ is not defined (or is defined but recoverable), then FEPI will not write to the TDQ. It is *strongly* recommended that the CSZX FEPI Global TDQ is always defined. If omitted, you lose potentially vital information about events such as session loss, etc. See Chapter 46 for what information is placed within CSZX.

The Pool-specific TDQs are defined via the `EXCEPTIONQ` parameter of the `EXEC CICS FEPI INSTALL PROPERTYSET` which sets the options for a Pool (see Sec. 16.2.5). Certain errors associated with SPI-type commands operating on the pool are sent to the Pool-specific TDQs. However, there is no restriction about sharing this TDQ between any number of Pools. See Chapter 45 for what information is placed therein.

# CHAPTER 44 Handler descriptions

**GUIDANCE**

This chapter describes the four Handlers. See Sec. 43.1.1 for the definitions required to run the Handlers, and Chapter 47 for information about using them in your application design.

The Handlers are CICS transactions started by FEPI when certain events occur. They are associated with Pools, and defined via the Pool's Propertyset (see Sec. 43.1). These are the Handlers:

- Begin Session (Sec. 44.1)
- End Session (Sec. 44.2)
- Unsolicited Data (Sec. 44.3)
- STSN (Sec. 44.4)

In all cases, information relevant for Handler operation is provided by Start Data. The Handler should issue an `EXEC CICS RETRIEVE` to obtain this information. (Beware of omitting this action, as CICS will reinitiate the Handler if the Start Data is not obtained.) The layout of the Start Data is described in Sec. D.2.

## 44.1 The Begin Session Handler

The Begin Session Handler is initiated as a nonterminal transaction when a Connection is Bound. A *Bind* occurs when the Connection is Acquired. (Contrast this with the End Session Handler which is invoked when the Connection is *Unbound* (or Released).)

The idea of the Handler is that it should do things that relate to the initialization of the partner system. It will usually be initiated on the first flow from the partner. However, what this first flow is depends on the definitions of the emulated terminal in the partner system. Therefore, the Begin Session Handler for a Datastream Connection may have to deal with things like Structured Field Queries (see Chapter 38) as well as the signon panel from the partner system. If the Begin Session Handler is working on a formatted Connection, then FEPI takes care of all of this for you.

A Structured Field Query is a 3270 Structured Field flow that requests the terminal to return certain attributes (like the screen size, and whether it supports colour, etc.). This raises a problem, as the Begin Session Handler is running nonterminal, and therefore there is no opportunity to send this request on to the real end-user terminal for it to supply the relevant attributes. Therefore, if communicating with CICS, you should either use RDO to define the TYPETERM of the emulated terminal as nonqueriable (IMS systems tend not to send this query flow), or research a suitable reply. A reply of 'null' is usually acceptable, and if CICS is the partner system, this is a cue to take defaults.

### 44.1.1 Circumstances generating the Handler

The Begin Session Handler is invoked after the Connection is bound. When it starts it is dependent on the INITIALDATA parameter of the Propertyset (see Sec. 16.2.8). With INITIALDATA(INBOUND) it will be initiated on the first flow from the partner. With INITIALDATA(NOTINBOUND) it will start immediately.

If the partner system sends a message upon its emulated terminal being 'turned on', then the Propertyset should specify INITIALDATA(INBOUND). IMS (on LU2 sessions) always sends an initial message; CICS usually does so (but you can easily alter this processing).

If INITIALDATA(NOTINBOUND) is specified, and a signon panel flows, this is classed as Unsolicited data.

There is no requirement that forces the usage of a Begin Session Handler with INITIALDATA(INBOUND). If the Begin Session Handler is not specified, then the data is queued until the first EXEC CICS FEPI RECEIVE on the Connection is issued (by an application program).

### 44.1.2 What the Handler should do

The Begin Session Handler should first EXEC CICS RETRIEVE the Start Data for the Handler, and then EXEC CICS FEPI ALLOCATE PASSCONVID on the Convid provided therein. Once it has finished processing, the Handler should EXEC CICS FEPI FREE the Conversation specifying HOLD or PASS. The layout of the Start Data is described in Sec. D.2.

The Begin Session Handler should process the first flow from the partner system. If this flow is a signon screen, then a suitable logonid and password should be specified to sign on the terminal. However, once the first flow has been EXEC CICS FEPI RECEIVEd (if there is initial data), full FEPI facilities are available, and, providing the partner accepts it, any flow can be sent to the partner.

If the FEPI application design is managing the Connections (as outlined in Chapter 61), then all the Begin Session Handler should do is save the Convid and then EXEC CICS FEPI FREE HOLD the Conversation.

## **44.2** The End Session Handler

The End Session Handler is invoked in two circumstances:

- At the end of a Conversation, or
- When a Connection is to be Unbound (that is, just before it is RELEASED).

The Handler is provided so that certain centrally-defined actions can be taken to clean up things before usage stops. The Start data (layout in Sec. D.2) indicates which circumstance has initiated the Handler.

### 44.2.1 End of Conversation

When a CICS transaction has finished running a FEPI Conversation, it issues an `EXEC CICS FEPI FREE` command to give up access. At this point, the End Session Handler is initiated (running as a nonterminal transaction) with `EVENTTYPE(FREE)` in the Start Data. The layout of the Start Data is described in Sec. D.2.

The End of Conversation flavour of the End Session Handler provides the opportunity to tidy up the emulated terminal in the partner system (perhaps by issuing a signoff sequence), and also the opportunity to override the type of `FREE` being performed.

Some FEPI application designs may involve managing the Connections, not letting FEPI allocate Connections randomly (see Chapter 61). In this case, the End Session Handler provides a convenient point at which to manage this process.

However, at this point, the Conversation has not been grabbed by another transaction, and so it is available for use within the Handler. Therefore, all the FEPI commands are available within the Handler, and so any suitable action can be taken (but beware of using `EXEC CICS FEPI START`s, and of using a long-running communications).

### 44.2.2 End of Connection

When the Connection to the partner system is to be released, then, after all existing FEPI Conversations have ended, the End Session Handler (with `EVENTTYPE(RELEASE)` in the Start Data) is started. The Connection can be released either because someone requested it (via usage of CEMT, executing an `EXEC CICS FEPI SET CONNECTION ACQSTATUS (RELEASED)`, or an `EXEC CICS FEPI FREE RELEASE`) or because CICS is undergoing a normal shutdown. These two cases are distinguished between via the `EVENTVALUE` field in the Start Data (which is set either to `RELEASE` or to `SHUTDOWN`).

As the idea of the Handler is to tidy things in the partner system before its terminal is 'turned off', it may be desirable to do a different set of actions in these two circumstances. The Handler is initiated before the Connection is actually Released, and so full FEPI facilities are available. However, note that certain commands will not operate during CICS shutdown, and CICS will not shutdown until the Handler has terminated.

Remember that if the End Session Handler is to run during CICS shutdown, it must be defined as such in the XLT.

### 44.2.3 What the Handler should do

The End Session Handler should first `EXEC CICS RETRIEVE` the Start Data for the Handler, and then `EXEC CICS FEPI ALLOCATE PASSCONVID` on the Convid provided within the Start Data. Once it has finished processing, it should `EXEC CICS FEPI FREE` the Conversation. The layout of the Start Data is described in Sec. D.2.

The End Session Handler should consider doing things like:

- Setting the state of the partner system's terminal into a known position, so that when the Connection is re-established a known panel will be presented.
- Signing off the emulated terminal in the partner system
- Taking some sort of action in the partner system to prevent it sending data to a terminal that is switched off (and so routing this information to elsewhere).
- Letting the partner system know that the FEPI system is shutting down, and the partmer system should adjust its processing accordingly. For example, if using Transaction Routing between the partner system back to the FEPI system, then this might be the opportunity to update a routing table, so that the partner system sends a routed transaction elsewhere.
- For the End Session Handler invoked as a result of End of Conversation (`EVENTTYPE(FREE)` in the Start Data), the opportunity exists to override the `EXEC CICS FEPI FREE` setting. Therefore, the FEPI application program could issue an `EXEC CICS FEPI FREE RELEASE`, and the End Session Handler could override this and say that the Connection is to be retained. This allows a centralized control of FEPI Connections.

## 44.3 The Unsolicited Data Handler

Before discussing the Handler, it is necessary to define what exactly *Unsolicited data* is. This is discussed in detail in Chapter 24, but is summarized here.

Data is *Unsolicited* when a flow arrives from the partner system on a Connection, and there is currently no FEPI application program using the Connection. Therefore, the Target system has decided to send a panel to its FEPI-emulated terminal when there is 'no one' sitting at the terminal.

FEPI cannot simply store the flow for reception on the next `EXEC CICS FEPI RECEIVE` command for the Connection for several reasons:

- The Receive may never be issued.
- The appearance of unknown data will upset the logic of the application running the FEPI communication.
- The partner system is expecting some 'keyed' response to the flow.
- The partner system that sent the flow may be awaiting a VTAM response flow to say that the data was received correctly.

Therefore, FEPI adopts the approach of either rejecting the flow completely (which is controlled by the `UNSOLDATACK` parameter on the pool owning the Connection, see Sec. 16.2.12), or starting a Handler transaction to process the flow. However, if the `UNSOLDATA` parameter which names the Handler transaction is invalid, or specifies a non-existent transaction, then the flow is lost (without any VTAM response, so this circumstance may lock the partner system, or cause it to resend the flow).

### 44.3.1 Circumstances generating the Handler

Unsolicited data occurs in situations such as the following:

- A partner system sends more data than the application program expected (because the first chunk has been successfully received and then the Conversation ended).

- When using Timeout facilities on an EXEC CICS FEPI RECEIVE, the Receive times out, and the Conversation ends before the partner system responds with the required panel.
- When communicating with CICS, the partner CICS system schedules a transaction at the emulated terminal, when there is no FEPI Conversation using the terminal, which transaction sends a panel for input.
- The partner system sends a broadcast message to all terminals (note that this falls into the category of Unexpected data (see Chapter 24) if there is a Conversation running on the Connection)
- When communicating with IMS, running a nonresponse mode transaction, and the Conversation that initiated the IMS process has ended when IMS responds.
- When communicating with IMS, general asynchronous output will also trigger the Unsolicited Data Handler if no Conversation is currently running on the Connection when IMS responds. This can also happen if IMS MFS is reassigning logical terminals to physical terminals.

### 44.3.2 What the Handler should do

The Unsolicited Data Handler should first EXEC CICS RETRIEVE the Start Data for the Handler, and then EXEC CICS FEPI ALLOCATE PASSCONVID on the Convid provided within the Start Data (layout in Sec. D.2). Once it has finished processing, it should EXEC CICS FEPI FREE the Conversation.

The Unsolicited Data Handler is not running at a terminal, so it is difficult to Send the flow from the partner system to a 'real' end user unless the whole of the FEPI emulation is designed to cope with this circumstance.

The Start Data which is EXEC CICS RETRIEVEd contains the Pool, Target, and Node names for the Connection upon which the Unsolicited data arrived (do not forget to EXEC CICS RETRIEVE this data, or else CICS will do the usual rescheduling of the Handler transaction). Therefore, it may be possible to tie up the FEPI Connection with the CICS terminal running the FEPI application (for example, by using the USERDATA field of the Connection (see Chapter 50). However, actually to obtain the Unsolicited flow within the Handler, the CONVID assigned from the Start Data is used in a normal EXEC CICS FEPI RETRIEVE command.

Once the data has been examined, the Conversation should be ended with an EXEC CICS FEPI FREE in the normal fashion. The choice of doing a HOLD/PASS or a RELEASE/FORCE depends upon whether you want the FEPI emulation to continue (see Chapter 36).

If the Unsolicited flow requires a VTAM response (as indicated by the RESPSTATUS field), then you should consider what response is needed (via an EXEC CICS FEPI ISSUE). If, after an analysis of the flow, you decide to discard it, then do you need to send a Negative Response to the partner system to let it know that you have done the rejection? If so, then the EXEC CICS FEPI ISSUE should be done. If not, then the usual response processing on the EXEC CICS FEPI FREE will respond Positively (see Chapter 53).

In general, you should consider that the Unsolicited Data Handler will only be initiated if the partner system does something which the FEPI application is not able to cope with. In this case, the Unsolicited Data Handler should simply log the data somewhere (perhaps in a Transient Data Queue) and `EXEC CICS FEPI FREE RELEASE` the Connection to prevent any further occurrences.

## 44.4 The STSN Handler

The STSN Handler is applicable only to SLUP (LU0) processing, and it deals with SNA Message Synchronization. It is started when the partner has issued the SNA *STSN* or *SDT* command. The detail of the processing is outside the scope of this book, but see Chapter 52 where it is briefly discussed.

# CHAPTER 45 Pool-specific Monitors

| GUIDANCE |
|---|
| This chapter contains information about Pool-specific Monitor programs. |

The Pool-specific Monitors are Transient Data Queues (TDQs) defined in the `EXCEPTIONQ` parameter of the Propertyset which defines the pool (see Sec. 16.2.5). When an error occurs, FEPI writes a record to the named TDQ, and that is all that happens. Once FEPI has written the record notifying the error, it is up to you to process it in the way most suitable for your application design. Note that if the named TDQ does not exist in the DCT, or if it is defined as recoverable, then FEPI will simply not write the TDQ record—no notification will be given of this absence.

Because the errors are recorded against the Pool, there is nothing stopping you from defining a single Pool-specific TDQ, and using this TDQ in all Pools. The format of the TDQ record is described in Sec. D.1, and it contains details about the Node, Target, and Pool involved in the failure. Therefore, you can readily detect the Pool in which the error occurred. However, it may simplify your application design to have different TDQs defined for each Pool, even though the same Triggered Transaction is started for each one.

To take this a step further, you could even define the Pool-specific TDQs to be the Global FEPI TDQ CSZX. However, this is not recommended, as the sorts of events logged to CSZX are really conceptually different to the Pool-specific TDQs.

Two types of TDQ records are written to the Pool-specific TDQs:

- Errors manipulating the Connections within the Pool
- Errors relating to the usability of Connections defined within the Pool

## 45.1 List errors

The `EXEC CICS FEPI ADD` and `DELETE` commands all accept lists of Nodes and Targets that are to be added or deleted from the Pool. However, this raises the problem of how an error within one of these lists is to be notified. FEPI solves this problem by returning EIBRESP2(119), and writing a record to the

Pool-specific TDQ naming the list item in error. See Sec. D.1 for details of the TDQ record, and Sec. 28.9 for information on EIBRESP2(119).

However, if a single Node or Target is being added or deleted from the Pool, and this operation fails, the TDQ record is not written, as the appropriate EIBRESP2 is directly returned in case of error.

### ADD ERRORS

In this case `EVENTTYPE(ADDFAIL)` is set in the TDQ record, which indicates that an attempt to add a new Connection (Target–Node pair) into the Pool has failed. The `EVENTVALUE` field contains the EIBRESP2 return code for the operation that would have been returned if the command was not in a list.

The most probable cause of this error is that the Connection is already defined in another Pool (`EVENTVALUE(175)`), but things like Unknown Node (`EVENTVALUE(117)`) or Unknown Target (`EVENTVALUE(116)`) are fairly common.

### DELETE ERRORS

In this case `EVENTTYPE(DELETEFAIL)` is set in the TDQ record, indicating that an attempt to delete an existing Connection (Target–Node pair) from the Pool has failed. The `EVENTVALUE` field contains the EIBRESP2 return code for the operation that would have been returned if the command was not in a list.

The most probable cause of this error is that the Connection is not defined in the Pool (`EVENTVALUE(118)`), but things like Unknown Node (`EVENTVALUE(117)`) or Unknown Target (`EVENTVALUE(116)`) are fairly common.

### 45.1.1 What the Monitor program should do (1)

Assuming that the Monitor program is initiated by a Transient Data Queue Trigger, then it should act as a normal CICS TD initiated program. It should do an `EXEC CICS ASSIGN STARTCODE` to ensure that it was TD initiated, and then do an `EXEC CICS ASSIGN QNAME` to obtain the name of the TDQ that caused the initiation. It should then issue an `EXEC CICS READQ TD` to obtain the record with failure information.

After examining the record the Monitor program has all the facilities of FEPI available to enact any suitable recovery operations. It is difficult to recommend any specific action, as an attempt to manipulate the contents of the Pool indicates some sort of logic error within the FEPI application.

The Monitor program should then reread the TDQ before ending so that any more failure records are immediately processed.

## 45.2 Usability errors

These Transient Data Queue records do not relate to any definitional errors for Connections within the Pool, but rather inform that something has happened to the Connection within the Pool. This is either that:

- The session has been lost or,
- The session could not be started.

### SESSION LOST

*Session Lost* indicates that the Connection to the partner system has failed. The first `EXEC CICS FEPI` command that detected this failure will return an indication of this error, but to assist in centralized recovery, an entry is also written to the Pool-specific TDQ.

The most common cause of Session Lost is that the partner system has abended. However, this condition will also be raised if an operator has cancelled the session. This could arise by either a system operator issuing an MVS `'V NET,INACT,FORCE'` command on the session, or (for example) a CICS operator `CEMT S TERM( ) REL`ing the emulated terminal in the partner system.

Some information about why the session failed is contained in the first part of the `EVENTDATA` field in the TDQ record (see Sec. D.1).

When the session is lost, FEPI will automatically try to restart it at periodic intervals (usually 1 minute for 30 retries). The progress of this recovery is indicated by the second part of the `EVENTDATA` field in the TDQ record. When FEPI decides that enough attempts have occurred, the second part of `EVENTDATA` contains 0.

### SESSION FAIL

*Session Fail* is generated when the Connection fails to start. The Connection is started when it is `ACQUIRED` either by a `CEMT S FECONN ACQ`, an `EXEC CICS FEPI SET CONNECTION ACQSTATUS(ACQUIRED)`, or by installing the Connection with `ACQSTATUS(ACQUIRED)`.

When a Connection fails to start, it could fail for reasons such as:

- An inconsistency between VTAM definitions, FEPI definitions or definitions within the partner system.
- VTAM could not contact the partner system.
- The partner system is not active.

Some information about why the Connection (the VTAM session) could not be started is contained in the first part of the `EVENTDATA` field in the TDQ record (see Sec. D.1 for the record layout).

When the session fails to start, FEPI will automatically retry the start at periodic intervals (usually 1 minute for 30 retries). The progress of this retry is indicated by the second part of the `EVENTDATA` field in the TDQ record. When FEPI decides that enough retries have occurred, the second part of `EVENTDATA` contains 0.

### 45.2.1 What the Monitor program should do (2)

Assuming that the Monitor program is initiated by a TDQ trigger, then it should act as a normal CICS TD Initiated program. It should do an `EXEC CICS ASSIGN STARTCODE` to ensure that it was TD initiated, and then do an `EXEC CICS ASSIGN QNAME` to obtain the name of the TDQ that caused the Monitor initiation. It should then issue an `EXEC CICS READQ TD` to obtain the record with the failure information.

After examining the record, the Monitor program has all the facilities of FEPI available to enact any suitable recovery operations.

You should view a Session Lost error as a serious occurrence, and should attempt to use the FEPI SPI-type commands to try and re-establish the session (but if you do not do this, FEPI will still be attempting to recontact the partner). However, if the failure is caused by the partner system abending, this will not be possible! If the partner system has abended, a Monitor TDQ record will be written for every active Connection to that target. If the partner is undergoing an XRF takeover, the situation may well recover itself without any intervention, as FEPI can cope with XRF takeovers of the partner system.

The only recommendation I can make is that some sort of Message be written to the CICS log (or MVS console) requesting investigation as to why the partner system is suddenly unavailable.

The case of Session Failure in establishing the Connection is a similar circumstance to Session Lost, except that it happens when the Connection is starting. Therefore, you should take similar actions to those mentioned for session loss.

CHAPTER 46

# CSZX Monitors

**GUIDANCE**

This chapter describes the unexpected events that are logged into the FEPI Global Transient Data Queue CSZX. You should always use a Triggered Monitor program to process these events.

In addition to the Pool-specific Monitors (see Chapter 45) FEPI writes data to CSZX, the FEPI Global TDQ. Although you can choose not to define CSZX, you are *strongly* recommended to do so (if the TDQ is not defined in the DCT, or it is defined as being recoverable, then FEPI will simply discard any information that would have been placed therein).

CSZX is used by FEPI to notify unexpected events that relate to the processing state of FEPI resources. The techniques for acting on the TDQ records are exactly the same as those for the Pool-specific TDQs. However, I would recommend that the Monitor program used to process CSZX TDQ records is different to the Monitors used to process the Pool-specific TDQs, as the actions to be taken are different.

The following types of events are notified in CSZX:

- Resource management errors
- A resource acquisition failure
- An Unsolicited Bind arrival

## 46.1 Resource management errors

Resource management errors are generated by FEPI resources failing to install or discard themselves, or because the resource has rejected an attempt to alter its state.

### INSTALL ERRORS

If an attempt to `EXEC CICS FEPI INSTALL` a FEPI resource fails, then an indication of this failure is sent to CSZX. This will occur even if only a single element-list is being used. The logic behind this is that, in a production environment, FEPI resources are assumed to be in a controlled environment. Consequently, if resource installation fails, then there may be some sort of unauthorized access going on, or there is a logic error in the installation process. Therefore, all installation failures are logged centrally for system programmer action to be taken.

### DISCARD ERRORS

If an attempt is made to `EXEC CICS FEPI DISCARD` a FEPI Resource and this operation fails, then an indication of this failure is sent to CSZX. This will occur even if only a single element-list is being used. The logic behind this is similar to that for installation errors.

However, a failure to discard the resource immediately does not generate a CSZX record. FEPI will mark the resource as being discardable at any time, but the resource will not actually disappear until usage of it is stopped. Consequently, the CSZX record is written only for things like an attempt to discard a non-existent FEPI resource.

### SET ERRORS

If a FEPI resource is being manipulated by an `EXEC CICS FEPI SET` command, and the request is rejected, a CSZX record will be generated. This will occur even if only a single element-list is being used. These entries usually indicate some sort of coding error.

However, FEPI resource state transitions do not happen immediately (see Sec. 18.1.1). The `EXEC CICS FEPI SET` may not alter the state to that requested immediately, but rather take effect once the transition is permitted (for example, setting a FEPI resource to `ACQUIRED` is not immediate, but occurs when the VTAM contact has succeeded). If this transition is not immediate, no CSZX TDQ record is written. The TDQ record will only be written if the transition fails.

## 46.1.1 What the Monitor program should do (1)

Assuming that the Monitor program is initiated by a TDQ trigger, then it should act as a normal CICS TD Initiated program. It should do an `EXEC CICS ASSIGN STARTCODE` to ensure that it was TD initiated, and then do an `EXEC CICS ASSIGN QNAME` to obtain the name of the TDQ that caused the Monitor initiation. It should then issue an `EXEC CICS READQ TD` to obtain the record with the failure information.

After examining the record the Monitor program has all the facilities of FEPI available to enact any suitable recovery operations. The `EVENTTYPE` field in the TDQ record (see Sec. D.1) identifies the failure, and the `EVENTVALUE` field contains the EIBRESP2 return code indicating why the TDQ record was generated.

These sort of resource management errors are usually caused by some sort of coding or logic error. They usually indicate that an attempt was made to install a duplicate resource, discard a non-existent resource, or do a set on a resource which does not exist. In these cases, all I can recommend is that you examine your code and application design to see why the errors were generated.

However, just because a CSZX TDQ record was generated, it does not necessarily mean that an error has occurred. If you are using Dynamic Resource Definition techniques (see Chapter 48), then you may well not bother to check that the named resource is actually installed before attempting to install it again! This is bad practice, but could be used as a mechanism to trigger certain processing actions in a Monitor.

Similarly, if attempting to remove FEPI resources prior to a shutdown sequence, then an attempt to discard a non-existent (but potentially existent) resource is not of any interest, providing all extant ones are discarded.

The Set Fail TDQ records could indicate some sort of VTAM failure, so these may be potentially interesting. However, in most cases they will be accompanied by another TDQ record indicating the precise reason for failure.

Therefore, what the CSZX Monitor program does with these resource management errors is completely up to your application design. However, as a first-case recommendation, it would not do too much harm simply to take no action on them, but just issue a message to record the occurrence.

## **46.2** Resource Acquisition Error

This error is raised when a FEPI resource cannot be `ACQUIRED`. The act of Acquisition involves VTAM actions on the resource. For a FEPI `NODE`, this means issuing a VTAM OPEN on the ACB which the Node represents. For a FEPI `CONNECTION`, this involves attempting to make contact with the partner system. This leads to the possibility that the failure does not reside within the CICS system running FEPI, but may be located within the partner system, or within VTAM definitions.

FEPI will retry the operation periodically (usually at 1 minute intervals for 30 retries), so there may be many occurrences of the same entry in the CSZX TDQ.

### 46.2.1 What the Monitor program should do (2)

Assuming that the Monitor program is initiated by a TDQ trigger, it should act as a normal CICS TD initiated program. It should do an `EXEC CICS ASSIGN STARTCODE` to ensure that it was TD initiated, and then do an `EXEC CICS ASSIGN QNAME` to obtain the name of the TDQ that caused the Monitor initiation. It should then issue an `EXEC CICS READQ TD` to obtain the record with the failure information.

After examining the record the Monitor program has all the facilities of FEPI available to enact any suitable recovery operations. The `EVENTTYPE` field in the TDQ record (see Sec. D.1) identifies the `ACQFAIL` failure, and the `EVENTVALUE` field contains the VTAM reason code for the failure, and an indication of which retry was being performed. The retry count is 0 when FEPI decides that enough retries have been made.

FEPI may well succeed in recontacting the resource, so no particular action needs to be taken until FEPI gives up. However, you can stop the retries happening by `EXEC CICS FEPI SET`ting the resource to `ACQSTATUS(RELEASED)`.

A Resource Acquisition Error CSZX TDQ record will be generated when the FEPI resource is defined with `ACQSTATUS(ACQUIRED)`, when an `EXEC CICS FEPI SET ACQSTATUS(ACQUIRED)` is processed, or when CEMT sets the resource to `ACQ`ed and the acquisition fails. However, if the resource is currently active when a VTAM failure occurs, then a Pool-specific TDQ record is made instead (see Chapter 45).

Assuming that there are no definitional errors, the main cause of this TDQ record will be that the partner system was not active when the Acquisition occurred. However, this will also occur if the partner system is undergoing an XRF takeover.

Therefore, I recommend that no action be taken on these CSZX TDQ records until the FEPI retries stop. Then you should send a message to either the MVS, network, or CICS operators to prompt them to investigate the situation.

## **46.3** Unsolicited Bind Arrival

An *Unsolicited Bind* is a VTAM *Bind* (an attempt to establish a session) that has flowed into FEPI from some external source. This means that some external partner is trying to make contact with FEPI. But FEPI processing always assumes that FEPI will be in control of this process. In other words, the act of generating a VTAM session to run an emulated terminal is under FEPI control. Consequently, FEPI will not process this VTAM flow, and puts it into the CSZX TDQ for a Monitor program to decide what to do with it.

When FEPI logs the Unsolicited *Bind* to CSZX, it has taken no action (either accepting or rejecting the Bind) to respond to the partner system that sent the Bind. (If, therefore, CSZX is not defined, then the Bind is left in limbo, and the partner never receives its expected response.)

However, the situation is not as bleak as this. An Unsolicited Bind will be logged in CSZX only if FEPI is expecting the Unsolicited Bind because CLSDST(PASS) processing is being performed (see Chapter 51). If FEPI does not expect the Unsolicited Bind, it will be unconditionally rejected, and will not be logged in CSZX.

Therefore, this type of CSZX TDQ record contains information for CLSDST(PASS) processing. This is the only mechanism that FEPI provides for CLSDST(PASS) processing.

### 46.3.1 What the Monitor program should do (3)

Assuming that the Monitor program is initiated by a TDQ trigger, it should act as a normal CICS TD initiated program. It should do an `EXEC CICS ASSIGN STARTCODE` to ensure that it was TD initiated, and then do an `EXEC CICS ASSIGN QNAME` to obtain the name of the TDQ that caused the Monitor initiation. It should then issue an `EXEC CICS READQ TD` to obtain the record with the failure information.

After examining the record, the Monitor program has all the facilities of FEPI available to enact any suitable recovery operations. The `EVENTTYPE` field in the TDQ record (see Sec. D.1) identifies the Unsolicited Bind arrival with a setting of `SESSION`, and the value in the `TARGET` field contains the Applid of the system from which the Bind flowed.

The action to be taken when processing CLSDST (PASS) operations for this Unsolicited Bind depends upon whether or not the partner Applid (in the `TARGET` field) is known. See Chapter 51 for the actions to be taken. However, the actions involve defining a Target for the Bind, together with other processing that depends upon application design. When the Target is defined and acquired, the VTAM flow that accepts the Bind is sent to the partner.

CHAPTER 47

# How to use Monitors and Handlers

| GUIDANCE |
|---|
| This chapter discusses the pros and cons of using Handlers and Monitors in your application design. |

## 47.1 Designing with Handlers

The Handlers are optional, and can be implemented on a Pool-by-Pool basis.

BEGIN SESSION HANDLER

The Begin Session Handler is initiated only when a Connection is `ACQUIRED`. Consequently, if it is not provided, whatever processing could potentially be done is postponed to the first use of the Connection in an application program

UNSOLICITED DATA HANDER

The Unsolicited Data Handler is invoked when data arrives on a Connection which is not currently active. If the Handler is not provided, the data is lost.

END SESSION HANDLER

The End Session Handler is invoked at the end of a Conversation, and at the end of a Connection. Consequently, the processing provided could, in principle, be located within application programs, but this assumes that facilities like CEMT are never used to release a FEPI resource.

STSN HANDLER

The use of the STSN Handler is outside the scope of this book. See Chapter 52 for information on this processing.

### 47.1.1 Design decisions

The crucial factor in considering whether or not to implement an Handler is: 'How can the required function be provided in another place?'

If a Handler is used, you have a guarantee that it is always invoked in the given circumstance, and therefore, that the processing is always performed. It may be the case that the Handler will be written by system programmers (who understand more of the FEPI Communication issues), whereas the application programs will be written by application programmers. Consequently, the location of processing within Handlers ensures that common standards are enforced, and that the partner systems are not upset when some sort of error occurs.

Some of the Handlers provide a mechanism for doing things that are not provided elsewhere (for example, the Unsolicited Data Handler). In this case, the design decision is an evaluation of the risk of the main line application program not working properly, and so having to code around the circumstance. Therefore, I recommend that you use the Handlers which provide function not located anywhere else. These Handlers are:

- The End Session Handler (for End of Connection)
- The Unsolicited Data Handler

The use of the other Handlers is dependent upon where you wish to provide the function (if at all). It may be convenient to centralize the function in a Handler, or to place it within application programs. This decision applies to these Handlers:

- The Begin Session Handler
- The End Session Handler (for End of Conversation)
- The STSN Handler

However, my main recommendation is that you should use the Handlers to the full.

### 47.1.2 The Begin Session Handler

The Begin Session Handler is invoked upon the first contact with a partner over a given Connection. Consequently, the Handler is involved with processing the first flow from the partner system. See Sec. 44.1 for details.

Therefore, the design decision involves:

- Processing Structured Field Queries
- Doing signons
- Managing Connections

#### STRUCTURED FIELD QUERIES

If the partner is sending Structured Field Queries, and if you are running the Begin Session Handler, you do not have a real end-user terminal from which an accurate response can be obtained. Thus, it might be better to avoid running the Handler, and to locate this function within each application program (note the duplication of function) that could use the Connection. Consequently, there is a significant overhead in removing the processing of Structured Field queries from the Begin Session Handler.

If you have followed the recommendation that partner CICS terminals be defined with `QUERY(NO)` in the `TYPETERM`, then CICS will not send the Structured Field Query, and so there is no problem. IMS does not send this query in any case. Therefore, it is possible to avoid this problem entirely.

It is entirely possible that a standard reply to the Structured Field Query can be made—indeed most partner systems will be quite happy to accept a 'null' response (but you have to send it; omitting the response will probably only result in the partner resending the query). In this case, you can send the standard reply from the Begin Session Handler.

If you do decide that you must query the real end user terminal, then you have no option to locate (and duplicate) the code in each program that issues an `EXEC CICS FEPI ALLOCATE` for the Pool. This logic is keyed by the `NEWSESSION` setting on the `SESSNSTATUS` parameter returned on the `EXEC CICS FEPI ALLOCATE` command.

To summarize this discussion on Structured Field Query:

- Use a Begin Session Handler if the Structured Field Query does not flow.
- Use a Begin Session Handler to cope with standard replies.
- Do not use a Begin Session Handler if an accurate response from a real end-user terminal is required.

## SIGNONS

The main problem of using Begin Session Handlers is processing signons. This question revolves around what security processing is required by the partner system, and how the FEPI application program is to comply with this edict. Note that I assume that the signon screen is the first panel to be presented (if it is not, then the Begin Session Handler can cope with all prior screens without any problem).

If your FEPI application is some sort of client–server arrangement, then it is quite possible that the partner system does not need a signon (as everything from a given terminal has come via FEPI, whose access has been authorized by the FEPI application), or that a fixed signon and password is acceptable. In this case, a Begin Session Handler can be used to do the signon processing.

However, if the partner terminal has to be signed on with the real end user logonid and password, then the Begin Session Handler cannot be used. This is because the Begin Session Handler runs nonterminal, and so does not know anything about userids, etc. Therefore, the processing of the signon screen has to be located within an application program. Section 21.1.2 contains information about the problems involved with doing this signon (in particular, the problem of the password).

To summarize this discussion of signon processing:

- Use a Begin Session Handler if the partner system does not require any special signons.
- Use a Begin Session Handler if the partner system can be signed on with a constant logonid and password.
- Do not use a Begin Session Handler if the partner system requires a signon with the correct logonid and password for the real end user.

## MANAGING CONNECTIONS

Having overcome the problems of Structured Field Queries and signons, some FEPI application designs manage the FEPI Conversations manually as described in Chapter 61. This is done to reduce RACF overheads on signon processing in the partner system. In this design, a FEPI Application Program *never* issues an `EXEC CICS FEPI FREE RELEASE` command, but *always* does an `EXEC CICS FEPI FREE PASS` at the end of each CICS application program to manage the Convids, and so control who is accessing what emulated terminal.

In this scenario, each FEPI Application program always gains access to the partner system via an `EXEC CICS FEPI ALLOCATE PASSCONVID` command. Consequently, there must be some mechanism which provides the Convid for this command. However, the Convids are obtained only by an `EXEC CICS FEPI ALLOCATE` command without the specification of the `PASSCONVID` option. The most suitable place to do this operation (i.e., to generate and capture the Convids) is within the Begin Session Handler, which then saves the Convids for subsequent use.

If the FEPI application design requires management of Convids to reduce partner signon overheads, the Begin Session Handler does not do any signon processing, but it should ensure that the emulated terminal is in a state such that the signon transaction can be easily issued.

To summarize this discussion of managing Connections:

- If managing Connections, you should use a Begin Session Handler.
- If not managing Connections, a Begin Session Handler is not necessarily necessary.

### 47.1.3 The Unsolicited Data Handler

The Unsolicited Data Handler is the only FEPI mechanism provided which notifies that a flow has occurred on a Connection that is not currently in use. Consequently, you should process this flow, or else the Connection will remain in an unexpected position when it next comes to be used.

What you do with the data is up to you. However, a properly structured partner system will not randomly send panels to working screens, so it is probable that the Unsolicited Data is some sort of broadcast message. Thus, it might take only a simple response (such as a Clear key) to remove it, and restore the previous screen.

If you are using the Unsolicited Data Handler to provide support for IMS nonresponse mode communications, then think about whether or not it would be better to use an `EXEC CICS FEPI RECEIVE TIMEOUT` to provide the equivalent function. However, contrary to this, you may need the Unsolicited Data Handler to avoid CICS resource constraints.

To summarize:

- *Always* provide an Unsolicited Data Handler.

### 47.1.4 The End Session Handler (End of Conversation)

The End Session Handler for End of Conversation is invoked each time a FEPI application program issues an `EXEC CICS FEPI FREE` (or the CICS task ends without this command being issued). The Handler provides the opportunity to alter the type of Free being processed, as well as allowing tidying up actions.

The End Session Handler for End of Conversation will typically be used to coordinate the state of the partner system's 'terminal' with that of the emulated terminal. For example, if the FEPI application program does an `EXEC CICS FEPI FREE RELEASE`, meaning that the current user has finished with the Connection and that another task can use it, it is desirable to enforce a signoff etc. in the partner system. If the application design guarantees that a signoff will always occur in this circumstance, then the Handler need not be provided.

However, if this guarantee cannot be given, the End Session Handler should be used.

If you need to take some sort of special action on transaction abend, then the End Session Handler provides the opportunity. If the CICS transaction abends, then the End Session Handler will be invoked with an indication that it was called by CICS End of Task Processing, rather than End of Conversation processing. In this case, FEPI is going to release the Connection, and you may well need to let the partner system know (or take some preventative action) before the drop occurs.

A special feature of the End Session Handler for End of Conversation permits the Handler to alter the type of `EXEC CICS FEPI FREE` being performed. Consequently, the opportunity exists to enforce a release/acquire operation on the connection, no matter what the FEPI application program says.

To summarize this discussion of the End Session Handler for End of Conversation:

- Use the Handler if you need to enforce signoff at End of Conversation.
- Use the Handler to take action on transaction abend.
- Use the Handler to coordinate partner 'terminal' status with FEPI Conversation status.
- Use the Handler if you need to police or override `EXEC CICS FEPI FREE` types.

### 47.1.5 The End Session Handler (End of Connection)

The End Session Handler for End of Connection will be invoked just before a Connection is to be released. Therefore, it provides the last possible opportunity to communicate with the partner before that partner receives an indication that its terminal has been turned off.

You should use this Handler to ensure that the partner system has been signed off. Additionally, if managing Conversations, then this Handler provides the only opportunity to note that the Connection is unavailable (you cannot rely on code in the FEPI application program, because the Connection may be dropped by an external agency like CEMT).

This Handler will also be invoked when CICS is doing a normal shutdown. Thus, this Handler provides the opportunity to tell the partner system that the FEPI CICS system is shutting down. This knowledge (before it actually happens) can be of use to the partner system (for example, in adjusting routing tables).

Although most FEPI facilities are available during shutdown, CICS shutdown will not proceed until the Handler has ended, so beware of locating long-running function in the Handler (and ensure that the Handler transaction name is in the CICS XLT).

To summarize this discussion of the End Session Handler for End of Conversation:

- Use the Handler if you need to sign off the partner system.
- Use the Handler if you need to do processing in the partner system before its terminal is 'switched off'.

- Use the Handler if you need to do processing in the partner during CICS normal shutdown

### 47.1.6 The STSN Handler

The use of the STSN Handler is outside the scope of this book. See Chapter 52 for information on this processing.

## 47.2 Designing with Monitors

The design decisions regarding the use of Monitors revolve around whether or not you are interested in the events placed therein. I would strongly recommend that both Pool-specific and CSZX Monitors are provided, even if they do not do anything with the notification.

However, if you decide not to use Pool-specific Monitors, you should *consider very carefully* the decision to omit provision of CSZX and its monitor. I emphasize that CSZX is vital for the smooth operation of FEPI and, in most cases, it should be used.

The general categories of notification provided in Monitor TDQ records are:

- Installation errors
- Pool manipulation errors
- VTAM-caused errors
- Unsolicited Bind processing

It is probable that you are not too interested in the errors logged because of a failure to `EXEC CICS FEPI INSTALL/DISCARD/ADD/DELETE/SET` a FEPI resource. Therefore, you could choose not to take any action on these occurrences. VTAM failures are of more interest, as they usually indicate that something has happened to the partner system. Unsolicited Bind processing via a Monitor is required if using CLSDST(PASS) processing (see Chapter 51).

### 47.2.1 Pool-specific Monitors

For a full description of Pool-specific Monitors, see Chapter 45.

Pool-specific Monitors can be shared between Pools. However, if you are allocating Pools to specific groups of users, then you need to provide separate Pool-specific TDQs and Monitor programs for each Pool.

There are two general categories of TDQ records written to the Pool specific TDQ:

- Failure to insert or remove a Connection from the Pool via `EXEC CICS FEPI ADD` and `EXEC CICS FEPI DELETE` commands
- VTAM failures on the Connections within the Pools

#### THE NUMBER OF CONNECTIONS

It is very probable that you are not too interested in knowing about failures to change the number of Connections in the Pool, because the error is reported on the issuing command. However, if you are doing this manipulation using lists, then you will need to take some notice of these entries (see Sec. 45.1), as they provide the only mechanism of reporting which element in the list has failed.

### VTAM FAILURES

On the other hand, you may be very interested in VTAM failures that cause the Connections to fail. FEPI distinguishes between the failure to Acquire the Connection (`SESSIONFAIL`) initially, and a failure while the Connection is active (`SESSIONLOST`).

These Connection failures should be used either to initiate recovery action, or to notify someone that the partner system is not contactable (so providing some sort of early warning or automated operations action).

Your FEPI Design may involve communicating with two partners: the first is used normally, while the second is used for backup purposes. If the first partner fails, then you route FEPI Communications to the other one. Therefore, you detect `SESSIONFAIL` TDQ records for the Pool, and then `EXEC CICS FEPI SET TARGET(T1) SERVSTATUS(OUTSERVICE)` followed by an `EXEC CICS FEPI SET TARGET(T2) SERVSTATUS(INSERVICE)`. This achieves the switching without any manual intervention by the CICS operator, and the end users do not know that they are talking to a different partner.

It should be noted that a DFHSZ message will usually be produced along with the Pool-specific TDQ record in these circumstances. Consequently, use of Netview automated operations may attempt to recover the situation before the FEPI retry occurs.

### GENERAL CONCLUSION

I recommend providing a Pool-specific TDQ and associated Monitor (triggered when a TDQ record is written by FEPI). If you are not interested in the failure, then simply take no action on the entry.

## 47.2.2 CSZX Monitors

For a full description of the FEPI Global CSZX Monitor, see Chapter 46.

The CSZX Monitor program provides the central point for FEPI error-reporting of central resources. It should always be provided, and the associated Monitor program should always take some action (even if it is to do nothing) for each entry.

There are four general types of records written to CSZX:

- Failure to create or destroy a FEPI resource via `EXEC CICS FEPI INSTALL` or `EXEC CICS FEPI DISCARD` commands (or their CEMT equivalents)
- A failure in an `EXEC CICS FEPI SET` operation (or CEMT equivalent)
- A failure to VTAM Acquire a resource
- The occurrence of an Unsolicited Bind

### INSTALL AND DISCARD ERRORS

It is very probable that you are not too interested in knowing about failures to Install or Discard a FEPI Resource, because the error is reported on the executing command (or the CEMT equivalent for a Discard). However, if you are doing this manipulation using lists, then you will need to take some notice of these entries (see Sec. 45.1), as they provide the only mechanism of reporting which element in the list has failed.

### SET FAILURES

It is very probable that you are not too interested in knowing about failures to change the status of a FEPI resource, because the error is reported on the executing command (or the CEMT equivalent). However, if you are doing this manipulation using lists, then you will need to take some notice of these entries (see Sec. 45.1), as they provide the only mechanism of reporting which element in the list has failed.

### VTAM ACQUISITION FAILURES

This notification shows that the FEPI Node or Connection has failed to connect with its VTAM equivalent. This probably means either a mismatch between VTAM and FEPI definitions, or that there is something not quite right with VTAM. Consequently, you are *very* interested in these records.

However, caution must be exercised in taking actions on the event. FEPI will attempt a recovery by retrying the failed action (usually after 1 minute for 30 retries). Thus, it may not be worth taking any action until FEPI decides that it has done enough retries. Contrariwise, you may need to inform as soon as the failure occurs.

If the Connection fails to acquire, it is possible that the partner system is undergoing an XRF takeover at the precise moment of contact. In this circumstance, taking no action is acceptable as the FEPI retry will establish contact when the partner becomes active.

As these errors involve VTAM (you get the VTAM response/error code in the CSZX TDQ record), it is possible that a resolution of the problem may involve issuing VTAM or Netview commands to resolve the situation.

It should be noted that a DFHSZ message will usually be produced along with a CSZX TDQ record in this circumstance. Consequently, use of Netview automated operations may attempt to recover the situation before the FEPI retry occurs.

To summarize: take some action, but you need to know what is going on as well!

### UNSOLICITED BIND OCCURRENCE

If your FEPI Application is involved with `CLSDST(PASS)` processing, then you are required to provide CSZX and process these records. See Chapter 51 for details of this processing.

### GENERAL CONCLUSION

I recommend providing the FEPI CSZX Global TDQ and associated Monitor (triggered when a TDQ record is written by FEPI). If you are not interested in the failure, then simply take no action on the entry.

# PART 7

# Hints and tips

## GUIDANCE

This part of the book contains an assortment of FEPI techniques and facilities.

The following are discussed:

- Resource tuning with the SPI
- Using STARTs effectively
- USERDATA
- FEPI and CLSDST(PASS) operation
- SLUP topics
- DRn responses, and how to cope with them
- IMS response and nonresponse modes
- Security
- Journalling
- Global User Exits
- Debugging
- Shutdown
- XRF
- Convid management

# CHAPTER 48 Resource tuning with the SPI

**GUIDANCE**

This chapter provides some hints about using the FEPI Dynamic Resource Definition facilities of the SPI-type commands for tuning purposes.

## 48.1 Pool organization

Each FEPI Pool contains many Connections. Each of these Connections' characteristics is defined by the Propertyset for the Pool. A crucial aspect of FEPI system design is how you arrange for the Pools to be used. For example, you can use Pools to separate different types of Users, or to provide differing classes of service. How you use the Pools is up to you, but bear in mind that their usage determines how you control the Connections therein.

If you are using Pools to separate different classes of user, then you will wish to provide different tuning facilities for each Pool. However, if you are using Pools to provide different classes of service, then you might be able to share tuning facilities.

Therefore, when thinking about using the SPI-type commands to tune resources as described in this chapter, you must think about what you wish to achieve for each Pool.

## 48.2 The number of Connections

The number of FEPI Connections within the Pool determines the bandwidth to the partner system (or systems). Therefore, there may well be situations when the number of Connections is insufficient for your needs.

This insufficiency will start to appear when the `EXEC CICS FEPI ALLOCATE` commands take a longer than expected time to acquire a Connection. If the `TIMEOUT` parameter is present on the Allocate, then they will start Timing out. Thus, there may well come a point during usage of your emulation when the number of Timeouts start becoming unacceptable, or the transactions take an unacceptably long time to start an emulation.

The equivalent extra definitions for FEPI are made by increasing the number of Connections initially put into the Pools. However, this may be wasteful of resources (if the increased number of Connections is required only during peak hour) and put an undesirable strain on the partner system.

Use of FEPI Dynamic Resource definition can tune your FEPI environment.

## 48.3 Detecting that there is a problem

If there are not enough Connections available for use, either the FEPI application programs will wait for ages on an `EXEC CICS FEPI ALLOCATE` command, or this command will timeout. However, it is not really the role of the application program to start defining some more Connections. This decision is properly in the system programming domain.

When there are not enough Connections in the Pool, the number of waiting `EXEC CICS FEPI ALLOCATE`s is available in the `WAITCONVNUM` parameter of the `EXEC CICS FEPI INQUIRE POOL` command (see Sec. 18.3.1). If the Pool contains multiple targets, then the `EXEC CICS FEPI INQUIRE CONNECTION` command (see Sec. 18.3.1) for the specific targets within the Pool has to be used to get hold of the number of queued Allocates to that specific target within the Pool.

Consequently, a FEPI application program can run (continuously) in background mode to scan the FEPI Pools and detect if there are not enough Connections defined for usage.

## 48.4 Needing more Connections

If you use a background transaction which continually scans all the Pools for lack of Connections, you can use the FEPI SPI-type commands to increase the number of Connections in the Pool. How you increase this number of Connections depends on your FEPI environment, and the capacity of the partner systems.

### 48.4.1 Adding more Connections

If you have some spare Nodes that are not present within the Pool, then you can simply `EXEC CICS FEPI ADD` them (see Sec. 14.3) into the Pool. The Nodes have to be `SERVSTATUS(INSERVICE)` and `ACQSTATUS(ACQUIRED)` before addition. It does not matter whether or not you initially set the Connections thus created to `ACQSTATUS(ACQUIRED)`, but the Connections must have `SERVSTATUS(INSERVICE)`.

When new Connections are added to a Pool, FEPI looks to see if there are any Allocates queued awaiting use of a Connection. If there are, then one of the newly defined Connections is grabbed (if the target matches). If this Connection is currently released, then FEPI will change its status to `ACQSTATUS (ACQUIRED)`, and after any Begin Session Handler processing, satisfy the queued `EXEC CICS FEPI ALLOCATE`.

### 48.4.2 Making more Connections usable

FEPI setup processing could have defined enough Connections within the Pool to cope with peak hour usage, but not all of them are usable at all times (perhaps because it is expensive to operate the Connection). Thus, when the Connections were created, some of them would have been defined with `SERVSTATUS(OUTSERVICE)`.

If a Connection is set Out of Service, then no FEPI Conversation is permitted to use the Connection (the same idea applies to the `SERVSTATUS` of Targets and Nodes). Therefore, if more Connections are needed, it is a simple matter to issue an `EXEC CICS FEPI SET CONNECTION SERVSTATUS(INSERVICE)`, or the CEMT equivalent (see Chapter 19) if operating manually, to allow usage of a Connection.

### 48.4.3 Adding another target to a Pool

It may be that you have defined the maximum number of Connections that the partner system can cope with. Therefore, if Allocates start queuing on the Pool, the problem is not that there are insufficient Connections, but that the partner system is getting too much usage. In this situation, the solution is to have *two* partner systems available for use. The second system acts exactly as the first one, but provides the extra capacity for the emulation.

It is not desirable for the extra Connections to be present in the Pool if the second partner system is not available (because FEPI will keep trying to contact the non-existent system, resulting in many irrelevant messages). Consequently, only when the second system is present do the additional Connections need to be available.

Thus, when the background transaction detects that more Connections are required, it could start up the second partner system (by submitting a job via the internal reader) and then add the new system's Applid to the Pool via the `EXEC CICS FEPI ADD` command (see Sec. 14.3) to create the extra Connections required. As both partner systems provide the same function, it does not matter with which one a FEPI emulation is communicating.

## **48.5** Removing Connections

In an equivalent fashion, the background transaction can detect that there are too many Connections for the Pool, and start removing them by `EXEC CICS FEPI DELETE` operations (see Sec. 15.3).

However, the detection of an excess of Connections is purely up to the background application program. I suggest that before removing a Connection you `EXEC CICS FEPI SET CONNECTION ACQSTATUS(RELEASED)` so that you have the chance to abort the removal if traffic suddenly increases.

## 48.6 Timed operations

Instead of running a background transaction to control the resources, you could use a transaction that is initiated at a given time to do the required operations. The transaction should do a specific set of operations, and not rely on the time of execution. In this way, you can manipulate the FEPI resources at any required time (you could pass the required operation via Start Data).

## 48.7 CEMT operations

CEMT (see Chapter 19) provides an ability to alter the `SERVSTATUS` and `ACQSTATUS` of FEPI resources. The number of queued Allocates is available on the CEMT I FEPOOL display. Note that the number of queued Allocates on the `CEMT I FECONN` display is the number of queued Allocates that could be satisfied by the Connection, *not* the total number queued on the Connection.

CEMT can be used to detect the fact that Allocates are queuing for the Pool. Similarly, it can be used to alter the usability of a FEPI Connection by keying INSERVICE/OUTSERVICE. However, CEMT cannot be used to Install new FEPI Resources.

# CHAPTER 49 Using STARTs effectively

**GUIDANCE**

This chapter describes problems with the asynchronous operation of FEPI as far as an end-user terminal is concerned, and how to get round them.

## 49.1 The problem

When using the EXEC CICS FEPI START asynchronous facilities of FEPI (see Chapter 35), you have a problem about what goes on at the real end-user terminal while awaiting the transaction to start.

To understand this problem, a digression on how CICS owns terminals. When CICS is running a transaction at a terminal, no other transactions can start at the terminal until the active transaction has ended. At that point, another transaction can start without keying (automatic terminal initiation, ATI), or the operator can key in another transaction id (terminal transaction initiation, TTI). When doing pseudo-conversational programming, the press of ENTER starts the second transaction without specifying a transaction ID, as CICS stores the next transaction ID required.

Therefore, when doing pseudo-conversational access, there is an opportunity for a third-party transaction to start running before the required transaction. This is the situation whereby a broadcast message can be sent to all terminals.

Now, back to FEPI. When you wish to continue a FEPI Conversation using EXEC CICS FEPI START TERMID(tttt) TRANSID(uuuu) you are implying that you are going to give up use of the end-user terminal until the flow comes in from the partner and starts transaction tttt at terminal uuuu. Consequently, you will end the transaction with an EXEC CICS RETURN *without* specifying NEXTTRAN.

Thus, there is a gap between the ending of the first transaction, and the initiation of the second tttt transaction. In this gap the terminal is not owned by any transaction, and so any other transaction can get in and corrupt the screen—upon whose image your FEPI application may well be dependent.

The following cases can be considered:

- If this invasion is due to a broadcast message, these transactions usually save the current screen before displaying the message, and restore it afterwards. Consequently, broadcast messages are not really a problem.
- If your FEPI application design precludes the circumstance where ATI (apart from `EXEC CICS FEPI START`ed ones) is used to start 'other' transactions at the terminal, then there is no problem. This is because there will be no 'alien' transactions intruding in the gap.
- The Terminal User may press 'RESET' and key in another transaction. There is nothing that prevents the terminal user from cancelling the keyboard lock, clearing the screen, and keying in a new transaction. As there is no transaction running at the terminal, CICS will accept it, run it, and so corrupt the screen image which your `EXEC CICS FEPI START`ed transaction may be relying upon.

What this means is that the FEPI application cannot be prevented from being corrupted by the terminal end user!

The use of an `EXEC CICS RETURN IMMEDIATE` can partially prevent an interruption, but it does not cover all the cases. However, for the majority of scenarios, this command may be perfectly adequate.

This problem can be resolved as described in Sec. 49.3, but Sec. 49.2 describes an attempt that will not work.

## 49.2 A failing work-around

Aha! says the system programmer, I know how to get round this inputting of data by the end user. I will set the terminal's TTI status so that CICS will not accept the input.

Sorry! This does not work for these reasons:

- At the time of writing, there is a CICS restriction that you cannot issue an `EXEC CICS SET TERMINAL(TTTT) TTISTATUS(NOTTI)` on the terminal at which the transaction is running. Consequently, this does not solve the problem. (You could still do the operation via a nonterminal transaction, but this still leaves open the gap until the transaction is scheduled, and you then have to schedule another transaction to turn `TTISTATUS(TTI)` on.)
- Even if you succeed in turning TTI off for the terminal, you have still corrupted the screen with the transaction Id—even though CICS has rejected it (with lots of important-sounding DFHZC messages to the CICS log)—and the `EXEC CICS FEPI START`ed transaction assumes that the real end-user screen is the same as it was at the end of the previous transaction.

This problem can be resolved as described in Sec. 49.3.

Another idea is that you attach a transaction to run at the terminal, and then do something complicated to cancel it to allow the `EXEC CICS FEPI START`ed transaction to run (perhaps using task class facilities). This will not work for an interesting reason.

The reason why you are using FEPI asynchronous facilities is that you are running more FEPI Connections than CICS can run transactions. CICS can run (about) 500 active transactions, so there can be only 500 transactions running FEPI Communications at any moment. However, FEPI allows more Connections than 500. Consequently, to use a larger number of active Connections, you are required to use FEPI asynchronous facilities to run the required number of emulations. Therefore, you cannot afford to waste 1/500th of allowable CICS processing simply to prevent terminal input.

So you are left with the solution in the following section!

## 49.3 The solution

What is required is the facility to accept a transaction from the end user, stick out a 'push off' message, and then restore the previous screen. There is no CICS-provided (or generic) facility to do this, but it can be performed with a little trick. The whole kit and caboodle depends on the operation of the (new) `EXEC CICS SET TERMINAL NEXTTRANSID` command. This command is conceptually similar to the use of `NEXTTRAN` on the `EXEC CICS RETURN` command, but is very different in operation.

When an `EXEC CICS SET TERMINAL NEXTTRANSID(oooo)` is done, whatever input is keyed on the terminal is sent to the `oooo` transaction. Consequently, the attempt to start any transid on the terminal by the end user is always sent to the given transaction. Thus, this feature can be used to prevent the screen corruption in the gap; but it cannot prevent the end user from attempting to do anything. However, this setting only lasts for one execution of the `oooo` transaction. Use of this facility does *not* prevent ATI starting a transaction at the terminal.

Therefore, the sequence is:

- First transaction
  - Gets the current screen via `EXEC CICS READ BUFFER`.
  - Saves the current screen (and cursor position) in a Temporary Storage Queue.
  - Requests continuation of the FEPI Conversation by `EXEC CICS FEPI START TRANSID(`second transaction`) TERMID(`ffff`)`.
  - Sets safety transaction via `EXEC CICS SET TERMINAL(`ffff`) NEXTTRANSID(`Safety Transaction`)`.
  - Ends the transaction with an `EXEC CICS RETURN` (without `NEXTTRAN`).
- When the partner responds, the second transaction
  - Clears the safety transaction via `EXEC CICS SET TERMINAL(`ffff`) NEXTTRANSID(' ')`.
  - Deletes the screen saver TSQ.
- The safety transaction
  - Receives all the screen input via `EXEC CICS RECEIVE`.
  - Sends a message to the end user saying 'input not allowed, FEPI transaction in progress'.
  - Waits for a short interval via `EXEC CICS DELAY`.
  - Reads the screen saver TSQ.
  - Recovers the screen by sending the image from the TSQ via `EXEC CICS SEND` (not forgetting to place the cursor correctly).
  - Reinstates itself via `EXEC CICS SET TERMINAL(`ffff`) NEXTTRANSID(`safety transaction`)`.
  - Ends via a plain `EXEC CICS RETURN`.

This sequence saves the screen status so that it can be used if the user enters a transaction in the gap. If the user does enter something, whatever transaction the user supplies, the safety transaction is run instead, which then recovers the prior screen. When the partner sends its flow, the required transaction gets going, and this then removes usage of the safety transaction. Hence, this code will protect against the end user invading the asynchronous FEPI application design.

However, if the safety transaction is not cleared by the `EXEC CICS SET TERMINAL(ffff) NEXTTRANSID(' ')` (perhaps because of a transaction abend or a cancellation caused by CICS stress conditions), then correct processing will never restart.

# CHAPTER 50 USERDATA

| GUIDANCE |
|---|
| This chapter describes how the USERDATA fields may be used. |

USERDATA is a 64-byte area that is provided on the following FEPI resources:

- Pools
- Nodes
- Targets
- Connections

The USERDATA is set via the execution of an EXEC CICS FEPI SET command, and is retrieved via an EXEC CICS FEPI INQUIRE command for the given resource. There are no facilities to set the USERDATA initially as part of an EXEC CICS FEPI INSTALL or an EXEC CICS FEPI ADD command.

The USERDATA field on the EXEC CICS FEPI START command is a different entity, and is discussed in Sec. 50.2.

| WARNING |
|---|
| Any data placed in this USERDATA field is generally available. Therefore, *placing confidential data therein is a Security Exposure.* |

## **50.1** Userdata on FEPI resources

The most useful usage of USERDATA is on a Connection. If you are managing the Convids in order to minimize partner signon operations (in the manner discussed in Chapter 61, you should think about holding the current signed on logonid as part of the Connection's USERDATA. However, *this is a security exposure.*

Thus, when you need to use a Connection, you scan down the list of Connections to see if one is 'unowned', and last used by the current user (by looking at the USERDATA). If this is found, then you can reaccess the given Conversation.

However, to do this reaccess, you need the CONVID. Therefore, the best place to store away the CONVID is to put this also in the Connection's USERDATA field.

At first sight this seems a little odd. You have put the CONVID for the Connection in the Connection's USERDATA. You need to do this because FEPI does not support any method of relating a Connection to a Convid. Note that when a Connection is in use, the Convid is locked to the current CICS task, and no other CICS task can use the Convid (this prevents any external interruptions of Conversation processing). The drawback to this method is the indication of a signed on partner terminal, which may constitute a security exposure.

Node USERDATA should be used to support CLSDST(PASS) processing as described in Chapter 51.

## 50.2 Userdata on FEPI starts

The USERDATA field on the EXEC CICS FEPI START command can be used to pass any data from the current transaction to that named in the start. The intention of this area is to provide COMMAREA-like facilities for the started transaction.

The length of the data area is anything up to 128 bytes, the length being specified on the EXEC CICS FEPI START command. However, as the USERDATA is passed to the started transaction as part of the Start Data (obtained via the execution of an EXEC CICS RETRIEVE command) which is a fixed-length item, there is no point in trying to manage the amount of data passed beneath 128 bytes.

# CHAPTER 51 FEPI and CLSDST(PASS) operation

**GUIDANCE**

This chapter discusses how to cope with partner systems that use VTAM CLSDST(PASS) processing.

If the partner system is CICS, CLSDST(PASS) processing is initiated via the `EXEC CICS ISSUE PASS` command.

Note that this discussion touches on the concepts mentioned in Chapter 46.

## 51.1 CLSDST(PASS) concepts

When a terminal is connected to a particular host system, the host can decide to connect the terminal to another system. This operation is called *CLSDST(PASS)* processing. If the original partner system is CICS, this operation is accomplished by the execution of an `EXEC CICS ISSUE PASS` command.

In the following discussion, the original partner system is referred to as the *second-party PLU*, and the system CLSDST(PASS)ed to as the *third-party PLU*. Figure 51.1 shows the switching.

In general, there are two cases to consider for CLSDST(PASS) processing:

- Where the Applid of the CLSDST(PASS)ed to a system is known, and
- Where this Applid is not known.

### 51.1.1 Known and unknown third-party systems

When you are CLSDST(PASS)ing to a new system, you may know the Applid of the new system. In this case, you can organize FEPI resources to make use of this information. If the third-party Applid is unknown (or is inherently variable), then FEPI processing is rather intricate, as described in Sec. 51.3.

In VTAM terms, when the CLSDST(PASS) switches the terminal, an *Unsolicited Bind* is received at the terminal.

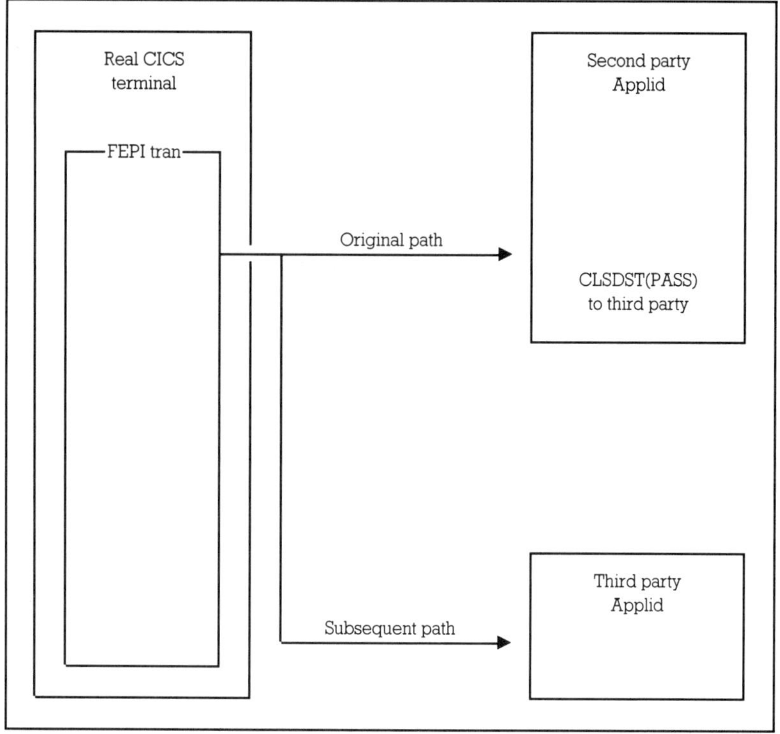


**Figure 51.1** CLSDST(PASS) processing

When FEPI receives a *Bind* for one of its Nodes, it rejects it. Therefore, a partner system cannot unilaterally decide to contact FEPI. The FEPI Node has to contact the partner system. However, exceptions to this rule apply to XRF-capable partners (see Chapter 60) as well as CLSDST(PASS) processing.

The reason why FEPI accepts the Bind from the third-party system is that FEPI knows that its Connection is undergoing CLSDST(PASS) processing, and so has special code in place to cope with this circumstance (as well as XRF processing).

### 51.1.2 Pool arrangements

The *CICS/ESA FEPI User's Guide* describes one way of coping with CLSDST(PASS) processing. I am going to outline an alternative method which is simpler, but more wasteful of resources.

Life is made considerably easier if you use a Pool with a single Connection when running a FEPI emulation to a system that CLSDST(PASS)es. The Node in the Pool *must* not be used by any other Connection, and the Target should be the system that does the CLSDST(PASS) switching.

## 51.2 Known third-party PLU name

If the Applid of the third-party system is known, then you create a Target with this Applid. Then, you place this Target into the Pool (which then has a single Node, the partner Target, and the third-party Target). However, the Connection to this third-party Target *must* be created with `ACQSTATUS(RELEASED)`.

You then `EXEC CICS FEPI ALLOCATE` the Connection to the partner system (second-party PLU) in the usual way. When the partner system does the CLSDST(PASS) processing, the *Bind* for the third-party PLU flows into FEPI. As a FEPI Connection to that third-party PLU is defined (because you have put the Target into the Pool) but inactive, FEPI will now Acquire the Connection.

Therefore, at the point of the partner system CLSDST(PASS)ing, there will be two active Connections in the Pool: the first to the partner system (which is being used), and the second to the third-party system (which is not being used).

When the CLSDST(PASS) actually happens, the current FEPI Connection will end, and the Session Lost Return Code will be raised on the FEPI Conversation. But, as FEPI knows that the FEPI Conversation is undergoing CLSDST(PASS) processing, the Conversation does not die, but recovery is attempted.

This recovery involves swapping the FEPI Conversation from the Connection to the second-party PLU (the system issuing the CLSDST(PASS) switching) to that for the third-party PLU (the CLSDST(PASS)ed to the system). Once that recovery has succeeded, then the Lost Session Response disappears and the FEPI Conversation continues as normal.

When Lost Session is raised, a looped execution of `EXEC CICS FEPI EXTRACT CONV` (see Sec. 27.11) can be used to detect when session recovery has ended.

### 51.2.1 Order of events

The order of events is thus:

- Create a FEPI Target for the known third-party PLU.
- Reserve a FEPI Node for use in a single Pool.
- Create the FEPI Connection in the Pool to the second-party system.
- Create a FEPI Connection to the third-party PLU in the Pool with `ACQSTATUS(RELEASED)`.
- `EXEC CICS FEPI ALLOCATE` the FEPI Connection to the second-party PLU in the normal way to start a FEPI Conversation.
- The second-party PLU does a CLSDST(PASS) operation.
- The FEPI Conversation starts returning 'Session Lost'.
- The third-party PLU's Bind flows into FEPI.
- FEPI knows about the third-party PLU, and activates the FEPI Connection in the Pool to that system.
- FEPI transfers the FEPI Conversation from the Connection to the second-party PLU to the third-party PLU's Connection.
- The FEPI Conversation stops returning 'Session Lost' and is again available for use.

Therefore, if the third-party PLU Applid is known, all the FEPI application program running the emulation has to know is that, at a certain point, the Conversation will enter a transient 'Session Lost' state, which ends when the CLSDST(PASS) operation has successfully transferred the emulated terminal to the new partner system.

Note that the existing second-party Connection is now available for reuse.

When the FEPI Conversation ends, it should be ended with an `EXEC CICS FEPI FREE RELEASE` to prevent subsequent Allocates from contacting the wrong system (i.e., the third-party system when the second-party was expected). Better still, Discard the Pool when access has ended to prevent accidental reuse.

## 51.3 Unknown third-party PLU name

If the third-party PLU's Applid is unknown, then the use of a CSZX Monitor program (see Chapter 46) is *required* to process the CLSDST(PASS). Again, you start from a Pool containing a single Node, and the Target of the second-party PLU. The Node must *not* be present in any other Pool.

When the CLSDST(PASS) bind flows into FEPI, its Applid is unknown. Therefore, there is no way for FEPI to know into which Pool it is to be placed. Therefore, FEPI creates a CSZX TDQ record, with the `EVENTTYPE (SESSION)` (see Sec. D.1).

The CSZX Monitor program reads the TDQ record, and then acts to create a new Target and a new Connection. In this TDQ record, the name of the third-party PLU (its Applid) is contained in the Target field. So the new Applid is known, but the Pool into which it should be placed is not known. However, the `NODE` field on the TDQ record contains the name of the Node which was involved in the CLSDST(PASS) operation.

A new Target should be created for the third-party PLU, quoting in the `APPLIST` parameter the `TARGET` from the CSZX TDQ record.

Unfortunately, FEPI does not provide any facilities for a determination of the Pool. However, it can be found in either of two ways, assuming the uniqueness of the Node:

1. As the Node is not being used in any other Pool (or Connection), apart from that involved in the CLSDST(PASS) operation, the use of an `EXEC CICS FEPI INQUIRE CONNECTION` browse can be performed until the Node is detected (use `NEXTNODE` scanning).

   The name of the Pool associated with the Connection is returned, and, as the Node is only being used in one Pool, you then know the Pool into which the Target is to be placed. Thus, you then `EXEC CICS FEPI ADD` the Target into the given Pool, ensuring that `ACQSTATUS(ACQUIRED)` is specified.

2. You could record in the Node's `USERDATA` (see Chapter 50) the name of the Pool in which the Node resides (remember that the Node must be in only one Pool). Thus, as the Node name is available in the CSZX TDQ record, you can do an `EXEC CICS FEPI INQUIRE NODE` to determine the Pool name from the associated `USERDATA`.

   You then EXEC CICS FEPI ADD the Target into the given Pool, ensuring that `ACQSTATUS(ACQUIRED)` is specified.

Once the third-party PLU name has been placed in the Pool, FEPI creates a new Connection, and activates it.

The FEPI Conversation which was running when the CLSDST(PASS) operation was made behaves in a similar manner to that described in Sec. 51.2. In other words, it gets a brief period of 'Session Lost' errors on the FEPI Conversation, which then disappear.

### 51.3.1 Order of events

The order of events is thus:

- Reserve a FEPI Node for use in a single Pool.
- Create the FEPI Connection in the Pool to the second-party system.
- `EXEC CICS FEPI ALLOCATE` the FEPI Connection to the second-party PLU in the normal way to start a FEPI Conversation.
- The second-party PLU does a CLSDST(PASS) operation.
- The FEPI Conversation starts returning 'Session Lost'.
- The third-party PLU's Bind flows into FEPI.
- A CSZX TDQ record appears with `EVENTTYPE(SESSION)`.
- A Monitor program reads the CSZX TDQ record, creates the new Target, and adds it to the Pool (by whatever means).
- FEPI activates the FEPI new Connection in the Pool to the third-party PLU.
- FEPI transfers the FEPI Conversation from the Connection to the second-party PLU to the third-party PLU's Connection.
- The FEPI Conversation stops returning 'Session Lost' and is again available for use.

Therefore, in the case where the Applid of the CLSDST(PASS)ed to system is not known, a Monitor program is used to create the required Target, and to add the new Connection into the Pool. The FEPI application program that is running the FEPI emulation receives a transient 'Session Lost' indication while this processing is occurring.

Note that the existing second-party Connection is now available for reuse.

When the FEPI Conversation ends, it should be ended with an `EXEC CICS FEPI FREE RELEASE` and then the Target `EXEC CICS FEPI DELETE`d to prevent subsequent Allocates from contacting the wrong system (i.e., the unknown third-party when the known second-party was expected). Better still, Discard the Pool when access has ended to prevent accidental reuse.

## 51.4 CLSDST(PASS) processing during EXEC CICS FEPI ALLOCATE processing

A special case of CLSDST(PASS) processing occurs when the act of Acquiring the Conversation causes the operation of a CLSDST(PASS) operation. In this case, all the processing described in Sec. 51.2 and 51.3 still applies for the management of the third-party PLU names, but the `EXEC CICS FEPI ALLOCATE` command will not complete until the switching has occurred. No 'Session Lost' indications are obtained.

In this environment, the act of CLSDST(PASS) processing is transparent to the FEPI application program. However, care has to be taken when `TIMEOUT` is specified in this arrangement, as switching will still be going on in the background. I recommend that `TIMEOUT` *not* be used on Pools that CLSDST(PASS) on Allocation.

Note that this scenario occurs when the FEPI Connection is Bound in VTAM terms. Therefore, in FEPI terms, this means that when the ACQSTATUS of the Connection changes from RELEASED to ACQUIRED, there may be no FEPI application program present to detect the CLSDST(PASS)ing. Consequently, care must be taken in this (rather rare) situation.

# CHAPTER 52 SLUP topics

**GUIDANCE**

This chapter outlines some information specific to SLUP (LU0) processing. However, this book is not primarily aimed at SLUP processing, and you should refer to IMS documentation or the *CICS/ESA FEPI User's Guide* for more information.

## 52.1 SLUP sequence numbers

The SLUP protocol uses *sequence numbers* to control the correct reception of data flows. Each end of a SLUP Conversation maintains sequence numbers for Inbound and Outbound flows. Periodic requests are made to ensure that both sides agree the number of flows.

These sequence numbers are returned on the `EXEC CICS FEPI ALLOCATE` command (see Sec. 27.2) and on the command `EXEC CICS FEPI RECEIVE DATASTREAM` (see Sec. 27.7) when they are operating on SLUP Connections.

### 52.1.1 SNA considerations

VTAM supports checking of these sequence numbers via the SNA `SDT` (*Start Data Traffic*) and `STSN` (*Set and Test Sequence Number*) commands (consult the *VTAM Programming Manual* for more information).

The `SDT` flows at session initiation (Bind time), but the `STSN` command can flow at any time.

### 52.1.2 FEPI STSN processing

When either a SNA `STSN` or a `SDT` command is received, FEPI will check the Pool's Propertyset for the presence of the STSN Handler (see Sec. 16.2.11). If the STSN handler is not defined, then FEPI will always respond positively to the sequence number checking. This is done by sending a STSN `TEST POSITIVE` flow.

### 52.1.3 The STSN Handler

If the STSN Handler is defined, then this is initiated (note that this can occur during Begin Session Processing), with the `EVENTTYPE` parameter of the Start Data set to `STSN` (see Sec. D.2).

The STSN Handler must issue an `EXEC CICS FEPI EXTRACT STSN` command (see Sec. 27.12) to determine which type of SNA flow was received.

### 52.1.4 The FEPI EXTRACT STSN command

The format of the `EXEC CICS FEPI EXTRACT STSN` command is:

```
EXEC CICS FEPI EXTRACT STSN
                CONVID(char8)
[SEQNUMIN(fixed31)]
[SEQNUMOUT(fixed31)]
[STSNSTATUS(cvda)]
```

The `SEQNUMIN` and `SEQNUMOUT` fields contain the *partner* system's view of its Send and Receive counts. They should correspond to your FEPI application program's view of its Receive and Send (respectively) counts.

The `STSNSTATUS` field's CVDA shows which flavour of SNA STSN command was received:

**STSNSET** An STSN *SET* command was received.

The partner system requested that the FEPI application program set its counts to the supplied values (with swapping!). Once this has been done, a positive response must be issued.

**STSNTEST** An STSN *TEST-AND-SET* command was received.

The partner system requested that the FEPI application program verify its sequence numbers (swapped around) with those the partner system supplied.

**NOSTSN** No SNA *STSN* command was received, rather it was a SDT command that was sent as part of session initiation.

When the FEPI LU0 (SLUP) Connection is started, the partner system will send its sequence numbers to the STSN Handler, which should verify that the local counts agree.

### 52.1.5 Responding to the STSN request

When the STSN Handler is started, the Handler should verify that the local sequence numbers agree with those sent from the partner system (local send =partner receive and local receive=partner send), and the appropriate response is transmitted by the `EXEC CICS FEPI ISSUE` command (see Sec. 27.13).

As the local sequence numbers have to be accessible from within FEPI application programs running the SLUP Conversation and the STSN Handler, I recommend considering using the `USERDATA` field (see Chapter 50) on the SLUP Connection to provide the required common addressability.

If the sequence numbers agree, then an `EXEC CICS FEPI ISSUE` command should be executed with `CONTROL(STSN) VALUE(POSITIVE)`. This sends a Positive Response to the received STSN Command.

If the sequence numbers disagree, then an `EXEC CICS FEPI ISSUE` command should be executed with `CONTROL(STSN) VALUE(NEGATIVE)`. This sends a Negative Response to the received STSN command.

If the STSN Handler was started due to the reception of a `STSN SET` request, then the local sequence numbers should be updated with those sent from the partner (local send=partner receive and vice versa), and an `EXEC CICS FEPI ISSUE CONTROL(NORMALRESP) VALUE(DEFRESP1)` issued.

If any other response is sent, then FEPI will release the connection (as if it were `EXEC CICS FEPI FREE RELEASE`d) after the response has been transmitted.

### 52.1.6 IMS and sequence numbers

IMS uses SLUP sequence numbers as part of Message Formatting Services (MFS) logging. When MFS tries to recover a SLUP connection, it sends the SNA `TEST-AND-SET STSN` command in order to determine whether or not all the messages got through to the FEPI terminal.

If IMS receives the positive response, then MFS uses this as the indication that all messages have been correctly sent and received. If MFS has any queued messages for the FEPI terminal, it then starts sending them (as normal).

If MFS receives the Negative Response, then message recovery is initiated.

## **52.2** SLUP VTAM definitions

The VTAM `LOGMODE` used for LU0 processing is IBM3600. However, the way this is used depends on how the partner system modifies the VTAM Bind that it receives when a FEPI LU0 Connection starts.

FEPI's LU0 support was designed to support only IMS SLUP access. Consequently, FEPI will only accept one of the many types of LU0 processing:

| ATTRIBUTE | REQUIRED SETTING |
|---|---|
| **Function Management Profile** | X'04' |
| **Transmission Services Profile** | X'04' |
| **Primary Profile** | X'B1' |
| **Secondary Profile** | X'B1' |
| **Common Protocols** | X'6080' |

This means that the LU0 Connection has the following characteristics:

- Multiple RU chains may be used by either side.
- The session operates in Immediate Request Mode.
- Brackets are used.
- End Brackets may be sent by both sides.
- The issuer of an End Bracket need not wait for a response.
- Compression is not used.
- Function Management Headers may flow.
- The send–receive mode is a strict half-duplex flip-flop.

Consequently, if you are attempting to run (an unsupported) FEPI emulation over LU0 to a partner other than IMS, the attempt will fail unless the above attributes are used.

# CHAPTER 53 DRn responses, and how to cope with them

| GUIDANCE |
|---|
| This chapter describes the SNA responses that flow with data. |

## 53.1 Overview

When a 3270 Datastream is sent over the network, the sender can request an acknowledgement from the receiver that the data arrived OK. The way this acknowledgement is requested is by the use of a SNA *Definite Response* indicator on the flow. The sender asks for acknowledgement from the receiver to come as an SNA *Response* tagged with either a *DR1* or a *DR2* indicator (or sometimes both). If the receiver likes the data, it sends an SNA *Normal Response* with the appropriate DRn indicator. If the receiver does not like the flow, then it will respond with an SNA *Exception Response* along with a DRn indicator.

When the sender receives the Normal Response (with the expected DRn), it knows that the data has reached the receiver, and that the receiver has checked it and found it acceptable. This results in the sender taking no more interest in the flow it sent. If the sender gets an Exception Response it knows that either the data did not all arrive, or it was corrupted on the way. The sender will usually resend the flow to the receiver.

## 53.2 FEPI and SNA responses

When FEPI receives a flow from the partner (whether running a Datastream or a Formatted Conversation), the `EXEC CICS FEPI RECEIVE` command's `RESPSTATUS` parameter contains an CVDA which says what the partner system expects in terms of an SNA response. If `RESPSTATUS` indicates that a response is required, then FEPI will automatically send the required acknowledgement along with the next flow to the partner system. This next flow is the first execution of:

- An `EXEC CICS FEPI SEND/CONVERSE` which causes a flow (i.e., one with the `INVITE` option, the `AID` parameter, or a `KEYSTROKE` sequence containing an Attention key)
- An `EXEC CICS FEPI RECEIVE`
- An `EXEC CICS FEPI FREE`
- An `EXEC CICS FEPI START`

Therefore, if you simply ignore RESPSTATUS, then FEPI will automatically acknowledge the flow on the next active FEPI command.

### 53.2.1 Responding manually

If you do not wish FEPI to respond automatically, you can do so manually within a FEPI application program via the EXEC CICS FEPI ISSUE command (see Sec. 27.13).

You might wish to consider doing the Normal Response yourself, if the FEPI application program will take a long time to issue the next active FEPI command, and you do not wish the partner system to be kept hanging about in the meantime. This might well fit in with a Passthrough Datastream design where the response will not flow until the user has responded to the partner's flow.

### 53.2.2 Responding negatively

If you receive data from the partner system, and decide that you do not like it, then you can use the EXEC CICS FEPI ISSUE command to send an Exception Response to the partner system. In this case, you must be aware of how the partner system is going to respond. Note that you can use this command only where the prior RESPSTATUS indicates that the partner system is using the protocol.

# CHAPTER 54 IMS response and nonresponse modes

**GUIDANCE**

This chapter provides a brief description of the distinction between IMS response mode and non-response mode transactions.

More IMS information can be found in Chapter 25.

## 54.1 Types of IMS transactions

IMS makes a distinction between *response mode* and *nonresponse mode* transactions.

### 54.1.1 IMS response mode

An IMS *response mode* transaction is equivalent to a normal CICS Conversation (whether CICS conversational or CICS pseudo-conversational). When a terminal sends something to an IMS response mode transaction, the next returned flow to that terminal comes from the same IMS transaction (and the terminal is locked until it arrives).

### 54.1.2 IMS nonresponse mode

An IMS *nonresponse mode* transaction does not have an exact equivalent within CICS.

IMS actually runs all transactions in background mode (see Chapter 25), so there is no real need to associate an IMS transaction with a terminal. (This is a gross simplification as IMS-knowledgeable readers will readily detect!)

An IMS nonresponse mode transaction does not run 'at' a terminal, and so when a flow is sent to a nonresponse mode transaction, the next flow to that terminal *need not* come from that same IMS transaction, but a response (even if it does not contain any data) *will* happen.

With IMS nonresponse mode transactions, data is sent to the terminal only after the terminal sends something to IMS. If there is any data awaiting delivery, then this is sent. If no data is ready, then IMS simply unlocks the terminal.

Thus, one of the characteristics of running nonresponse mode transactions at a terminal is that you can initiate many IMS transactions, which then respond in a random fashion.

### 54.1.3 IMS definitions

An IMS transaction's characteristics are defined by a combination of attributes on the IMS `TERMINAL` and `TRANSACTION` definitions. In particular, you should be aware that the `TERMINAL` definition will override some of the `TRANSACTION`'s definition. Thus, an IMS `TRANSACTION` could say response mode, but the `TERMINAL` could say that whatever the `TRANSACTION` definition says, it is going to run all transactions in nonresponse mode.

## **54.2** Coping with IMS response mode transactions

IMS response mode transactions behave in a like manner to CICS transactions, therefore you cope with them in exactly the same fashion as for CICS transactions.

## **54.3** Coping with IMS nonresponse mode transactions

As IMS nonresponse mode transactions send data to the FEPI emulated terminal in a (perhaps) disordered fashion, the behaviour of the FEPI application program must be complex enough to cope with whatever comes back, and process it correctly.

The setting of the `CONTENTION` parameter (see Sec. 16.2.2) has important implications when running IMS nonresponse mode transactions.

Use of the `TIMEOUT` parameter on an `EXEC CICS FEPI RECEIVE` command *cannot* be used to detect the arrival of a panel from an IMS non-response mode transaction, as IMS will send something back regardless.

I *strongly recommend* using the IMS `TERMINAL` definitions for FEPI emulated terminals to force all IMS transactions to run as response mode transactions. This will ensure that only one IMS transaction is running 'at' the terminal at any time, and so the FEPI application program always knows what is going on.

However, there is nothing stopping your FEPI application program from running IMS nonresponse mode transactions, but be sure you understand the IMS concepts involved, and do not make any unwarranted assumptions about IMS behaviour in the FEPI application program.

CHAPTER

# 55 Security

| GUIDANCE |
| --- |
| This chapter discusses the (minimal) security provided by FEPI. |

FEPI provides a minimal set of security checking. The only facilities provided are to authorize the SPI-type commands. No security checking is performed on any of the API-type commands, nor is any resource name checking done.

Access to the SPI-commands requires RACF (or other External Security Manager) authorization for the CICS SPCOMMAND resource which is called FEPIRESOURCE. The usual CICS mechanisms are used to control whether or not SPCOMMAND is active for security checking, and you should refer to the *CICS/ESA RACF Security Guide* for details at this high level.

The following shows what authorization level is required for each of the SPI commands:

| EXEC CICS FEPI VERB | RACF AUTHORIZATION REQUIRED |
| --- | --- |
| **ADD** | UPDATE |
| **DELETE** | UPDATE |
| **DISCARD** | UPDATE |
| **INQUIRE** | READ |
| **INSTALL** | UPDATE |
| **SET** | UPDATE |
| **SP NOOP** | READ |

If doing a browse, only the START command is security checked (for read authority), the NEXT and END operations are assumed to have been validated by the start of the browse.

The FEPI CEMT commands (see Chapter 19) call the SPI-type commands internally, so CICS operators will need to be authorized for FEPIRESOURCE access. As with the rest of CICS, the accessibility for the current user can be determined by issuing the command EXEC CICS QUERY SECURITY RESTYPE('SPCOMMAND') RESID('FEPIRESOURCE').

Note that as the Monitors and Handlers run in CICS non-terminal mode, if they issue SPI-type commands, the default CICS logonids will require authorization to `FEPIRESOURCE`.

If extra security checking is required (perhaps to authorize the `EXEC CICS FEPI ALLOCATE` Pool names), then the XSZBRQ Global User Exit (see Chapter 57) can be used to provide this function.

A security violation will result in the `NOTAUTH` condition (with EIBRESP2(100)), which should be handled in the normal fashion for security violations.

# CHAPTER 56 Journalling

## GUIDANCE

This chapter discusses journalling of FEPI flows. FEPI's journalling facilities are controlled by the MSGJRNL and FJOURNALNUM settings in the Propertyset defining the characteristics of a Pool (see Secs 16.2.6 and 16.2.10). Consequently, each Pool can have a tailored set of journalling options.

FEPI journalling enables copies of the flow sent or received over a Connection to be recorded. You would want to journal these flows for reasons like:

- Audit trailing
- Performance monitoring
- Debugging

## 56.1 Journalling facilities

The flows that are journalled are controlled by the MSGJRNL option:

**NONE** No FEPI journalling is to be performed.

**INPUT** All FEPI Inbound data is to be journalled.

**OUTPUT** All FEPI Outbound data is to be journalled.

**INOUT** Both FEPI Inbound and FEPI Outbound data are to be journalled.

FEPI Inbound data is a flow from the partner to FEPI, while FEPI Outbound data is a flow from FEPI to the partner system. Table 56.1 on page 256 shows what data FEPI will journal, and what constitutes Inbound and Outbound data.

The crucial thing to note about Table 56.1 is that EXEC CICS FEPI EXTRACT FIELD data is classed as an Inbound Flow. This is because, conceptually, you are obtaining information from the partner system, and so it is a data flow which should be journalled.

The journal in which the records are placed is determined by the parameter FJOURNALNUM—but you cannot journal to the system log (FJOURNALNUM(1) is not allowed).

If either MSGJRNL(NONE) or FJOURNALNUM(0) is specified, then no journalling is performed. As is usual within CICS, if the requested journal is not present, or not active, FEPI will not complain; it will simply not write the record.

## 56.2 Layout of FEPI journal records

The layout of the FEPI journal records follows that for CICS (see *CICS/ESA Data Areas Book* for details). In particular, some new definitions have been added to the prefix to identify FEPI records, as shown in Table 56.2 on page 256.

After the standard CICS prefix, the layout of the FEPI records (those with a module identifier of MODIDFEP(X'5D')) is described in Table 56.3 on page 256.

## 56.3 Printing FEPI journal records

The manipulation of FEPI journal records is performed in the usual fashion for CICS (see the *CICS/ESA Operations Guide* and the *CICS/ESA Customisation Guide*). This section shows a few fragments for printing the FEPI records with DFHJUP.

- Each fragment first selects the FEPI record by examining the module identifier (position 6 in the DFHJUP record).
- Selection is then made on either the Inbound or Outbound record. This is done on the function identifier field (position 5 in the DFHJUP record). This immediately precedes the module identifier in the record layout, so these two tests are usually combined.
- Once the FEPI journal record has been selected, manipulation is done on the actual FEPI data.
- If more than one selection is made, then do not forget to use the grouping facilities of DFHJUP provided by the COND parameter.

**Table 56.1** FEPI journalled data

| FEPI command | Data flow | Format of data journalled |
|---|---|---|
| `CONVERSE` | Inbound | ← Datastream<br>← Formatted.Screen Image |
| `CONVERSE` | Outbound | → Datastream<br>→ Formatted.Screen Image<br>→ Formatted.Keystroke |
| `EXTRACT FIELD` | Inbound | ← Extract Field data |
| `SEND` | Outbound | → Datastream<br>→ Formatted.Screen Image<br>→ Formatted.Keystroke |
| `RECEIVE` | Inbound | ← Datastream<br>← Formatted.Screen Image |

**Table 56.2** FEPI identifers in CICS journal records

| Type of Identifier | Identifier name | Value | Description of setting |
|---|---|---|---|
| Module | `MODIDFEP` | X'5D' | Shows the journal record was generated by FEPI |
| Function | `FIDFEPIN`<br>`FIDFEPOU` | X'F0'<br>X'F1' | Shows FEPI Inbound data<br>Shows FEPI Outbound data |

**Table 56.3** FEPI journal record layout for DFHJUP processing

| Position | Format | Description | Settings |
|---|---|---|---|
| 31 | `XL1` | Shows the format of data in the record | X'01' Datastream<br>X'02' Formatted.Screen Image<br>X'03' Formatted.Keystroke<br>X'04' Extract Field data |
| 32 | `CL1` | `ESCAPE` character for Keystrokes | |
| 35 | `CL8` | Pool name | |
| 43 | `CL8` | Target name | |
| 51 | `XL8` | Conversation ID | |

*Note:* The offsets given in this table may easily change owing to maintenance or a new release of CICS or FEPI. Consult the *CICS/ESA Data Areas Book* for accurate positions.

## DFHJUP JCL FRAGMENT

```
//JPRINT    EXEC PGM=DFHJUP
//*
//*         Print a CICS Journal
//*
//STEPLIB   DD  DSN=CICS.loadlib,DISP=SHR
//SYSUT1    DD  DSN=CICS.journal,DISP=SHR,
//              DCB=RECFM=VB
//SYSPRINT  DD  SYSOUT=*
//SYSIN     DD  *
    .......... DFHJUP OPTION records .........
/*
```

## PRINT ALL FEPI RECORDS

```
OPTION PRINT OFFSET=6,FLDTYPE=X,VALUE=5D,FLDLEN=1,COND=E
```

## PRINT ALL FEPI RECORDS WITH INBOUND DATA

```
OPTION PRINT OFFSET=5,FLDTYPE=X,VALUE=F05D,FLDLEN=2,COND=E
```

## PRINT ALL FEPI RECORDS FOR A GIVEN POOL

```
OPTION PRINT OFFSET=6,FLDTYPE=X,VALUE=5D,FLDLEN=1,COND=M
OPTION PRINT OFFSET=35,FLDTYPE=C,VALUE=pppppppp,FLDLEN=8,COND=E
```

## PRINT ALL FEPI KEYSTROKE FLOWS

```
OPTION PRINT OFFSET=6,FLDTYPE=X,VALUE=5D,FLDLEN=1,COND=M
OPTION PRINT OFFSET=32,FLDTYPE=X,VALUE=03,FLDLEN=1,COND=E
```

CHAPTER 57

# Global User Exits

**GUIDANCE**

This chapter describes the operations of the FEPI CICS Global User Exits XSZBRQ and XSZARQ.

See the *CICS/ESA Customisation Guide* and the *CICS/ESA System Programming Reference Book* for details of CICS GLUEs.

## 57.1 FEPI Global User Exits

FEPI provides two CICS Global User Exits (GLUEs):

**XSZBRQ** is invoked immediately before FEPI processes an `EXEC CICS FEPI` command (or upon certain internal CICS events that enact FEPI processing).

**XSZARQ** is invoked after FEPI has processed the `EXEC CICS FEPI` command or CICS/FEPI event (and after FEPI has done any journalling required).

These GLUEs are standard CICS GLUEs, and so behave in a similar manner to all the other CICS GLUEs. However, note that the CICS XPI commands may *not* be used in the two FEPI GLUEs.

The parameter lists passed to both these exits are in the standard CICS GLUE format. These structures are listed in Appendix H. Table 57.1 describes the parameters for `XSZBRQ` and Table 57.2 those for `XSZARQ`.

As the exits are invoked for every FEPI command (or event), a command code (documented in Table 57.4) describes the operation.

The exits can use the usual GLUE return codes to alter subsequent processing. These are documented in Table 57.3, but only `XSZBRQ` can decide to reject the request. However, some CICS/FEPI events cannot be bypassed, and are shown in reverse within Table 57.4.

**Table 57.1** XSZBRQ exit parameters (before FEPI request processed)

| Field Name | Type | Updatable | Description |
|---|---|---|---|
| UEPSZACT | XL2 | N | FEPI Command Code |
| UEPSZCNV | CL8 | N | CONVID |
| UEPSZALP | CL8 | Y | POOL |
| UEPSZALT | CL8 | Y | TARGET |
| UEPSZTIM | F | Y | TIMEOUT |
| UEPSZSND | AL4 | N | Address of Outbound data |
| UEPSZSNL | F | N | Length of Outbound data |
| UEPSZSTT | CL4 | Y | Transid for Start |
| UEPSZSTM | CL4 | Y | Termid for Start |
| UEPSZSNK | XL1 | N | Keystroke flag<br>X'80' (UEPSZSNK_ON )-Active<br>X'00' (UEPSZSNK_OFF)-InActive |
| UEPSZSNE | XL1 | N | ESCAPE Byte |

**Table 57.2** XSZARQ exit parameters (after FEPI request processed)

| Field name | Type | Updatable | Description |
|---|---|---|---|
| UEPSZACN | XL2 | N | FEPI Command Code |
| UEPSZCON | CL8 | N | CONVID |
| UEPSZRP2 | F | N | Response Code |
| UEPSZRVD | AL4 | N | Address of Inbound data |
| UEPSZRVL | F | N | Length of Inbound data |

**Table 57.3** XSZBRQ and XSZARQ exit Return Codes

| Return Code | Valid exits | Description |
|---|---|---|
| UERCNORM | XSZBRQ<br>XSZARQ | Continue processing (the default) |
| UERCBYP | XSZBRQ | Ignore the command, return INVREQ to the FEPI application program with EIBRESP2(10) |

**Table 57.4** Settings of UEPSZACT (exit XSZBRQ) and UEPSZACN (exit XSZARQ)

| Name | Value | FEPI command (or event) |
|---|---|---|
| UEPSZNOA | X'820E' | AP NOOP |
| UEPSZOAL | X'8210' | ALLOCATE |
| UEPSZOCF | X'8212' | CONVERSE FORMATTED |
| UEPSZOCD | X'8214' | CONVERSE DATASTREAM |
| UEPSZOXC | X'8216' | EXTRACT CONV |
| UEPSZOXF | X'8218' | EXTRACT FIELD |
| UEPSZOXS | X'821A' | EXTRACT STSN |
| UEPSZOFR | X'821C' | FREE |
| UEPSZOSU | X'821E' | ISSUE |
| UEPSZORF | X'8220' | RECEIVE FORMATTED |
| UEPSZORD | X'8222' | RECEIVE DATASTREAM |
| UEPSZOSF | X'8224' | SEND FORMATTED |
| UEPSZOSD | X'8226' | SEND DATASTREAM |
| UEPSZOST | X'8228' | START |
| UEPSZSDN | X'8402' | NORMAL SHUTDOWN |
| UEPSZSDI | X'8404' | IMMEDIATE SHUTDOWN |
| UEPSZSDF | X'8406' | FORCED SHUTDOWN |
| UEPSZEOT | X'8408' | CICS END OF TASK |
| UEPSZNOS | X'840E' | SP NOOP |
| UEPSZOQY | X'8422' | INQUIRE PROPERTYSET |
| UEPSZOIY | X'8428' | INSTALL PROPERTYSET |
| UEPSZODY | X'8430' | DISCARD PROPERTYSET |
| UEPSZOQN | X'8442' | INQUIRE NODE |
| UEPSZOTN | X'8444' | SET NODE |
| UEPSZOIN | X'8448' | INSTALL NODE |
| UEPSZOAD | X'844A' | ADD POOL |
| UEPSZODE | X'844C' | DELETE POOL |
| UEPSZODN | X'8450' | DISCARD NODE |
| UEPSZOQP | X'8462' | INQUIRE POOL |
| UEPSZOTP | X'8464' | SET POOL |
| UEPSZOIP | X'8468' | INSTALL POOL |
| UEPSZODP | X'8470' | DISCARD POOL |
| UEPSZOQT | X'8482' | INQUIRE TARGET |
| UEPSZOTT | X'8484' | SET TARGET |
| UEPSZOIT | X'8488' | INSTALL TARGET |
| UEPSZODT | X'8490' | DISCARD TARGET |
| UEPSZOQC | X'84A2' | INQUIRE CONNECTION |
| UEPSZOTC | X'84A4' | SET CONNECTION |

*Note:* Events in REVERSE cannot be bypassed

The exits do not provide any information for the EXEC CICS FEPI SPI-type commands, apart from the fact that a command was issued. However, for the EXEC CICS FEPI API-type commands, the exits provide some information relating to the command. The most useful information available is the data sent between FEPI and the partner system.

The FEPI GLUEs can be used for all the normal CICS-type things. However, you could use the exits to enhance FEPI facilities in the following arenas:

- Check individual EXEC CICS FEPI ALLOCATE commands for Pool authority (by issuing the appropriate External Security Manager call).
- Provide Pool routing when an EXEC CICS FEPI ALLOCATE is issued. You could use an empty Pool on the Allocate, and then decide in the XSZBRQ exit which real Pool to use. This decision could be done on a timing, or performance basis for example.
- Scan data sent to and from the partner system.

Note that the CICS XPI commands are not available within the XSZARQ and XSZBRQ exits.

## 57.2 Usage of the Global User Exits

### 57.2.1 Usage of XSZBRQ

XSZBRQ is invoked before FEPI processes an EXEC CICS FEPI command (or CICS/FEPI event). You can, therefore, modify some of the parameters of the command in the exit:

**Transaction id** UEPSZSTT can be altered to amend the transaction ID provided in an EXEC CICS FEPI START command.

FEPI does not check that the transaction exists, so if XSZBRQ changes it, ensure that the new transaction exists (and runs locally).

**Terminal id** UEPSZSTM can be updated to alter the termid that an EXEC CICS FEPI STARTed transaction will run at.

If this field is set to X'00000000', then the transaction will run nonterminal.

**Timeouts** The interval specified via a TIMEOUT parameter can be changed by XSZBRQ.

If the field is set to F'0', then the command will wait forever for event completion.

**Pool name** The name of a Pool specified on an EXEC CICS FEPI ALLOCATE (for normal FEPI Conversations) or on an EXEC CICS FEPI CONVERSE (for a temporary Conversation) can be changed by XSZBRQ.

In addition to changing some of the parameters of the EXEC CICS FEPI command, the XSZBRQ exit can decide that it does not want the command to be executed. It indicates this (in the standard CICS fashion) by returning `UERCBYP` instead of `UERCNORM`. If the request is rejected, then the issuing FEPI application program is informed of this by `EIBRESP2`(10).

### 57.2.2 Usage of XSZARQ

`XSZARQ` is invoked after FEPI has processed the command. It is primarily provided for completeness, but it does give the opportunity to examine the flow sent from the partner before a FEPI application program sees it.

You could use XSZBRQ and XSZARQ together to provide timing-related information for a FEPI command (by time-stamping within both exits).

# CHAPTER 58 Debugging

**GUIDANCE**

This chapter outlines the debugging facilities provided by FEPI. However, before these are discussed, a description of the FEPI environment is provided.

## 58.1 The FEPI environment

FEPI is actually implemented as a CICS system transaction, and so it runs under the control of the CICS dispatcher. However, the way the FEPI transaction is executed is different from other CICS transactions. In particular, it runs under its own MVS TCB (called the SZ TCB). Normal CICS transactions run under the QR TCB.

### 58.1.1 FEPI as a CICS transaction

FEPI is implemented as a CICS transaction called CSZI. CSZI is started as part of CICS initialization (if `FEPI=YES` is coded in the SIT), and shutdown as part of CICS termination.

CSZI runs the `DFHSZRMP` program, which is called the FEPI Resource Manager. The Resource Manager is implemented as a CICS system task (so it is protected against cancellation, and does not appear in a CEMT display).

Requests are passed to the FEPI Resource Manager from FEPI application programs' `EXEC CICS FEPI` commands via the FEPI Adapter. The FEPI Adapter is the `DFHSZATR` program.

As the FEPI Resource Manager is running under the SZ TCB, a queuing mechanism is used to communicate between the FEPI Adapter (running under the usual CICS QR TCB) and the FEPI Resource Manager.

## **58.2** FEPI tracing

### 58.2.1 Controlling the FEPI trace

FEPI tracing is controlled by the `SZ` keyword on the usual CICS methods of activating trace. There is only one level of `SZ` tracing, so FEPI either traces or it does not.

The methods of setting the trace are:

- Via `STNTRSZ` and `SPCTRSZ` parameters (`STNTR` and `SPCTR` also affect FEPI) at CICS initialization
- Via the `SZ` parameter of CETR
- Via `EXEC CICS SET TRACETYPE STANDARD/SPECIAL SZ()`

If CETR is used to control the trace, then trace selectivity does not operate upon the FEPI Resource Manager (the CSZI transaction), because CSZI runs before CETR can get in to control tracing. However, trace selectivity can be used to affect how FEPI applications take trace information (but as this affects only FEPI Adapter processing, not FEPI Resource Manager processing, this is not usually very informative).

FEPI trace entries are in the range from X'1200' to X'16FF'.

When FEPI trace is enabled, FEPI will generate a huge quantity of output. You must ensure that the CICS trace table is big enough to contain all the FEPI entries necessary for problem determination. The size depends on the usage of FEPI, but anything under 8 Mb is probably too small.

If you are doing something fancy with `DFHTRAP`, then you should *not* do anything that affects the SZ TCB upon which the FEPI Resource Manager is executing.

### 58.2.2 Printing the trace

FEPI trace entries are printed in the usual CICS ways (via IPCS, etc.). Both short and long listings are supported.

### 58.2.3 Interpreting the FEPI trace

In order to interpret the FEPI trace, you need to understand the concepts outlined in Sec. 58.1.1. In particular, commands executed in a FEPI application program are not immediately executed by the FEPI Resource Manager. This is because of the queuing mechanism used to communicate between the FEPI Adapter (running under the CICS QR TCB) and the FEPI Resource Manager (running under the SZ TCB).

Therefore, the FEPI Adapter will produce very few trace entries before the issuing FEPI application program enters a wait state. When the FEPI Resource Manager has finished processing the request, the wait is ended, and then the FEPI Adapter resumes processing to return the results of the request to the FEPI application program.

Consequently, the trace entries from the FEPI Adapter do not usually contain any vitally interesting diagnostic information.

### FEPI RESOURCE MANAGER TRACE ENTRIES

When the FEPI Resource Manager processes a request, several subcomponents of the FEPI Resource Manager are invoked. In general, these subcomponents are invoked by passing around a control block within the Resource Manager. These control blocks are placed on various queues internal to the Resource Manager to schedule the required processing (these queues may be interpreted by dump processing).

All the component modules of the FEPI Resource Manager generate the usual entry and exit trace points if FEPI tracing is active. Additionally, exception trace entries are always generated if a problem is detected.

## 58.3 FEPI dump interpretation

The FEPI control blocks can be interpreted via the usual CICS mechanisms under the control of the SZ keyword:

```
IPCS VERBX DFHPD330 'SZ=1,IND'
```

The SZ settings are:

0 No FEPI areas are interpreted.
1 All FEPI areas are interpreted.
2 All FEPI areas are interpreted, together with FEPI execution stacks.

### 58.3.1 FEPI control blocks

Figure 58.1 on page 266 shows the overall layout of FEPI control blocks. The major FEPI control block is the `COMMON AREA`, which anchors all the other FEPI areas. The common area is addressed by the `STATIC AREA`, which is itself chained from the CSA static area. The `STATIC AREA` is obtained as part of CICS initialization (as it is addressed from the CSA), and is present whether or not FEPI is active in the CICS system.

The FEPI Propertysets, Pools, Nodes, and Targets are all in chains anchored from the `COMMON AREA`. In addition, each of these objects are linked to other objects via a `SURROGATE` control block (this has nothing to do with CICS surrogate terminals!).

FEPI Connections and Conversations are treated rather differently. Although a Chain of Conversations is maintained from the `COMMON AREA`, the most common route for them is via the connection control blocks (which are anchored from the `COMMON AREA`).

All these Chains are followed by the FEPI dump interpretation routines. These routines check for chaining errors during the interpretation.

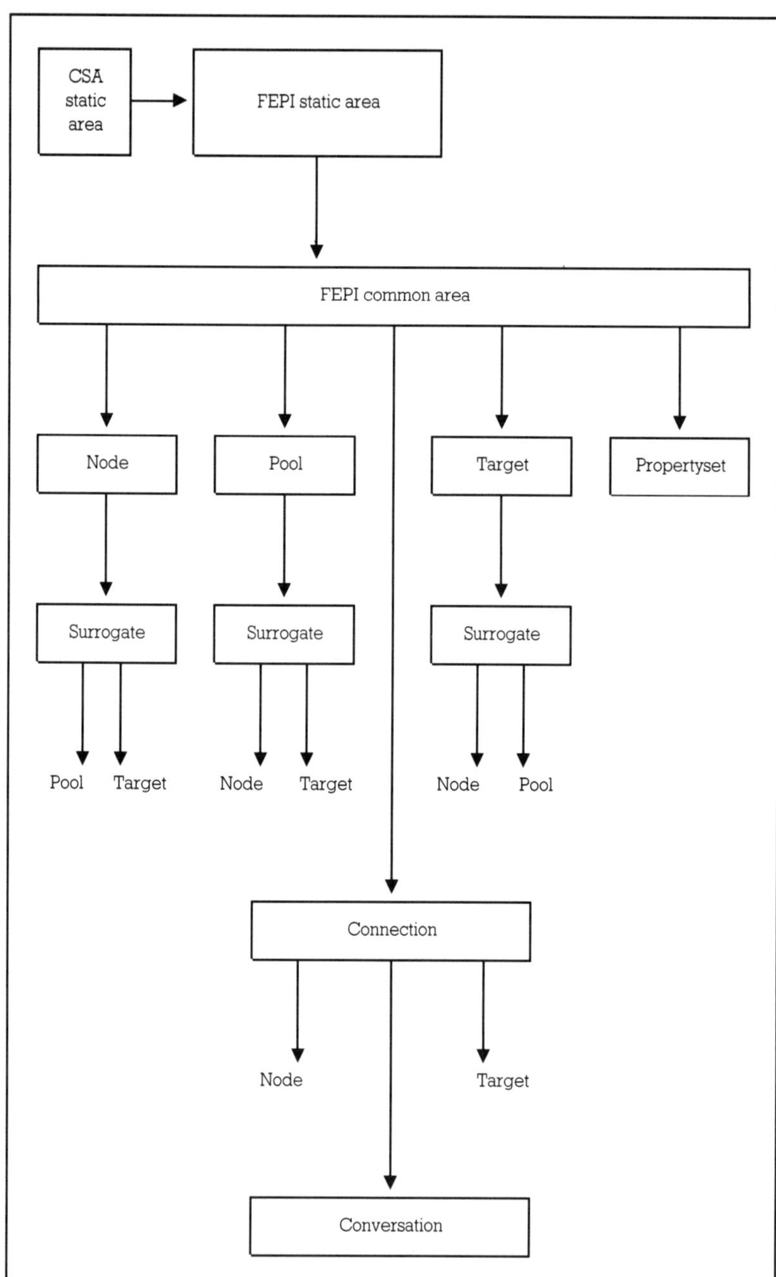


**Figure 58.1** FEPI control block relationships

## **58.4** FEPI and CICS debugging facilities

### Storage Manager

FEPI uses the standard CICS mechanisms to control storage. Therefore, FEPI uses some CICS Storage Pools which can be debugged via CICS Storage Manager facilities. The FEPI storage subpools all have names starting SPSZV for variable-length items or SPSZF for fixed-length. The great majority of FEPI storage is above the line, but there is a small quantity of 24-bit storage which is required for VTAM operation.

### DISPATCHER

As the FEPI Resource Manager runs as a transaction, it is under the control of the CICS Dispatcher. FEPI appears as the `CSZI` transaction.

### KERNEL

The CICS kernel knows about the SZ TCB used to run the FEPI Resource Manager. Therefore, the kernel dump interpretation should show the presence of this TCB. Additionally, there will be a kernel entry for CSZI, the FEPI Resource Manager.

### WAITS

FEPI processing involves two waits:

- That used when a FEPI application program is waiting for a request to complete, and
- that used when the FEPI Resource Manager is not doing anything.

The application wait uses a resource name of `FEPI_RQE` on the `ADAPTER` type. The FEPI Resource Manager idle wait uses a resource name of `SZRDP` on the `FEPRM` type. These waits will appear on the dispatcher dump interpretation (and also on CEMT).

## **58.5** GTF tracing

When attempting to diagnose a FEPI problem, you may need to have an explicit knowledge of the VTAM flows (particularly when you have problems in deciding when all of a flow has been received, see Chapter 23). Certainly IBM Service will usually need a GTF trace to debug FEPI problems. In this case, you will need to turn GTF tracing on for VTAM flows. Note that the GTF file will wrap around if it is not big enough, so you should ensure that GTF VTAM tracing is fairly restrictive.

# CHAPTER 59 Shutdown

| GUIDANCE |
|---|
| This chapter outlines what happens to FEPI during CICS shutdown. |

FEPI is started and shut down as part of CICS initialization and shutdown. This chapter discusses how FEPI behaves during the different types of CICS shutdown.

These are the cases to consider:

**Normal shutdown** is what CICS does in response to a `CEMT P SHUT`. It is often referred to as a *warm shutdown* (because you can warm restart CICS).

**Immediate shutdown** is initiated by a CEMT P `SHUT IMMEDIATE` operation. It stops all running CICS transactions as soon as possible, and CICS will have to be *emergency* restarted after its execution.

**Forced shutdown** This occurs when CICS abends (or suffers XRF takeover, see Chapter 60).

## 59.1 Normal shutdown

A normal shutdown of CICS will request a FEPI normal shutdown. In this situation, FEPI will not permit any new FEPI Conversations to start, nor any passing of Conversations, but will allow existing Conversations to continue. FEPI will not shut down until all the FEPI Conversations have ended. Therefore, be warned, FEPI can stop a normal CICS shutdown.

When FEPI receives the request for a normal shutdown from CICS, all FEPI resources that are not being used are terminated (by the operation of the equivalents of `EXEC CICS FEPI DELETE` and `EXEC CICS FEPI DISCARD` commands). Similarly, Conversations that are awaiting a flow from the partner are also ended (so the transaction to be `EXEC CICS FEPI START`ed never runs—this is because CICS would not normally schedule it).

Once FEPI has removed all inactive resources, it waits until all the existing Conversations have ended. Once they have all ended, then FEPI stops, so permitting CICS normal shutdown to continue.

FEPI transactions that are currently executing when CICS normal shutdown commences receive an indication (via EIBRESP2(12)) that CICS normal shutdown is proceeding. Attempts to do an `EXEC CICS FEPI START` or an `EXEC CICS FEPI FREE PASS` are rejected.

Handlers can start during shutdown (in particular the End Session Handler for End of Connection), but as they are CICS transactions, they have to be defined in the CICS XLT for them to run. The End Session Handler receives an indication that it was called during CICS shutdown, so it can take the appropriate action (such as signing off from the partner system) before the emulated terminal is 'switched off'.

Consequently, if a FEPI transaction does not complete during CICS normal shutdown, FEPI will not terminate, and so CICS will not shut down. To remedy this situation, try doing the following:

- `CEMT DISCARD FExxxx(*)` to remove all stuck FEPI resources.
- `CEMT S FECONN(*) REL` to cancel any stuck Connections.
- `CEMT SET TASK(nnn) FORCE` *twice* for each transaction stuck on a FEPI resource.
- Issue an MVS `V NET,INACT,FORCE,ID=...` for any FEPI Node that is still active.

If these actions still fail to get a FEPI shutdown, you are stuck, and a normal CICS shutdown cannot occur.

Consider taking a dump of both CICS and VTAM before doing a `CEMT PERFORM SHUTDOWN IMMEDIATE` to attempt a CICS shutdown. If this fails, then you will have to Cancel CICS.

## 59.2 Immediate shutdown

When CICS undergoes an immediate shutdown, FEPI endeavours to terminate immediately, but in a controlled fashion. All active VTAM resources (the Nodes and the Connections) are terminated (by issuing the appropriate VTAM macros), and then the FEPI transaction (`CSZI`) ends. No Handlers are run for an immediate shutdown.

As FEPI manages to close the VTAM resources before it ends, no drastic VTAM messages will be produced upon the console. However, a VTAM *Session Outage Notification* (SON) is received by the partner system's 'terminal'. This will result in the terminal becoming unavailable, and the abending of whatever is running on it.

## 59.3 Forced shutdown

FEPI runs in the CICS address space as a separate MVS TCB (called the SZ TCB) under the control of the main CICS TCB. Consequently, when CICS abends, the SZ TCB will be cancelled by either MVS or CICS in a radical fashion. Thus, FEPI does not get a chance to clean up its resources.

In particular, all active Connections will suddenly be cancelled (as the owning TCB is cancelled). This will result in a VTAM Session Outage Notification (SON) being received on the partner system's 'terminal', and lots of VTAM messages on the MVS console complaining about session loss. However, these messages will probably be swamped by other CICS-related messages, and in general can be ignored.

A XRF takeover is discussed in Chapter 60.

# CHAPTER 60 XRF

**GUIDANCE**

This chapter discusses the impact of XRF upon FEPI. The discussion refers to a CICS/XRF system for the partner system, but the same principles apply to an IMS/XRF partner system.

You should refer to the *CICS/ESA XRF Guide* and the *VTAM Programming Manual* for more information on XRF processing.

## 60.1 VTAM and XRF concepts

An XRF-capable system is one which can recover from a failure by either switching terminals to a backup system, or restarting itself. This chapter discusses the impact upon FEPI operation when an XRF-capable system undergoes an XRF takeover.

The following concepts are discussed in this section:

- Section 60.1.1 explains the various VTAM Applids used in an XRF environment.
- Section 60.1.2 discusses how FEPI interacts with CICS/XRF, and explains how the VTAM requests issued during a CICS/XRF takeover affect FEPI operation.
- Section 60.1.3 discusses how FEPI resource definition is affected by operation in a CICS/XRF environment.

### 60.1.1 XRF and VTAM Applids

When you set up a host system to be XRF capable, you actually start two systems:

- The *active*
- The *alternate*

The *active system* is that to which a terminal is initially connected. The *alternate system* does not (usually) have any terminals connected to it, and is ready to take over all terminals used by the active if it fails.

Both the active and alternate systems have an unique Applid (the *specific Applid*). However, they additionally share another applid, the *generic Applid*. This generic Applid is used to enable the terminal switching when a failure occurs.

In the case of a CICS/XRF arrangement, the active systems will have an applid of (say)

```
APPLID(RAHXRF,HURAPPL1)
```

and an alternate one of

```
APPLID(RAHXRF,HURAPPL2)
```

where the generic Applid is `RAHXRF`, and the specific Applids are `HURAPPL1` and `HURAPPL2`. The terminals all sign on to the `RAHXRF` Applid, not to the specific Applid of either the active or alternate system.

In order to tie up the generic Applid to whichever of the specific Applids is required, the VTAM USERVAR facility is used. When the XRF setup starts, the generic Applid points to active's specific Applid (`RAHXRF->HURAPPL1`). When an XRF takeover occurs, the generic Applid becomes the specific Applid of the alternate system (`RAHXRF->HURAPPL2`). In a CICS/XRF system, this switching is accomplished when the alternate CICS system detects the failure of the active CICS system. The alternate CICS issues a VTAM `USERVAR` command to change the specific Applid to which the generic Applid points.

### 60.1.2 VTAM XRF terminal classes and CICS/XRF

VTAM supports three classes of terminals for XRF operation:

**Class 1 terminals** are automatically switched between systems when an XRF takeover occurs. This requires the use of a 3725/3745 controller.

**Class 2 terminals** support XRF via manual switching (which is not the same as the USERVAR processing described in Sec. 60.1.1). CICS/XRF systems use a tracking mechanism to achieve this manual switching.

**Class 3 terminals** do not support XRF operation at all.

FEPI uses VTAM *SECONDARY LU* support for communication. Consequently, the FEPI 'terminals' with which a partner CICS system is communicating behave in a slightly different fashion to 'real' devices. This is only of interest when operating in an XRF environment.

In the CICS/XRF environment, the 'terminals' in the partner system cannot behave as VTAM class 1 terminals (because there is no 3745 controller acting as the Boundary Network Node). Consequently, the FEPI 'terminals' behave like VTAM class 2 terminals. Therefore, FEPI 'terminals' are not VTAM XRF-capable, and CICS/XRF facilities are provided by TRACKING mechanisms (this is all explained in the *CICS/ESA XRF Guide*).

Thus, when a FEPI Connection is acquired, the partner CICS generates a TCTTE via the usual AutoInstall mechanism (or there is one present already if AutoInstall is not being used). At this point, in the CICS/XRF environment, the active informs the alternate that a terminal has been defined. If the active is then taken over, the alternate knows what terminals are defined, and so can take actions to recover the linkage.

This means that as part of the alternate takeover processing, a VTAM Bind will be issued to re-establish the session for the FEPI terminal. However, FEPI will have detected that the Connection has ended, and will be attempting to contact the (now being taken over) partner system by issuing a similar Bind. This results in a *Bind Race*.

The consequences of this race depend upon the circumstances of the exchange. However, the alternate CICS will probably have its Bind rejected, and the FEPI Bind accepted. This will result in rather strange DFHZC messages being produced during the takeover. If FEPI re-establishes the Connection, these messages can be ignored.

These Bind Races can be prevented by making the TYPETERM for the partner CICS FEPI 'terminals' into a VTAM class 3 terminal by setting RECOVOPTION(NONE).

In IMS terms, the BACKUP parameter on the TERMINAL definition macro controls the VTAM XRF class:

| BACKUP SETTING | VTAM XRF CLASS |
|---|---|
| **(n,YES)** | 1 |
| **(n,NO)** | 2 |
| **NO** | 3 |

### 60.1.3 FEPI resource definition and CICS/XRF

In the XRF environment, the APPLID quoted in the EXEC CICS INSTALL TARGET command must be the partner's generic Applid. Usages of a specific Applid for Target will result in processing errors. If you use the generic Applid, FEPI will be able to cater for the partner system's undergoing an XRF takeover.

However, you can define a Pool containing both the active and alternate specific Applids. In this case, the alternate Targets cannot be contacted until the XRF takeover has been performed. Equivalently, the active Target cannot be contacted after takeover. If you choose to define Pools in this fashion (perhaps to provide backup support without XRF), you should arrange to manage the ACQUIRED/RELEASED status yourself to minimize FEPI retry processing. Note that this method is not recommended in preference to 'proper' XRF usage.

## 60.2 XRF takeover of FEPI CICS

What happens when the CICS system containing FEPI undergoes an XRF takeover depends on what is currently going on in FEPI.

### 60.2.1 Effect on partner transactions

Partner transactions will be abended due to the loss of the 'terminal'—which will mostly be the principal facility for the task. Consequently, the ATNI (or equivalent) abend processing will be unable to send the usual message indicating transaction abend to the principal facility.

Transactions that attempt to handle terminal control errors should already be coded to cope with this circumstance, and should not need alteration.

### 60.2.2 Effect on partner 'terminals'

As FEPI is acting as the 'terminal', the XRF takeover of the FEPI system results in the loss of the 'terminal' in the partner system. The usual CICS actions are taken for the loss of a (real) terminal.

There are three scenarios to consider:

- 'Terminals' not running a Conversation
- 'Terminals' running a Conversation, but data has not yet flowed
- 'Terminals' running a Conversation, with data flow

#### 'TERMINALS' WITHOUT A CONVERSATION

The 'terminal' behaves just as if a real terminal were switched off while not doing anything. The TCTTEs representing these 'terminals' will be deleted (if using AutoInstall).

#### 'TERMINALS' WITHOUT DATA FLOW

The 'terminal' behaves just as if a real terminal were switched off while not doing anything. The TCTTEs representing these 'terminals' will be deleted (if using AutoInstall).

#### 'TERMINALS' WITH DATA FLOW

These 'terminals' will usually be running a transaction when the 'terminal' is lost. This will result in the transaction being abended with the usual CICS abend code for a terminal failure (usually ATNI). This abend will, probably, be accompanied by `DFHZC` messages indicating that the 'terminal' has suffered an unrecoverable failure.

The processing CICS takes within the Node Error Program may have to be amended to prevent retry loops, but normally the default action not to retry will be taken. When this processing has ended, the 'terminal' will be deleted (if using AutoInstall).

### 60.2.3 Effect in the alternate

The alternate FEPI CICS will take over operation of the failed CICS in the normal fashion. However, FEPI resources are not XRF-aware, and are not recovered by a takeover. FEPI will restart at a late stage of takeover, after all RDO resources have been reinstalled.

Consequently, when the second phase of the PLTPI is entered, FEPI is ready to action requests. Therefore, if you are following my recommendation to initiate FEPI resource definition from within a transaction started from a PLTPI program (see Chapter 13), the FEPI resources will be installed as part of the takeover. If you are not doing FEPI resource definition in this fashion, then after a takeover you must manually arrange for FEPI resources to be defined.

However you handle FEPI resource definition in the XRF environment, you must be prepared to cope with the possibility that FEPI resources have been manipulated in the failed CICS, so that the environment after takeover is not the same as that immediately before takeover (i.e., resources may have been EXEC CICS FEPI INSTALLed, or EXEC CICS FEPI DISCARDed and SERVSTATUS/ACQSTATUS altered).

## 60.3 XRF takeover of partner CICS

What happens when the CICS system communicating with FEPI undergoes a XRF takeover depends on what is currently going on in a FEPI emulation.

### 60.3.1 Effect on FEPI application programs

Conversations that are active to a partner that undergoes an XRF takeover are unable to distinguish between the case of Session Lost due to XRF or to failure. In general, upon the next EXEC CICS FEPI command after the takeover has started, an EIBRESP2 of 215 (Session Lost) will typically be returned. Alternatively, you may get an indication of a state error, meaning that the command cannot be issued as the connection is not active. The application program should then *immediately* EXEC CICS FEPI FREE the Conversation.

If an End Session handler (see Sec. 44.2) is active for the Connection's pool, then it will be invoked (even though the Conversation has ended).

If the FEPI application program has reason to believe that the partner is undergoing an XRF takeover, then it should reissue an EXEC CICS FEPI ALLOCATE for the partner. When the takeover has completed, and FEPI has re-established contact, the EXEC CICS FEPI ALLOCATE will successfully complete (with any required Begin Session (see Sec. 44.1) processing). If the TIMEOUT parameter (see Chapter 34) is used, then consider its setting in relation to how long you expect the partner system to complete takeover.

It is then the responsibility of the application program to perform any necessary processing in the ex-standby partner necessitated by the XRF takeover.

### 60.3.2 Effect on FEPI Connections

In general, FEPI will successfully cope with the XRF takeover of a partner system with which it is communicating. However, when the partner alternate system attempts to re-establish its terminal sessions, communication with FEPI will produce some strange DFHZC terminal control messages. These should be ignored until FEPI has had a chance to contact the partner system.

While FEPI is attempting to re-establish contact with the partner:

- CEMT will show the Connections as 'BEING ACQUIRED'.
- CEMT will show a 'LASTACQCODE' of (probably) X'320C0000'.
- Message DFHSZ4155I may be produced with reason codes (typically X'320C0000' or X'81062900') showing that FEPI is attempting to re-establish contact with the partner system.

There are three scenarios to consider:

- Connections not running a Conversation
- Connections running a Conversation, but data has not yet flowed
- Connections running a Conversation, with data flow

## CONNECTIONS WITHOUT A CONVERSATION

These Connections will re-establish contact with the ex-alternate partner when the partner's *ACB* (its specific Applid) is opened, without any problems.

## CONNECTIONS WITHOUT DATA FLOW

These Connections will re-establish contact with the ex-standby partner when the partner's VTAM *ACB* (its specific Applid) is opened, without any problems. You may get some messages in the partner system indicating that the TCTTE was deleted and reinstalled.

## CONNECTIONS WITH DATA FLOW

These Connections will generate errors in the partner system when it attempts to re-establish contact with the 'terminal'. You could see messages DFHZC3492I, DFHZC2411E, DFHZC3422E, DFHZC3437I, and DFHZC3462I being generated—all of which say that the standby partner could not re-establish contact with the 'terminal'. However, as long as the Conversation that was running on the Connection has been freed, FEPI will subsequently re-establish contact and reinstall the 'terminal'.

# CHAPTER 61 Convid management

**GUIDANCE**

This chapter outlines a method for reducing partner system signon processing, *at the expense of a potential security exposure.*

## 61.1 Partner signons

One of the major facilities of FEPI, the ability for FEPI Connections to be maintained over FEPI Conversations, also poses one of the more interesting problems. When a FEPI Connection is used for a FEPI Conversation, the first thing that will usually happen is that a user will be signed on to the partner's 'terminal'. To do a signon, you (normally) need a logonid and a password.

The logonid can easily be determined, there is an `EXEC CICS` command to obtain the current userid (`EXEC CICS ASSIGN USERID`), but there is no way for the current password to be determined (for obvious security reasons). Therefore, if the partner system's 'terminal' has to be signed on for each user that is using the Conversation, there are two problems:

- How to determine the correct password
- How to minimize processing overheads

### 61.1.1 Obtaining the password

The password for the currently signed-on user cannot, in general, be obtained. Therefore, you could:

- Ask the user for the password whenever a new FEPI access is done. This is not terribly friendly.
- Manually intercept the CICS signon processing and save the supplied password somewhere (*and accept the increased risk of a security violation*). This could be done within your own CICS signon processing.
- Persuade the partner system to not check the password supplied with the logonid. This is usually impossible.
- Use RACF exits to generate a temporary time-based password which is used for the partner system signon. This may be difficult to implement.

Consequently, the signon problems affecting a FEPI emulation are exactly the same as for a PC-based connection to a host system. Thus, you may already have processes in place to authenticate PC-based host users, which can be adapted for FEPI use.

### 61.1.2 Signon overheads

Whenever you sign on in the partner system, you will be calling the external security manager (such as RACF) to do the signon. Therefore, databases will be read to determine if the quoted logonid is known, and the supplied password is correct.

This processing may involve considerable ESM processing (perhaps depending upon the release of the ESM) at an operating system environment level. It may be desirable to reduce this OSE overhead to a minimum.

### 61.1.3 Security implications

- Saving the password implies that it becomes generally available.
- Access to a Convid implies access to a signed-on partner system's terminal.

## 61.2 Reducing signon overhead by Convid management

The idea behind Convid management is to reduce the partner system signon overhead by minimizing the number of times a signon occurs. This is done by seeing if the FEPI Connection (not Conversation) last used by the currently signed-on user is available for use. If it is, then it can be reused without doing the signon processing in the partner. This technique is called *Convid management*.

Convid management crucially depends on never changing the Convid which represents a Connection. The technique involves selecting a Convid for the relevant Connection.

Convid management does not affect the problem of obtaining the password, but it does reduce partner system overhead.

### 61.2.1 Convid management code overview

Convid management always maintains a Convid for a Connection. The most suitable Convid is then returned to the user for FEPI application program usage.

If there is a Connection in the requested Pool that is inactive, but was last used (and so signed on) for the current user, then this Connection is the one to use, and so the relevant Convid is returned for usage. If there is not an inactive Connection for the user, then one must be selected. If there is a Connection that has not yet been used, then this is the Connection most suitable for the user (as its usage does not affect anyone else).

However, once all the Connections in the Pool have a signed-on user, then the case reduces to picking a Connection, signing off the last user, and signing on the new one. This operation affects the old user, so an efficient algorithm should be used to pick the best (i.e. worst!) Connection for reuse. Ideally, the longest inactive connection should be picked, but this choice really depends on how you are utilizing your FEPI emulations (for example, you might wish to base the choice according to partner system).

### 61.2.2 Saving away the last userid

In order for Convid management to reduce the partner system overhead, you need to record for each FEPI Connection within the Pool, the userid of the last user running over it (along with the Convid for the Connection). This can be done in the usual fashion for a CICS lookup table, or the data could be held in the USERDATA (see Chapter 50) for the Connection. I assume a table is being used.

However, in addition to the logonid, you need to record the usage state of the Connection (whether running a Conversation or not), and also whether or not anyone is signed on to the Connection.

#### 61.2.3 Pool arrangement

No special arrangement need be made in the Pool setup for Convid management.

#### 61.2.4 EXEC CICS FEPI FREE processing

To provide Convid management, you *never* issue an EXEC CICS FEPI FREE HOLD command; an EXEC CICS FEPI FREE PASS (see Chapter 36) is *always* performed. This is required because Convid management reuses known Convids.

#### 61.2.5 Begin Session and End Session processing

The Begin Session Handler should merely ensure that the 'terminal' is set up so that a signon transaction can be issued. It should end its processing via the usual EXEC CICS FEPI FREE HOLD command.

The End Session (End of Conversation) Handler should ensure that an EXEC CICS FEPI FREE HOLD is turned into an EXEC CICS FEPI FREE PASS command (see Chapter 43), and that for End of Session (End of Connection) it signs off the current user and updates the table accordingly.

## **61.3** Convid management coding

The processing which a FEPI application program performs should be as follows. The processing should simply return the Convid to be used:

- Scan the table (for the given Pool) for the current user with a Connection in use.
- If this is found:
  - Update the table to say that the Connection is now in use for the userid.
  - Use the associated Convid in the table for future FEPI access.
- If this is not found then:
  - If there is an unused Connection.
    - —EXEC CICS FEPI ALLOCATE this unused Connection.
    - —Save the Convid in the table together with the logonid.
    - —Update the table status to say the Connection is in use for the quoted logonid.
    - —Sign on the current user to the partner system.
    - —Use the associated Convid in the table for future FEPI access.
  - If there is not a spare Connection:
    - —Select (by scanning the table for the pool) a Connection that is not currently being used (perhaps by picking the earliest Connection not in active use).
    - —Sign off the partner system (if a signon does not automatically sign off a prior user).
    - —Sign on the new user to the partner system.
    - —Use the associated Convid in the table for future FEPI access.

The End Session (End of Conversation) Handler can be used to update the table (for the Convid) to show that the Connection is not currently being used for the named signed-on user. Alternatively, this coding can be provided as a utility which takes a FEPI Convid, updates the table, and does an `EXEC CICS FEPI FREE PASS`.

The End Session (End of Connection) Handler will be called only if the Connection is dropped from the Convid management scheme (via CEMT releasing the Connection). It should ensure that the partner system is signed off, and that the Convid is removed from the table.

PART 8

# Reference material

**GUIDANCE**

This part of the book provides a reference section for FEPI.

The following topics are presented:

- Listing of the API and SPI
- Listing of CVDAs used by FEPI
- Listing of FEPI Return Codes and names
- Start Data and Transient Data Queue Record layouts
- Listing of FEPI Command Codes
- FEPI states
- Listing of FEPI formatted keystrokes escape sequences
- Listing of FEPI XSZARQ and XSZBRQ GLUE parameter lists

# APPENDIX A Listing of the API and SPI

## A.1 The API-type commands

### A.1.1 Allocate new Conversation

```
EXEC CICS FEPI ALLOCATE

POOL(char8)
[TARGET(char8)]
[TIMEOUT(fixed31)]

CONVID(char8)
[SEQNUMIN(fixed31)]
[SEQNUMOUT(fixed31)]
[SESSNSTATUS(cvda)]
```

### A.1.2 Allocate existing Conversation

```
EXEC CICS FEPI ALLOCATE

PASSCONVID(char8)
```

### A.1.3 Converse Datastream

```
EXEC CICS FEPI CONVERSE DATASTREAM

CONVID(char8)
  |{POOL(char8)  [TARGET(char8)]}
FROM(char) [FROMFLENGTH(fixed31)]
[MAXFLENGTH(fixed31)]
[TIMEOUT(fixed31)]
[CHAIN|RU|UNTILCDEB]
[FMH]

[ENDSTATUS(cvda)]
[FMHSTATUS(cvda)]
[INTO(char)] [TOFLENGTH(fixed31)]
[REMFLENGTH(fixed31)]
[RESPSTATUS(cvda)]
[SEQNUMIN(fixed31)]
[SEQNUMOUT(fixed31)]
```

### A.1.4 Converse Formatted

```
EXEC CICS FEPI CONVERSE FORMATTED

CONVID(char8)
   |{POOL(char8)  [TARGET(char8)]}
FROM(char)  [FROMFLENGTH(fixed31)]
{AID(char1)  [FROMCURSOR(fixed31)]
  |KEYSTROKES  [ESCAPE(char1)]}
[MAXFLENGTH(fixed31)]
[TIMEOUT(fixed31)]

[ALARMSTATUS(cvda)]
[ENDSTATUS(cvda)]
[FIELDS(fixed31)]
[INTO(char)] [TOFLENGTH(fixed31)]
[LINES(fixed31)] [COLUMNS(fixed31)]
[RESPSTATUS(cvda)]
[TOCURSOR(fixed31)]
```

### A.1.5 Get Conversation status

```
EXEC CICS FEPI EXTRACT CONV

CONVID(char8)

[DEVICE(cvda)]
[FORMAT(cvda)]
[NODE(char8)]
[POOL(char8)]
[SENSEDATA(fixed31)]
[TARGET(char8)]
```

### A.1.6 Get field information

```
EXEC CICS FEPI EXTRACT FIELD

CONVID(char8)
FIELDLOC(fixed31)|FIELDNUM(fixed31)
[MAXFLENGTH(fixed31)]

[BACKGROUND(char1)]
[COLOR(char1)]
[FIELDATTR(char1)]
[HILIGHT(char1)]
[INPUTCONTROL(char1)]
[INTO(char)]  [FLENGTH(fixed31)]
[MDT(cvda)]
[OUTLINE(char1)]
[POSITION(fixed31)]
[PROTECT(cvda)]
[PS(char1)]
[SIZE(fixed31)]
[TRANSPARENCY(char1)]
[VALIDATION(char1)]
```

### A.1.7 Get STSN data

```
EXEC CICS FEPI EXTRACT STSN

CONVID(char8)

[SEQNUMIN(fixed31)]
[SEQNUMOUT(fixed31)]
[STSNSTATUS(cvda)]
```

### A.1.8 Free Conversation

```
EXEC CICS FEPI FREE

[HOLD|RELEASE|FORCE|PASS]
CONVID(char8)
```

### A.1.9 Issue control data

```
EXEC CICS FEPI ISSUE

CONVID(char8)
CONTROL(cvda)
[SENSEDATA(fixed31)]
[VALUE(cvda)]
```

### A.1.10 Receive Datastream

```
EXEC CICS FEPI RECEIVE DATASTREAM

CONVID(char8)
[MAXFLENGTH(fixed31)]
[TIMEOUT(fixed31)]
[CHAIN|RU|UNTILCDEB]

[ENDSTATUS(cvda)]
[FMHSTATUS(cvda)]
[INTO(char)]  [FLENGTH(fixed31)]
[REMFLENGTH(fixed31)]
[RESPSTATUS(cvda)]
[SEQNUMIN(fixed31)]
[SEQNUMOUT(fixed31)]
```

### A.1.11 Receive Formatted

```
EXEC CICS FEPI RECEIVE FORMATTED

CONVID(char8)
[MAXFLENGTH(fixed31)]
[TIMEOUT(fixed31)]

[ALARMSTATUS(cvda)]
[COLUMNS(fixed31)]
[CURSOR(fixed31)]
[ENDSTATUS(cvda)]
[FIELDS(fixed31)]
[INTO(char)]  [FLENGTH(fixed31)]
[LINES(fixed31)]
[RESPSTATUS(cvda)]
```

### A.1.12 Send Datastream

```
EXEC CICS FEPI SEND DATASTREAM

CONVID(char8)
FROM(char)  [FLENGTH(fixed31)]
[FMH]
[INVITE]

[SEQNUMIN(fixed31)]
[SEQNUMOUT(fixed31)]
```

### A.1.13 Send Formatted

```
EXEC CICS FEPI SEND FORMATTED

CONVID(char8)
FROM(char)  [FLENGTH(fixed31)]
{AID(char1)  [CURSOR(fixed31)]
  |KEYSTROKES  [ESCAPE(char1)]}
```

### A.1.14 Start

```
EXEC CICS FEPI START

CONVID(char8)
TRANSID(char4)
[TERMID(char4)]
[USERDATA(char) [FLENGTH(fixed31)]]
[TIMEOUT(fixed31)]
```

## A.2 The SPI-type commands

### A.2.1 Install Propertyset

```
EXEC CICS FEPI INSTALL

PROPERTYSET(char8)
[BEGINSESSION(char4)]
[CONTENTION(cvda)|LOSE|WIN]
[DEVICE(cvda)|T3278M2|T3278M3|T3278M4|T3278M5|
              T3279M2|T3279M3|T3279M4|T3279M5|
              TPS55M2|TPS55M3|TPS55M4|LUP]
[ENDSESSION(char4)]
[EXCEPTIONQ(char4)]
[FJOURNALNUM(fixed31)]
[FORMAT(cvda)|FORMATTED|DATASTREAM]
[INITIALDATA(cvda)|NOTINBOUND|INBOUND]
[MAXFLENGTH(fixed31)]
[MSGJRNL(cvda)|NOMSGJRNL|INPUT|OUTPUT|INOUT]
[STSN(char4)]
[UNSOLDATA(char4)|UNSOLDATACK(cvda)|NEGATIVE|POSITIVE]
```

### A.2.2 Install Node

```
EXEC CICS FEPI INSTALL

NODELIST(char)  NODENUM(fixed31)
[ACQSTATUS(cvda)|ACQUIRED|RELEASED]
[PASSWORDLIST(char)]
[SERVSTATUS(cvda)|INSERVICE|OUTSERVICE]
```

### A.2.3 Install Target

```
EXEC CICS FEPI INSTALL

TARGETLIST(char)  TARGETNUM(fixed31)
APPLLIST(char)
[SERVSTATUS(cvda)|INSERVICE|OUTSERVICE]
```

### A.2.4 Install Pool

```
EXEC CICS FEPI INSTALL

POOL(char8)
PROPERTYSET(char8)
[NODELIST(char)  NODENUM(fixed31)]
[TARGETLIST(char)  TARGETNUM(fixed31)]
[ACQSTATUS(cvda)|ACQUIRED|RELEASED]
[SERVSTATUS(cvda)|INSERVICE|OUTSERVICE]
```

### A.2.5 Add to Pool

```
EXEC CICS FEPI ADD

POOL(char8)
[NODELIST(char)  NODENUM(fixed31)]
[TARGETLIST(char)  TARGETNUM(fixed31)]
[ACQSTATUS(cvda)|ACQUIRED|RELEASED]
[SERVSTATUS(cvda)|INSERVICE|OUTSERVICE]
```

### A.2.6 Discard Propertyset

```
EXEC CICS FEPI DISCARD

PROPERTYSET(char8)
```

### A.2.7 Discard Node

```
EXEC CICS FEPI DISCARD

NODELIST(char)  NODENUM(fixed31)
```

### A.2.8 Discard Target

```
EXEC CICS FEPI DISCARD

TARGETLIST(char)  TARGETNUM(fixed31)
```

### A.2.9 Discard Pool

```
EXEC CICS FEPI DISCARD

POOL(char8)
```

### A.2.10 Delete from Pool

```
EXEC CICS FEPI DELETE

POOL(char8)
[NODELIST(char)  NODENUM(fixed31)]
[TARGETLIST(char)  TARGETNUM(fixed31)]
```

### A.2.11 Inquire Propertyset

```
EXEC CICS FEPI INQUIRE

PROPERTYSET(char8)

[BEGINSESSION(char4)]
[CONTENTION(cvda)]
[DEVICE(cvda)]
[ENDSESSION(char4)]
[EXCEPTIONQ(char4)]
[FJOURNALNUM(fixed31)]
[FORMAT(cvda)]
[INITIALDATA(cvda)]
[MAXFLENGTH(fixed31)]
[MSGJRNL(cvda)]
[STSN(char4)]
[UNSOLDATA(char4)]
[UNSOLDATACK(cvda)]
```

### A.2.12 Inquire Node

```
EXEC CICS FEPI INQUIRE

NODE(char8)

[ACQNUM(fixed31)]
[ACQSTATUS(cvda)]
[INSTLSTATUS(cvda)]
[LASTACQCODE(fixed31)]
[SERVSTATUS(cvda)]
[USERDATA(char64)]
```

### A.2.13 Inquire Target

```
EXEC CICS FEPI INQUIRE

TARGET(char8)

[APPL(char8)]
[INSTLSTATUS(cvda)]
[SERVSTATUS(cvda)]
[USERDATA(char64)]
```

### A.2.14 Inquire Pool

```
EXEC CICS FEPI INQUIRE

POOL(char8)

[BEGINSESSION(char4)]
[CONTENTION(cvda)]
[DEVICE(cvda)]
[ENDSESSION(char4)]
[EXCEPTIONQ(char4)]
[FJOURNALNUM(fixed31)]
[FORMAT(cvda)]
[INITIALDATA(cvda)]
[INSTLSTATUS(cvda)]
[MAXFLENGTH(fixed31)]
[MSGJRNL(cvda)]
[PROPERTYSET(char8)]
[SERVSTATUS(cvda)]
[STSN(char4)]
[UNSOLDATA(char4)]
[UNSOLDATACK(cvda)]
[USERDATA(char64)]
[WAITCONVNUM(fixed31)]
```

### A.2.15 Inquire Connection

```
EXEC CICS FEPI INQUIRE CONNECTION

NODE(char8)  TARGET(char8)

[ACQNUM(fixed31)]
[ACQSTATUS(cvda)]
[CONVNUM(fixed31)]
[INSTLSTATUS(cvda)]
[LASTACQCODE(fixed31)]
[POOL(char8)]
[SERVSTATUS(cvda)]
[STATE(cvda)]
[USERDATA(char64)]
[WAITCONVNUM(fixed31)]
```

### A.2.16 Set Node

```
EXEC CICS FEPI SET

NODE(char8)
  |NODELIST(char)  NODENUM(fixed31)
[ACQSTATUS(cvda)|ACQUIRED|RELEASED]
[SERVSTATUS(cvda)|INSERVICE|OUTSERVICE]
[USERDATA(char64)]
```

### A.2.17 Set Target

```
EXEC CICS FEPI SET

TARGET(char8)
  |TARGETLIST(char)  TARGETNUM(fixed31)
[SERVSTATUS(cvda)|INSERVICE|OUTSERVICE]
[USERDATA(char64)]
```

### A.2.18 Set Pool

```
EXEC CICS FEPI SET

POOL(char8)
  |POOLLIST(char)  POOLNUM(fixed31)
[SERVSTATUS(cvda)|INSERVICE|OUTSERVICE]
[USERDATA(char64)]
```

### A.2.19 Set Connection

```
EXEC CICS FEPI SET

CONNECTION
TARGET(char8)
  |TARGETLIST(char)  TARGETNUM(fixed31)
NODE(char8)
  |NODELIST(char)  NODENUM(fixed31)
[ACQSTATUS(cvda)|ACQUIRED|RELEASED]
[SERVSTATUS(cvda)|INSERVICE|OUTSERVICE]
[USERDATA(char64)]
```

### A.2.20 Browse start

```
EXEC CICS FEPI INQUIRE PROPERTYSET START
                       NODE
                       TARGET
                       POOL
```

### A.2.21 Browse next

```
EXEC CICS FEPI INQUIRE PROPERTYSET NEXT
                       NODE
                       TARGET
                       POOL

PROPERTYSET(char8)|NODE(char8)|TARGET(char8)
                  |POOL(char8)
          and fields as for INQUIRE
```

### A.2.22 Browse end

```
EXEC CICS FEPI INQUIRE PROPERTYSET END
                       NODE
                       TARGET
                       POOL
```

### A.2.23 Browse Connection

```
EXEC CICS FEPI INQUIRE CONNECTION START
                                  NEXTTARGET|NEXTNODE
                                  END

NEXTTARGET and/or NEXTNODE return TARGET(char(8)
                                  NODE(char8)
                                  and fields as
                                  for INQUIRE
```

### A.2.24 AP NOOP

```
EXEC CICS FEPI AP NOOP
```

### A.2.25 SP NOOP

```
EXEC CICS FEPI SP NOOP
```

## A.3 EXEC CICS FEPI syntax diagrams

### A.3.1 EXEC CICS FEPI AP NOOP

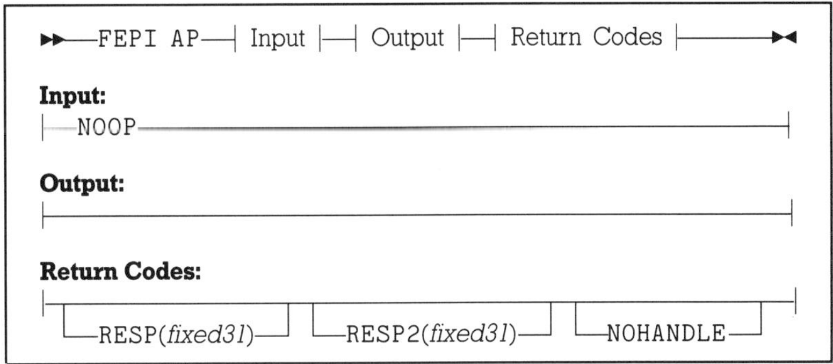


### A.3.2 EXEC CICS FEPI ALLOCATE new Conversation

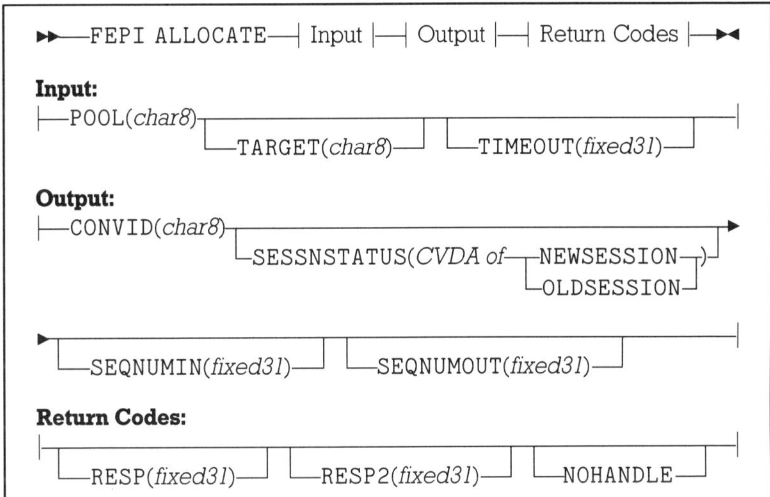


### A.3.3 EXEC CICS FEPI ALLOCATE existing Conversation

```
▶▶──FEPI ALLOCATE──┤ Input ├──┤ Output ├──┤ Return Codes ├──▶◀

Input:
├──PASSCONVID(char8)──────────────────────────────────────┤

Output:
├─────────────────────────────────────────────────────────┤

Return Codes:
├─┬───────────────────┬─┬────────────────────┬─┬────────────┬─┤
  └─RESP(fixed31)─────┘ └─RESP2(fixed31)─────┘ └─NOHANDLE───┘
```

## A.3.4 EXEC CICS FEPI CONVERSE DATASTREAM

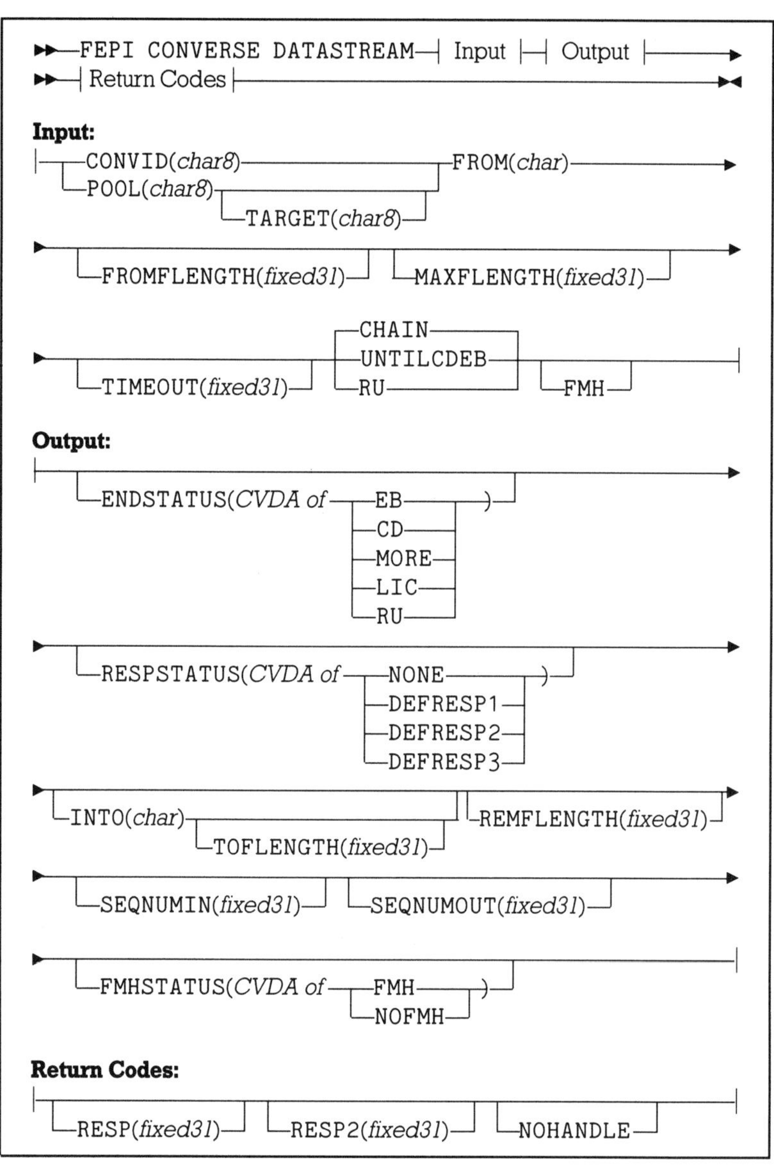

### A.3.5 EXEC CICS FEPI CONVERSE FORMATTED

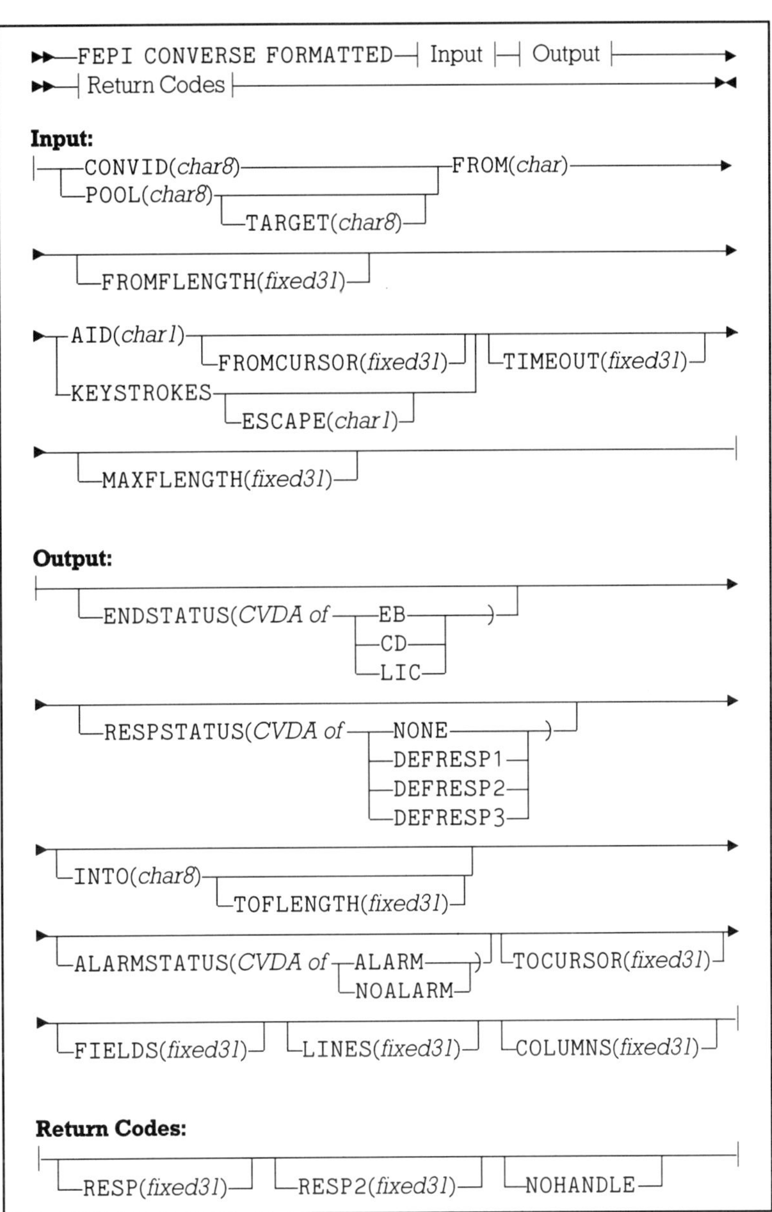

## A.3.6 EXEC CICS FEPI EXTRACT CONV

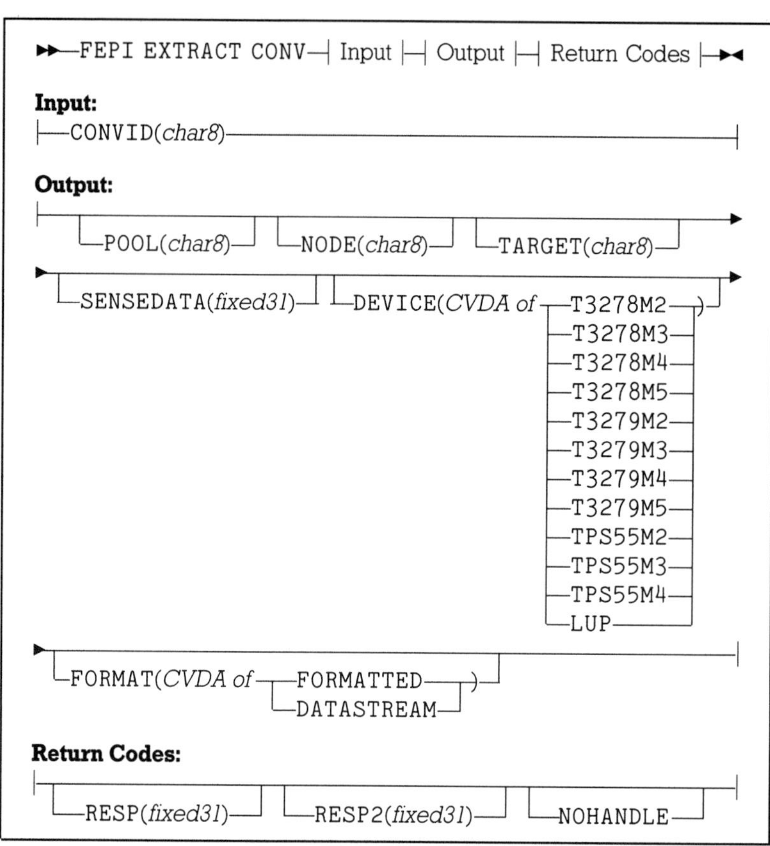

## A.3.7 EXEC CICS FEPI EXTRACT FIELD

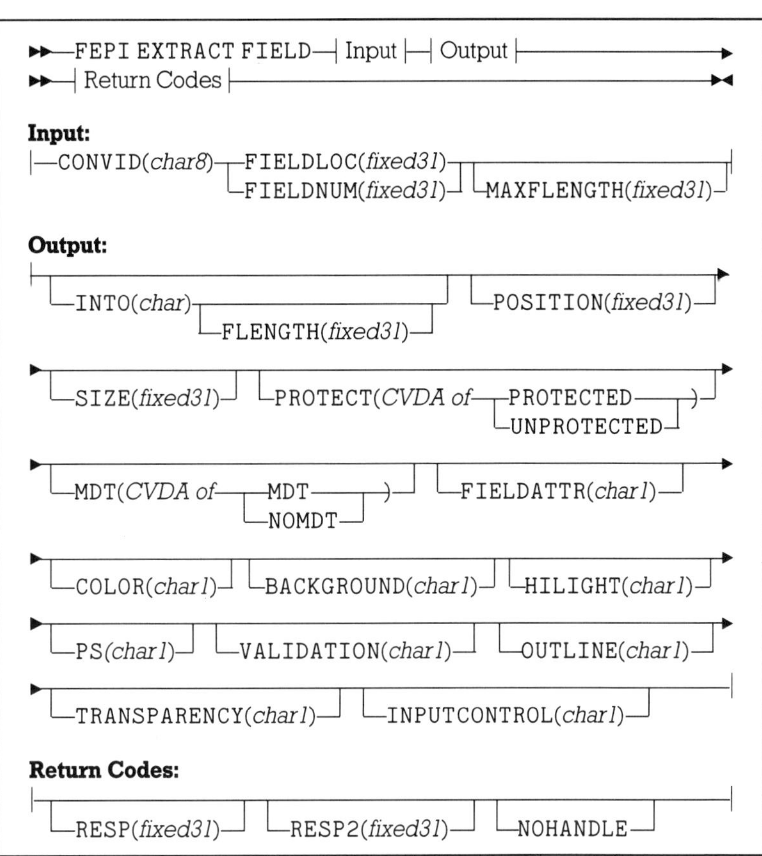

### A.3.8 EXEC CICS FEPI EXTRACT STSN

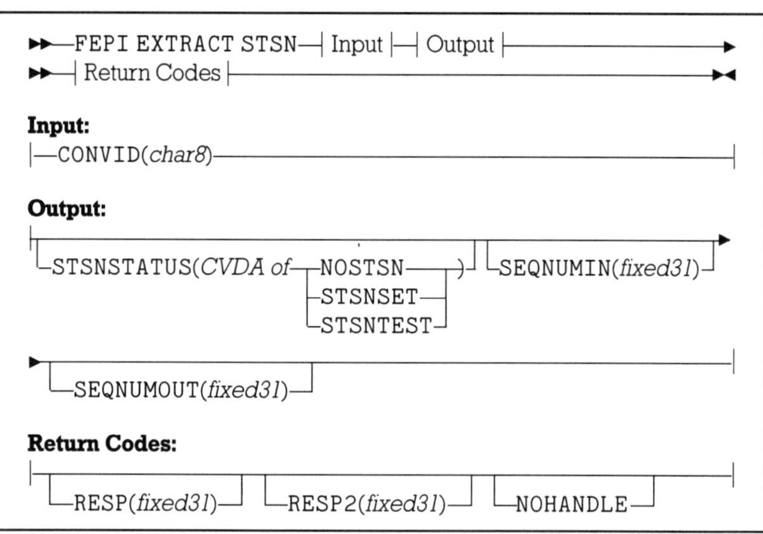


### A.3.9 EXEC CICS FEPI FREE

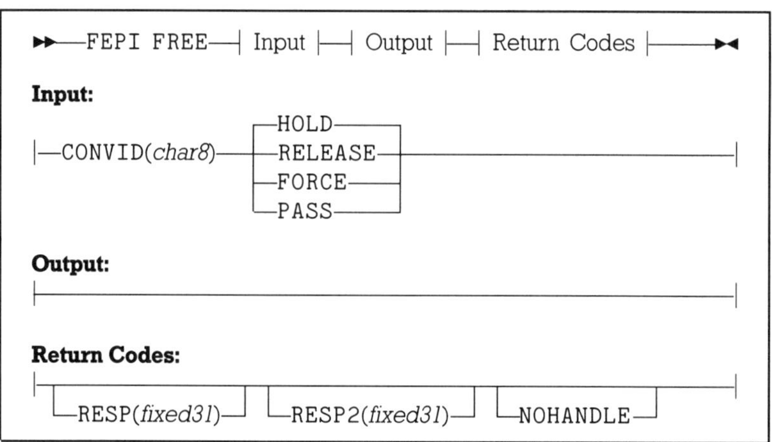

## A.3.10 EXEC CICS FEPI ISSUE

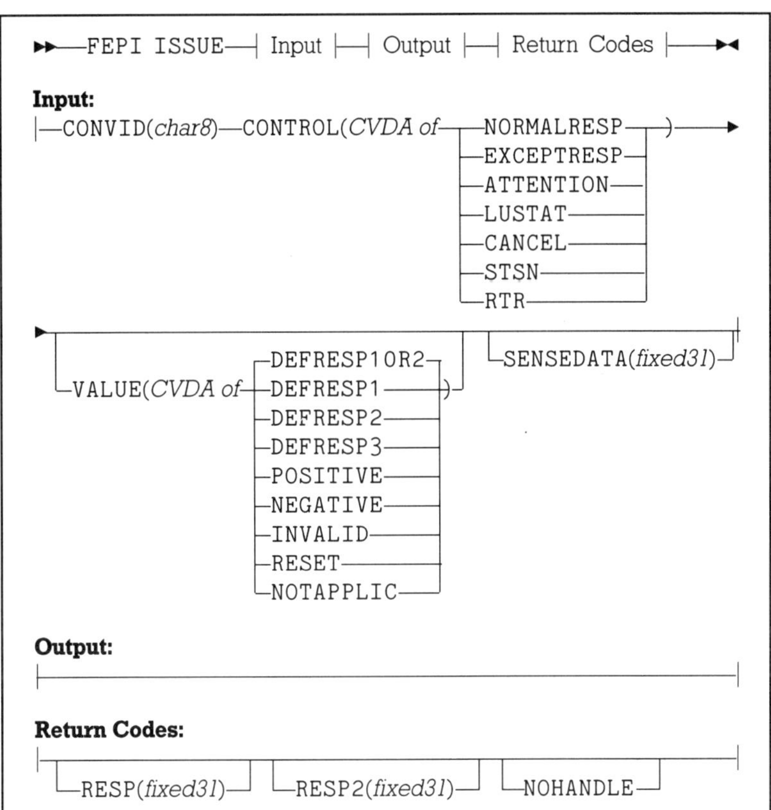

## A.3.11 EXEC CICS FEPI RECEIVE FORMATTED

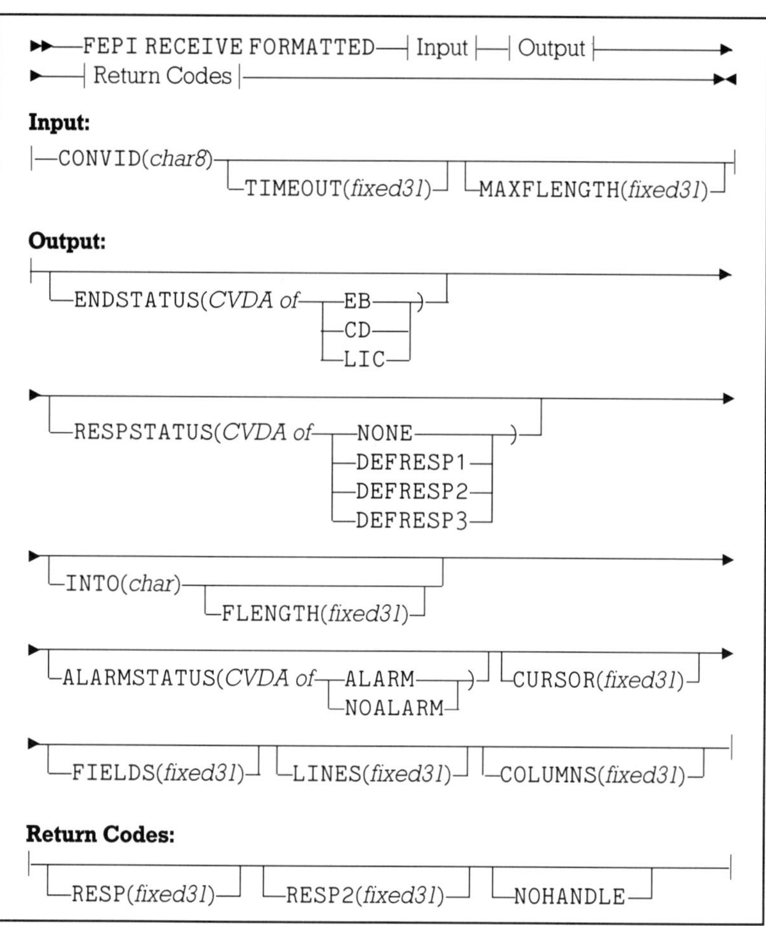

## A.3.12 EXEC CICS FEPI RECEIVE DATASTREAM

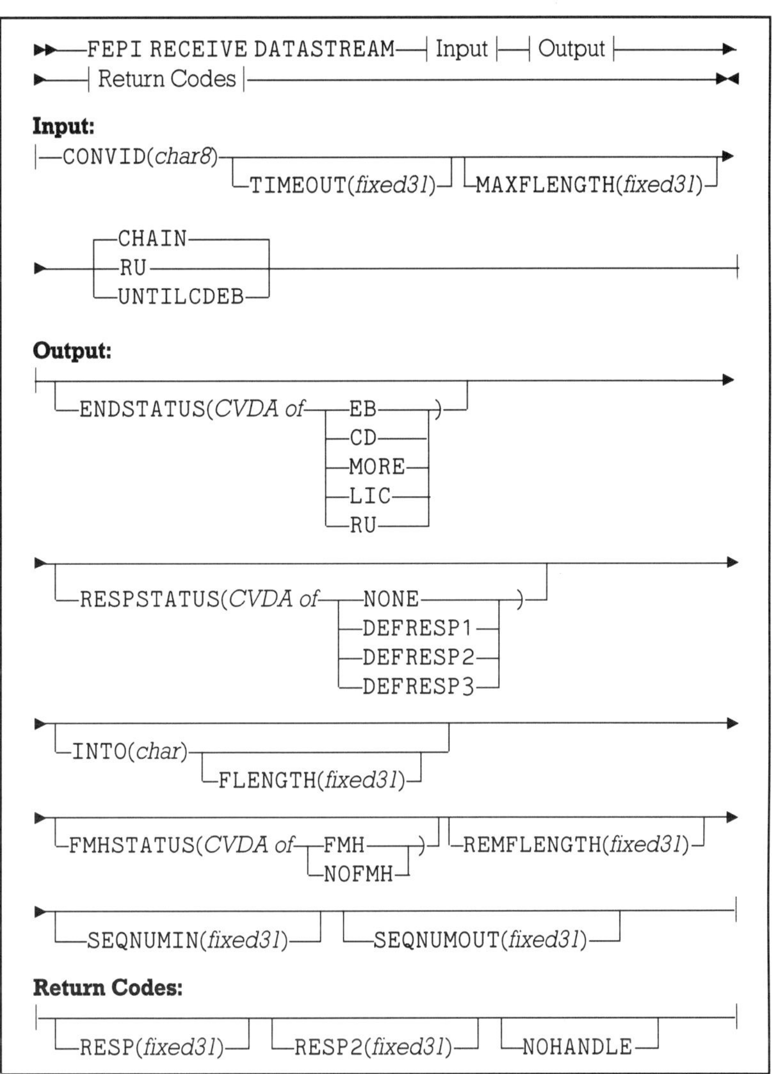

### A.3.13 EXEC CICS FEPI SEND FORMATTED

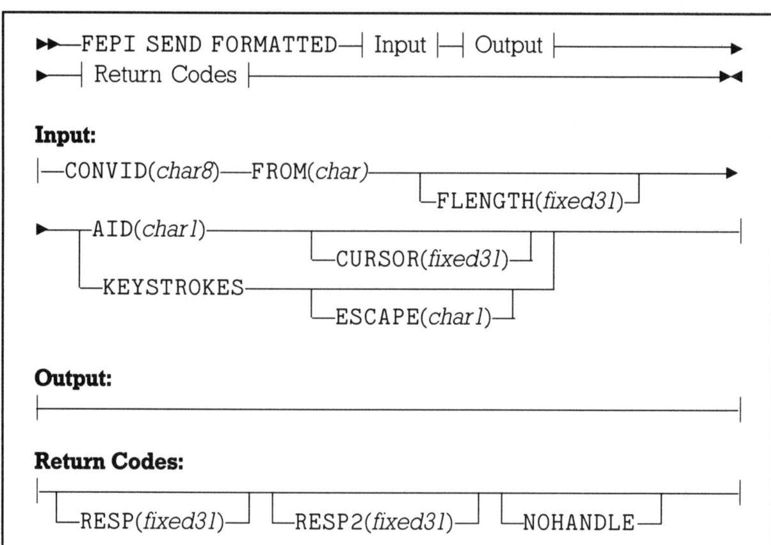


### A.3.14 EXEC CICS FEPI SEND DATASTREAM

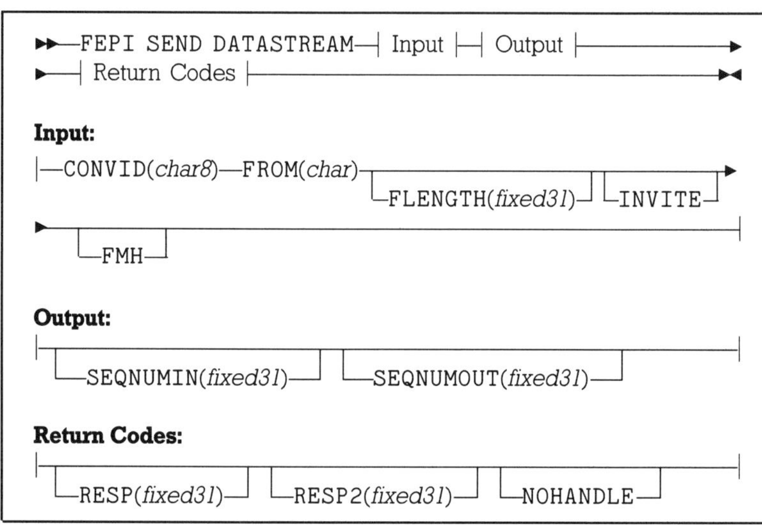

### A.3.15 EXEC CICS FEPI START

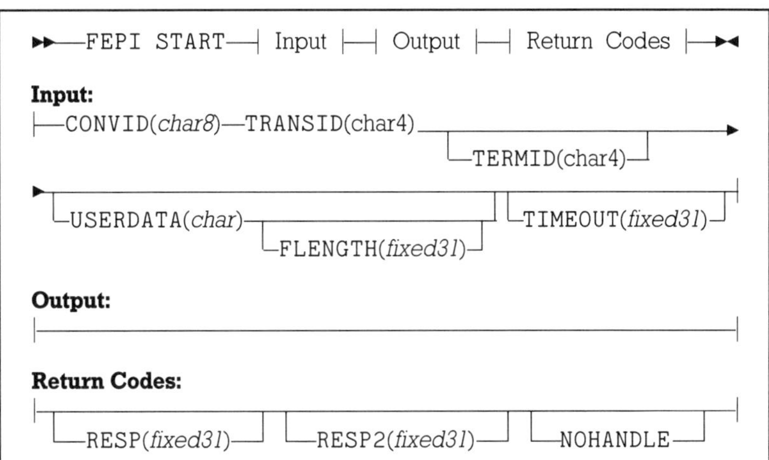


### A.3.16 EXEC CICS FEPI SP NOOP

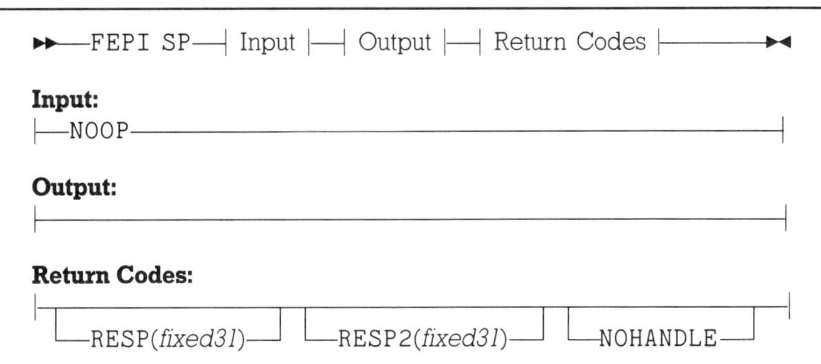


### A.3.17 EXEC CICS FEPI INSTALL TARGET

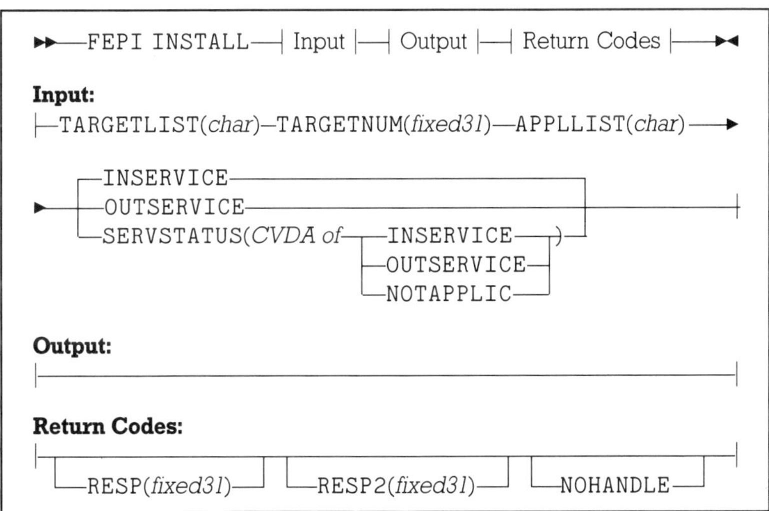

### A.3.18 EXEC CICS FEPI DISCARD TARGET

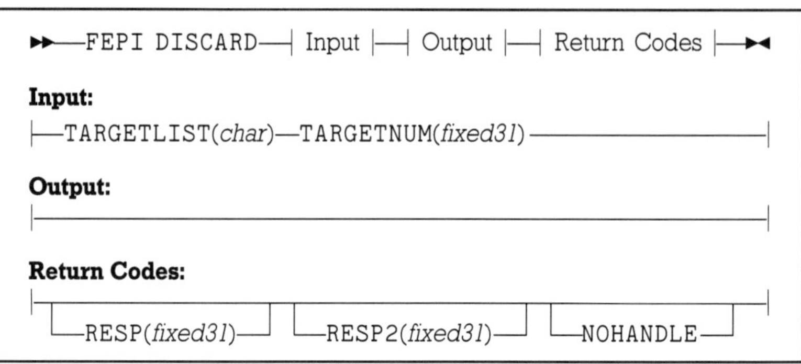


### A.3.19 EXEC CICS FEPI INSTALL NODE

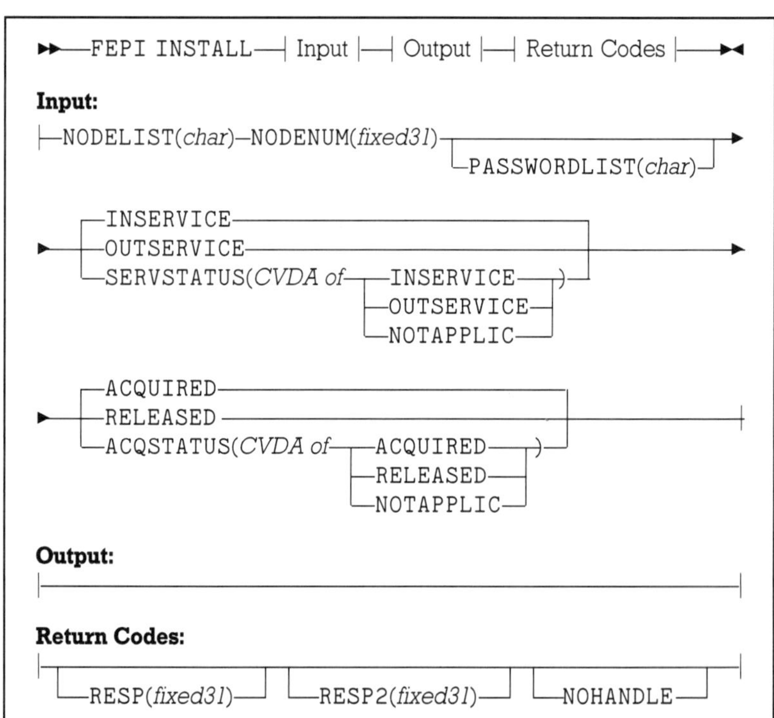


### A.3.20 EXEC CICS FEPI DISCARD NODE

```
►►──FEPI DISCARD──┤ Input ├──┤ Output ├──┤ Return Codes ├──►◄

Input:
├──NODELIST(char)──NODENUM(fixed31)─────────────────────────┤

Output:
├───────────────────────────────────────────────────────────┤

Return Codes:
├─┬──────────────────┬─┬───────────────────┬─┬──────────────┬─┤
  └──RESP(fixed31)───┘ └──RESP2(fixed31)───┘ └──NOHANDLE────┘
```

## A.3.21 EXEC CICS FEPI INSTALL PROPERTYSET

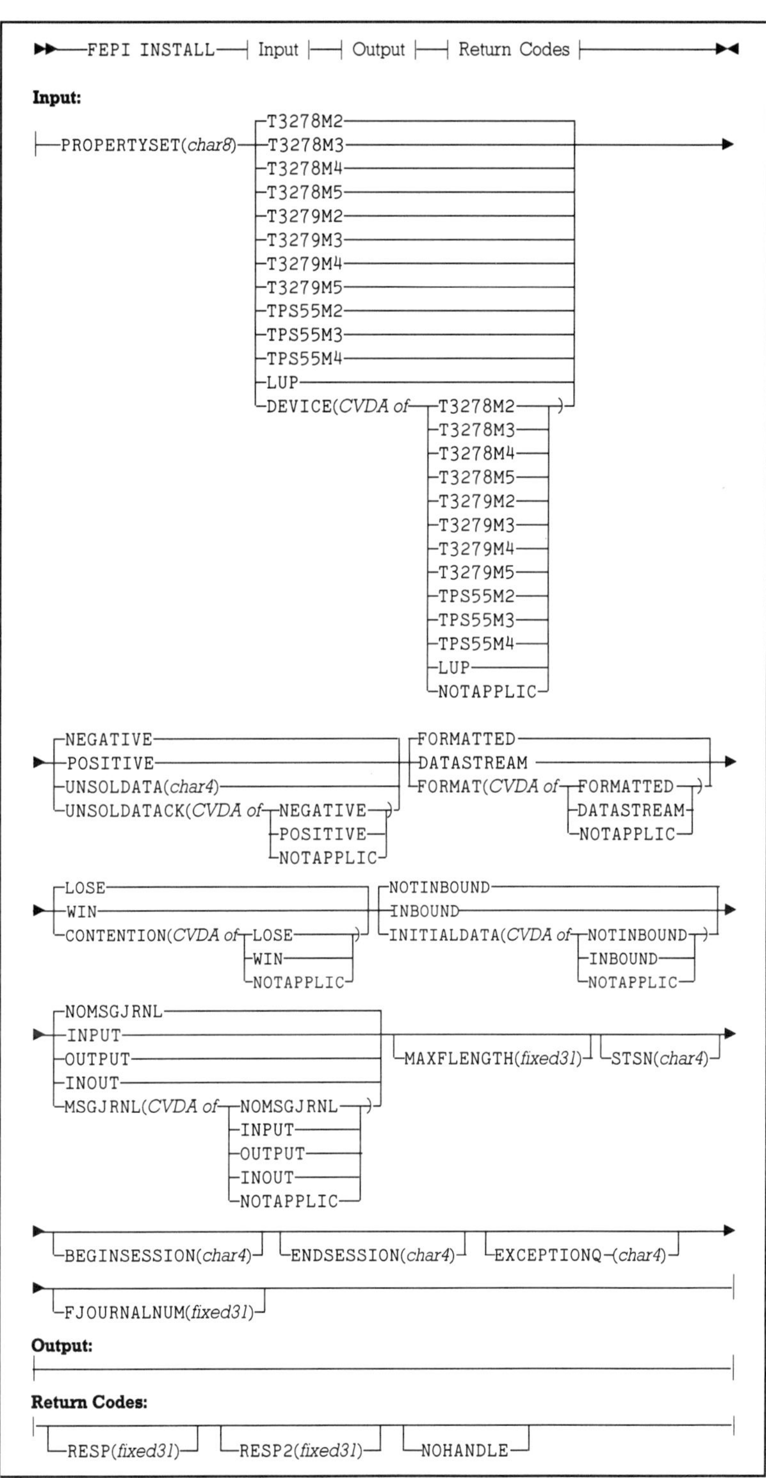

### A.3.22 EXEC CICS FEPI DISCARD PROPERTYSET

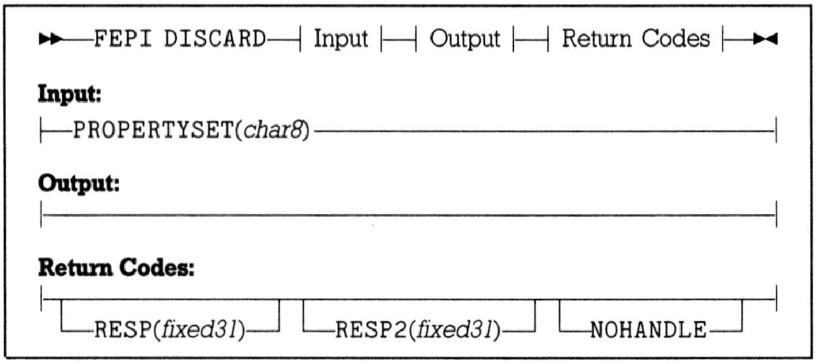

```
▶▶──FEPI DISCARD──┤ Input ├──┤ Output ├──┤ Return Codes ├──▶◀
```

**Input:**

```
├──PROPERTYSET(char8)──────────────────────────────────────┤
```

**Output:**

```
├──────────────────────────────────────────────────────────┤
```

**Return Codes:**

```
├──┬──────────────────┬──┬───────────────────┬──┬────────────┬──┤
   └──RESP(fixed31)───┘  └──RESP2(fixed31)───┘  └──NOHANDLE──┘
```

## A.3.23 EXEC CICS FEPI INQUIRE PROPERTYSET

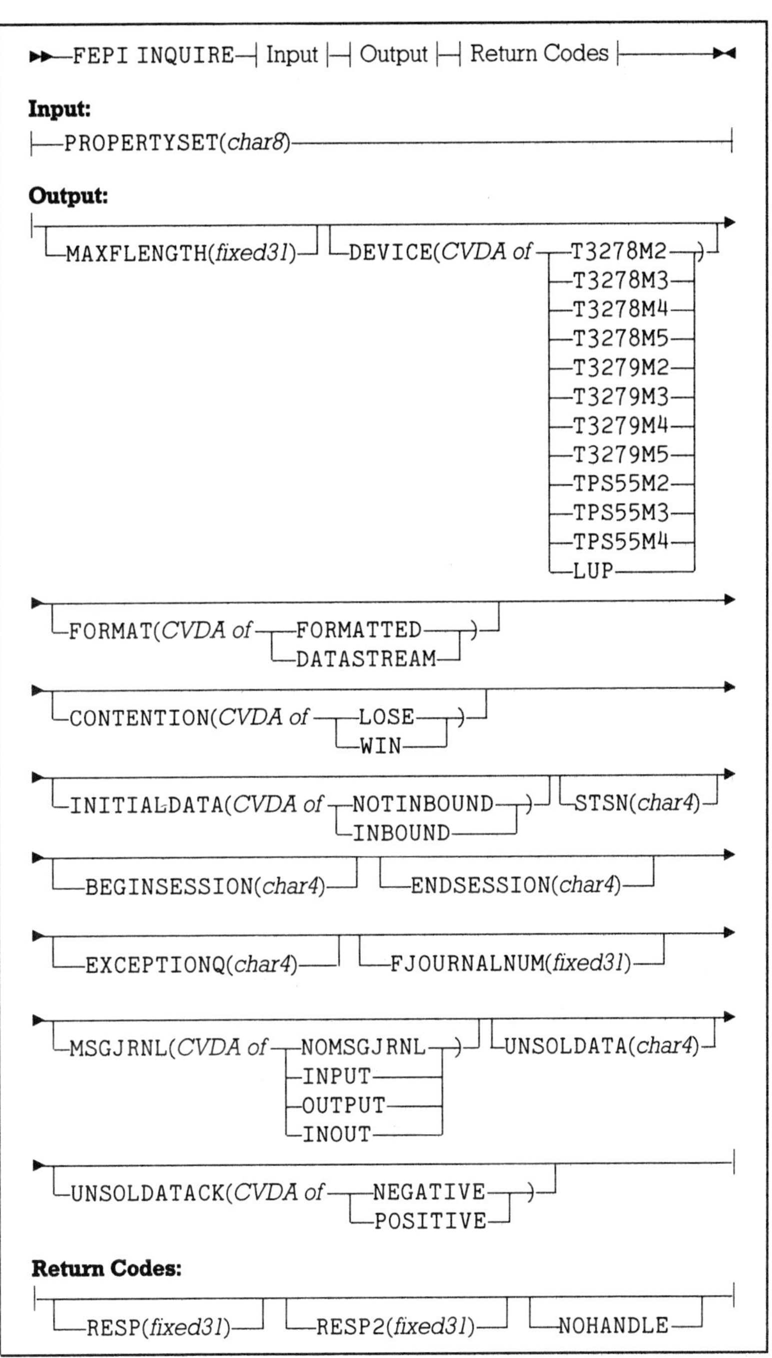

## A.3.24 EXEC CICS FEPI INSTALL POOL

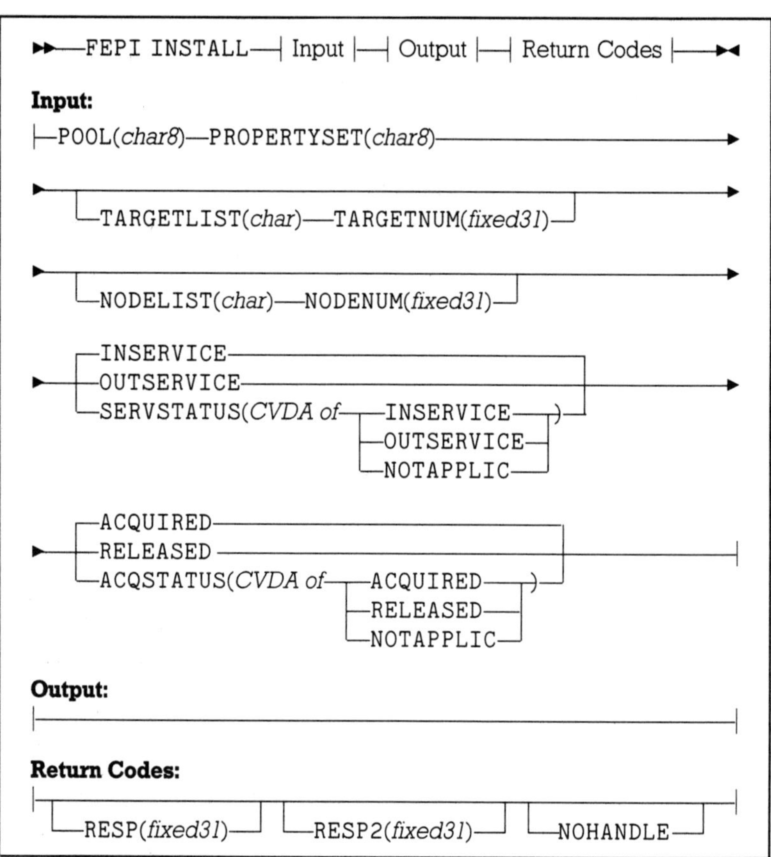


## A.3.25 EXEC CICS FEPI DISCARD POOL

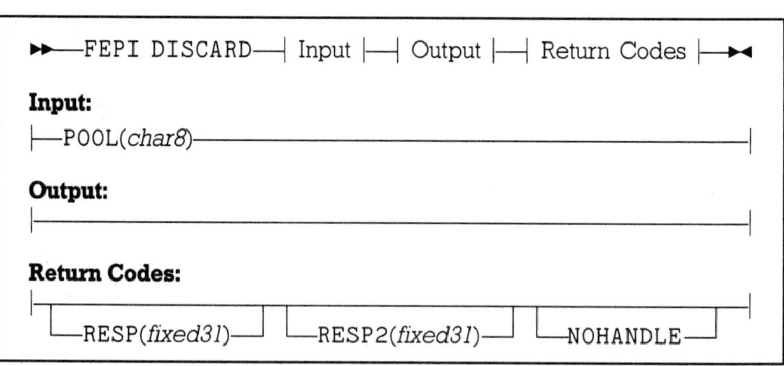

### A.3.26 EXEC CICS FEPI ADD POOL

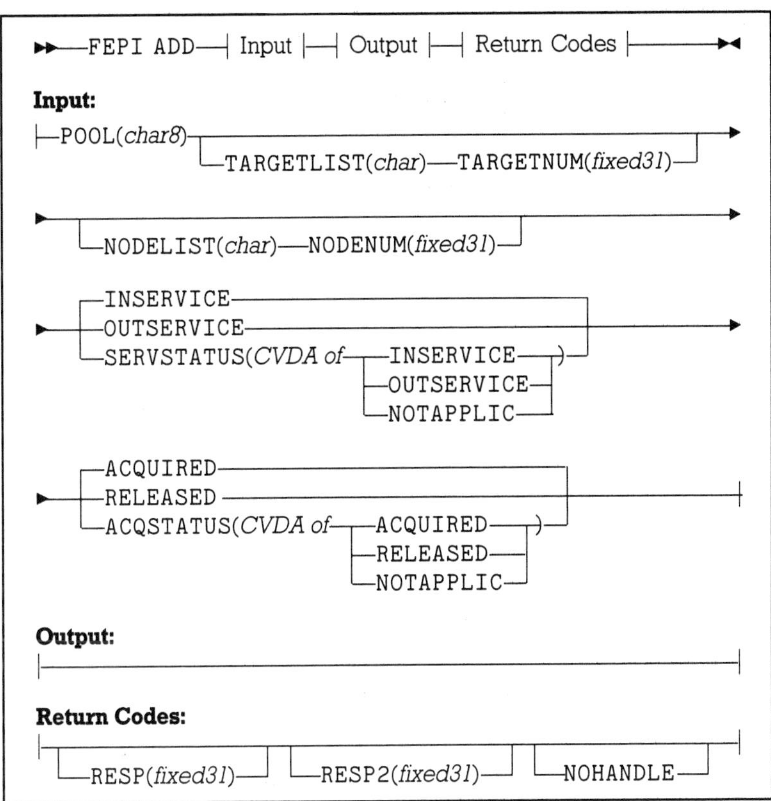


### A.3.27 EXEC CICS FEPI DELETE POOL

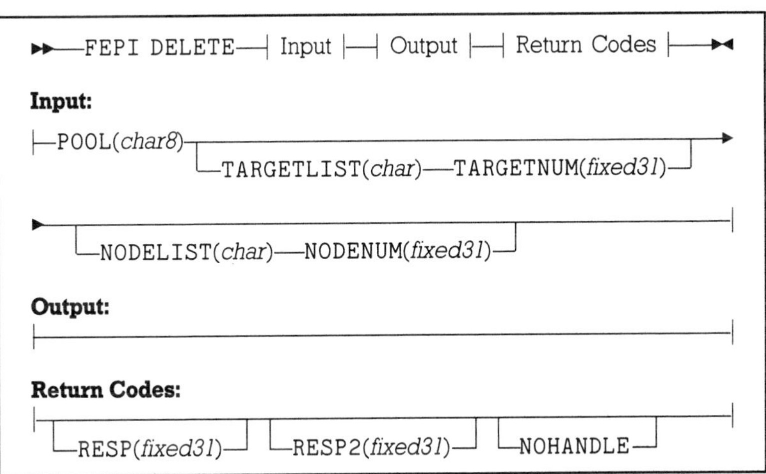

### A.3.28 EXEC CICS FEPI INQUIRE NODE

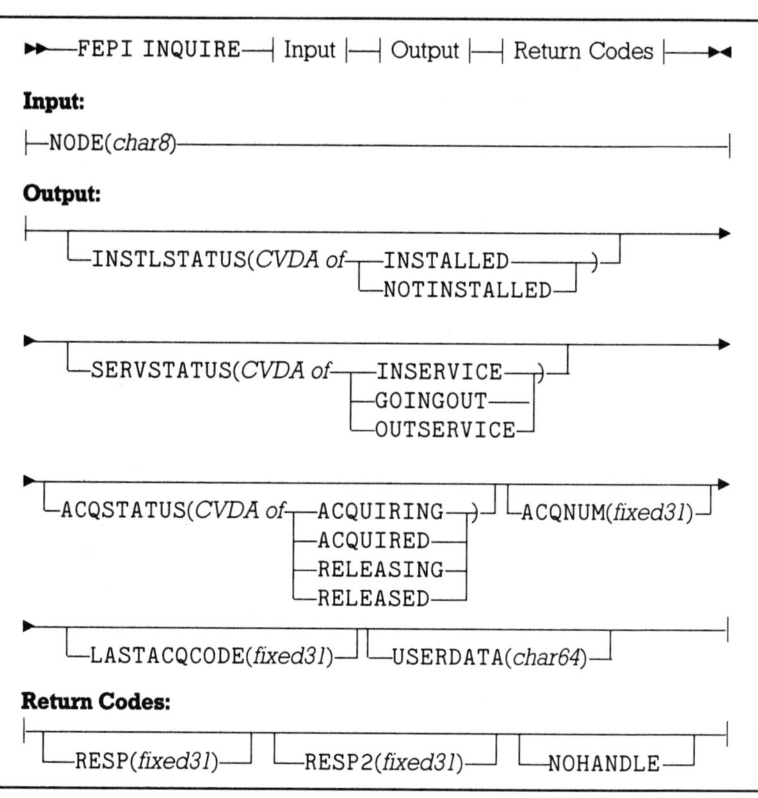


### A.3.29 EXEC CICS FEPI SET NODE

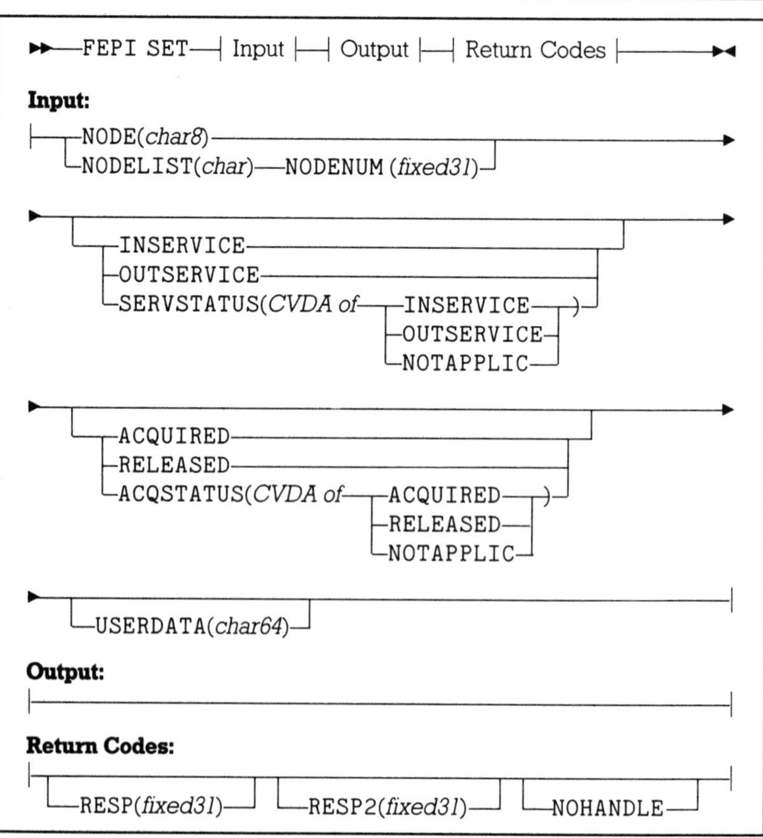

### A.3.30 EXEC CICS FEPI INQUIRE POOL

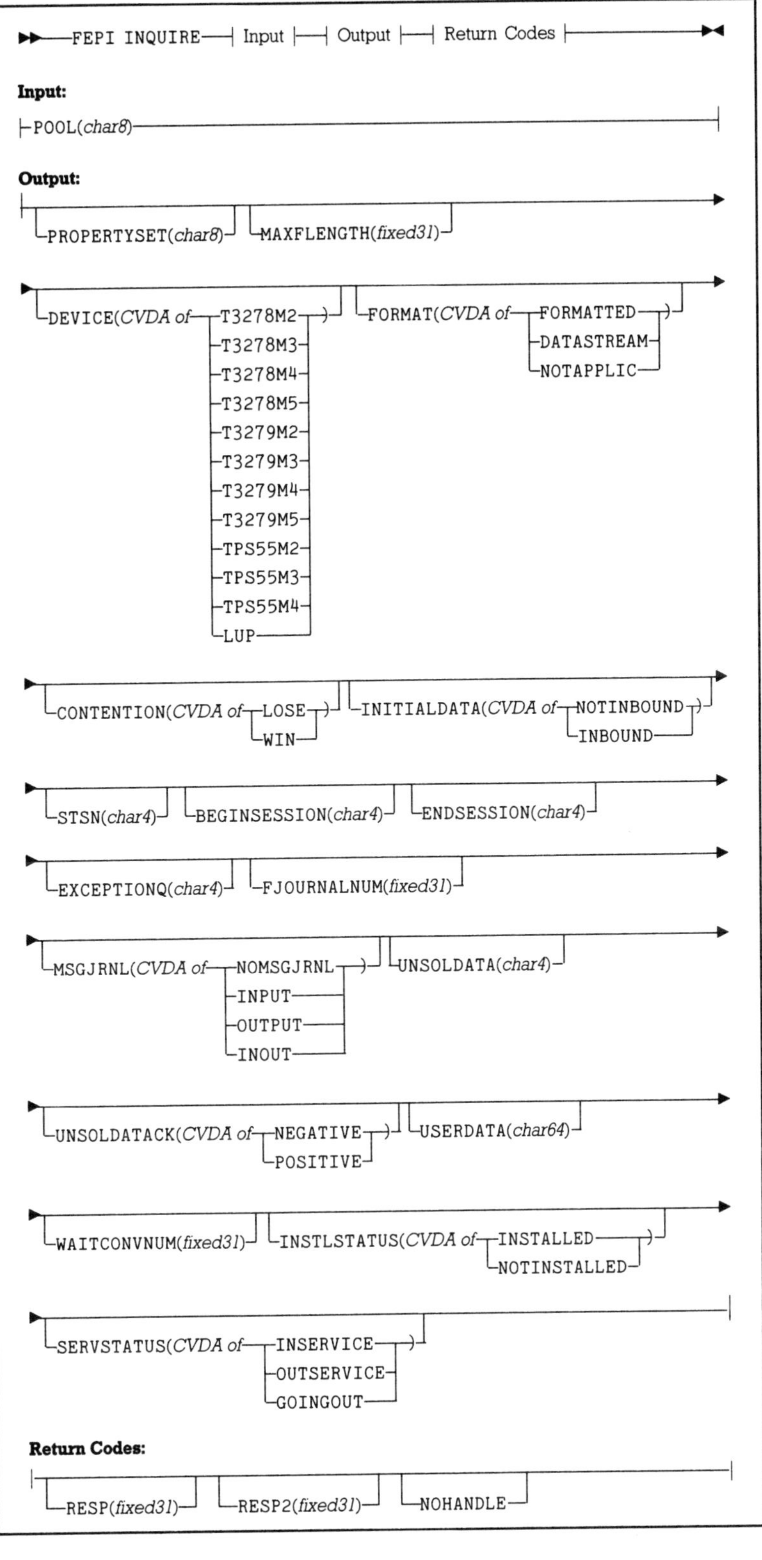

## A.3.31 EXEC CICS FEPI SET POOL

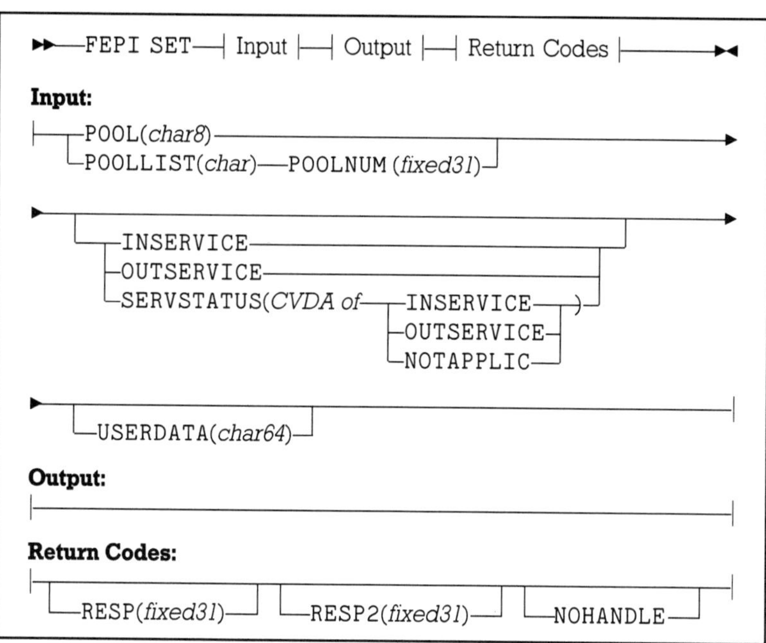


## A.3.32 EXEC CICS FEPI INQUIRE TARGET

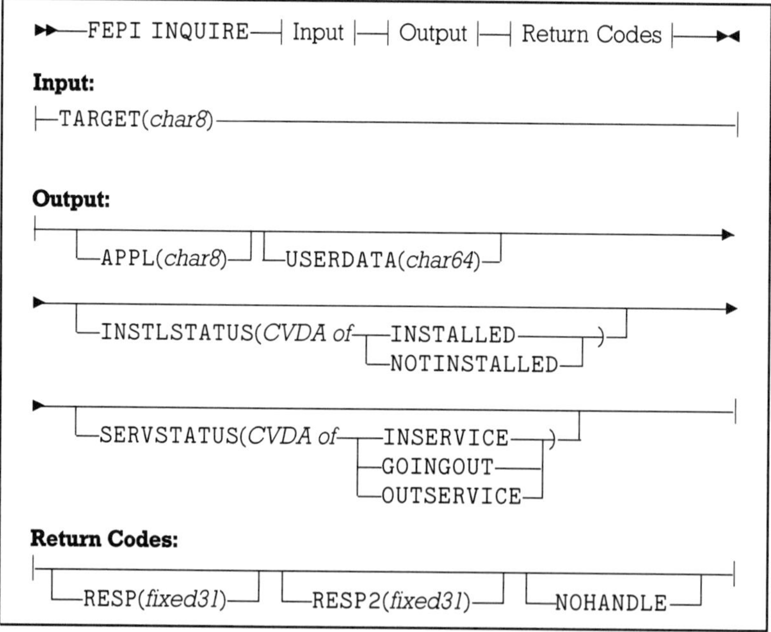

### A.3.33 EXEC CICS FEPI SET TARGET

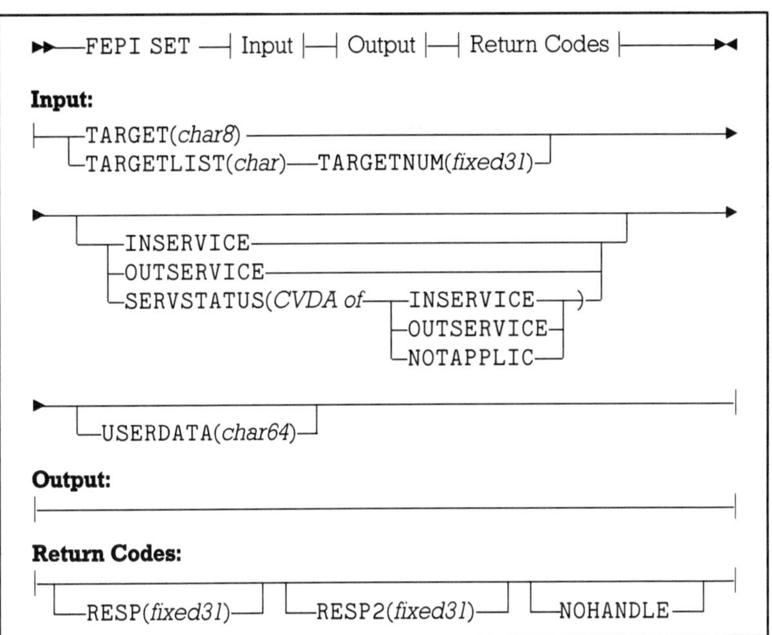

## A.3.34 EXEC CICS FEPI INQUIRE CONNECTION

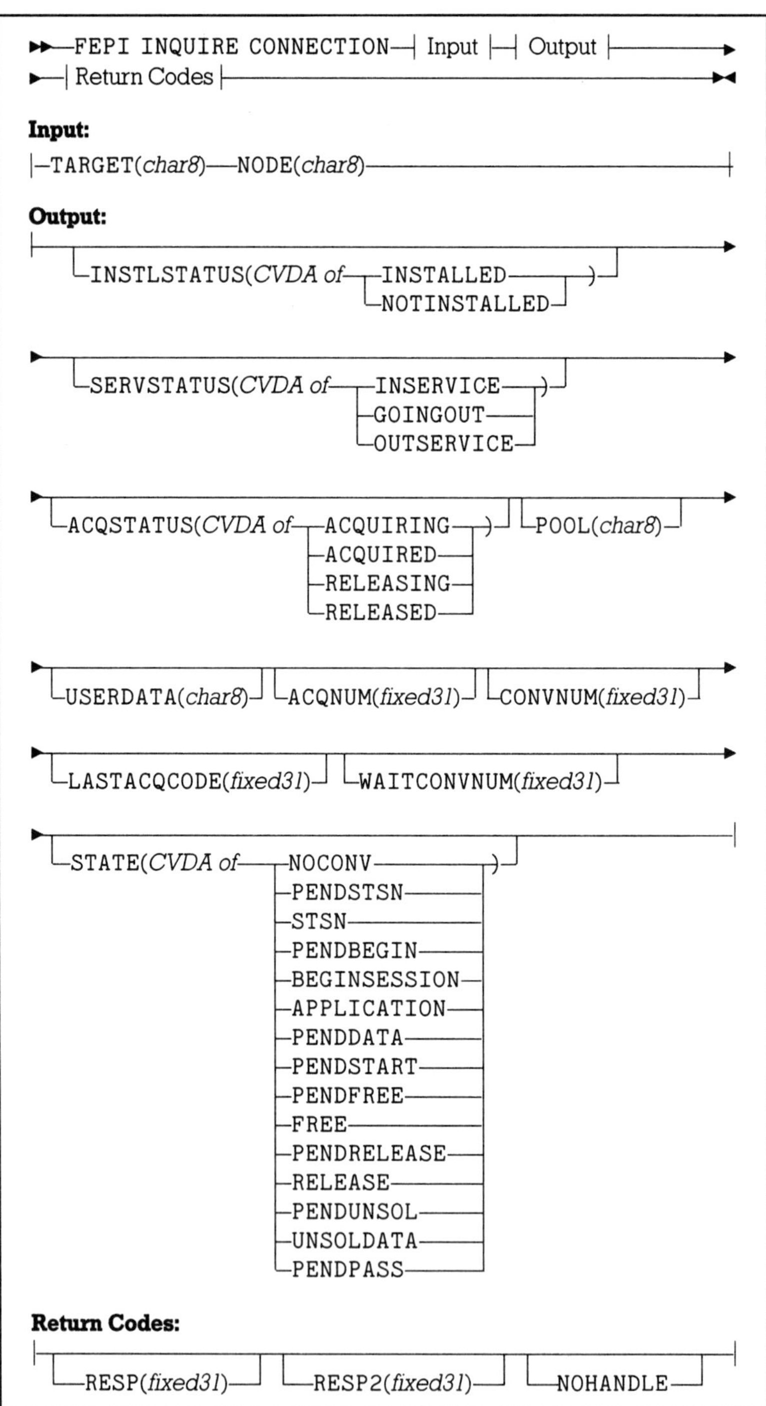

## A.3.35 EXEC CICS FEPI SET CONNECTION

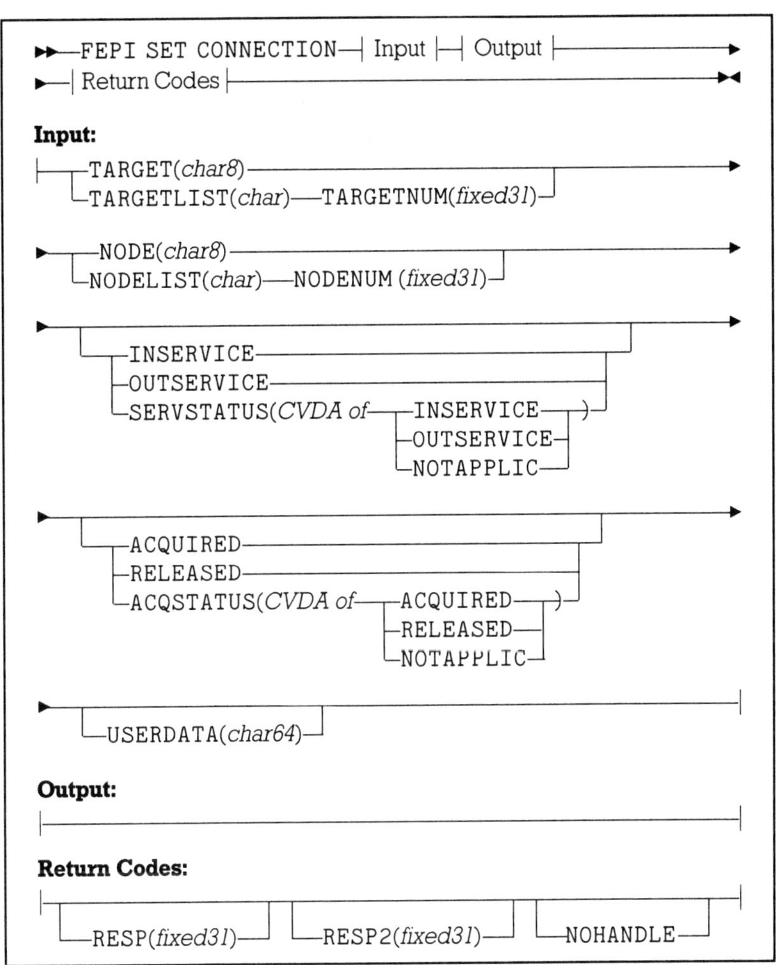

APPENDIX B

# Listing of CVDAs used by FEPI

| | | | |
|---|---|---|---|
| ACQFAIL | 515 | NORMALRESP | 522 |
| ACQUIRED | 69 | NOSTSN | 487 |
| ACQUIRING | 71 | NOTINBOUND | 546 |
| ADDFAIL | 519 | NOTINSTALLED | 551 |
| ALARM | 501 | OLDSESSION | 486 |
| APPLICATION | 559 | OUTPUT | 227 |
| ATTENTION | 524 | OUTSERVICE | 74 |
| BEGINSESSION | 510 | PENDBEGIN | 558 |
| CANCEL | 526 | PENDDATA | 560 |
| CD | 491 | PENDFREE | 86 |
| DATA | 508 | PENDPASS | 565 |
| DATASTREAM | 543 | PENDRELEASE | 562 |
| DEFRESP1 | 497 | PENDSTART | 561 |
| DEFRESP1OR2 | 528 | PENDSTSN | 557 |
| DEFRESP2 | 498 | PENDUNSOL | 564 |
| DEFRESP3 | 499 | POSITIVE | 529 |
| DELETEFAIL | 520 | PROTECTED | 504 |
| DISCARDFAIL | 513 | RELEASE | 563 |
| EB | 490 | RELEASED | 70 |
| EXCEPTRESP | 523 | RELEASING | 549 |
| FMH | 502 | RESET | 290 |
| FORCE | 342 | RTR | 527 |
| FORMATTED | 542 | RU | 494 |
| FREE | 85 | SESSION | 372 |
| GOINGOUT | 172 | SESSIONFAIL | 517 |
| HOLD | 163 | SESSIONLOST | 516 |
| INBOUND | 547 | SETFAIL | 514 |
| INOUT | 532 | SHUTDOWN | 288 |
| INPUT | 226 | STSN | 509 |
| INSERVICE | 73 | STSNSET | 488 |
| INSTALLED | 550 | STSNTEST | 489 |
| INSTALLFAIL | 512 | TASK | 233 |
| INVALID | 359 | TIMEOUT | 511 |
| LIC | 493 | TPS55M2 | 552 |
| LOSE | 544 | TPS55M3 | 553 |
| LUP | 541 | TPS55M4 | 554 |
| LUSTAT | 525 | T3278M2 | 533 |
| MDT | 506 | T3278M3 | 534 |
| MORE | 492 | T3278M4 | 535 |
| NEGATIVE | 530 | T3278M5 | 536 |
| NEWSESSION | 485 | T3279M2 | 537 |
| NOALARM | 500 | T3279M3 | 538 |
| NOCONV | 556 | T3279M4 | 539 |
| NOFMH | 503 | T3279M5 | 540 |
| NOMDT | 507 | UNPROTECTED | 505 |
| NOMSGJRNL | 531 | UNSOLDATA | 521 |
| NONE | 496 | WIN | 545 |

| | | | |
|---|---|---|---|
| 69 | ACQUIRED | 516 | SESSIONLOST |
| 70 | RELEASED | 517 | SESSIONFAIL |
| 71 | ACQUIRING | 519 | ADDFAIL |
| 73 | INSERVICE | 520 | DELETEFAIL |
| 74 | OUTSERVICE | 521 | UNSOLDATA |
| 85 | FREE | 522 | NORMALRESP |
| 86 | PENDFREE | 523 | EXCEPTRESP |
| 163 | HOLD | 524 | ATTENTION |
| 172 | GOINGOUT | 525 | LUSTAT |
| 226 | INPUT | 526 | CANCEL |
| 227 | OUTPUT | 527 | RTR |
| 233 | TASK | 528 | DEFRESP1OR2 |
| 288 | SHUTDOWN | 529 | POSITIVE |
| 290 | RESET | 530 | NEGATIVE |
| 342 | FORCE | 531 | NOMSGJRNL |
| 359 | INVALID | 532 | INOUT |
| 372 | SESSION | 533 | T3278M2 |
| 485 | NEWSESSION | 534 | T3278M3 |
| 486 | OLDSESSION | 535 | T3278M4 |
| 487 | NOSTSN | 536 | T3278M5 |
| 488 | STSNSET | 537 | T3279M2 |
| 489 | STSNTEST | 538 | T3279M3 |
| 490 | EB | 539 | T3279M4 |
| 491 | CD | 540 | T3279M5 |
| 492 | MORE | 541 | LUP |
| 493 | LIC | 542 | FORMATTED |
| 494 | RU | 543 | DATASTREAM |
| 496 | NONE | 544 | LOSE |
| 497 | DEFRESP1 | 545 | WIN |
| 498 | DEFRESP2 | 546 | NOTINBOUND |
| 499 | DEFRESP3 | 547 | INBOUND |
| 500 | NOALARM | 549 | RELEASING |
| 501 | ALARM | 550 | INSTALLED |
| 502 | FMH | 551 | NOTINSTALLED |
| 503 | NOFMH | 552 | TPS55M2 |
| 504 | PROTECTED | 553 | TPS55M3 |
| 505 | UNPROTECTED | 554 | TPS55M4 |
| 506 | MDT | 556 | NOCONV |
| 507 | NOMDT | 557 | PENDSTSN |
| 508 | DATA | 558 | PENDBEGIN |
| 509 | STSN | 559 | APPLICATION |
| 510 | BEGINSESSION | 560 | PENDDATA |
| 511 | TIMEOUT | 561 | PENDSTART |
| 512 | INSTALLFAIL | 562 | PENDRELEASE |
| 513 | DISCARDFAIL | 563 | RELEASE |
| 514 | SETFAIL | 564 | PENDUNSOL |
| 515 | ACQFAIL | 565 | PENDPASS |

APPENDIX C

# Listing of FEPI Return Codes and names

## C.1 Return Code numbers

| RC no. | Meaning |
|---|---|
| 1 | INQUIRE START, NEXT, or END command not valid here:<br>START Browse of this resource type already in progress.<br>NEXT INQUIRE START not issued.<br>END INQUIRE START not issued. |
| 2 | All resource definitions have been retrieved. |
| 10 | Command bypassed by user exit. |
| 11 | FEPI not installed or not active. |
| 12 | CICS shutting down, command not allowed. |
| 13 | FEPI not available. |
| 14 | FEPI busy or cannot get storage. |
| 15 | Unknown command. |
| 16 | Internal problem. |
| 17 | FEPI cannot get storage for user exit parameters. |
| 18 | Command failed because of operator or system action. |
| 30 | POOL name not known. |
| 31 | POOL name out of service. |
| 32 | TARGET name not known. |
| 33 | TARGET name out of service. |
| 34 | TARGET name required but not specified. |
| 35 | Pool name is unsuitable for Temporary Conversations. It has CONTENTION(LOSE) or INITIALDATA(INBOUND) but no Begin Session Handler. |
| 36 | No suitable session available and inservice. |
| 40 | [FROM]FLENGTH value is negative, zero, or more than MAXFLENGTH value for Pool. |
| 41 | ESCAPE value not valid. |
| 50 | Inbound data with 'begin bracket' to be received. |
| 51 | Attention identifier (AID) not valid. |
| 52 | Cursor position not valid. |
| 53 | Code points in Formatted data not valid. |
| 54 | Attribute positions or values in Send data not valid. |
| 55 | Keystroke Escape sequence in Send data not valid. |
| 56 | Field validation (mandatory fill, mandatory enter, trigger) failed. |
| 57 | Input is inhibited. |
| 58 | VTAM SEND failed. |
| 59 | DBCS data rules violated. |
| 60 | MAXFLENGTH value negative or greater than MAXFLENGTH value for Pool. |
| 61 | FLENGTH value negative or greater than 128. |
| 62 | TRANSID name not valid. |
| 63 | TERMID name not valid. |
| 70 | FIELDLOC or FIELDNUM value negative or not valid. |
| 71 | VTAM *RECEIVE* failed. |

| RC no. | Meaning |
|---|---|
| 80 | `CONTROL` value not valid. |
| 81 | `VALUE` not valid: omitted when required; included when not required; or unsuitable for specified `CONTROL`. |
| 82 | `SENSEDATA` option omitted when required, or specified when not required. |
| 90 | Definite Response type did not match what was required. |
| 91 | Only `NORMALRESP` or `EXCEPTRESP` allowed at this point in conversation. |
| 92 | Response to `STSN` *SET* was not positive. |
| 93 | Only `STSN` allowed at this point in conversation. |
| 94 | Only `STSN` or `NORMALRESP` allowed at this point in conversation. |
| 95 | `CONTROL` value not allowed at this point in conversation. |
| 100 | Not authorized to issue request. |
| 110 | `SERVSTATUS` value not valid. |
| 111 | `ACQSTATUS` value not valid. |
| 115 | `POOL` name not known. |
| 116 | `TARGET` name not known. |
| 117 | `NODE` name not known. |
| 118 | Unknown connection (`TARGET` and `NODE` names known, but not in a common POOL). |
| 119 | Request failed for one or more items in list. Detailed errors reported to TD queue for monitor to handle. |
| 130 | `TARGETNUM` value negative, zero, or not valid. |
| 131 | `NODENUM` value negative, zero, or not valid. |
| 132 | `POOLNUM` value negative, zero, or not valid. |
| 140 | `DEVICE` value not valid. |
| 141 | `CONTENTION` value not valid. |
| 142 | `INITIALDATA` value not valid. |
| 143 | `UNSOLDATACK` value not valid. |
| 144 | `MSGJRNL` value not valid. |
| 150 | `FORMAT` value not valid or unsuitable for specified device. |
| 153 | `STSN` name not valid or `STSN` unsuitable for specified device. |
| 154 | `BEGINSESSION` value not valid. |
| 155 | `UNSOLDATA` value not valid. |
| 156 | `EXCEPTIONQ` value not valid. |
| 157 | `FJOURNALNUM` value not valid. |
| 158 | `MAXFLENGTH` value not valid. |
| 159 | `ENDSESSION` value not valid. |
| 160 | `PROPERTYSET` name not valid. |
| 162 | `POOL` name not valid. |
| 163 | `NODE` name not valid. |
| 164 | `TARGET` name not valid. |
| 167 | `APPL` name not valid. |
| 170 | `PROPERTYSET` name already exists. |
| 171 | `PROPERTYSET` name not known. |
| 172 | `POOL` name already exists. |
| 173 | `NODE` name already exists. |
| 174 | `TARGET` name already exists. |
| 175 | Connection already exists. |
| 176 | VTAM *OPEN NODE* failed. |
| 177 | VTAM *APPLID* already known. |
| 182 | Session unbound, unrecoverable. |
| 183 | Session *unbound*, recoverable. |
| 184 | Session *unbound*, error. |
| 185 | Session *unbound*, *bind* coming. |
| 186 | Session *unbound*. |
| 187 | Lost terminal. |
| 188 | *CLEANUP*, abnormal. |
| 189 | *CLEANUP*. |
| 190 | *UNBIND*, error. |
| 191 | *SETUP* error. |
| 192 | *SSCP* error. |
| 193 | *SLU* error. |
| 194 | *PLU* error. |
| 195 | *BIND* error. |
| 196 | *CINIT* error. |
| 197 | *REQSESS* error. |
| 198 | *REQSESS* inhibited. |
| 199 | *REQSESS* not available. |
| 210 | Option not valid for SLUP. |
| 211 | Option not valid for SLU2. |
| 212 | Wrong data format for conversation. |
| 213 | Command has timed out. |
| 214 | CICS shutting down, conversation should be ended. |
| 215 | Session lost. |

| RC no. | Meaning | RC no. | Meaning |
|---|---|---|---|
| 216 | Error occurred on previous `SEND` command. | 230 | SNA *CLEAR* command received. |
| 220 | `SEND` or `CONVERSE` command not allowed at this point in conversation. | 231 | SNA *CANCEL* command received. |
| 221 | `RECEIVE` command not allowed at this point in conversation. | 232 | SNA *CHASE* command received. |
| 223 | `START` command not allowed at this point in conversation. | 233 | Exception Response received. |
| 224 | Only `ISSUE` or `FREE` allowed at this point in conversation. | 234 | Exception Request received. |
| | | 240 | Conversation ID unknown or not owned by task. |
| | | 241 | `TIMEOUT` value negative or not valid. |

## C.2 Return Code names

These definitions are contained in the following copybooks:

**DFHSZAPA** Assembler programs
**DFHSZAPC** C programs
**DFHSZAPO** Cobol programs (a '_' is a '-')
**DFHSZAPP** PL/1 programs (a '_' is a '-')

| RC no. | Name | RC no. | Name |
|---|---|---|---|
| 000 | DFSHZ_RESPX_OK | 117 | DFHSZ_RESPS_UNK_NODE |
| 001 | DFHSZ_RESPS_SEQ_BROWSE | 118 | DFHSZ_RESPS_UNK_CONN |
| 002 | DFHSZ_RESPS_END_BROWSE | 119 | DFHSZ_RESPS_ERR_LIST |
| 010 | DFHSZ_RESPX_BYPASS | 130 | DFHSZ_RESPS_INV_TARGETNUM |
| 011 | DFHSZ_RESPX_NOFEPI | 131 | DFHSZ_RESPS_INV_NODENUM |
| 012 | DFHSZ_RESPX_SHUTDOWN | 132 | DFHSZ_RESPS_INV_POOLNUM |
| 013 | DFHSZ_RESPX_OUT_FEPI | 140 | DFHSZ_RESPI_INV_DEVICE |
| 014 | DFHSZ_RESPX_BUSY | 141 | DFHSZ_RESPI_INV_CONTENTION |
| 015 | DFHSZ_RESPX_UNK_COMMAND | 142 | DFHSZ_RESPI_INV_INITLDATA |
| 016 | DFHSZ_RESPX_ERR_INTERNAL | 143 | DFHSZ_RESPI_INV_UNSOLACK |
| 017 | DFHSZ_RESPX_BUSYEXIT | 144 | DFHSZ_RESPI_INV_MSGJRNL |
| 018 | DFHSZ_RESPX_OPSYS | 150 | DFHSZ_RESPI_INV_FORMAT |
| 030 | DFHSZ_RESPA_UNK_POOL | 153 | DFHSZ_RESPI_INV_STSN |
| 031 | DFHSZ_RESPA_OUT_POOL | 154 | DFHSZ_RESPI_INV_BEGINSESS |
| 032 | DFHSZ_RESPA_UNK_TARGET | 155 | DFHSZ_RESPI_INV_UNSOLDATA |
| 033 | DFHSZ_RESPA_OUT_TARGET | 156 | DFHSZ_RESPI_INV_EXCEPTIONQ |
| 034 | DFHSZ_RESPA_REQ_TARGET | 157 | DFHSZ_RESPI_INV_JOURNAL |
| 035 | DFHSZ_RESPA_BAD_POOL | 158 | DFHSZ_RESPI_INV_MAXLEN |
| 036 | DFHSZ_RESPA_NOSESSION | 159 | DFHSZ_RESPI_INV_ENDSESS |
| 040 | DFHSZ_RESPA_INV_FROMLEN | 160 | DFHSZ_RESPI_INV_PROPSET |
| 041 | DFHSZ_RESPA_INV_ESCAPE | 162 | DFHSZ_RESPI_INV_POOL |
| 050 | DFHSZ_RESPA_INBOUNDDATA | 163 | DFHSZ_RESPI_INV_NODE |
| 051 | DFHSZ_RESPA_INV_AID | 164 | DFHSZ_RESPI_INV_TARGET |
| 052 | DFHSZ_RESPA_INV_CURSOR | 167 | DFHSZ_RESPI_INV_APPL |
| 053 | DFHSZ_RESPA_INV_CODE | 170 | DFHSZ_RESPI_DUP_PROPSET |
| 054 | DFHSZ_RESPA_INV_ATTR | 171 | DFHSZ_RESPI_UNK_PROPSET |
| 055 | DFHSZ_RESPA_INV_KEYESC | 172 | DFHSZ_RESPI_DUP_POOL |
| 056 | DFHSZ_RESPA_ERR_VALIDATION | 173 | DFHSZ_RESPI_DUP_NODE |
| 057 | DFHSZ_RESPA_INPUTINHIBIT | 174 | DFHSZ_RESPI_DUP_TARGET |
| 058 | DFHSZ_RESPA_ERR_SEND | 175 | DFHSZ_RESPI_DUP_CONN |
| 059 | DFHSZ_RESPA_ERR_DBCS | 176 | DFHSZ_RESPI_ERR_OPENNODE |
| 060 | DFHSZ_RESPA_INV_MAXLEN | 177 | DFHSZ_RESPI_DUP_APPL |
| 061 | DFHSZ_RESPA_INV_STARTLEN | 210 | DFHSZ_RESPA_BAD_PARMP |
| 062 | DFHSZ_RESPA_INV_TRANSID | 211 | DFHSZ_RESPA_BAD_PARM2 |
| 063 | DFHSZ_RESPA_INV_TERMID | 212 | DFHSZ_RESPA_BAD_DATAFMT |
| 070 | DFHSZ_RESPA_INV_FIELD | 213 | DFHSZ_RESPA_TIMEOUT |
| 071 | DFHSZ_RESPA_ERR_RECEIVE | 214 | DFHSZ_RESPA_FREECONV |
| 080 | DFHSZ_RESPA_INV_CONTROL | 215 | DFHSZ_RESPA_LOSTSESSION |
| 081 | DFHSZ_RESPA_INV_VALUE | 216 | DFHSZ_RESPA_ERR_LASTSEND |
| 082 | DFHSZ_RESPA_BAD_SENSEDATA | 220 | DFHSZ_RESPA_SEQ_SEND |
| 090 | DFHSZ_RESPA_BAD_DEFRESP | 221 | DFHSZ_RESPA_SEQ_RECEIVE |
| 091 | DFHSZ_RESPA_NOT_RESPONSE | 223 | DFHSZ_RESPA_SEQ_START |
| 092 | DFHSZ_RESPA_NOT_POSITIVE | 224 | DFHSZ_RESPA_NOT_ISSUEFREE |
| 093 | DFHSZ_RESPA_NOT_STSN | 230 | DFHSZ_RESPA_RCV_CLEAR |
| 094 | DFHSZ_RESPA_NOT_STSNRESP | 231 | DFHSZ_RESPA_RCV_CANCEL |
| 095 | DFHSZ_RESPA_BAD_CONTROL | 232 | DFHSZ_RESPA_RCV_CHASE |
| 100 | DFHSZ_RESPS_NOTAUTH | 233 | DFHSZ_RESPA_RCV_EXCEPTRESP |
| 110 | DFHSZ_RESPS_INV_SERV | 234 | DFHSZ_RESPA_RCV_EXCEPTREQ |
| 111 | DFHSZ_RESPS_INV_ACQ | 240 | DFHSZ_RESPA_UNK_CONVID |
| 115 | DFHSZ_RESPS_UNK_POOL | 241 | DFHSZ_RESPA_INV_TIMEOUT |
| 116 | DFHSZ_RESPS_UNK_TARGET | | |

APPENDIX

# D Start Data and Transient Data Queue Record layouts

## D.1 TDQ records

The following structure describes the TDQ records written to either Pool-specific TDQs or the FEPI Global TDQ CSZX. They are mapped by the DFHSZAPA/O/P/C copybooks.

**Table D.1** TDQ record format (Continues)

| Field name | Format | Description | Settings | |
|---|---|---|---|---|
| DATATYPE | F | Identification of the structure | Always set to 2 | |
| EVENTTYPE | CVDA (F) | Shows what the event was | **CVDA** | **Meaning** |
| | | | ACQFAIL | Node could not be acquired (VTAM could not open the ACB). |
| | | | ADDFAIL | Connection in list not added to Pool. |
| | | | DELETEFAIL | Connection in list not deleted from Pool. |
| | | | DISCARDFAIL | Resource in a list not discarded. |
| | | | INSTALLFAIL | Resource in a list not installed. |
| | | | SESSION | An Unsolicited Bind received. |
| | | | SESSIONFAIL | Connection could not be started. |
| | | | SESSIONLOST | Active Connection failed. |
| | | | SETFAIL | Connection or resource in a list could not be set by EXEC CICS FEPI SET or EXEC CICS FEPI INSTALL. |
| EVENTVALUE | F | Provides more information about the event | **Event** | **Value** |
| | | | ACQFAIL | 0 |
| | | | ADDFAIL | EIBRESP2 failure value |
| | | | DELETEFAIL | EIBRESP2 failure value |
| | | | DISCARDFAIL | EIBRESP2 failure value |
| | | | INSTALLFAIL | EIBRESP2 failure value |
| | | | SESSION | 0 |
| | | | SESSIONFAIL | EIBRESP2 failure value |
| | | | SESSIONLOST | EIBRESP2 failure value |
| | | | SETFAIL | EIBRESP2 failure value |

**Table D.1** TDQ record format (Continued)

| Field name | Format | Description | Settings |
|---|---|---|---|
| EVENTDATA | XL8 | Information about the event in two fullwords | **Event** / **Data**<br>ACQFAIL: 1 VTAM Reason code, 2 Retry count<br>SESSIONFAIL: 1 VTAM Reason code, 2 Retry count<br>SESSIONLOST: 1 VTAM Reason code, 2 Retry count<br>**Other events**: 1 0, 2 0 |
| PADDING | XL4 | | |
| POOL | CL8 | The applicable Pool | |
| TARGET | CL8 | The applicable Target | For the SESSION event this is the VTAM applid, not the FEPI Target name |
| NODE | CL8 | The applicable Node | |
| CONVID | XL8 | If relevant, the Conversation Convid | |
| DEVICE | CVDA (F) | If relevant, the DEVICE CVDA for the Pool | |
| FORMAT | CVDA (F) | If relevant, the FORMAT CVDA for the Pool | FORMATTED or DATASTREAM |
| PADDING | XL8 | | |

*Note:* F → fullword, CLn → Character field of *n* bytes, XLn → Hex field of *n* bytes, CVDA(F) → CVDA value of format fullword. See Appendix B for the CVDA numbers.

## D.2 Start Data format

The following structure describes the Start Data format used for FEPI transaction initiation. It is mapped by the DFHSZAPA/O/P/C copybooks.

**Table D.2** Start Data format (Continues)

| Field name | Format | Description | Settings | |
|---|---|---|---|---|
| DATATYPE | F | Identification of the structure | Always set to 1 | |
| EVENTTYPE | CVDA (F) | Shows what the event was | **CVDA** | **Meaning** |
| | | | BEGINSESSION | Transaction is a Begin Session Handler |
| | | | DATA | START transaction run because of data arrival |
| | | | FREE | Transaction is an End Session Handler for End of Conversation |
| | | | RELEASE | Transaction is an End Session Handler for End of Connection |
| | | | SESSIONLOST | START transaction run because Connection lost |
| | | | STSN | Transaction is an STSN Handler |
| | | | TIMEOUT | START transaction run because of Timeout |
| | | | UNSOLDATA | Transaction is an Unsolicited Data Handler |
| EVENTVALUE | F | Provides more information about the free and release events | For a FREE: | |
| | | | **FORCE** | EXEC CICS FEPI FREE FORCE issued |
| | | | **HOLD** | EXEC CICS FEPI FREE HOLD issued |
| | | | **RELEASE** | EXEC CICS FEPI FREE RELEASE issued |
| | | | **SHUTDOWN** | CICS is undergoing a Normal Shutdown |
| | | | **TASK** | The Conversation is being freed by CICS End of task processing |
| | | | For a RELEASE: | |
| | | | **SHUTDOWN** | CICS is undergoing a Normal Shutdown |
| | | | **RELEASE** | All other reasons |
| EVENTDATA | XL8 | Information about the event in two fullwords | **Event** | **Data** |
| | | | ACQFAIL | 1 VTAM Reason code<br>2 Retry count |
| | | | SESSIONFAIL | 1 VTAM Reason code<br>2 Retry count |
| | | | SESSIONLOST | 1 VTAM Reason code<br>2 Retry count |
| | | | **Other events** | 1 0<br>2 0 |

**Table D.2** Start data format (Continued)

| **Field name** | **Format** | **Description** | **Settings** |
|---|---|---|---|
| PADDING | XL4 | | |
| POOL | CL8 | The applicable Pool | |
| TARGET | CL8 | The applicable Target | |
| NODE | CL8 | The applicable Node | |
| CONVID | XL8 | If relevant, the Conversation Convid | |
| DEVICE | CVDA (F) | If relevant, the DEVICE CVDA for the Pool | |
| FORMAT | CVDA (F) | If relevant, the FORMAT CVDA for the Pool | FORMATTED DATASTREAM |
| PADDING | XL8 | | |
| FLENGTH | F | Length of the USERDATA area | |
| USERDATA | XL128 | User data as set in the EXEC CICS FEPI START command | |

*Note:* F → Fullword, CLn → Character field of *n* bytes, XLn → Hex field of *n* bytes, CVDA(F) → CVDA value of format fullword. See Appendix B for the CVDA numbers.

APPENDIX E

# Listing of FEPI Command Codes

| | |
|---|---|
| 820E | AP NOOP |
| 8210 | ALLOCATE |
| 8212 | CONVERSE FORMATTED |
| 8214 | CONVERSE DATASTREAM |
| 8216 | EXTRACT CONV |
| 8218 | EXTRACT FIELD |
| 821A | EXTRACT STSN |
| 821C | FREE |
| 821E | ISSUE |
| 8220 | RECEIVE FORMATTED |
| 8222 | RECEIVE DATASTREAM |
| 8224 | SEND FORMATTED |
| 8226 | SEND DATASTREAM |
| 8228 | START |
| 8402 | CICS Normal shutdown |
| 8404 | CICS Immediate shutdown |
| 8406 | CICS Forced shutdown |
| 8408 | CICS End of task |
| 840E | SP NOOP |
| 8422 | INQUIRE PROPERTYSET |
| 8428 | INSTALL PROPERTYSET |
| 8430 | DISCARD PROPERTYSET |
| 8442 | INQUIRE NODE |
| 8444 | SET NODE |
| 8448 | INSTALL NODELIST |
| 844A | ADD POOL |
| 844C | DELETE POOL |
| 8450 | DISCARD NODE |
| 8462 | INQUIRE POOL |
| 8464 | SET POOL |
| 8468 | INSTALL POOL |
| 8470 | DISCARD POOL |
| 8482 | INQUIRE TARGET |
| 8484 | SET TARGET |
| 8488 | INSTALL TARGETLIST |
| 8490 | DISCARD TARGET |
| 84A2 | INQUIRE CONNECTION |
| 84A4 | SET CONNECTION |

# APPENDIX F FEPI States

| | |
|---|---|
| APPLICATION | A normal FEPI application task owns the Conversation. |
| BEGINSESSION | A Begin Section Handler owns the Conversation. |
| FREE | An End Session (End of Conversation) Handler owns the Conversation. |
| NOCONV | No Conversation is active on the Connection. |
| PENDBEGIN | A Begin Session Handler has been scheduled. |
| PENDDATA | FEPI is waiting for Inbound data, following a START request. |
| PENDFREE | An End Session (End of Conversation) Handler has been scheduled. |
| PENDPASS | The Conversation is unowned following an EXEC CICS FEPI FREE PASS command. |
| PENDRELEASE | An End Session (End of Connection) Handler has been scheduled. |
| PENDSTART | Inbound Data arrived, so a START transaction has been scheduled. |
| PENDSTSN | An STSN Handler has been scheduled. |
| PENDUNSOL | An Unsolicited Data Handler has been scheduled. |
| RELEASE | An End Session (End of Connection) Handler owns the Conversation. |
| STSN | An STSN Handler owns the Conversation. |
| UNSOLDATA | An Unsolicited Data Handler Task owns the Conversation. |

APPENDIX G

# Listing of FEPI formatted keystroke escape sequences

CURSOR KEYS

**&Bn** Backtab, *n* times

**&Dn** Cursor down, *n* times

**&HO** Home

**&Ln** Cursor left, *n* times

**&Nn** Newline, *n* times

**&Rn** Cursor right, *n* times

**&Tn** Tab, *n* times

**&Un** Cursor up, *n* times

($n = 1 \ldots 9$)

SPECIAL KEYS

**&DL** Delete

**&DU** DUP

**&EF** Erase end-of-field

**&EI** Erase input

**&ES** Escape character

**&FM** Field mark

**&IN** Insert

**&MS** Start secure Magnetic Strip Reader

**&RS** Reset

**&SI** Shift in

**&SO** Shift out

ATTENTION KEYS

**&AT** Attention

**&An** PA*n* (*n* = 1 . . . 3)

**&CL** Clear

**&CS** Cursor select (light pen)

**&EN** Enter

**&ME** End secure MSR

**&nn** PF*nn* (*nn* = 01 . . . 24, a leading 0 must be specified)

# APPENDIX H Listing of FEPI XSZARQ and XSZBRQ GLUE parameter lists

## XSZBRQ Parameter list

```
*** XSZBRQ PARAMETERS    *************************************
*
* VALID RETURN CODES FOR XSZBRQ ARE:
*
*       UERCNORM EQU  X'00'        NORMAL
*       UERCBYP  EQU  X'04'        NOOP THE CALL
*
UEPSZACT DS    XL2                      FEPI Command Code
         DS    XL2                           Unused
UEPSZCNV DS    CL8                           CONVID
UEPSZALP DS    CL8                           POOL
UEPSZALT DS    CL8                           TARGET
UEPSZTIM DS    F                             TIMEOUT
UEPSZSND DS    AL4                           Addr of Outbound Data
UEPSZSNL DS    F                             Len  of Outbound Data
UEPSZSTT DS    CL4                           TRANSID for START
UEPSZSTM DS    CL4                           TERMID  for START
UEPSZSNK DS    XL1                           KEYSTROKE Flag
UEPSZSNK_ON    EQU X'80'                                    Active
UEPSZSNK_OFF   EQU X'00'                                    InActive
UEPSZSNE DS    XL1                           ESCAPE    Byte
```

## XSZARQ Parameter List

```
*** XSZARQ PARAMETERS    *************************************
*
* VALID RETURN CODES FOR XSZARQ ARE:
*
*       UERCNORM EQU  X'00'        NORMAL
*
UEPSZACN DS    XL2                      FEPI Command Code
         DS    XL2                           Unused
UEPSZCON DS    CL8                           CONVID
UEPSZRP2 DS    F                             Response Code
UEPSZRVD DS    AL4                           Addr of Inbound Data
UEPSZRVL DS    F                             Len  of Inbound Data
```

## UEPSZACN and UEPSZACT Parameter Settings

```
UEPSZNOA EQU   X'820E'                 AP NOOP
UEPSZOAL EQU   X'8210'                 ALLOCATE
UEPSZOCF EQU   X'8212'                 CONVERSE FORMATTED
UEPSZOCD EQU   X'8214'                 CONVERSE DATASTREAM
UEPSZOXC EQU   X'8216'                 EXTRACT CONV
UEPSZOXF EQU   X'8218'                 EXTRACT FIELD
UEPSZOXS EQU   X'821A'                 EXTRACT STSN
UEPSZOFR EQU   X'821C'                 FREE
UEPSZOSU EQU   X'821E'                 ISSUE
UEPSZORF EQU   X'8220'                 RECEIVE FORMATTED
UEPSZORD EQU   X'8222'                 RECEIVE DATASTREAM
UEPSZOSF EQU   X'8224'                 SEND FORMATTED
UEPSZOSD EQU   X'8226'                 SEND DATASTREAM
UEPSZOST EQU   X'8228'                 START
UEPSZSDN EQU   X'8402'                 Normal Shutdown
UEPSZSDI EQU   X'8404'                 Immediate Shutdown
UEPSZSDF EQU   X'8406'                 Forced Shutdown
UEPSZEOT EQU   X'8408'                 CICS End of Task
UEPSZNOS EQU   X'840E'                 SP NOOP
UEPSZOQY EQU   X'8422'                 INQUIRE PROPERTYSET
UEPSZOIY EQU   X'8428'                 INSTALL PROPERTYSET
UEPSZODY EQU   X'8430'                 DISCARD PROPERTYSET
UEPSZOQN EQU   X'8442'                 INQUIRE NODE
UEPSZOTN EQU   X'8444'                 SET NODE
UEPSZOIN EQU   X'8448'                 INSTALL NODE
UEPSZOAD EQU   X'844A'                 ADD POOL
UEPSZODE EQU   X'844C'                 DELETE POOL
UEPSZODN EQU   X'8450'                 DISCARD NODE
UEPSZOQP EQU   X'8462'                 INQUIRE POOL
UEPSZOTP EQU   X'8464'                 SET POOL
UEPSZOIP EQU   X'8468'                 INSTALL POOL
UEPSZODP EQU   X'8470'                 DISCARD POOL
UEPSZOQT EQU   X'8482'                 INQUIRE TARGET
UEPSZOTT EQU   X'8484'                 SET TARGET
UEPSZOIT EQU   X'8488'                 INSTALL TARGET
UEPSZODT EQU   X'8490'                 DISCARD TARGET
UEPSZOQC EQU   X'84A2'                 INQUIRE CONNECTION
UEPSZOTC EQU   X'84A4'                 SET CONNECTION
```

# Glossary

**A**

**ACB** (1) A VTAM Access Control Block which allows usage of a resource. (2) The VTAM representation of a FEPI node.

**ACQSTATUS** The VTAM status of a FEPI resource (either `ACQUIRED`, `ACQUIRING`, `RELEASED` or `RELEASING`).

**Acquired** A FEPI resource is said to be Acquired when it is active in VTAM terms.

**Acquiring** The `ACQSTATUS` of a FEPI resource that is being Acquired.

**Active Connection** A FEPI Connection which is being used by a FEPI application program.

**AID** (1) The CICS Automatic Initiator Descriptor which is used to schedule transactions on a time basis. (2) The 'key' pressed on a terminal to send the screen to the host.

**APAR** The way you report a problem to IBM.

**API** (1) The set of FEPI commands that is not security protected, and is used for normal FEPI communication. (2) More generally, an Application Programming Interface providing a way of invoking some function.

**APPL** The definition in the VTAM 'SYS1.VTAMLST' file used to define FEPI nodes.

**Application Minor Node** The VTAM name for a FEPI Node.

**Application Program** (1) A CICS command-level program that issues `EXEC CICS FEPI` commands. (2) An MVS program that issues VTAM operations (in FEPI terms, the FEPI code).

**APPLID** The VTAM name of the CICS system that terminals use to connect to the system.

**Asynchronous** Things that are executed in parallel or at a later time to other things.

**ATI** Automatic Transaction Initiation is the way a CICS transaction is scheduled to run on a time basis. ATI covers both `EXEC CICS START` operations, and Transient Data Triggered Transactions.

**Attention Identifier** See *AID*.

**Attribute Bytes** Part of the 3270 protocol which defines the layout of a *Formatted Screen*.

**AutoInstall** The method of creating CICS terminals without defining them explicitly to CICS.

## B

**Back end** The CICS or IMS system with which FEPI communicates (as opposed to *Front End*). See also *Partner*.

**Background** A CICS transaction that is not executing at a terminal.

**BB** Begin Bracket is an SNA indicator that flows on the first RU of a sequence of flows. See also *Bracket*.

**Begin Session Handler** A CICS transaction which is optionally run when a FEPI Connection is Bound.

**Between Brackets** A FEPI Connection is Between Brackets when no flow is being sent or received upon it. This is closely aligned with *Contention State*.

**Bind** The VTAM flow that occurs when a FEPI Connection is acquired. It activates the SNA session between the FEPI LU and the partner system's LU.

**Bind Race** That situation which occurs when both FEPI and the partner system are generating *Binds* (only occurs for FEPI during XRF processing).

**BMP** A Batch Message Program is the IMS process that executes IMS transactions.

**Bound** A FEPI Connection is Bound when a *Bind* has successfully flowed on the Connection and the underlying VTAM session completed.

**Bracket** A Bracket is a group of RUs that form a logical sequence. It starts with a BB (Begin Bracket) and ends with an EB (End Bracket). If a Bracket is not in progress, then the session is *Between Brackets* and in *Contention State*. The Bracket contains a number of *Chains*.

**Browsing** Scanning through FEPI Resources via `EXEC CICS FEPI INQUIRE` commands.

**Buffer Address** The encoded position of a byte on a 3270 terminal screen.

## C

**CD** (1) The Change Direction indicator flows as part of a *Bracket* to show which side can send a flow (the end with the CD has permission to send). (2) An SNA half-duplex protocol using the CD indicator to indicate which side will next send a flow.

**CEDA** The CICS transaction that creates CICS resources for RDO in the CSD.

**CEMT** The CICS master terminal transaction.

**CETR** The CICS trace control transaction.

**Chain** A Chain is a set of RUs that together comprise a flow to and from a terminal. The chain is a component of a *Bracket*. A chain starts with a first-in-Chain indicator on an RU, and ends with a last-in-Chain indicator on an RU.

**CLSDST(PASS)** A VTAM programming facility for changing the host system to which a terminal is connected.

**Coded Application** A FEPI application program running a FEPI Formatted Conversation.

**Command code** The first byte of a FEPI 3270 Inbound Datastream that controls the disposition of the rest of the Datastream.

**Connection** (1) The FEPI Target–Node pair that is used to send and receive flows to the partner system. (2) The FEPI resource upon which FEPI Conversations run. (3) Another name for a VTAM *session*.

**Contention State** Contention State results when both ends of a VTAM session (or FEPI Connection) try to Send a flow at the same time. The `CONTENTION` parameter on the Pool's Propertyset controls what FEPI does in this situation.

**Conversation** (1) The FEPI object which lasts between an `EXEC CICS FEPI ALLOCATE` command and an `EXEC CICS FEPI FREE HOLD`. (2) The FEPI object which runs over a FEPI Connection to provide Communication with partner systems.

**Conversational Program** A program which contains all interactions with an end user or a partner system in a single CICS task.

**CONVID** The identifier for a FEPI Conversation, which is quoted on most `EXEC CICS FEPI` commands.

**Convid Management** A FEPI technique used to control usage of FEPI connections on a user basis.

**CSD** The CICS file that contains RDO entries.

**CSZI** The CICS transaction under which FEPI runs.

**CSZL** A CICS TDQ to which FEPI sends messages.

**CSZX** The FEPI Global TDQ for monitoring special events.

**CVDA** A CICS Value Data Area name that is interpreted by the `DFHVALUE` translator operation.

## D

**Datastream** A flow over a VTAM session.

**Datastream Data** The FEPI protocol which allows a FEPI application program to access VTAM Datastreams.

**DBCS** Double Byte Character Set, used in Japanese and Asian language flows.

**DCT** The CICS Destination Control Table used to define TDQs.

**Definite Response** The VTAM flow used to indicate acknowledgement of a flow from a partner. See *DR*.

**DFHSZATR** The FEPI Adapter.

**DFHSZRMP** The FEPI Resource Manager.

**Dispatcher** The CICS component that controls how CICS tasks are run.

**DR** (1) The VTAM protocol used to ensure that a flow has reached its destination. (2) The VTAM indicator which is used in this acknowledgement process.

**DSA** CICS managed storage that is below the line.

**Dynamic Resource Definition** Using FEPI SPI-type commands to define FEPI resources rather than via RDO or RDM techniques.

## E

**EB** End Bracket in an SNA indicator that flows on the last RU of a sequence of flows. See also *Bracket*.

**EDSA** CICS managed storage that is above the line.

**End Session Handler** A CICS transaction that optionally runs when either a FEPI Conversation is ended, or a FEPI Connection is released.

**End user** A real terminal operator.

**ENDSTATUS** The reason why an `EXEC CICS FEPI RECEIVE` terminated.

**Escape character** The prefix character used to indicate a 3270 terminal key-sequence when using keystroke access.

**ESM** An External Security Manager, such as RACF, which provides security processing.

**Exception Response** The VTAM flow used to tell the sender of a flow that the data was not successfully received. See also *DR*.

## F

**FEPI** The CICS/ESA Front End Programming Interface.

**FIC** First-in-Chain, see *Chain*.

**First Flow** See *Initial data*.

**Flow** Any set of bytes which travel over a VTAM session.

**FMH** The VTAM Function Management Header is part of a flow which contains SNA control information.

**Forced shutdown** The type of CICS shutdown initiated when CICS is cancelled, or suffers an XRF takeover.

**Foreground** A CICS transaction that is executing at a terminal.

**Formatted data** The FEPI protocol which hides most of 3270 from the FEPI application programmer.

**Formatted Screen** A 3270 terminal whose display contains Attribute Bytes.

**Front End** The CICS or IMS system that contains FEPI (as opposed to *Back End*). See also *Partner*.

## G

**Generic Applid** The shared Applid used to coordinate between XRF active and alternate systems.

**GLUE** A CICS Global User Exit, which provides facilities for system programmers to affect CICS function.

**Goingout** The `SERVSTATUS` of a FEPI resource that is being placed `OUTSERVICE`.

**GTF** The MVS-provided way of recording system trace entries.

## H

**Handler** CICS transactions that FEPI optionally runs to provide facilities for processing certain events.

## I

**Immediate shutdown** The type of CICS shutdown initiated by a `CEMT PERFORM SHUTDOWN IMMEDIATE` operation.

**Inactive Connection** A FEPI Connection which is not being used by a FEPI application program.

**Inbound** Data that flows into FEPI from a partner system.

**Initial data** The initial flow sent from a partner system when a FEPI Connection is acquired. This is commonly a Start-of-Day panel, but may contain a *Structured Field Query*.

**Inservice** A FEPI resource is said to be Inservice when it is available for FEPI use.

**INVREQ** The CICS condition returned upon an `EXEC CICS FEPI` command when FEPI raises an error.

**IPCS** The Interactive Problem Control System used to provide CICS dump interpretation facilities (usually run under TSO/E).

**IRC** CICS MRO facilities.

**ISC** CICS LU6.2 facilities.

## J

**Journalling** A special CICS facility for logging flows and records.

## K

**Kernel** The CICS component that controls CICS task processing.

**Keystroke** A way of specifying FEPI *formatted data* via a sequence of key presses.

## L

**LASTACQCODE** A field containing VTAM Return Code information.

**LIC** Last-in-Chain, see *Chain*.

**Lists** A way of defining multiple FEPI resources in one `EXEC CICS FEPI` command. I recommend *not* using lists.

**LOGMODE** A way of defining VTAM characteristics for a FEPI Node.

**LU** A Logical Unit is an SNA object through which a user access the network. In FEPI terms, a FEPI connection is one LU, and the partner system another LU.

**LU name** The network name of a FEPI node.

**LU0** A low-level VTAM protocol. Often referred to as *SLUP*.

**LU2** The 3270 protocol.

## M

**Mapin** Conventionally taken to mean getting data from a 'real' terminal and giving it to a FEPI emulated 'terminal'.

**Mapout** Conventionally taken to mean getting data from a FEPI 'terminal' and giving it to a 'real' terminal.

**MDT** The 3270 Modified Data Tag shows whether or not the following field has been updated.

**MFS** IMS Message Formatting Services.

**MODETABLE** A VTAM table that contains LOGMODEs.

**Monitor** CICS TDQ triggered transactions that FEPI optionally runs to provide facilities for processing certain events.

**MRO** CICS Multi-Region Operation.

**MVS** An IBM operating system for mainframes.

## N

**NCCF** A component of Netview used to control networks.

**Netview** An IBM product used to monitor networks.

**Node** (1) The FEPI resource that represents an emulated terminal. (2) The VTAM object representing a Secondary LU.

**Nonresponse Mode** An IMS way of running transactions that are not associated with a terminal.

**Normal shutdown** The type of CICS shutdown initiated by a `CEMT PERFORM SHUTDOWN` operation.

**NOTAUTH** The CICS condition returned upon an `EXEC CICS FEPI` SPI-type command when the user is not permitted to issue that command.

## O

**OCO** Object Code Only rules restrict the documentation of IBM products.

**Order** Part of a 3270 Datastream that positions fields on a screen.

**Outbound data** Data that is sent from FEPI to a partner system.

**Outservice** A FEPI resource is said to be Out of Service when it is unavailable for FEPI use.

## P

**Partner** (1) The system to which FEPI is communicating. (2) Generally, the process on the other end of a VTAM session.

**Passthrough program** A FEPI application program that takes a 3270 Datastream to and from a real terminal and a partner.

**PF key** A key on a 3270 keyboard that sends data to the host.

**PLT** The CICS Program List Table used to define programs that are to be run during CICS initialization, or CICS termination.

**PLU** The VTAM Primary Logical Unit. In FEPI terms, this is the partner system.

**Pool** The FEPI resource that contains groups of FEPI Connections.

**Propertyset** The FEPI resource that defines the characteristics of a Pool.

**PS/55** A Japanese terminal.

**Pseudo-conversational program** A program which does not contain all interactions with an end user or a partner system in single CICS task. As many CICS tasks are used as required.

## Q

**QR TCB** The CICS-managed TCB that all CICS application programs run upon.

## R

**RACF** An IBM External Security Manager.

**RDM** The CICS method of defining resources via resource definition macros (such as the DCT or SIT).

**RDO** The CICS method of defining resources via resource definition online techniques, using the CEDA transaction.

**Read Partition Query** See *Structured Field Query*.

**Released** A FEPI resource is said to be Released when it is inactive in VTAM terms.

**Releasing** The ACQSTATUS of a FEPI resource that is being Released.

**Response mode** The way IMS runs transactions that are associated with an IMS terminal.

**RESPSTATUS** The VTAM Response required to acknowledge receipt of a flow.

**RU** A Request/Response Unit is the lowest level chunk of VTAM/SNA data that is a component of a *Chain*.

## S

**Scatter/Gather** A single request can generate multiple requests (*scattering*) which are then merged (*gathered*) into a single result.

**Screen image** That part of FEPI *Formatted data* that uses a buffer to represent a terminal's screen.

**SDT** The VTAM Start-Data-traffic flow used to indicate that a VTAM session has been established.

**SERVSTATUS** The FEPI usability of a resource (either INSERVICE, OUTSERVICE, or GOINGOUT).

**Session** The VTAM concept of a linkage between two objects (a PLU and a SLU), which is the underlying representation of a FEPI Connection.

**Session Failure** A Session Failure results when a FEPI Connection fails.

**Session Loss** See *Session Failure*.

**Setup program** A transaction that is initiated from a *PLT* program which installs FEPI resources.

**SIT** The CICS System Initialization Table.

**SLU** The VTAM Secondary Logical Unit. A FEPI Node is represented in VTAM terms as an SLU.

**SLUP** An IMS implementation of the LU0 protocol used mainly by automatic teller machines.

**SLU2** See *LU2*.

**SNA** Systems Network Architecture.

**SON** A Session Outage Notification is received by both partners when a session fails.

**SPA** An IMS mechanism for continuing IMS transactions. The nearest CICS equivalent is use of `EXEC CICS RETURN NEXTTRAN`.

**Specific Applid** The unique nonshared Applid used by XRF active and alternate systems.

**SPI** The set of `EXEC CICS FEPI` commands that are security protected and are used to process FEPI resources.

**Start-of-Day flow** See *Initial data*.

**Structured Field Query** A 3270 flow which requests a terminal to respond with details about itself (such as screen size).

**Structured Fields** Part of the 3270 protocol which provides special features.

**STSN** The Set-and-Test-Sequence number flow used by SLUP.

**STSN Handler** A CICS transaction that optionally runs when an STSN flow is received from a partner system.

**Synchronous** Tasks that get executed sequentially to other things.

**Syncpoint** A CICS procedure that ensures all updated resources have been committed.

**SZ** The CICS identifier used for FEPI modules, etc.

**SZ TCB** The CICS-managed TCB that the FEPI Resource Manager runs upon.

**T**

**Target** The FEPI resource that represents a partner system.

**Task** Another term for a CICS transaction (as used in this book).

**TCB** The MVS task control block which MVS uses to run its tasks.

**TCTTE** The CICS Terminal Control Block.

**TDQ** A CICS Transient Data Queue, as defined in the CICS DCT.

**Temporary Conversation** A FEPI Conversation that lasts only during a single `EXEC CICS FEPI CONVERSE` command.

**Timeout** (1) The FEPI facility whereby `EXEC CICS FEPI` commands can complete without the requested operation having finished. (2) The state resulting when the above action occurs.

**Translator** The program which converts `EXEC CICS` commands into executable code.

**Triggered Transaction** A CICS transaction initiated via the DCT when a given number of records are in the owning TDQ.

**TYPETERM** The CICS AutoInstall mechanism for defining the characteristics of a terminal.

**U**

**Unbind** The SNA operation that results when a FEPI Connection is released. It removes the VTAM session.

**Unbound** A VTAM session that has been '*unbind*-ed'.

**Unexpected data** A flow that is sent by the partner system which is not that which usually occurs. The classic example is when an abend message is generated.

**Unsolicited Bind** The (rejected) attempt for a partner system to contact FEPI.

**Unsolicited Data** A flow that arrives from a partner system when no FEPI Conversation is using the FEPI Connection. The classic example is a broadcast message.

**Unsolicited Data Handler** A CICS transaction which is optionally run when a FEPI Connection receives Unsolicited Data.

**USERDATA** An area contained within FEPI Resources that can hold application-supplied data.

**V**

**Virtual terminal** The FEPI emulated terminal (whose screen is maintained for Formatted accesses).

**VTAM** The Virtual Telecommunications Access Method used by CICS and FEPI for communications.

**VTAM indicator** See *Definite Response* and *Exception Response*.

**VTAM response** The VTAM indicators required to acknowledge receipt of a flow.

## W

**WCC** The 3270 Write Control Character that controls how the following Datastream is used.

## X

**XLT** The CICS transaction list table that contains a list of transactions that can run during CICS shutdown.

**XOPTS(FEPI)** The CICS translator option that is required to process `EXEC CICS FEPI` commands.

**XRF** The Extended Recovery Facility. This is a method of providing backup for system failures.

**XSZARQ** The FEPI After-Command GLUE.

**XSZBRQ** The FEPI Before-Command GLUE.

## Special characters

**&** The default Escape character used in keystroke sequences.

## Numerics

**12-bit cursor position** A method of specifying a position on the screen via B'00efghij 00klmnop' instead of a full halfword B'abcdefgh ijklmnop'.

**3270** Another name for the LU2 protocol.

**3278** A 3270 monochrome terminal.

**3279** A 3270 colour terminal.

# Index


3270 Attribute Bytes:
  Datastream Access, 174
3270 Command Codes, 166
  Datastream Access, 166
  Datastream Coding techniques, 177
3270 Datastream:
  12-bit Cursor Position, 167
  3270 Attribute Bytes, 174
  3270 Extended Attribute Bytes, 175
  3270 Format Control Orders, 174
  3270 Inbound Data, 167
  3270 Inbound Structured Fields, 168
  3270 Orders, 172
  3270 Outbound Structured Fields, 169
  Asynchronous operation, 175
  Bracket, 164
  Chain 163, 164
  Coding Techniques for 3270 Command Codes, 177
  Coding Techniques for Datastream access, 176
  Contention, 164
  Contention State, 164
  Datastream Errors, 175
  EXEC CICS CONVERSE command, 171
  EXEC CICS CONVERSE STRFIELD command, 178
  EXEC CICS FEPI RECEIVE DATASTREAM command, 165
  EXEC CICS RECEIVE command, 170, 178
  EXEC CICS SEND command, 170, 177
  EXEC CICS SEND STRFIELD command, 178
  FEPI Inbound Structured Fields, 168
  FEPI Outbound Data, 167
  FEPI Outbound Structured Fields, 169
  Overview, 77
  Query Structured Field, 78
  RU, 163
  Structured Fields Overview, 168
  VTAM Indicators, 78
3270 Extended Attribute Bytes:
  Datastream Access, 175
3270 Format Control Orders:
  Datastream Access, 174
3270 Inbound Structured Fields, 168
3270 Orders:
  Datastream Access, 172
3270 Outbound Structured Fields, 169
3270 Structured Fields, 168
3270 Write Control Character, 166
  Datastream Access, 166

ACQNUM, 63,65
  EXEC CICS FEPI INQUIRE CONNECTION command, 63
  EXEC CICS FEPI INQUIRE NODE command, 65
ACQSTATUS:
  and Connection usability, 44
  and Connections VTAM status, 44
  and Node usability, 43
  and Nodes VTAM status, 43
  and the Begin Session, 45
  and the End Session (End of Connection) Handler, 45
  CEMT, 61
ACQSTATUS *continued*
  EXEC CICS FEPI ADD command, 43
  EXEC CICS FEPI INQUIRE CONNECTION command, 63
  EXEC CICS FEPI INQUIRE NODE command, 65
  EXEC CICS FEPI INSTALL NODELIST command, 42
  EXEC CICS FEPI INSTALL POOL command, 40
  EXEC CICS FEPI SET CONNECTION command, 61
  EXEC CICS FEPI SET NODE command, 62
  Settings, 61
  Status Transitions, 61
ACQUIRED, 61
  CEMT, 71
  EXEC CICS FEPI ADD command, 43
  EXEC CICS FEPI INSTALL NODELIST command, 42
  EXEC CICS FEPI INSTALL POOL command, 40
ACQUIRING, 61
Adapter, 263
AID:
  EXEC CICS FEPI SEND FORMATTED command, 103
ALARM:
  EXEC CICS FEPI RECEIVE FORMATTED command, 105
ALARMSTATUS:
  EXEC CICS FEPI RECEIVE FORMATTED command, 105
APPL:
  CEMT, 71
  EXEC CICS FEPI INQUIRE TARGET command, 66
APPLICATION:
  and STATE parameter of EXEC CICS FEPI INQUIRE CONNECTION, 64
Application Program General, 95
APPLIDs:
  and Targets, 33, 41
  and XRF, 42, 271, 273
APPLLIST:
  and Targets, 41
  EXEC CICS FEPI INSTALL TARGETLIST command, 41
Asynchronous Operation, 81
  Datastream Access, 175
  EXEC CICS FEPI START command, 154, 233
  problems with User Input, 233
  Transaction considerations, 155
  use of a Screen Saver Transaction, 235
ATTENTION:
  EXEC CICS FEPI ISSUE command, 113
Attribute Bytes:
  and the EXEC CICS FEPI SEND FORMATTED command, 142
  Formatted Access, 142

BACKGROUND:
  EXEC CICS FEPI EXTRACT FIELD command, 110
Begin Session Handler, 205
  and First Flow processing, 81
  Convid Management, 221
  defining, 204
  design, 219, 220
  EXEC CICS FEPI FREE command, 158
  Signons, 221
  specification, 50
  Structured Field Query, 220
  Timeouts and the First Flow, 153

Begin Session Handler *continued*
- what the Handler should do, 206
- when FEPI generates the Handler, 206

BEGINSESSION:
- and STATE parameter of EXEC CICS FEPI INQUIRE CONNECTION, 64
- EXEC CICS FEPI INQUIRE POOL command, 67
- EXEC CICS FEPI INQUIRE PROPERTYSET command, 67
- EXEC CICS FEPI INSTALL PROPERTYSET command, 40
- Propertyset parameter, 50

Bracket, 164
- EB Indicator, 79

Browsing FEPI Resources, 68, 290
- Connections, 69
- Nodes, 68
- Pools, 68
- Propertysets, 68
- Targets, 68

CANCEL:
- EXEC CICS FEPI ISSUE command, 113

CD:
- 3270 Datastream, 79
- ENDSTATUS, 165
- EXEC CICS FEPI RECEIVE DATASTREAM command, 107
- EXEC CICS FEPI RECEIVE FORMATTED command, 105

CEMT:
- ACQSTATUS, 61
- ACQUIRED, 71
- APPL, 71
- Connection example, 74
- Connection Inquiry, 71
- Connection Setting, 71
- DEVICE, 71
- INSERVICE, 71
- INSTALLED, 71
- LASTACQCODE, 71
- NODE, 71
- Node Discarding, 71
- Node example, 72
- Node Inquiry, 71
- Node Setting, 71
- NOTINSTALLED, 71
- OUTSERVICE, 71
- POOL, 71
- Pool Discarding, 71
- Pool example, 73
- Pool Inquiry, 71
- Pool Setting, 71
- Propertyset Discarding, 71
- Propertyset example, 72
- Propertyset Inquiry, 71
- RELEASED, 71
- SERVSTATUS, 61
- STATE, 71
- TARGET, 71
- Target Discarding, 71
- Target example, 73
- Target Inquiry, 71
- Target Setting, 71
- WAITCONVNUM, 71

CETR:
- FEPI Trace, 264

CHAIN, 164
- EXEC CICS FEPI RECEIVE DATASTREAM command, 107, 165
- RU, 163

Change Direction, 165

CICS Inbound data:
- Datastream Coding techniques, 179

CICS Outbound data:
- Datastream Coding techniques, 177

CICS Resource Constraints, 17

CICS Shutdown:
- FEPI stops CICS from Shutting Down, 268
- Forced, 269
- Immediate, 269
- Normal, 268
- Types of Shutdown, 268

CLSDST(PASS) processing:
- and EXEC CICS ISSUE PASS command, 239
- Concepts, 239
- during EXEC CICS FEPI ALLOCATE processing, 243
- Known Third party PLU name, 240
- Pool arrangement, 240
- Third party PLU names, 239

CLSDST(PASS) processing *continued*
- Unknown Third party PLU name, 242

Coded Design, 12

COLOR:
- EXEC CICS FEPI EXTRACT FIELD command, 110

Color Node, 32

COLUMNS:
- EXEC CICS FEPI RECEIVE FORMATTED command, 105

Connection, 29
- Browsing, 69
- CEMT example, 74
- CLSDST(PASS) processing, 240, 242
- Creation, 44
- Creation Failures and Pool Specific Monitors, 212
- Deletion, 48
- Deletion Failures and Pool Specific Monitors, 212
- Guidance for creation, 45
- How EXEC CICS FEPI ALLOCATE picks a Connection, 133
- Installing, 44
- Lost Session and Pool Specific Monitors, 213
- Not enough, 229
- Obtaining Status, 63
- Session Failure and Pool Specific Monitors, 213
- Setting Status, 61
- State, 64, 324
- Tuning, 229
- VTAM Sense Code, 64
- Waits on obtaining, 229
- XRF processing, 275

CONTENTION:
- and First Flow processing, 82
- Bracket, 165
- EXEC CICS FEPI INQUIRE POOL command, 67
- EXEC CICS FEPI INQUIRE PROPERTYSET command, 67
- EXEC CICS FEPI INSTALL PROPERTYSET command, 40
- Propertyset parameter, 50
- Contention State, 79
- and First Flow processing, 82
- and Positioning, 82
- and the CONTENTION parameter, 51
- and the EB indicator, 79
- Bracket, 165

CONTROL:
- EXEC CICS FEPI ISSUE command, 112

Conversation, 30
- Continuing, 135
- EXEC CICS FEPI ALLOCATE command (Existing Conversation), 135
- Handlers, 135
- PASSCONVID, 135
- Starting, 131

CONVID:
- EXEC CICS FEPI ALLOCATE command (new Conversation), 102
- EXEC CICS FEPI EXTRACT CONV command, 111
- EXEC CICS FEPI EXTRACT FIELD command, 109
- EXEC CICS FEPI EXTRACT STSN command, 112
- EXEC CICS FEPI FREE command, 108
- EXEC CICS FEPI ISSUE command, 112
- EXEC CICS FEPI RECEIVE DATASTREAM command, 106
- EXEC CICS FEPI RECEIVE FORMATTED command, 105
- EXEC CICS FEPI SEND DATASTREAM command, 104
- EXEC CICS FEPI SEND FORMATTED command, 103
- EXEC CICS FEPI START command, 108
- Obtaining on EXEC CICS FEPI ALLOCATE command (New Conversation), 132

Convid Management, 277
- Code design, 279
- MVS Signon overhead, 278
- MVS Signon overhead reduction, 278
- Password considerations, 277
- Security implications, 278
- Techniques, 278

Convid Passing, 156

CONVNUM, 63
- EXEC CICS FEPI INQUIRE CONNECTION command, 63

CSZI Transaction, 263

CSZX Monitor, 215, 225
- CLSDST(PASS) processing, 242
- Defining within FEPI, 204
- EXEC CICS FEPI DISCARD errors, 216
- EXEC CICS FEPI INSTALL errors, 215
- EXEC CICS FEPI SET errors, 216
- Record Layout, 319
- Resource Acquisition Errors, 217
- Resource Management Errors, 215

CSZX Monitor *continued*
Unsolicited Bind, 218
what the Monitor Program should do for Resource Acquisition Errors, 217
what the Monitor Program should do for Resource Manipulation errors, 216
what the Monitor Program should do for Unsolicited Binds, 218
CSZX TDQ:
Record Layout, 319
CURSOR:
EXEC CICS FEPI RECEIVE FORMATTED command, 105
EXEC CICS FEPI SEND FORMATTED command, 103
Cursor position:
Formatted Access, 142
CVDA reference, 314

DATA:
EXEC CICS FEPI STARTed Transaction, 155
DATASTREAM:
EXEC CICS FEPI EXTRACT CONV command, 111
EXEC CICS FEPI INSTALL PROPERTYSET command, 40
Propertyset parameter, 52
Datastream access, 10
12-bit Cursor Position, 167
3270 Attribute Bytes, 174
3270 Command Codes, 166
3270 Considerations, 163
3270 Extended Attribute Bytes, 175
3270 Format Control Orders, 174
3270 Inbound Data, 167
3270 Inbound Structured Fields, 168
3270 Orders, 172
3270 Outbound Structured Fields, 169
3270 Write Control Character, 166
Asynchronous operation, 175
Bracket, 165
CD, 165
Chain, 163, 164
Change Direction, 165
Coding techniques, 176
Coding techniques for 3270 Command Codes, 177
Contention, 165
Contention State, 165
Datastream Errors, 175
EB, 165
End Bracket, 165
ENDSTATUS, 163
EXEC CICS CONVERSE command, 171
EXEC CICS CONVERSE STRFIELD command, 179
EXEC CICS FEPI RECEIVE DATASTREAM command, 165
EXEC CICS RECEIVE command, 170, 178
EXEC CICS SEND command, 170, 177
EXEC CICS SEND STRFIELD command, 178
FEPI Inbound Structured Fields, 168
FEPI Outbound Data, 167
FEPI Outbound Structured Fields, 169
RU, 163
Structured Fields Overview, 168
Datastream Conversation and Unsolicited Data, 89
Datastream Errors:
Datastream Access, 175
Debugging:
CETR, 264
CICS Dispatcher (DS) facilities, 267
CICS Kernel (KE) facilities, 267
CICS Storage Manager (SM) facilities, 267
DFHSZATR program, 263
DFHSZRMP program, 263
Dump interpretation, 265
EXEC CICS INQUIRE/SET TRACETYPE SZ command, 264
FEPI Control Block Layouts, 265
FEPI Trace, 264
GTF Tracing, 267
SIT Tracing, 264
The CSZI Transaction, 263
The FEPI Adapter, 263
The FEPI Resource Manager, 263
The SZ TCB, 263
Trace interpretation, 264
Trace Printing, 264
Waits, 267
Definite Response:
EXEC CICS FEPI ISSUE command, 249
FEPI Automatic operation, 249

Definite Response *continued*
Manual operation, 249
DEFRESP1:
EXEC CICS FEPI ISSUE command, 113
EXEC CICS FEPI RECEIVE DATASTREAM command, 107
EXEC CICS FEPI RECEIVE FORMATTED command, 106
DEFRESP1OR2:
EXEC CICS FEPI ISSUE command, 113
DEFRESP2:
EXEC CICS FEPI ISSUE command, 113
EXEC CICS FEPI RECEIVE DATASTREAM command, 107
EXEC CICS FEPI RECEIVE FORMATTED command, 106
DEFRESP3:
EXEC CICS FEPI ISSUE command, 113
EXEC CICS FEPI RECEIVE DATASTREAM command, 107
EXEC CICS FEPI RECEIVE FORMATTED command, 106
DEVICE:
CEMT, 71
EXEC CICS FEPI EXTRACT CONV command, 111
EXEC CICS FEPI INQUIRE POOL command, 67
EXEC CICS FEPI INQUIRE PROPERTYSET command, 67
EXEC CICS FEPI INSTALL PROPERTYSET command, 40
Propertyset parameter, 51
DFHJUP:
Printing FEPI Journal Records, 257
DFHSZAPA, 116, 318
DFHSZAPC, 116, 318
DFHSZAPO, 116, 318
DFHSZAPP, 116, 318
Allocation Errors, 122
Browse Errors, 128
Datastream Errors, 121
General API Errors, 119
General SPI Errors, 125
Install Errors, 126
Issue Errors, 124
Receive/Start Errors, 123
Send Errors, 122
Sequence Errors, 121
Universal Errors, 118
DFHSZATR program:
the FEPI Adapter, 263
DFHSZRMP program, 263
Dump Interpretation:
FEPI Control Block Layouts, 266
Printing FEPI Control Blocks, 265
Dynamic Resource Definition:
Concepts, 35
Timed Operations, 229
Tuning, 229

EB:
3270 Datastream, 79
and IMS, 92
ENDSTATUS, 165
EXEC CICS FEPI RECEIVE DATASTREAM command, 107
EXEC CICS FEPI RECEIVE FORMATTED command, 105
EIBRESP2s, 116, 315, 318
DFHSZAPA, 116, 318
DFHSZAPC, 116, 318
DFHSZAPO, 116, 318
DFHSZAPP, 116, 318
Enabling FEPI from the SIT, 36
END:
EXEC CICS FEPI INQUIRE CONNECTION command, 69
EXEC CICS FEPI INQUIRE NODE command, 68
EXEC CICS FEPI INQUIRE POOL command, 68
EXEC CICS FEPI INQUIRE PROPERTYSET command, 68
EXEC CICS FEPI INQUIRE TARGET command, 68
End Bracket, 165
End Session Handler, 204, 206, 219
Design for End of Connection processing, 223
Design for End of Conversation processing, 222
EXEC CICS FEPI FREE command, 158
Specification, 51
what the Handler should do, 207
End Session Handler (End of Connection), 207, 223
End Session Handler (End of Conversation), 207, 222
ENDSESSION:
EXEC CICS FEPI INQUIRE POOL command, 67
EXEC CICS FEPI INQUIRE PROPERTYSET command, 67
EXEC CICS FEPI INSTALL PROPERTYSET command, 40
Propertyset parameter, 51

ENDSTATUS:
 CD, 165
 EB, 165
 EXEC CICS FEPI RECEIVE DATASTREAM command, 107
 EXEC CICS FEPI RECEIVE FORMATTED command, 105
 Formatted Access, 146
 LIC, 163, 165
 RU, 163
ESCAPE:
 EXEC CICS FEPI SEND FORMATTED command, 103
EVENTTYPE:
 EXEC CICS FEPI STARTed Transaction, 155
EXCEPTION:
 EXEC CICS FEPI INQUIRE POOL command, 67
 EXEC CICS FEPI INQUIRE PROPERTYSET command, 67
 EXEC CICS FEPI INSTALL PROPERTYSET command, 40
 Propertyset parameter, 52
EXCEPTRESP:
 EXEC CICS FEPI ISSUE command, 112
EXEC CICS ASSIGN STARTCODE command:
 SZ Startcode, 155
EXEC CICS CONVERSE command:
 Datastream usage, 171
EXEC CICS CONVERSE STRFIELD command:
 Datastream Coding techniques, 179
EXEC CICS FEPI ADD command, 43, 287
 ACQSTATUS, 43
 ACQUIRED, 43
 Failures and Pool Specific Monitors, 212
 INSERVICE, 43
 NODELIST, 43
 NODENUM, 43
 OUTSERVICE, 43
 POOL, 43
 RELEASED, 43
 SERVSTATUS, 43
 Syntax diagram, 307
 TARGETLIST, 43
 TARGETNUM, 43
EXEC CICS FEPI ALLOCATE command (existing Conversation), 103, 283
 and Handlers, 135
 PASSCONVID, 103
 Syntax diagram, 291
 usage, 135
EXEC CICS FEPI ALLOCATE command (new Conversation), 102, 283
 CLSDST(PASS) processing, 243
 Connection selection, 133
 CONVID, 102
 Convid usage, 132
 how the Connection Started, 134
 NEWSESSION, 102, 135
 OLDSESSION, 102, 135
 POOL, 102
 SEQNUMIN, 102
 SEQNUMOUT, 102
 SESSNSTATUS, 102, 135
 Syntax diagram, 291
 TARGET, 102
 Target selection, 132
 TIMEOUT, 102
 Timeout usage, 131
 Usage, 131
EXEC CICS FEPI AP NOOP command, 115, 290
 Syntax diagram, 291
EXEC CICS FEPI CONVERSE DATASTREAM command, 14, 283
 Syntax diagram, 292
 Warning, 87
EXEC CICS FEPI CONVERSE FORMATTED command, 114, 284
 Syntax diagram, 293
 Warning, 87
EXEC CICS FEPI DELETE command, 48, 288
 Failures and Pool Specific Monitors, 212
 NODELIST, 48
 NODENUM, 48
 POOL, 48
 Syntax diagram, 307
 TARGETLIST, 48
 TARGETNUM, 48
EXEC CICS FEPI DISCARD commands, 47
EXEC CICS FEPI DISCARD NODELIST command, 47, 287
 Errors and the FEPI Global Monitor, 216
 NODELIST, 47
 NODENUM, 47
 Syntax diagram, 302
EXEC CICS FEPI DISCARD POOL command, 48, 287
 Errors and the FEPI Global Monitor, 216
 POOL, 48
 Syntax diagram, 306
EXEC CICS FEPI DISCARD PROPERTYSET command, 47, 287
 Errors and the FEPI Global Monitor, 216
 PROPERTYSET, 47
 Syntax diagram, 304
EXEC CICS FEPI DISCARD TARGETLIST command, 47, 287
 Errors and the FEPI Global Monitor, 216
 Syntax diagram, 302
 TARGETLIST, 47
 TARGETNUM, 47
EXEC CICS FEPI EXTRACT CONV command, 111, 284
 CONVID, 111
 DATASTREAM, 111
 DEVICE, 111
 FORMAT, 111
 FORMATTED, 111
 LUP, 111
 NODE, 111
 POOL, 111
 SENSEDATA, 111
 Syntax diagram, 294
 T3278M2, 111
 T3278M3, 111
 T3278M4, 111
 T3278M5, 111
 T3279M2, 111
 T3279M3, 111
 T3279M4, 111
 T3279M5, 111
 TARGET, 111
 TPS55M2, 111
 TPS55M3, 111
 TPS55M4, 111
EXEC CICS FEPI EXTRACT FIELD command, 109, 284
 BACKGROUND, 110
 COLOR, 110
 CONVID, 109
 Field Information, 149
 FIELDATTR, 110
 FIELDLOC, 109
 FIELDNUM, 109
 FLENGTH, 109
 Formatted Access, 149
 HILIGHT, 110
 INPUTCONTROL, 111
 INTO, 109
 MAXFLENGTH, 109
 MDT, 110
 NOMDT, 110
 OUTLINE, 110
 POSITION, 110
 PROTECT, 110
 PROTECTED, 110
 PS, 110
 SIZE, 110
 Syntax diagram, 295
 TRANSPARENCY, 110
 UNPROTECTED, 110
 VALIDATION, 110
 EXEC CICS FEPI EXTRACT STSN command, 111, 285
 CONVID, 112
 LUO considerations, 246
 SEQNUMIN, 112
 SEQNUMOUT, 112
 SLUP considerations, 246
 STSNSET, 112
 STSNSTATUS, 112
 STSNTEST, 112
 Syntax diagram, 296
EXEC CICS FEPI FREE command, 108, 285
 Begin Session Handler, 158
 CONVID, 108
 End Session Handler, 158
 FORCE, 108, 156
 HOLD, 108, 156
 PASS, 108, 156
 RELEASE, 108, 156
 STSN Handler, 159
 Syntax diagram 296
 Unsolicited Data Handler, 158
 usage, 156

EXEC CICS FEPI INQUIRE commands, 63
and Resource Manipulation, 60
EXEC CICS FEPI INQUIRE CONNECTION command, 63, 289
ACQNUM, 63
ACQSTATUS, 63
CONVNUM, 63
END, 69
INSTLSTATUS, 64
LASTACQCODE, 64
NEXTNODE, 69
NEXTTARGET, 69
NODE, 63
POOL, 64
SERVSTATUS, 64
START, 69
STATE, 64
Syntax diagram, 312
TARGET, 63
USERDATA, 65
WAITCONVNUM, 65
EXEC CICS FEPI INQUIRE NODE command, 65, 288
ACQNUM, 65
ACQSTATUS, 65
END, 68
INSTLSTATUS, 66
LASTACQCODE, 66
NEXT, 68
NODE, 65
SERVSTATUS, 66
START, 68
Syntax diagram, 308
USERDATA, 66
EXEC CICS FEPI INQUIRE POOL command, 289
BEGINSESSION, 67
CONTENTION, 67
DEVICE, 67
END, 68
ENDSESSION, 67
EXCEPTIONQ, 67
FJOURNALNUM, 67
FORMAT, 67
INITIALDATA, 67
INSTLSTATUS, 68
MAXFLENGTH, 67
MSGJRNL, 67
NEXT, 68
POOL, 67
PROPERTYSET, 68
SERVSTATUS, 68
START, 68
STSN, 67
Syntax diagram, 309
UNSOLDATA, 67
UNSOLDATACK, 67
USERDATA, 68
WAITCONVNUM 68
EXEC CICS FEPI INQUIRE PROPERTYSET command, 67, 288
BEGINSESSION, 67
CONTENTION, 67
DEVICE, 67
END, 68
ENDSESSION, 67
EXCEPTIONQ, 67
FJOURNALNUM, 67
FORMAT, 67
INITIALDATA, 67
MAXFLENGTH, 67
MSGJRNL, 67
NEXT, 68
PROPERTYSET, 67
START, 68
STSN, 67
Syntax diagram, 305
UNSOLDATA, 67
UNSOLDATACK, 67
USERDATA, 67
EXEC CICS FEPI INQUIRE TARGET command, 66, 288
APPL, 66
END, 68
INSTLSTATUS, 66
NEXT, 68
SERVSTATUS, 67
START, 68
EXEC CICS FEPI INQUIRE TARGET command *continued*
Syntax diagram, 310
TARGET, 66
USERDATA, 67
EXEC CICS FEPI INSTALL commandS, 39
Errors and the FEPI Global Monitor, 215
EXEC CICS FEPI INSTALL NODELIST command, 42, 287
ACQSTATUS, 42
ACQUIRED, 42
Errors and the FEPI Global Monitor, 215
INSERVICE, 42
NODELIST, 42
NODENUM, 42
OUTSERVICE, 42
PASSWORDLIST, 42
RELEASED, 42
SERVSTATUS, 42
Syntax diagram, 302
EXEC CICS FEPI INSTALL POOL command, 40, 287
ACQSTATUS, 40
ACQUIRED, 40
Errors and the FEPI Global Monitor, 215
INSERVICE, 40
NODELIST, 40
NODENUM, 40
OUTSERVICE, 40
PROPERTYSET, 40
RELEASED, 40
SERVSTATUS, 40
Syntax diagram, 306
TARGETLIST, 40
TARGETNUM, 40
EXEC CICS FEPI INSTALL PROPERTYSET command, 40, 286
BEGINSESSION, 40
CONTENTION, 40
DATASTREAM, 40
DEVICE, 40
ENDSESSION, 40
Errors and the FEPI Global Monitor, 215
EXCEPTIONQ, 40
FJOURNALNUM, 40
FORMAT, 40
FORMATTED, 40
INITIALDATA, 40
INOUT, 40
INPUT, 40
LOSE, 40
LUP, 40
MAXFLENGTH, 40
MSGJRNL, 40
NEGATIVE, 40
NOMSGJRNL, 40
NOTINBOUND, 40
OUTPUT, 40
POSITIVE, 40
STSN, 40
Syntax diagram, 303
T3278M2, 40
T3278M3, 40
T3278M4, 40
T3278M5, 40
T3279M2, 40
T3279M3, 40
T3279M4, 40
T3279M5, 40
TPS55M2, 40
TPS55M3, 40
TPS55M4, 40
UNSOLDATA, 40
UNSOLDATACK, 40
WIN, 40
EXEC CICS FEPI INSTALL TARGETLIST command, 41, 287
APPLLIST, 41
Errors and the FEPI Global Monitor, 215
INSERVICE, 41
OUTSERVICE, 41
SERVSTATUS, 41
Syntax diagram, 301
TARGETLIST, 41
TARGETNUM, 41
EXEC CICS FEPI ISSUE command, 112, 285
ATTENTION, 113
CANCEL, 113
CONTROL, 112

EXEC CICS FEPI ISSUE command *continued*
CONVID, 112
Definite Response, 249
DEFRESP1, 113
DEFRESP1OR2, 113
DEFRESP2, 113
DEFRESP3, 113
EXCEPTRESP, 112
INVALID, 113
LUSTAT, 113
NEGATIVE, 113
Negative Response, 249
NORMALRESP, 112
POSITIVE, 113
RESET, 113
RTR, 113
SENSEDATA, 113
STSN, 113
Syntax diagram, 297
VALUE, 113
EXEC CICS FEPI RECEIVE DATASTREAM command, 106, 285
CD, 107
CHAIN, 107, 165
CONVID, 106
DEFRESP1, 107
DEFRESP2, 107
DEFRESP3, 107
EB, 107
ENDSTATUS, 107
FLENGTH, 106
FMH, 107
INTO, 106
LIC, 107
MAXFLENGTH, 106
MORE, 107
NOFMH, 107
NONE, 107
REMFLENGTH, 107
RESPSTATUS, 107
RU, 107, 165
SEQNUMIN, 108
SEQNUMOUT, 108
Syntax diagram, 299
TIMEOUT, 106
UNTILCDEB, 107, 165
usage, 165
EXEC CICS FEPI RECEIVE FORMATTED command, 104, 285
ALARM, 105
ALARMSTATUS, 105
CD, 105
COLUMNS, 105
CONVID, 105
CURSOR, 105
DEFRESP1, 106
DEFRESP2, 106
DEFRESP3, 106
EB, 105
ENDSTATUS, 105
FIELDS, 105
FLENGTH, 105
INTO, 105
LIC, 105
LINES, 105
MAXFLENGTH, 105
NOALARM, 105
NONE, 106
RESPSTATUS, 106
Syntax diagram, 298
TIMEOUT, 105
usage, 145
EXEC CICS FEPI SEND DATASTREAM command, 104, 286
CONVID, 104
FLENGTH, 104
FMH, 104
FROM, 104
INVITE, 104
SEQNUMIN, 104
SEQNUMOUT, 104
Syntax diagram, 300
EXEC CICS FEPI SEND FORMATTED command, 103, 286
AID, 103
CONVID, 103
CURSOR, 103
ESCAPE, 103
EXEC CICS FEPI SEND FORMATTED command *continued*
FLENGTH, 103
FROM, 103
KEYSTROKES, 103
Syntax diagram, 300
usage, 142
EXEC CICS FEPI SEND KEYSTROKES command, 138
EXEC CICS FEPI SET commands, 61
and Resource Manipulation, 61
Errors and the FEPI Global Monitor, 216
EXEC CICS FEPI SET CONNECTION command, 61, 290
ACQSTATUS, 61
Errors and the FEPI Global Monitor, 216
NODE, 61
NODELIST, 61
NODENUM, 61
SERVSTATUS, 61
Syntax diagram, 313
TARGET, 61
TARGETLIST, 61
TARGETNUM, 61
USERDATA, 61
EXEC CICS FEPI SET NODE command, 62, 289
ACQSTATUS, 62
Errors and the FEPI Global Monitor, 216
NODE, 62
NODELIST, 62
NODENUM, 62
SERVSTATUS, 62
Syntax diagram, 308
USERDATA, 62
EXEC CICS FEPI SET POOL command, 62, 290
Errors and the FEPI Global Monitor, 216
POOL, 62
POOLLIST, 62
POOLNUM, 62
SERVSTATUS, 62
Syntax diagram, 310
USERDATA, 62
EXEC CICS FEPI SET TARGET command, 62, 289
Errors and the FEPI Global Monitor, 216
SERVSTATUS, 62
Syntax diagram, 311
TARGET, 62
TARGETLIST, 62
TARGETNUM, 62
USERDATA, 62
EXEC CICS FEPI SP NOOP command, 115, 290
Syntax diagram, 301
EXEC CICS FEPI START command, 108, 286
Asynchronous operation, 233
CONVID, 108
Effective use of, 233
FLENGTH, 109
Problems with User Input, 233
Syntax diagram, 301
TERMID, 109
TIMEOUT, 109
TRANSID, 109
usage, 154
use of a Screen Saver Transaction, 235
USERDATA, 109
EXEC CICS FEPI STARTed Transaction:
DATA, 155
EVENTTYPE, 155
Operation, 155
SESSIONLOST, 155
TIMEOUT, 155
Timeouts and the First Flow in the Started transaction, 152
EXEC CICS INQUIRE/SET TRACETYPE SZ command:
FEPI Trace, 264
EXEC CICS RECEIVE command:
Datastream Coding techniques, 178, 179
Datastream usage, 170
EXEC CICS SEND command:
Datastream Coding techniques, 177
Datastream usage, 170
EXEC CICS SEND STRFIELD command:
Datastream Coding techniques, 179

FEPI access type, 52
FEPI Command Code Reference, 323
FEPI Concepts:
Background Functions, 4

FEPI Concepts *continued*
Change Control, 3
Changing PF Keys, 5
Corporate Takeover, 4
Esoteric usage, 5
Function Bundling, 4
Integrational, 3
Linkage Functions, 4
Parallelism, 4
Risk, 3
FEPI Connections:
and FEPI Conversations, 22
FEPI Conversations:
and CICS Tasks, 16
and EXEC CICS FEPI FREE, 23
and EXEC CICS FEPI START, 17, 23
and FEPI Connections, 22
Fully Asynchronous Conversations, 23
Handler Conversations, 24
Normal Conversations, 22
Pseudo Conversational, 17
Single Transaction Conversations, 23
Temporary Conversations, 24
FEPI Emulation:
Datastream, 6, 8
Flow completeness, 86
Formatted, 6, 8
Special, 6, 8
the importance of position, 80
FEPI Global Monitor, 215, 225
defining within FEPI, 204
EXEC CICS FEPI DISCARD errors, 216
EXEC CICS FEPI INSTALL errors, 215
EXEC CICS FEPI SET errors, 216
Record Layout, 319
Resource Acquisition Errors, 217
Resource Management Errors, 215
Unsolicited Bind, 218
what the Monitor Program should do for Resource Acquisition Errors, 217
what the Monitor Program should do for Resource Manipulation errors, 216
what the Monitor Program should do for Unsolicited Binds, 218
FEPI Global TDQ:
Record Layout, 319
FEPI Inbound 3270 Structured Fields, 168
FEPI Inbound data:
Datastream Coding techniques, 177
FEPI Outbound 3270 Structured Fields, 169
FEPI Outbound data:
Datastream Coding techniques, 179
FEPI Shutdown:
FEPI stops CICS from Shutting Down, 268
Forced, 269
Immediate, 269
Normal, 268
Types of Shutdown, 268
FEPI SIT parameter, 36
Field Information:
Formatted Access, 147
FIELDATTR:
EXEC CICS FEPI EXTRACT FIELD command, 110
FIELDLOC:
EXEC CICS FEPI EXTRACT FIELD command, 109
FIELDNUM:
EXEC CICS FEPI EXTRACT FIELD command, 109
FIELDS:
EXEC CICS FEPI RECEIVE FORMATTED command, 105
First Flow Processing, 80
and CONTENTION, 82
Begin Session Handler, 81
IMS, 92
Signon, 81
specification, 53
First Receive:
Begin Session Handler, 153
EXEC CICS FEPI STARTed Transaction, 152
Unsolicited Data Handler, 152
FJOURNALNUM:
EXEC CICS FEPI INQUIRE POOL command, 67
EXEC CICS FEPI INQUIRE PROPERTYSET command, 67
EXEC CICS FEPI INSTALL PROPERTYSET command, 40
Journalling Journal number, 254
Propertyset parameter, 52
FLENGTH:
EXEC CICS FEPI EXTRACT FIELD command, 109
FLENGTH *continued*
EXEC CICS FEPI RECEIVE DATASTREAM command, 106
EXEC CICS FEPI RECEIVE FORMATTED command, 105
EXEC CICS FEPI SEND DATASTREAM command, 104
EXEC CICS FEPI SEND FORMATTED command, 103
EXEC CICS FEPI START command, 109
FMH:
EXEC CICS FEPI RECEIVE DATASTREAM command, 107
EXEC CICS FEPI SEND DATASTREAM command, 104
FORCE:
EXEC CICS FEPI FREE command, 108, 156
FORMAT:
EXEC CICS FEPI EXTRACT CONV command, 111
EXEC CICS FEPI INQUIRE POOL command, 67
EXEC CICS FEPI INQUIRE PROPERTYSET command, 67
EXEC CICS FEPI INSTALL PROPERTYSET command, 40
Propertyset parameter, 52
FORMATTED:
EXEC CICS FEPI EXTRACT CONV command, 111
EXEC CICS FEPI INSTALL PROPERTYSET command, 40
Formatted Access, 136
Attribute Bytes, 142
Buffer reception, 145
Buffer techniques, 141
Cursor Position, 142
Data Reception Concepts, 144
ENDSTATUS, 146
EXEC CICS FEPI EXTRACT FIELD command, 149
EXEC CICS FEPI RECEIVE FORMATTED command, 145
EXEC CICS FEPI SEND FORMATTED command, 142
EXEC CICS FEPI SEND KEYSTROKES command, 138
Field Information, 147, 148, 149
Keystroke Errors, 140
Keystroke Interface, 136
Keystroke Multiple Attentions, 139
Keystroke sequences, 137
Keystroke Stacking, 139
knowing when everything has been received, 146
Protected and Unprotected Fields, 142
RESPSTATUS, 147
Screen Parameters, 145
VTAM Responses, 147
Formatted Conversation:
and Unsolicited Data, 90
Formatted CVDA:
Propertyset parameter, 52
FREE:
and STATE parameter of EXEC CICS FEPI INQUIRE CONNECTION, 64
FROM:
EXEC CICS FEPI SEND DATASTREAM command, 104
EXEC CICS FEPI SEND FORMATTED command, 103

GLUE:
After FEPI Command execution Exit, 258
Before FEPI Command execution Exit, 258
Command codes, 260
Parameter lists, 327
XSZARQ GLUE, 258
XSZARQ parameter, 259
XSZARQ Return codes, 259
XSZARQ usage, 262
XSZBRQ GLUE, 258
XSZBRQ parameter, 259
XSZBRQ Return codes, 259
XSZBRQ usage, 261
GOINGOUT, 61

Handlers, 20, 203, 205, 219
Begin Session, 20
defining, 203
defining within FEPI, 204
End Session (End of Connection), 20
End Session (End of Conversation), 20
EXEC CICS FEPI ALLOCATE command (Existing Conversation), 135
STSN, 20
Unsolicited Data, 20
HILIGHT:
EXEC CICS FEPI EXTRACT FIELD command, 110
HOLD:
EXEC CICS FEPI FREE command, 108, 156

IMS:
and EB, 92
First flow processing, 92
IMS Definitions, 250

IMS *continued*
IMS Transactions, 92, 94, 250, 251
Message logging, 93
MFS, 92
Non-Response Mode Transactions, 250, 251
Response Mode Transactions, 250
Unexpected Data, 91
Unsolicited Data, 91
IMS Non-Response Mode:
Coding for, 251
Transaction behaviour, 250
IMS Response Mode:
Coding for, 251
Transaction behaviour, 250
INBOUND:
Propertyset parameter, 53
INITIALDATA:
EXEC CICS FEPI INQUIRE POOL command, 67
EXEC CICS FEPI INQUIRE PROPERTYSET command, 67
EXEC CICS FEPI INSTALL PROPERTYSET command, 40
Propertyset parameter, 53
INOUT:
EXEC CICS FEPI INSTALL PROPERTYSET command, 40
Journalling flows, 254
INPUT:
EXEC CICS FEPI INSTALL PROPERTYSET command, 40
Journalling flows, 254
Propertyset parameter, 55
INPUTCONTROL:
EXEC CICS FEPI EXTRACT FIELD command, 111
INSERVICE, 61
CEMT, 71
EXEC CICS FEPI ADD command, 43
EXEC CICS FEPI INSTALL NODELIST command, 42
EXEC CICS FEPI INSTALL POOL command, 40
EXEC CICS FEPI INSTALL TARGETLIST command, 41
INSTALLED:
and INSTLSTATUS, 64, 66, 68
CEMT, 71
INSTLSTATUS, 64, 66, 68
EXEC CICS FEPI INQUIRE CONNECTION command, 64
EXEC CICS FEPI INQUIRE NODE command, 66
EXEC CICS FEPI INQUIRE POOL command, 68
EXEC CICS FEPI INQUIRE TARGET command, 66
INTO:
EXEC CICS FEPI EXTRACT FIELD command, 109
EXEC CICS FEPI RECEIVE DATASTREAM command, 106
EXEC CICS FEPI RECEIVE FORMATTED command, 105
INVALID:
EXEC CICS FEPI ISSUE command, 113
INVITE:
EXEC CICS FEPI SEND DATASTREAM command, 104

Journalling:
DFHJUP, 257
FJOURNALNUM, 254
INOUT, 254
INPUT, 254
MSGJRNL, 254
NONE, 254
OUTPUT, 254
Printing Journal Records, 255
Record Layout, 255
Specification of flows, 55, 254
Specification of Journal, 52, 254

Keystroke, 325
Keystroke Interface, 9, 136
Errors, 140
Keystroke sequences, 137
Multiple Attentions, 139
Stacking sequences, 139
KEYSTROKES:
EXEC CICS FEPI SEND FORMATTED command, 103

LASTACQCODE:
and Connections, 64
and Nodes, 66
CEMT, 71
EXEC CICS FEPI INQUIRE CONNECTION command, 64
EXEC CICS FEPI INQUIRE NODE command, 66

LIC:
ENDSTATUS, 163, 165
EXEC CICS FEPI RECEIVE DATASTREAM command, 107
EXEC CICS FEPI RECEIVE FORMATTED command, 105
LINES:
EXEC CICS FEPI RECEIVE FORMATTED command, 105
List Errors:
Detection via Pool Specific Monitors, 211
Logonid:
and Signon processing, 81
LOSE:
EXEC CICS FEPI INSTALL PROPERTYSET command, 40
Propertyset parameter, 50
LUO Access, 7
discussion of special topics, 245
EXEC CICS FEPI EXTRACT STSN command, 246
Sequence numbers, 245
STSN processing, 245
VTAM definition, 247
VTAM/SNA Considerations, 245
LU2 Access, 6
LUP:
EXEC CICS FEPI EXTRACT CONV command, 111
EXEC CICS FEPI INSTALL PROPERTYSET command, 40
Propertyset parameter, 51
LUSTAT:
EXEC CICS FEPI ISSUE command, 113

MAXFLENGTH:
EXEC CICS FEPI EXTRACT FIELD command, 109
EXEC CICS FEPI INQUIRE POOL command, 67
EXEC CICS FEPI INQUIRE PROPERTYSET command, 67
EXEC CICS FEPI INSTALL PROPERTYSET command, 40
EXEC CICS FEPI RECEIVE DATASTREAM command, 106
EXEC CICS FEPI RECEIVE FORMATTED command, 105
Propertyset parameter, 54
Maximum Data Size for a pool, 54
MDT:
EXEC CICS FEPI EXTRACT FIELD command, 110
Monitors, 21, 203, 224
defining, 203
defining within FEPI, 204
Monochrome Node, 32
MORE:
EXEC CICS FEPI RECEIVE DATASTREAM command, 107
MSGJRNL:
EXEC CICS FEPI INQUIRE POOL command, 67
EXEC CICS FEPI INQUIRE PROPERTYSET command, 67
EXEC CICS FEPI INSTALL PROPERTYSET command, 40
Journalling flows, 254
Propertyset parameter, 55

NEGATIVE:
EXEC CICS FEPI INSTALL PROPERTYSET command, 40
EXEC CICS FEPI ISSUE command, 113
Propertyset parameter, 55
Rejecting Unsolicited Data, 89
NEWSESSION:
and the EXEC CICS FEPI ALLOCATE command (new Conversation), 102, 135
NEXT:
EXEC CICS FEPI INQUIRE NODE command, 68
EXEC CICS FEPI INQUIRE POOL command, 68
EXEC CICS FEPI INQUIRE PROPERTYSET command, 68
EXEC CICS FEPI INQUIRE TARGET command, 68
NEXTNODE:
EXEC CICS FEPI INQUIRE CONNECTION command, 69
NEXTTARGET:
EXEC CICS FEPI INQUIRE CONNECTION command, 69
NOALARM:
EXEC CICS FEPI RECEIVE FORMATTED command, 105
NOCONV:
and STATE parameter of EXEC CICS FEPI INQUIRE CONNECTION, 64
Node, 28
and VTAM Application Minor Node names, 42
Browsing, 68
CEMT, 71, 72
Discarding, 47
EXEC CICS FEPI EXTRACT CONV command, 111
EXEC CICS FEPI INQUIRE CONNECTION command, 63
EXEC CICS FEPI INQUIRE NODE command, 65
EXEC CICS FEPI SET CONNECTION command, 61
EXEC CICS FEPI SET NODE command, 62
Installing, 42

Node *continued*
Obtaining Status, 65
Setting Status, 62
VTAM activation, 32
VTAM APPL statement, 31
VTAM definition, 31
VTAM LOGMODE, 32
VTAM MODETAB, 33
VTAM Sense Code, 66
NODELIST:
EXEC CICS FEPI ADD command, 43
EXEC CICS FEPI DELETE command, 48
EXEC CICS FEPI DISCARD NODELIST command, 47
EXEC CICS FEPI INSTALL NODELIST command, 42
EXEC CICS FEPI INSTALL POOL command, 40
EXEC CICS FEPI SET CONNECTION command, 61
EXEC CICS FEPI SET NODE command, 62
NODENUM:
EXEC CICS FEPI ADD command, 43
EXEC CICS FEPI DELETE command, 48
EXEC CICS FEPI DISCARD NODELIST command, 47
EXEC CICS FEPI INSTALL NODELIST command, 42
EXEC CICS FEPI INSTALL POOL command, 40
EXEC CICS FEPI SET CONNECTION command, 61
EXEC CICS FEPI SET NODE command, 62
NOFMH:
EXEC CICS FEPI RECEIVE DATASTREAM command, 107
NOMDT:
EXEC CICS FEPI EXTRACT FIELD command, 110
NOMSGJRNL:
EXEC CICS FEPI INSTALL PROPERTYSET command, 40
Propertyset parameter, 55
NONE:
EXEC CICS FEPI RECEIVE DATASTREAM command, 107
EXEC CICS FEPI RECEIVE FORMATTED command, 106
Journalling flows, 254
NORMALRESP:
EXEC CICS FEPI ISSUE command, 112
NOTINBOUND:
EXEC CICS FEPI INSTALL PROPERTYSET command, 40
Propertyset parameter, 53
NOTINSTALLED:
and INSTLSTATUS, 64, 66, 68
CEMT, 71

OLDSESSION
and the EXEC CICS FEPI ALLOCATE command (new Conversation), 102, 135
OUTLINE:
EXEC CICS FEPI EXTRACT FIELD command, 110
OUTPUT:
EXEC CICS FEPI INSTALL PROPERTYSET command, 40
Journalling flows, 254
Propertyset parameter, 55
OUTSERVICE, 61
CEMT, 71
EXEC CICS FEPI ADD command, 43
EXEC CICS FEPI INSTALL NODELIST command, 42
EXEC CICS FEPI INSTALL POOL command, 40
EXEC CICS FEPI INSTALL TARGETLIST command, 41

PASS:
EXEC CICS FEPI FREE command, 108, 156
PASSCONVID:
EXEC CICS FEPI ALLOCATE command (existing Conversation), 103, 135
Passthrough Design, 11
Password:
and Nodes, 43
and Signon processing, 81
on VTAM APPL statement, 31
VTAM definition, 43
PASSWORDLIST:
EXEC CICS FEPI INSTALL NODELIST command, 42
PENDBEGIN:
and STATE parameter of EXEC CICS FEPI INQUIRE CONNECTION, 64
PENDDATA:
and STATE parameter of EXEC CICS FEPI INQUIRE CONNECTION, 64
PENDFREE:
and STATE parameter of EXEC CICS FEPI INQUIRE CONNECTION, 64
PENDPASS:
and STATE parameter of EXEC CICS FEPI INQUIRE CONNECTION, 64
PENDRELEASE:
and STATE parameter of EXEC CICS FEPI INQUIRE CONNECTION, 64
PENDSTART:
and STATE parameter of EXEC CICS FEPI INQUIRE CONNECTION, 65
PENDSTSN:
and STATE parameter of EXEC CICS FEPI INQUIRE CONNECTION, 65
PENDUNSOL:
and STATE parameter of EXEC CICS FEPI INQUIRE CONNECTION, 65
PLT, 36
Pool, 29
arrangement for CLSDST(PASS) processing, 240
Browsing, 68
CEMT, 71, 73
Discarding, 48
EXEC CICS FEPI ADD command, 43
EXEC CICS FEPI ALLOCATE command (new Conversation), 102
EXEC CICS FEPI DELETE command, 48
EXEC CICS FEPI DISCARD POOL command, 48
EXEC CICS FEPI EXTRACT CONV command, 111
EXEC CICS FEPI INQUIRE CONNECTION command, 64
EXEC CICS FEPI INQUIRE POOL command, 67
EXEC CICS FEPI SET POOL command, 62
Installing, 40
Setting Status, 62
Pool Specific Error TDQ, 52
Pool Specific Monitor, 211, 224
Add Errors, 212
defining within FEPI, 204
Delete Errors, 212
List Errors, 211
Lost Session, 213
Record Layout, 319
Session failure, 213
what the Monitor program should do for EXEC CICS FEPI ADD Errors, 212
what the Monitor program should do for EXEC CICS FEPI DELETE Errors, 212
what the Monitor program should do for List Errors, 212
what the Monitor program should do for Lost Session, 213
what the Monitor program should do for Session Loss, 213
Pool Specific TDQ:
Record Layout, 319
POOLLIST:
EXEC CICS FEPI SET POOL command, 62
POOLNUM:
EXEC CICS FEPI SET POOL command, 62
POSITION:
EXEC CICS FEPI EXTRACT FIELD command, 110
POSITIVE:
EXEC CICS FEPI INSTALL PROPERTYSET command, 40
EXEC CICS FEPI ISSUE command, 113
Ignoring Unsolicited Data, 89
Propertyset parameter, 55
Propertyset, 29
BEGINSESSION, 40
Browsing, 68
CEMT, 72
CONTENTION, 40
DATASTREAM, 40
DEVICE, 32, 40
Discarding, 47
ENDSESSION, 40
EXCEPTIONQ, 40
EXEC CICS FEPI DISCARD PROPERTYSET command, 47
EXEC CICS FEPI INQUIRE POOL COMMAND, 67
EXEC CICS FEPI INQUIRE PROPERTYSET command, 67
EXEC CICS FEPI INSTALL POOL command, 40
FJOURNALNUM, 40
FORMAT, 40
FORMATTED, 40
INITIALDATA, 40
INOUT, 40
INPUT, 40
Installing, 40
LOSE, 40
LUP, 32, 40
MAXFLENGTH, 40
MSGJRNL, 40
NEGATIVE, 40
NOMSGJRNL, 40
NOTINBOUND, 40
Obtaining Status, 67
OUTPUT, 40
POSITIVE, 40
STSN, 40
T3278M2, 32, 40

Propertyset *continued*
  T3278M3, 32, 40
  T3278M4, 32, 40
  T3278M5, 32, 40
  T3279M2, 32, 40
  T3279M3, 32, 40
  T3279M4, 32, 40
  T3279M5, 32, 40
  TPS55M2, 32, 40
  TPS55M3, 32, 40
  TPS55M4, 32, 40
  UNSOLDATA, 40
  UNSOLDATACK, 40
  WIN, 40
PROTECT:
  EXEC CICS FEPI EXTRACT FIELD command, 110
  PROTECTED:
  EXEC CICS FEPI EXTRACT FIELD command, 110
Protected and Unprotected Fields:
  Formatted Access, 142
PS:
  EXEC CICS FEPI EXTRACT FIELD command, 110

RDM, 34
RDO, 34
RELEASE:
  and STATE parameter of EXEC CICS FEPI INQUIRE CONNECTION, 65
  EXEC CICS FEPI FREE command, 108, 156
RELEASED, 61
  CEMT, 71
  EXEC CICS FEPI ADD command, 43
  EXEC CICS FEPI INSTALL NODELIST command, 42
  EXEC CICS FEPI NSTALL POOL command, 40
RELEASING, 61
REMFLENGTH:
  EXEC CICS FEPI RECEIVE DATASTREAM command, 107
RESET:
  EXEC CICS FEPI ISSUE command, 113
Resource Acquisition:
  CSZX Monitor, 217
  FEPI Global monitor, 217
  Resource Definition, 34
  Connection, 44
  examples, 57
  EXEC CICS FEPI command, 38
  IMS Definitions, 250
  in a Startup Program, 36
  Node, 42
  Ordering, 36
  Pool, 40
  Propertyset, 40
  Target, 41
Resource Manager, 263
Resource Manipulation, 60
  CEMT, 60
  Connection, 61, 63
  CSZX Monitor, 215
  FEPI Global monitor, 215
  Node 62, 65
  Pool, 62
  Propertyset, 67
  Target, 62, 66
Resource Removal, 60
  CEMT, 60
  Connection, 48
  EXEC CICS FEPI command overview, 46
  Node, 47
  Pool, 48
  Propertyset, 47
  Target, 47
Resource Tuning, 229
RESP2s, 116, 315, 318
  DFHSZAPA, 116, 318
  DFHSZAPC, 116, 318
  DFHSZAPO, 116, 318
  DFHSZAPP, 116, 318
RESPSTATUS:
  EXEC CICS FEPI RECEIVE DATASTREAM command, 107
  EXEC CICS FEPI RECEIVE FORMATTED command, 106
  Formatted Access, 147
Return Codes, 116, 315, 318
  DFHSZAPA, 116, 318
  DFHSZAPC, 116, 318
  DFHSZAPO, 116, 318

Return Codes *continued*
  DFHSZAPP, 116, 318
RTR:
  EXEC CICS FEPI ISSUE command, 113
RU, 163
  Chain, 163
  ENDSTATUS, 163
  EXEC CICS FEPI RECEIVE DATASTREAM command, 107, 165

Scatter/Gather, 13, 83
  Gathering the data, 85
  Multiple Transactions, 83
  Returning the results, 84
  Scattered updates, 85
  Screen Image Interface, 9
Security:
  FEPI's facilities, 252
SENSEDATA:
  EXEC CICS FEPI EXTRACT CONV command, 111
  EXEC CICS FEPI ISSUE command, 113
SEQNUMIN:
  EXEC CICS FEPI ALLOCATE command (new Conversation), 102
  EXEC CICS FEPI EXTRACT STSN command, 112
  EXEC CICS FEPI RECEIVE DATASTREAM command, 108
  EXEC CICS FEPI SEND DATASTREAM command, 104
SEQNUMOUT:
  EXEC CICS FEPI ALLOCATE command (new Conversation), 102
  EXEC CICS FEPI EXTRACT STSN command, 112
  EXEC CICS FEPI RECEIVE DATASTREAM command, 108
  EXEC CICS FEPI SEND DATASTREAM command, 104
SERVSTATUS:
  and Connection usability, 44
  and Node usability, 43
  and Pool usability, 40
  and Target usability, 41
  CEMT, 61
  EXEC CICS FEPI ADD command, 43
  EXEC CICS FEPI INQUIRE CONNECTION command, 64
  EXEC CICS FEPI INQUIRE NODE command, 66
  EXEC CICS FEPI INQUIRE POOL command, 67
  EXEC CICS FEPI INQUIRE TARGET command, 67
  EXEC CICS FEPI INSTALL NODELIST command, 42
  EXEC CICS FEPI INSTALL POOL command, 40
  EXEC CICS FEPI INSTALL TARGETLIST command, 41
  EXEC CICS FEPI SET CONNECTION command, 61
  EXEC CICS FEPI SET NODE command, 62
  EXEC CICS FEPI SET POOL command, 62
  EXEC CICS FEPI SET TARGET command, 62
  Settings, 61
  Status Transitions, 61
SESSIONLOST:
  EXEC CICS FEPI STARTed Transaction, 155
SESSNSTATUS:
  and the EXEC CICS FEPI ALLOCATE command (new Conversation), 102, 135
Signoff, 81
Signon, 81
  Logonid, 81
  Password, 81
SIT, 36
  FEPI Trace, 264
SIZE:
  EXEC CICS FEPI EXTRACT FIELD command, 110
SLUP Access, 7
  discussion of special topics, 245
  EXEC CICS FEPI EXTRACT STSN command, 246
  Sequence numbers, 245
  STSN processing, 245
  VTAM definition, 247
  VTAM/SNA considerations, 245
SNA:
  Bracket, 164
  Chain, 163, 164
  Definite Response, 249
  DRn, 249
  EXEC CICS FEPI ISSUE command, 249
  LUO considerations, 245
  Negative Response, 249
  RU, 163
  SLUP considerations, 245
START:
  EXEC CICS FEPI INQUIRE CONNECTION command, 69
  EXEC CICS FEPI INQUIRE NODE command, 68
  EXEC CICS FEPI INQUIRE POOL command, 68

START *continued*
EXEC CICS FEPI INQUIRE PROPERTYSET command, 68
EXEC CICS FEPI INQUIRE TARGET command, 68
START Data:
Record Layout, 321
Start of Day Flow, 53
STATE:
APPLICATION, 64
BEGINSESSION, 64
CEMT, 71
EXEC CICS FEPI INQUIRE CONNECTION command, 64
FREE, 64
NOCONV, 64
PENDBEGIN, 64
PENDDATA, 64
PENDFREE, 64
PENDPASS, 64
PENDRELEASE, 64
PENDSTART, 65
PENDSTSN, 65
PENDUNSOL, 65
RELEASE, 65
STSN, 65
UNSOLDATA, 65
STSN:
and STATE parameter of EXEC CICS FEPI INQUIRE CONNECTION, 65
EXEC CICS FEPI INQUIRE POOL command, 67
EXEC CICS FEPI INQUIRE PROPERTYSET command, 67
EXEC CICS FEPI INSTALL PROPERTYSET command, 40
EXEC CICS FEPI ISSUE command, 113
LUO considerations, 245
Propertyset parameter, 55
SLUP considerations, 245
STSN Handler, 245
STSN Handler, 55, 210, 219, 224
Defining, 204
EXEC CICS FEPI EXTRACT STSN command, 246
EXEC CICS FEPI FREE command, 159
LUO processing, 245
SLUP processing, 245
STSNSET:
EXEC CICS FEPI EXTRACT STSN command, 112
STSNSTATUS:
EXEC CICS FEPI EXTRACT STSN command, 112
STSNTEST:
EXEC CICS FEPI EXTRACT STSN command, 112
SZ TCB, 263

T3278M2:
EXEC CICS FEPI EXTRACT CONV command, 111
EXEC CICS FEPI INSTALL PROPERTYSET command, 40
Propertyset parameter, 51
T3278M3:
EXEC CICS FEPI EXTRACT CONV command, 111
EXEC CICS FEPI INSTALL PROPERTYSET command, 40
Propertyset parameter, 51
T3278M4:
EXEC CICS FEPI EXTRACT CONV command, 111
EXEC CICS FEPI INSTALL PROPERTYSET command, 40
Propertyset parameter, 51
T3278M5:
EXEC CICS FEPI EXTRACT CONV command, 111
EXEC CICS FEPI INSTALL PROPERTYSET command, 40
Propertyset parameter, 51
T3279M2:
EXEC CICS FEPI EXTRACT CONV command, 111
EXEC CICS FEPI INSTALL PROPERTYSET command, 40
Propertyset parameter, 51
T3279M3:
EXEC CICS FEPI EXTRACT CONV command, 111
EXEC CICS FEPI INSTALL PROPERTYSET command, 40
Propertyset parameter, 51
T3279M4:
EXEC CICS FEPI EXTRACT CONV command, 111
EXEC CICS FEPI INSTALL PROPERTYSET command, 40
Propertyset parameter, 51
T3279M5:
EXEC CICS FEPI EXTRACT CONV command, 111
EXEC CICS FEPI INSTALL PROPERTYSET command, 40
Propertyset parameter, 51
Target, 28
Browsing, 68
CEMT, 71, 73
Discarding, 47

Target *continued*
EXEC CICS FEPI ALLOCATE command (new Conversation), 102
EXEC CICS FEPI ALLOCATEing to a specific Target, 132
EXEC CICS FEPI EXTRACT CONV command, 111
EXEC CICS FEPI INQUIRE CONNECTION command, 63
EXEC CICS FEPI INQUIRE TARGET command, 66
EXEC CICS FEPI SET CONNECTION command, 61
EXEC CICS FEPI SET TARGET command, 62
Installing, 41
Obtaining Status, 66
Setting Status, 62
TARGETLIST:
EXEC CICS FEPI ADD command, 43
EXEC CICS FEPI DELETE command, 48
EXEC CICS FEPI DISCARD TARGETLIST command, 47
EXEC CICS FEPI INSTALL POOL command, 40
EXEC CICS FEPI INSTALL TARGETLIST command, 41
EXEC CICS FEPI SET CONNECTION command, 61
EXEC CICS FEPI SET TARGET command, 62
TARGETNUM:
EXEC CICS FEPI ADD command, 43
EXEC CICS FEPI DELETE command, 48
EXEC CICS FEPI DISCARD TARGETLIST command, 47
EXEC CICS FEPI INSTALL POOL command, 40
EXEC CICS FEPI INSTALL TARGETLIST command, 41
EXEC CICS FEPI SET CONNECTION command, 61
EXEC CICS FEPI SET TARGET command, 62
TDQ records, 319
TERMID:
EXEC CICS FEPI START command, 109
Terminal Type:
and the DEVICE parameter 32, 51
TIMEOUT:
and EXEC CICS FEPI STARTed transactions First Receive Handler, 152
Begin Session Handler, 153
EXEC CICS FEPI ALLOCATE command (new Conversation), 102
EXEC CICS FEPI RECEIVE DATASTREAM command, 106
EXEC CICS FEPI RECEIVE FORMATTED command, 105
EXEC CICS FEPI START command, 109
EXEC CICS FEPI STARTed Transaction, 155
Recovering from a Timeout, 151
Unsolicited data Handler, 152
usage, 151
usage on EXEC CICS FEPI ALLOCATE command (new Conversation), 132
Timeouts, 18
and EXEC CICS FEPI ALLOCATE, 19
and EXEC CICS FEPI RECEIVE, 19
and EXEC CICS FEPI START, 19
on the EXEC CICS FEPI ALLOCATE command (new Conversation), 132
TPS55M2:
EXEC CICS FEPI EXTRACT CONV command, 111
EXEC CICS FEPI INSTALL PROPERTYSET command, 40
Propertyset parameter, 51
TPS55M3:
EXEC CICS FEPI EXTRACT CONV command, 111
EXEC CICS FEPI INSTALL PROPERTYSET command, 40
Propertyset parameter, 51
TPS55M4:
EXEC CICS FEPI EXTRACT CONV command, 111
EXEC CICS FEPI INSTALL PROPERTYSET command, 40
Propertyset parameter, 51
Trace:
CETR, 264
EXEC CICS INQUIRE/SET TRACETYPE SZ command, 264
GTF Tracing, 267
Printing, 264
SIT Tracing, 264
Trace Interpretation:
Printing, 264
TRANSID:
EXEC CICS FEPI START command, 109
TRANSPARENCY:
EXEC CICS FEPI EXTRACT FIELD command, 110

Unexpected Data, 90
and IMS, 91
UNPROTECTED:
EXEC CICS FEPI EXTRACT FIELD command, 110
UNSOLDATA:
and STATE parameter of EXEC CICS FEPI INQUIRE CONNECTION, 65
EXEC CICS FEPI INQUIRE POOL command, 67
EXEC CICS FEPI INQUIRE PROPERTYSET command, 67
EXEC CICS FEPI INSTALL PROPERTYSET command, 40

UNSOLDATA *continued*
  Propertyset parameter, 55
UNSOLDATACK:
  EXEC CICS FEPI INQUIRE POOL command, 67
  EXEC CICS FEPI INQUIRE PROPERTYSET command, 67
  EXEC CICS FEPI INSTALL PROPERTYSET command, 40
  Ignoring Unsolicited Data, 89
  Propertyset parameter, 55
  Rejecting Unsolicited Data, 89
Unsolicited Bind:
  CSZX Monitor, 218
  FEPI Global monitor, 218
Unsolicited Data, 88
  and IMS, 91
  Ignoring with UNSOLDATACK, 89
  Implications for Datastream Conversations, 89
  Implications for Formatted Conversations, 90
  NEGATIVE, 89
  POSITIVE, 89
  Processing, 89
  Rejecting with UNSOLDATACK, 89
Unsolicited Data Handler, 208, 219, 222
  Defining, 204
  EXEC CICS FEPI FREE command, 159
  specification, 55
  Timeouts and the First Flow, 152
  usage, 89
  what the Handler should do, 209
  when FEPI generates the Handler, 208
UNTILCDEB:
  EXEC CICS FEPI RECEIVE DATASTREAM command, 107, 165
USERDATA, 237
  and FEPI Resources, 61
  CLSDST(PASS) processing 242
  EXEC CICS FEPI INQUIRE CONNECTION command, 65
  EXEC CICS FEPI INQUIRE NODE command, 66
  EXEC CICS FEPI INQUIRE POOL command, 68
  EXEC CICS FEPI INQUIRE PROPERTYSET command, 67
  EXEC CICS FEPI INQUIRE TARGET command, 67
  EXEC CICS FEPI SET CONNECTION command, 61
  EXEC CICS FEPI SET NODE command, 62
  EXEC CICS FEPI SET POOL command, 62
  EXEC CICS FEPI SET TARGET command, 62
  EXEC CICS FEPI START command, 109, 238
  usage, 65, 66, 67, 68

VALIDATION:
  EXEC CICS FEPI EXTRACT FIELD command, 110
VALUE:
  EXEC CICS FEPI ISSUE command, 113
VTAM:
  and Application Minor Node names, 31
  APPLIDs and Targets, 33
  APPLIDs and XRF, 271, 273
  CD, 79
  CLSDST(PASS) processing, 239
  Connection Sense Code, 64
  D4A32782, 32
  D4A32783, 32
  D4A32784, 32
  D4A32785, 32
  Definite Response, 248
  DRn, 249

VTAM *continued*
  EB, 79, 92
  EXEC CICS FEPI ISSUE command, 249
  IBM3600, 32
  LOGMODE, 32
  LOGMODE and Node, 32
  LUO considerations, 245
  LUO definitions, 247
  MODETAB and Node, 33
  Negative Response, 248
  Node activation, 32
  Node definition, 31
  Node Password, 31
  Node Sense Code, 66
  Resource Acquisition Errors, 217
  SLUP considerations, 245
  SLUP definitions, 247
  SNX32702, 32
  SNX32703, 32
  SNX32704, 32
  SNX32705, 32
  Third party PLU names and CLSDST(PASS) processing, 239
  VTAM indicators, 78
  XRF concepts, 271
  XRF Terminal Classes, 272

WAITCONVNUM, 65
  CEMT, 71
  EXEC CICS FEPI INQUIRE CONNECTION command, 65
  EXEC CICS FEPI INQUIRE POOL command, 68
Waits:
  Connection, 229
  Debugging, 267
WIN:
  EXEC CICS FEPI INSTALL PROPERTYSET command, 40
  Propertyset parameter, 50

XRF:
  Active System, 271, 273
  Alternate System, 271, 273
  and APPLIDs, 42
  Applids, 271, 273
  Concepts, 271
  takeover of FEPI's CICS system:
    effect in Alternate system, 274
    effect on Partner systems' terminals, 274
    effect on partner systems' transactions, 274
  takeover of partner CICS system:
    effect on FEPI Application Programs, 275
    effect on FEPI Connections, 275
  Terminal Classes, 272
XSZARQ GLUE, 258
  Command Codes, 260
  Parameter descriptions, 259
  Parameter List, 327
  Return Codes, 259
  usage, 262
XSZBRQ GLUE, 258
  Command Codes, 260
  Parameter descriptions, 259
  Parameter List, 327
  Return Codes, 259
  usage, 261